THE ALL NEW ATOM

My Life in Miniature

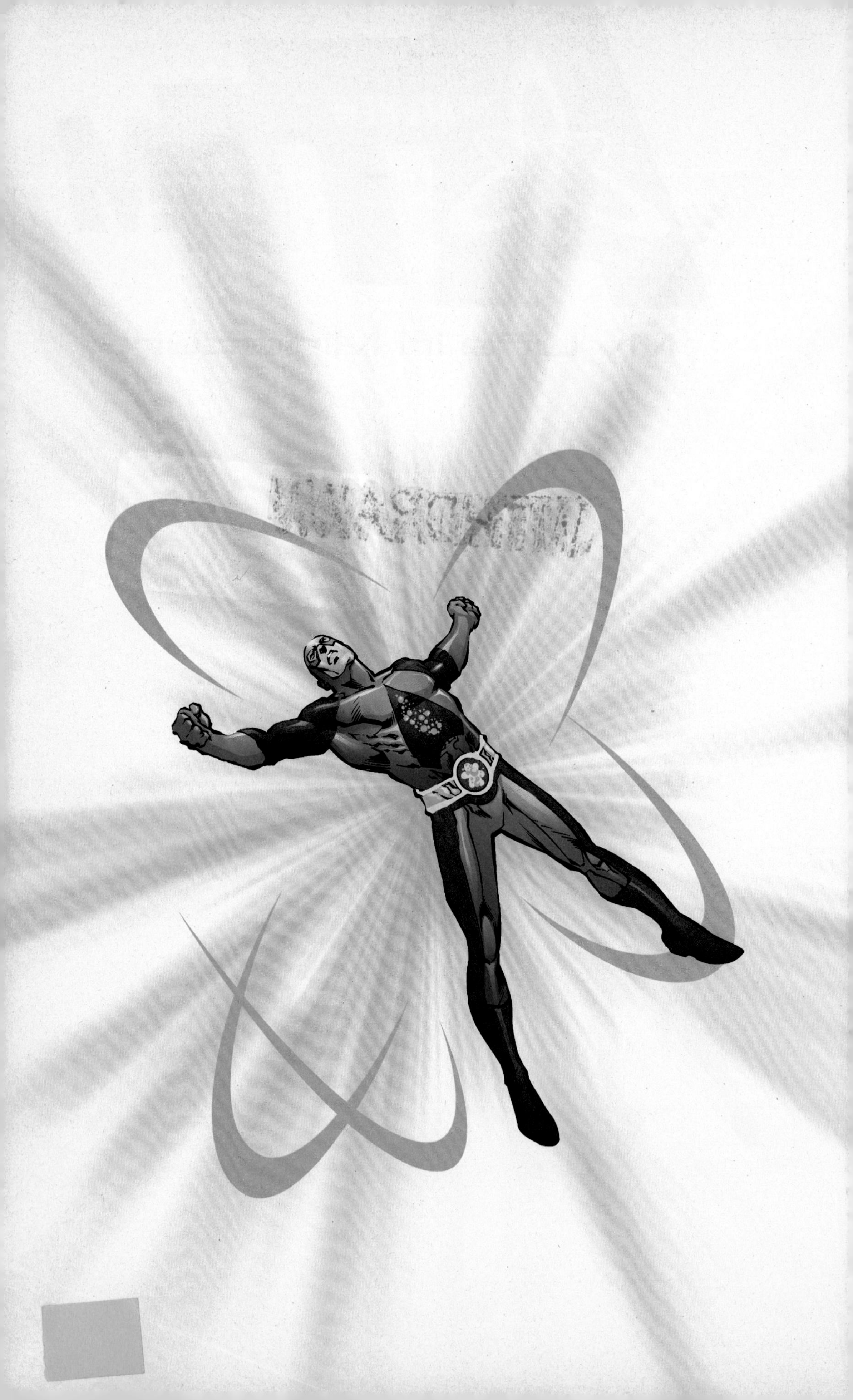

THE ALL NEW ATOM

My Life in Miniature

Gail Simone
Writer

John Byrne
Eddy Barrows
Pencils

Trevor Scott
Inks

Travis Lanham
Letters

Alex Bleyaert
Colors

Based on ideas and concepts developed
by **Grant Morrison.**

Dan DiDio
Senior VP-Executive Editor

Mike Carlin
Editor-original series

Tom Palmer Jr.
Associate Editor-original series

Bob Joy
Editor-collected edition

Robbin Brosterman
Senior Art Director

Paul Levitz
President & Publisher

Georg Brewer
VP-Design & DC Direct Creative

Richard Bruning
Senior VP-Creative Director

Patrick Caldon
Executive VP-Finance & Operations

Chris Caramalis
VP-Finance

John Cunningham
VP-Marketing

Terri Cunningham
VP-Managing Editor

Alison Gill
VP-Manufacturing

Hank Kanalz
VP-General Manager, WildStorm

Jim Lee
Editorial Director-WildStorm

Paula Lowitt
Senior VP-Business & Legal Affairs

MaryEllen McLaughlin
VP-Advertising & Custom Publishing

John Nee
VP-Business Development

Gregory Noveck
Senior VP-Creative Affairs

Sue Pohja
VP-Book Trade Sales

Cheryl Rubin
Senior VP-Brand Management

Jeff Trojan
VP-Business Development, DC Direct

Bob Wayne
VP-Sales

Cover art by Ariel Olivetti
Logo design by Rian Hughes

**THE ALL NEW ATOM:
MY LIFE IN MINIATURE**

Published by DC Comics.
Cover and compilation
copyright © 2007 DC Comics.
All Rights Reserved.

Originally published in single magazine
form as: BRAVE NEW WORLD 1, THE ALL
NEW ATOM 1-6 Copyright © 2006, 2007
DC Comics. All Rights Reserved.
All characters, their distinctive
likenesses and related elements
featured in this publication are
trademarks of DC Comics.
The stories, characters and incidents
featured in this publication are entirely
fictional. DC Comics does not read or
accept unsolicited submissions of
ideas, stories or artwork.

DC Comics, 1700 Broadway,
New York, NY 10019
A Warner Bros. Entertainment Company
Printed in Canada. First Printing.

ISBN: 1-4012-1325-1
ISBN 13: 978-1-4012-1325-1

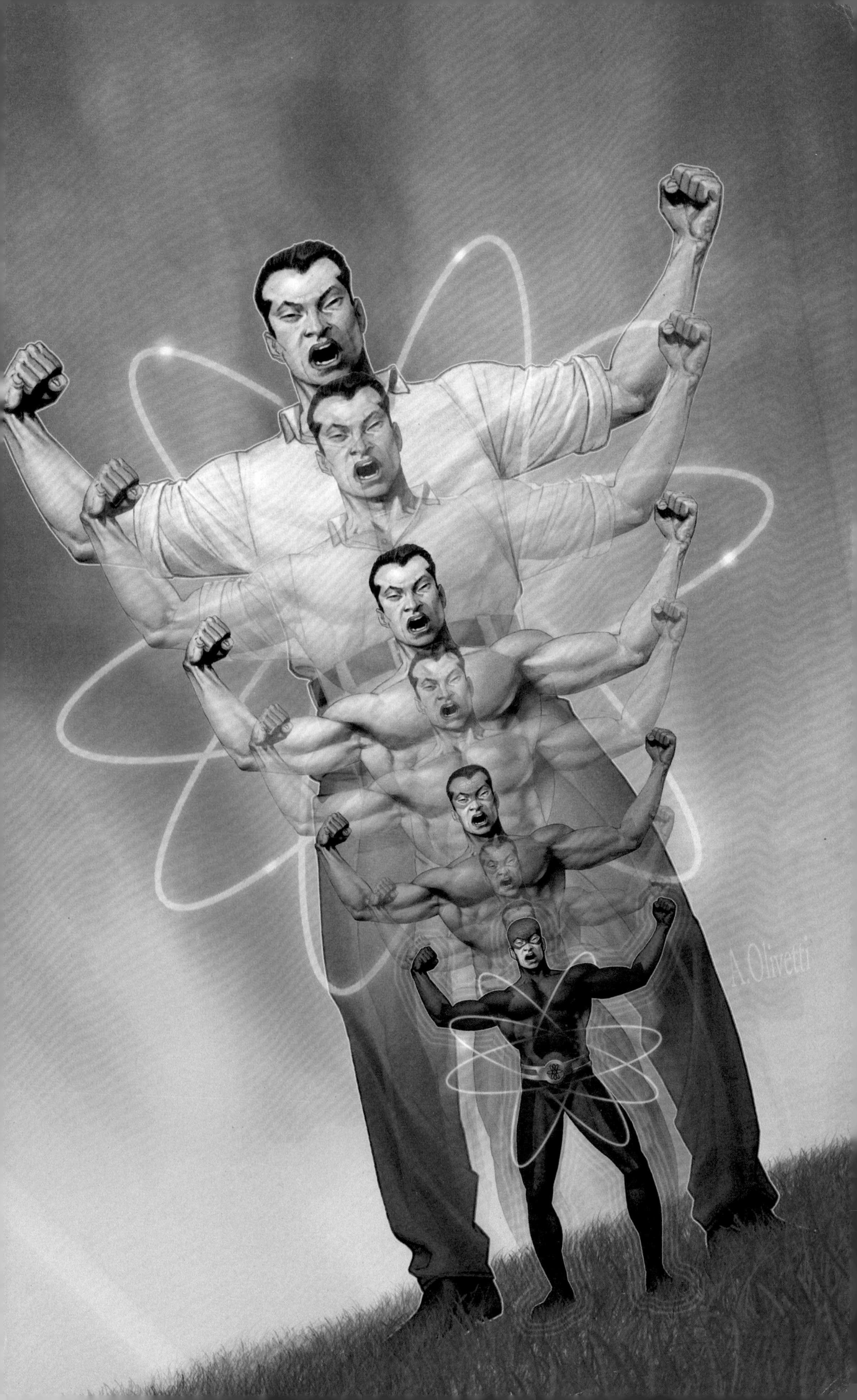
A.Olivetti

MY LIFE IN MINIATURE: PART ONE
INDIVISIBLE

from **THE ALL NEW ATOM #1**
Cover by **Ariel Olivetti**

INTRODUCTION TO CHRONOLOGY

Chapter One

Study the following three prologues, which are presented in non-linear fashion. Discuss how the sequence of events differs from traditional story-telling methods. Why did the author choose to present the epilogues out of chronological order?

Professor Palmer says size isn't matter!

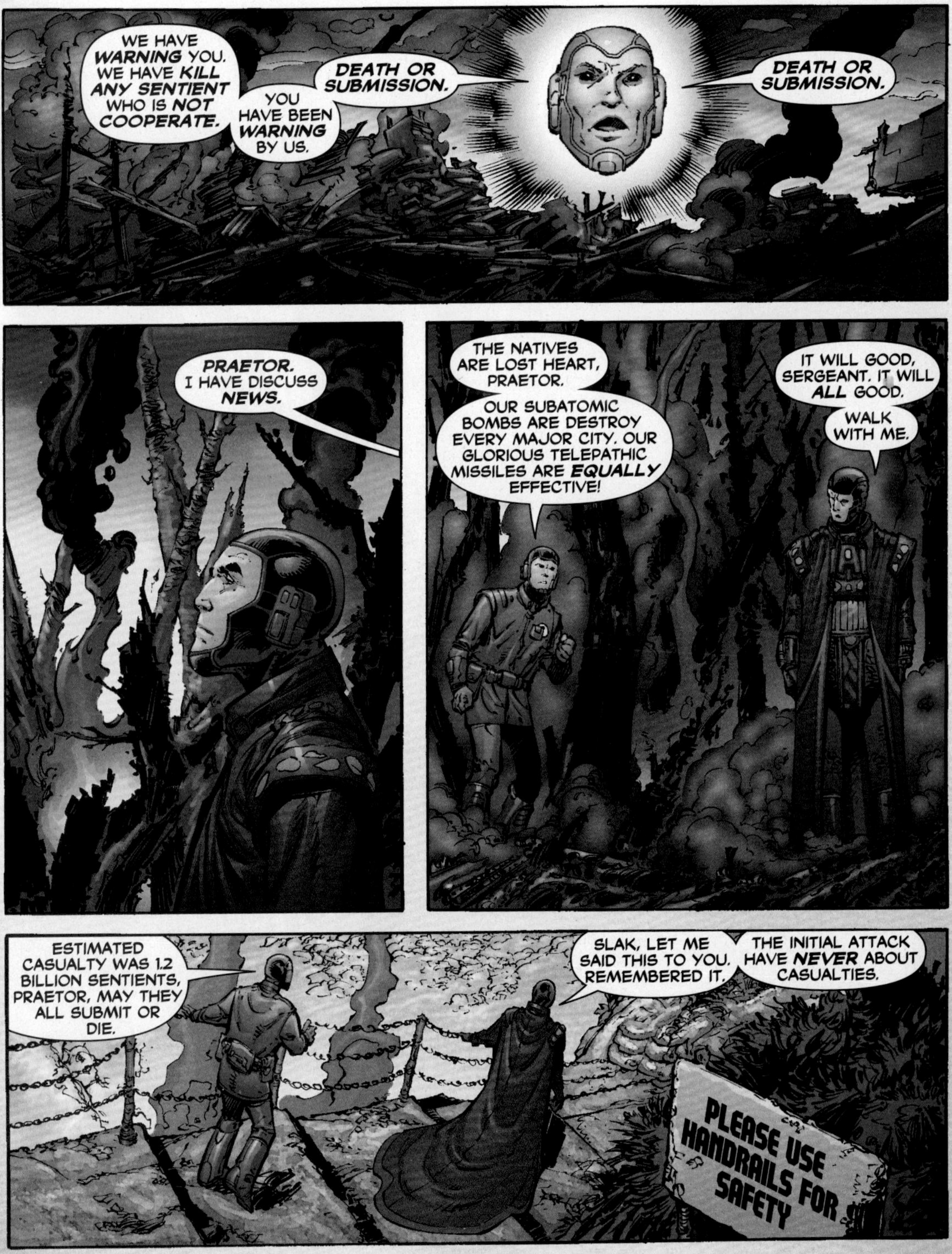

WE HAVE WARNING YOU. WE HAVE KILL ANY SENTIENT WHO IS NOT COOPERATE.
YOU HAVE BEEN WARNING BY US.
DEATH OR SUBMISSION.
DEATH OR SUBMISSION.
PRAETOR. I HAVE DISCUSS NEWS.
THE NATIVES ARE LOST HEART, PRAETOR.
OUR SUBATOMIC BOMBS ARE DESTROY EVERY MAJOR CITY. OUR GLORIOUS TELEPATHIC MISSILES ARE EQUALLY EFFECTIVE!
IT WILL GOOD, SERGEANT. IT WILL ALL GOOD.
WALK WITH ME.
ESTIMATED CASUALTY WAS 1.2 BILLION SENTIENTS, PRAETOR, MAY THEY ALL SUBMIT OR DIE.
SLAK, LET ME SAID THIS TO YOU. REMEMBERED IT.
THE INITIAL ATTACK HAVE NEVER ABOUT CASUALTIES.
PLEASE USE HANDRAILS FOR SAFETY

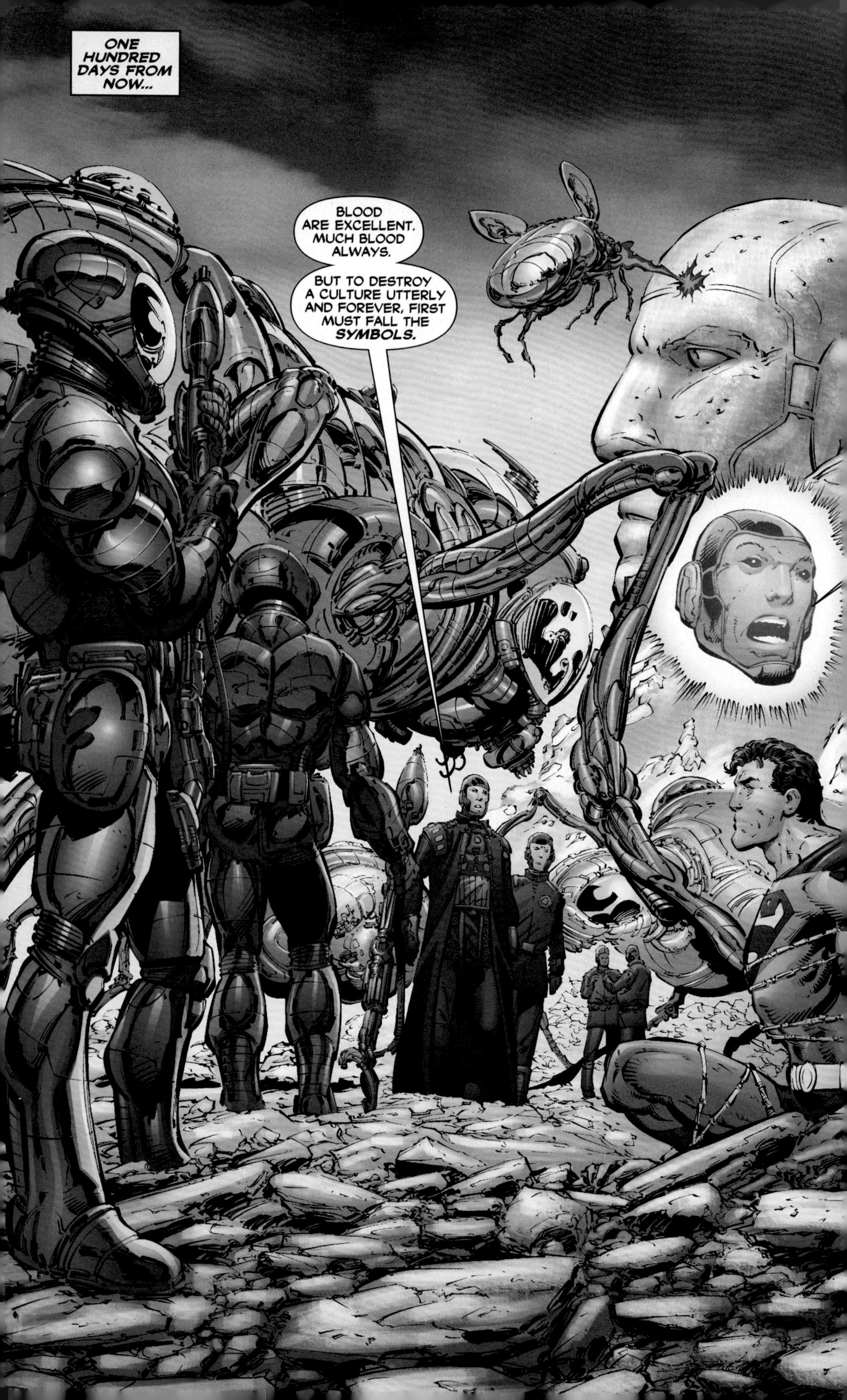
ONE HUNDRED DAYS FROM NOW...
BLOOD ARE EXCELLENT. MUCH BLOOD ALWAYS.
BUT TO DESTROY A CULTURE UTTERLY AND FOREVER, FIRST MUST FALL THE SYMBOLS.

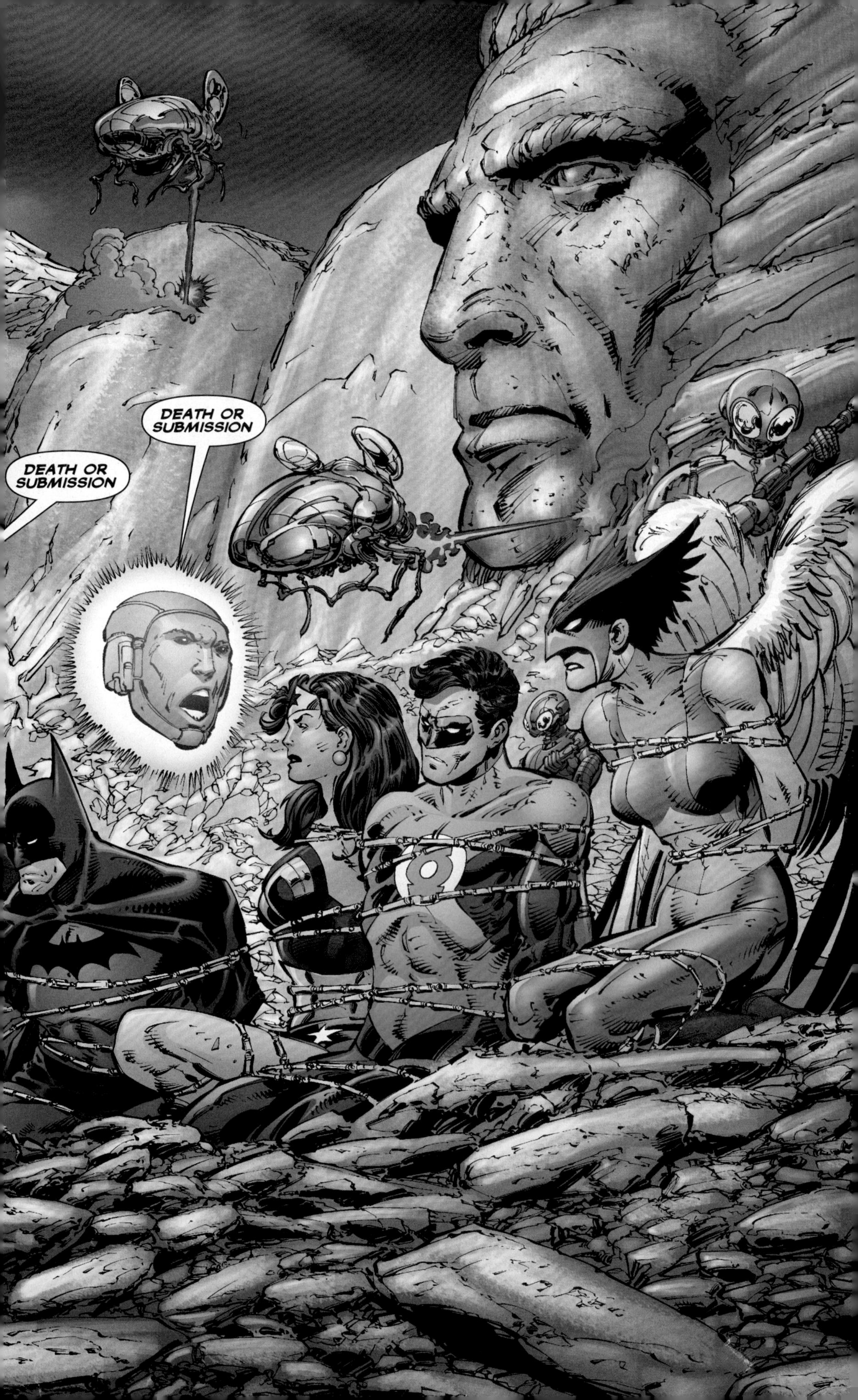
DEATH OR SUBMISSION
DEATH OR SUBMISSION

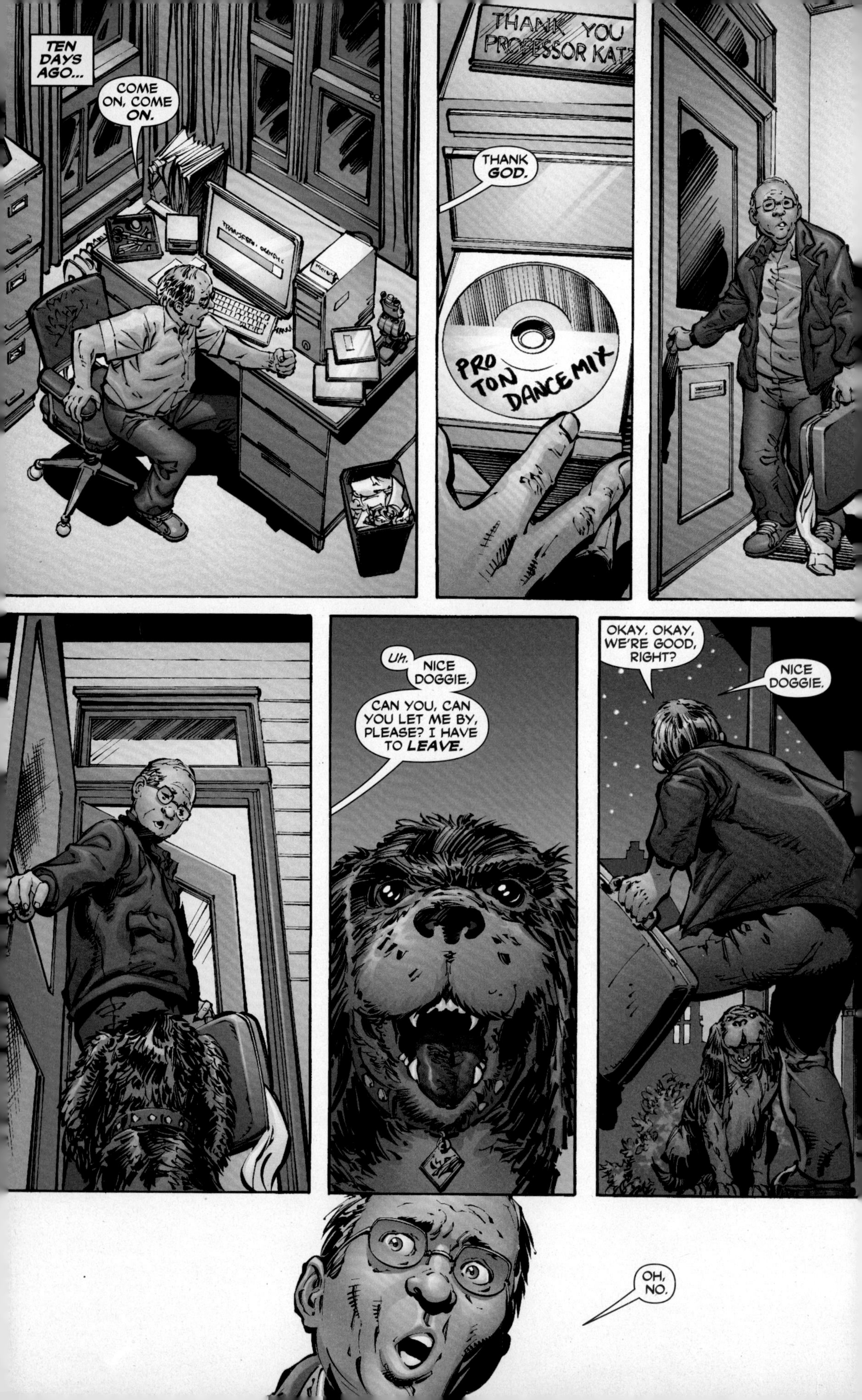
TEN DAYS AGO...
COME ON, COME ON.
THANK YOU PROFESSOR KATZ
THANK GOD.
PRO TON DANCE MIX
Uh. NICE DOGGIE.
CAN YOU, CAN YOU LET ME BY, PLEASE? I HAVE TO LEAVE.
OKAY. OKAY, WE'RE GOOD, RIGHT?
NICE DOGGIE.
OH, NO.

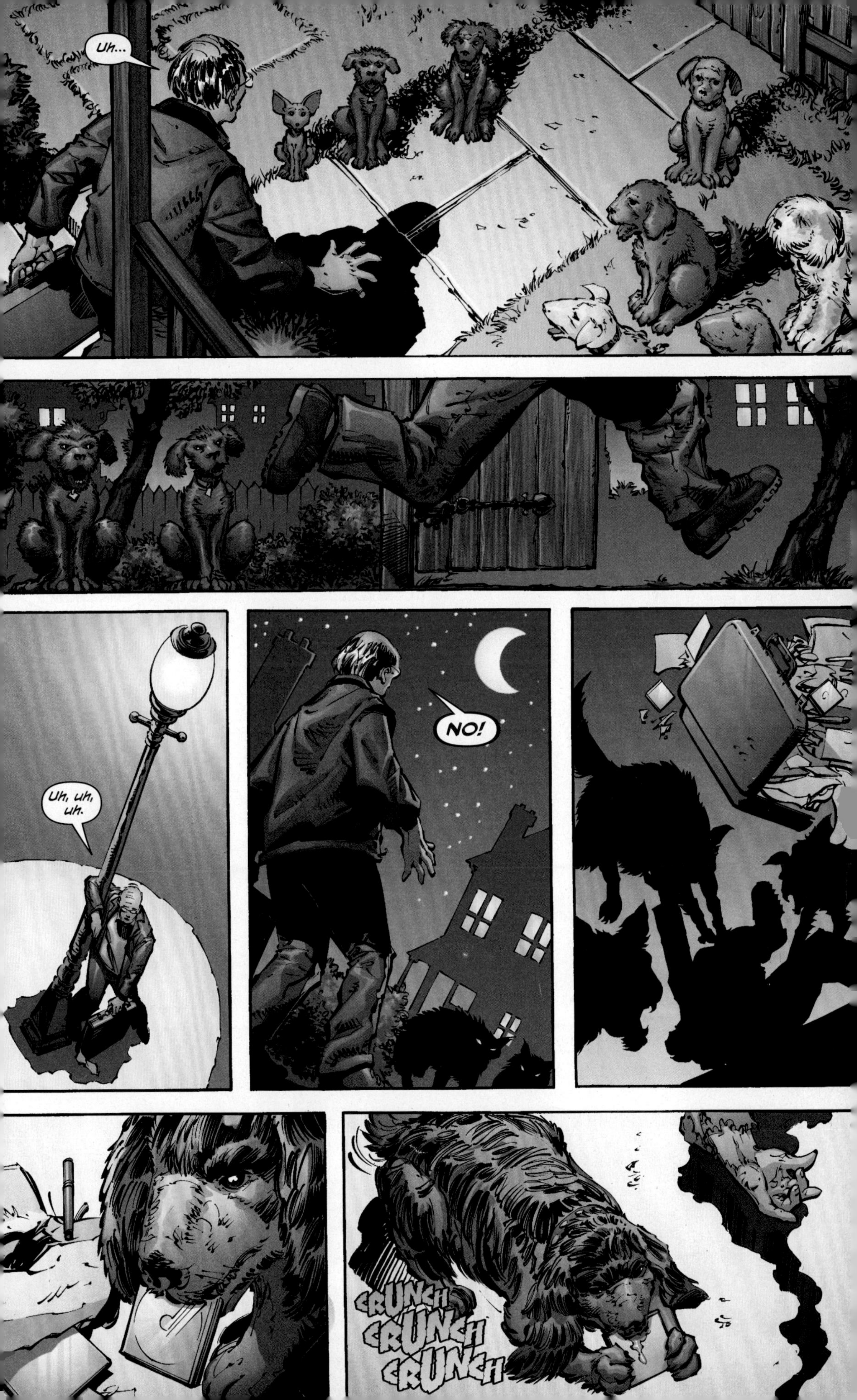
Uh...
Uh, uh, uh.
NO!
CRUNCH
CRUNCH
CRUNCH

KOWLOON PARK, HONG KONG...

FOURTEEN YEARS AGO...

<I ASK FOR SUCH A SMALL THING, REALLY.>

<A TINY BIT OF DISCIPLINE, A MINUSCULE AMOUNT OF CONCENTRATION.>

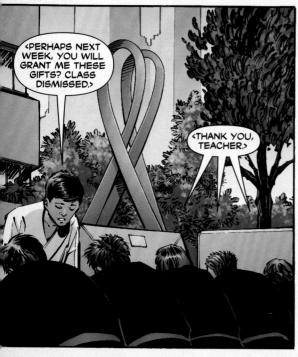

<PERHAPS NEXT WEEK, YOU WILL GRANT ME THESE GIFTS? CLASS DISMISSED.>

<THANK YOU, TEACHER.>

<"I ASK ONLY TO BORE YOU A TINY BIT. A LITTLE BIT OF SPIRIT-CRUSHING DULLNESS!">

<HE'LL HEAR YOU!>

<YEAH? WELL, WHAT WOULD HE DO ABOUT IT, RYAN? DOESN'T HE KNOW THAT I'M NOT ACTUALLY ERIK CHOW...>

<...BUT BRUCE LEE IN DISGUISE!>

<AND I'LL BE JACKIE CHAN!>

<WHO ARE YOU, RYAN?>

Uh...

<I'M FENG JISHEN!>

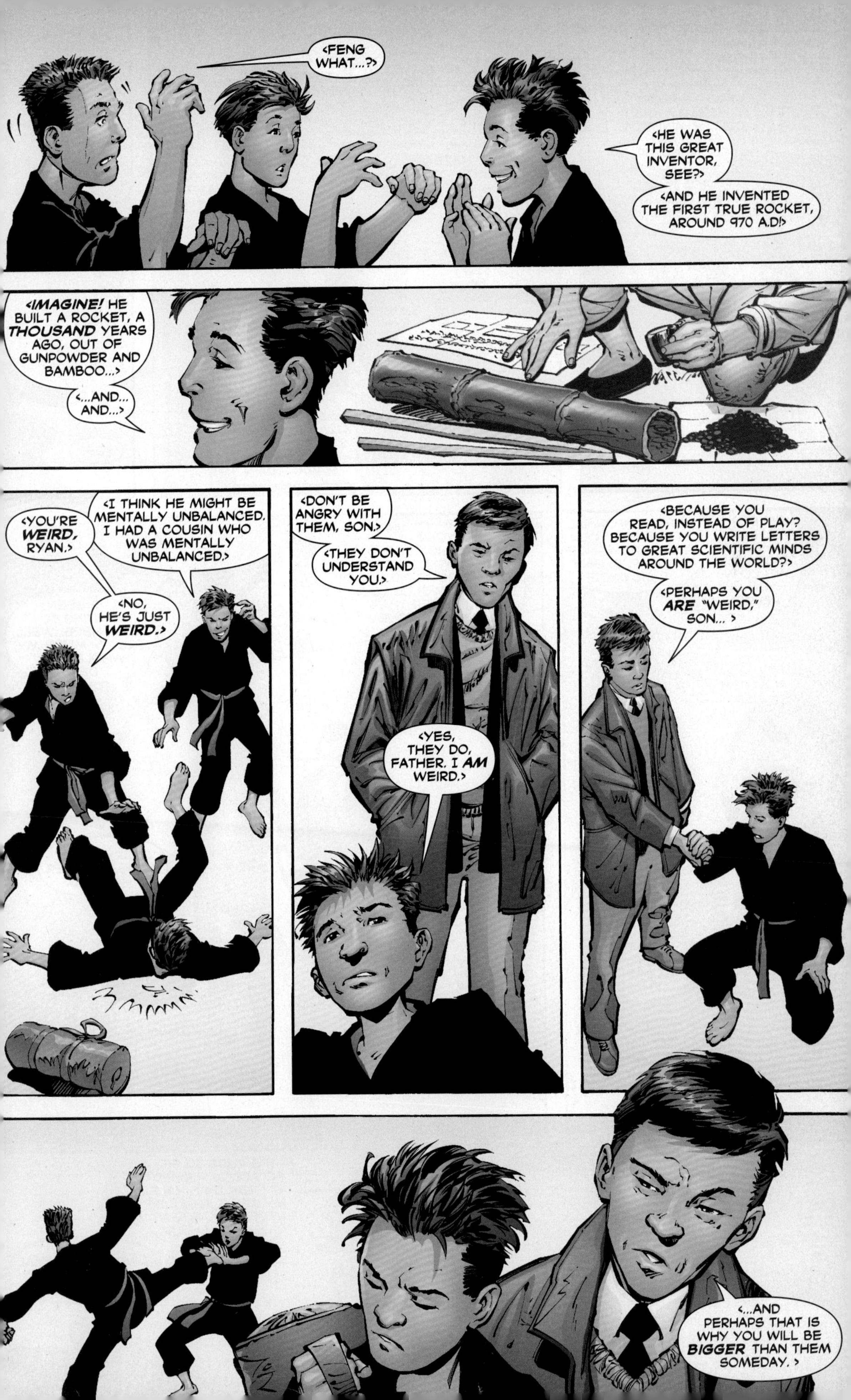

‹FENG WHAT...?›
‹HE WAS THIS GREAT INVENTOR, SEE?›
‹AND HE INVENTED THE FIRST TRUE ROCKET, AROUND 970 A.D!›
‹IMAGINE! HE BUILT A ROCKET, A THOUSAND YEARS AGO, OUT OF GUNPOWDER AND BAMBOO...›
‹...AND... AND...›
‹YOU'RE WEIRD, RYAN.›
‹I THINK HE MIGHT BE MENTALLY UNBALANCED. I HAD A COUSIN WHO WAS MENTALLY UNBALANCED.›
‹NO, HE'S JUST WEIRD.›
‹DON'T BE ANGRY WITH THEM, SON.›
‹THEY DON'T UNDERSTAND YOU.›
‹YES, THEY DO, FATHER. I AM WEIRD.›
‹BECAUSE YOU READ, INSTEAD OF PLAY? BECAUSE YOU WRITE LETTERS TO GREAT SCIENTIFIC MINDS AROUND THE WORLD?›
‹PERHAPS YOU ARE "WEIRD," SON... ›
‹...AND PERHAPS THAT IS WHY YOU WILL BE BIGGER THAN THEM SOMEDAY. ›

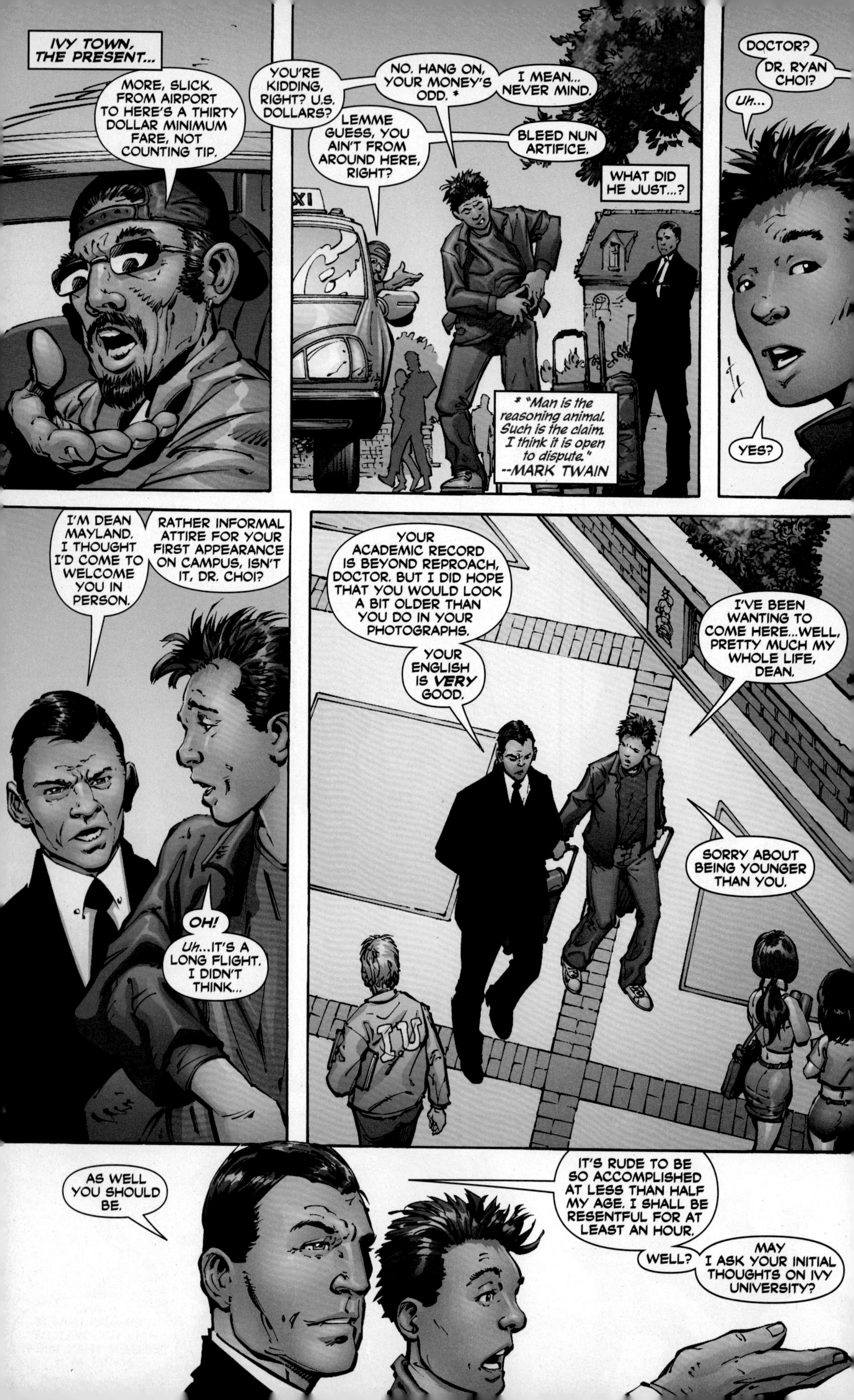
IVY TOWN, THE PRESENT...
MORE, SLICK. FROM AIRPORT TO HERE'S A THIRTY DOLLAR MINIMUM FARE, NOT COUNTING TIP.
YOU'RE KIDDING, RIGHT? U.S. DOLLARS?
NO. HANG ON, YOUR MONEY'S ODD. *
I MEAN... NEVER MIND.
LEMME GUESS, YOU AIN'T FROM AROUND HERE, RIGHT?
BLEED NUN ARTIFICE.
WHAT DID HE JUST...?
* "Man is the reasoning animal. Such is the claim. I think it is open to dispute." --MARK TWAIN
DOCTOR? DR. RYAN CHOI?
Uh...
YES?
I'M DEAN MAYLAND. I THOUGHT I'D COME TO WELCOME YOU IN PERSON.
RATHER INFORMAL ATTIRE FOR YOUR FIRST APPEARANCE ON CAMPUS, ISN'T IT, DR. CHOI?
OH!
Uh...IT'S A LONG FLIGHT. I DIDN'T THINK...
YOUR ACADEMIC RECORD IS BEYOND REPROACH, DOCTOR. BUT I DID HOPE THAT YOU WOULD LOOK A BIT OLDER THAN YOU DO IN YOUR PHOTOGRAPHS.
YOUR ENGLISH IS VERY GOOD.
I'VE BEEN WANTING TO COME HERE...WELL, PRETTY MUCH MY WHOLE LIFE, DEAN.
SORRY ABOUT BEING YOUNGER THAN YOU.
AS WELL YOU SHOULD BE.
IT'S RUDE TO BE SO ACCOMPLISHED AT LESS THAN HALF MY AGE. I SHALL BE RESENTFUL FOR AT LEAST AN HOUR.
WELL?
MAY I ASK YOUR INITIAL THOUGHTS ON IVY UNIVERSITY?

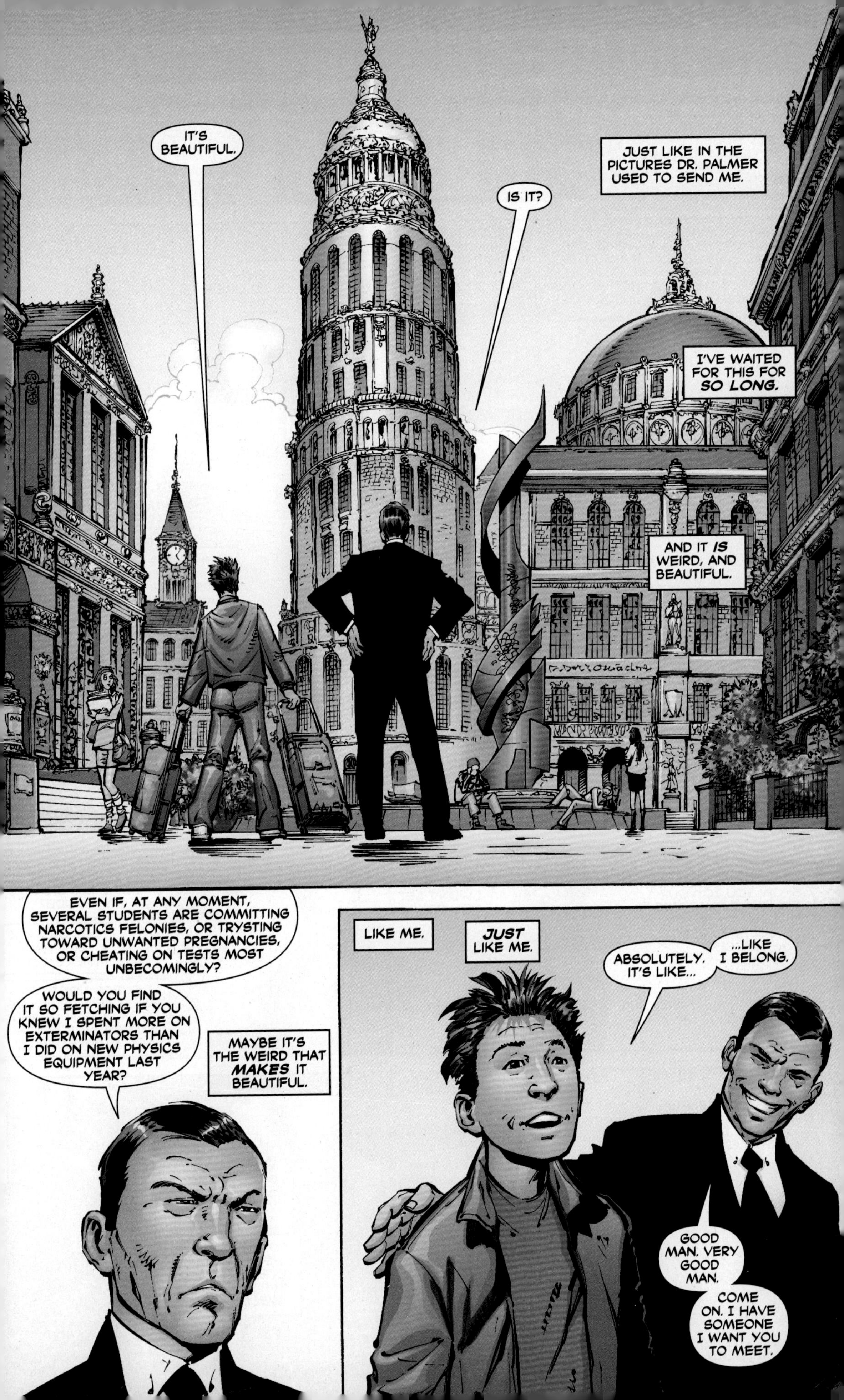
IT'S BEAUTIFUL.
IS IT?
JUST LIKE IN THE PICTURES DR. PALMER USED TO SEND ME.
I'VE WAITED FOR THIS FOR SO LONG.
AND IT IS WEIRD, AND BEAUTIFUL.
EVEN IF, AT ANY MOMENT, SEVERAL STUDENTS ARE COMMITTING NARCOTICS FELONIES, OR TRYSTING TOWARD UNWANTED PREGNANCIES, OR CHEATING ON TESTS MOST UNBECOMINGLY?
WOULD YOU FIND IT SO FETCHING IF YOU KNEW I SPENT MORE ON EXTERMINATORS THAN I DID ON NEW PHYSICS EQUIPMENT LAST YEAR?
MAYBE IT'S THE WEIRD THAT MAKES IT BEAUTIFUL.
LIKE ME.
JUST LIKE ME.
ABSOLUTELY. IT'S LIKE...
...LIKE I BELONG.
GOOD MAN. VERY GOOD MAN.
COME ON. I HAVE SOMEONE I WANT YOU TO MEET.

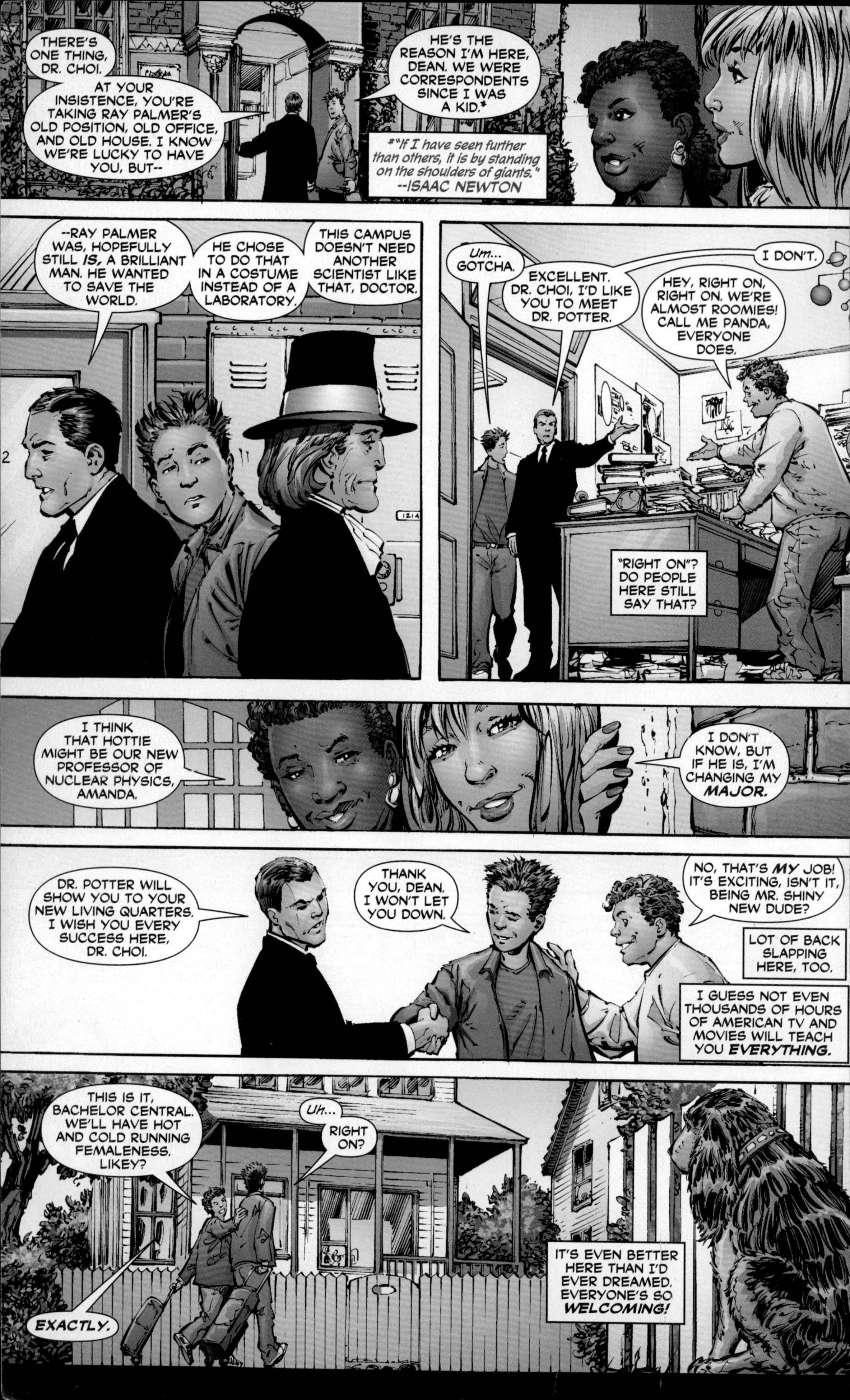
THERE'S ONE THING, DR. CHOI.
AT YOUR INSISTENCE, YOU'RE TAKING RAY PALMER'S OLD POSITION, OLD OFFICE, AND OLD HOUSE. I KNOW WE'RE LUCKY TO HAVE YOU, BUT--
HE'S THE REASON I'M HERE, DEAN. WE WERE CORRESPONDENTS SINCE I WAS A KID.*
*"If I have seen further than others, it is by standing on the shoulders of giants." --ISAAC NEWTON
--RAY PALMER WAS, HOPEFULLY STILL *IS,* A BRILLIANT MAN. HE WANTED TO SAVE THE WORLD.
HE CHOSE TO DO THAT IN A COSTUME INSTEAD OF A LABORATORY.
THIS CAMPUS DOESN'T NEED ANOTHER SCIENTIST LIKE THAT, DOCTOR.
Um... GOTCHA.
EXCELLENT. DR. CHOI, I'D LIKE YOU TO MEET DR. POTTER.
I DON'T.
HEY, RIGHT ON, RIGHT ON. WE'RE ALMOST ROOMIES! CALL ME PANDA, EVERYONE DOES.
"RIGHT ON"? DO PEOPLE HERE STILL SAY THAT?
I THINK THAT HOTTIE MIGHT BE OUR NEW PROFESSOR OF NUCLEAR PHYSICS, AMANDA.
I DON'T KNOW, BUT IF HE IS, I'M CHANGING MY ***MAJOR.***
DR. POTTER WILL SHOW YOU TO YOUR NEW LIVING QUARTERS. I WISH YOU EVERY SUCCESS HERE, DR. CHOI.
THANK YOU, DEAN. I WON'T LET YOU DOWN.
NO, THAT'S *MY* JOB! IT'S EXCITING, ISN'T IT, BEING MR. SHINY NEW DUDE?
LOT OF BACK SLAPPING HERE, TOO.
I GUESS NOT EVEN THOUSANDS OF HOURS OF AMERICAN TV AND MOVIES WILL TEACH YOU ***EVERYTHING.***
THIS IS IT, BACHELOR CENTRAL. WE'LL HAVE HOT AND COLD RUNNING FEMALENESS. LIKEY?
Uh... RIGHT ON?
EXACTLY.
IT'S EVEN BETTER HERE THAN I'D EVER DREAMED. EVERYONE'S SO ***WELCOMING!***

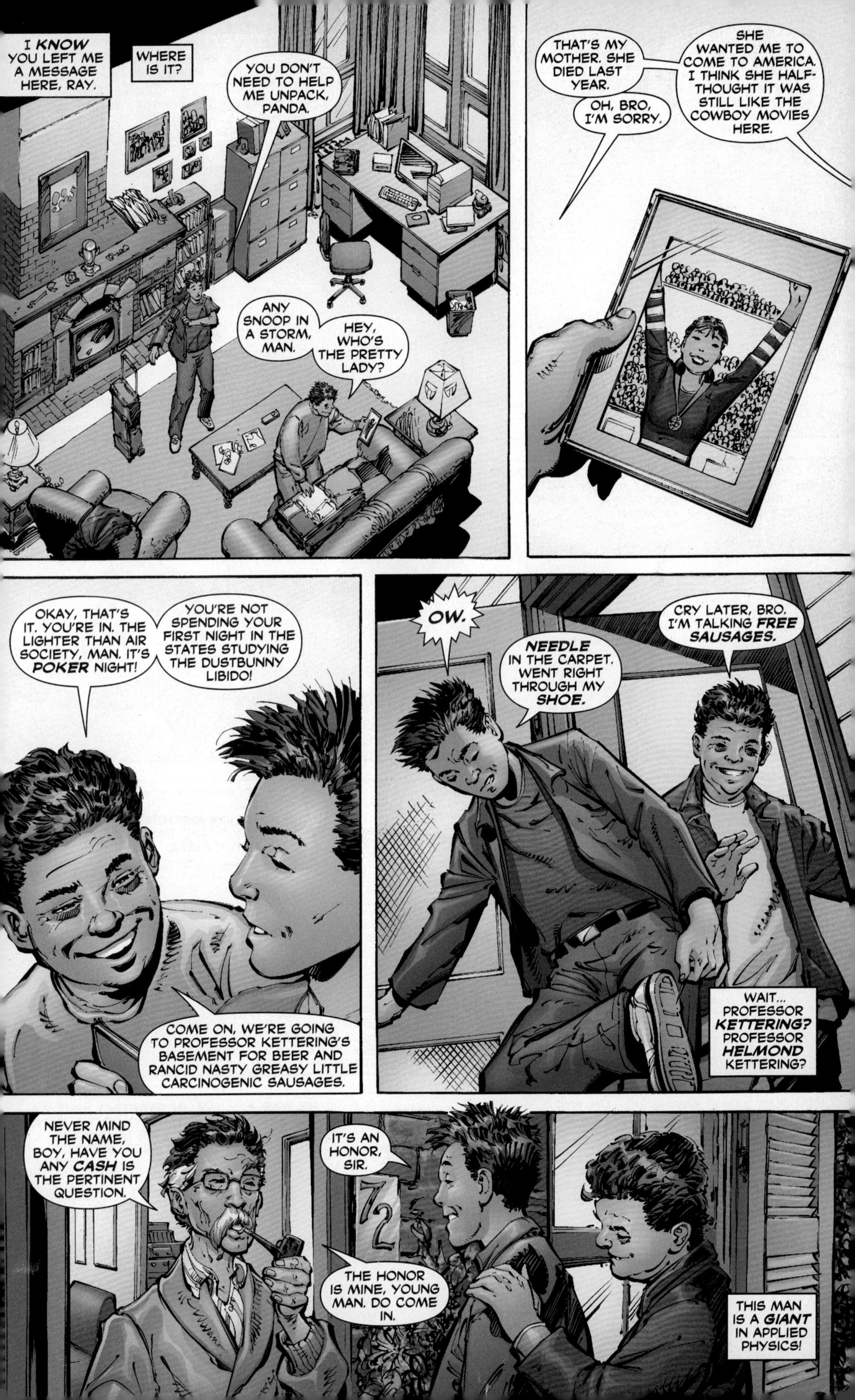
I KNOW YOU LEFT ME A MESSAGE HERE, RAY.
WHERE IS IT?
YOU DON'T NEED TO HELP ME UNPACK, PANDA.
ANY SNOOP IN A STORM, MAN.
HEY, WHO'S THE PRETTY LADY?
THAT'S MY MOTHER. SHE DIED LAST YEAR.
OH, BRO, I'M SORRY.
SHE WANTED ME TO COME TO AMERICA. I THINK SHE HALF-THOUGHT IT WAS STILL LIKE THE COWBOY MOVIES HERE.
OKAY, THAT'S IT. YOU'RE IN. THE LIGHTER THAN AIR SOCIETY, MAN. IT'S POKER NIGHT!
YOU'RE NOT SPENDING YOUR FIRST NIGHT IN THE STATES STUDYING THE DUSTBUNNY LIBIDO!
COME ON, WE'RE GOING TO PROFESSOR KETTERING'S BASEMENT FOR BEER AND RANCID NASTY GREASY LITTLE CARCINOGENIC SAUSAGES.
OW.
NEEDLE IN THE CARPET. WENT RIGHT THROUGH MY SHOE.
CRY LATER, BRO. I'M TALKING FREE SAUSAGES.
WAIT... PROFESSOR KETTERING? PROFESSOR HELMOND KETTERING?
NEVER MIND THE NAME, BOY, HAVE YOU ANY CASH IS THE PERTINENT QUESTION.
IT'S AN HONOR, SIR.
72
THE HONOR IS MINE, YOUNG MAN. DO COME IN.
THIS MAN IS A GIANT IN APPLIED PHYSICS!

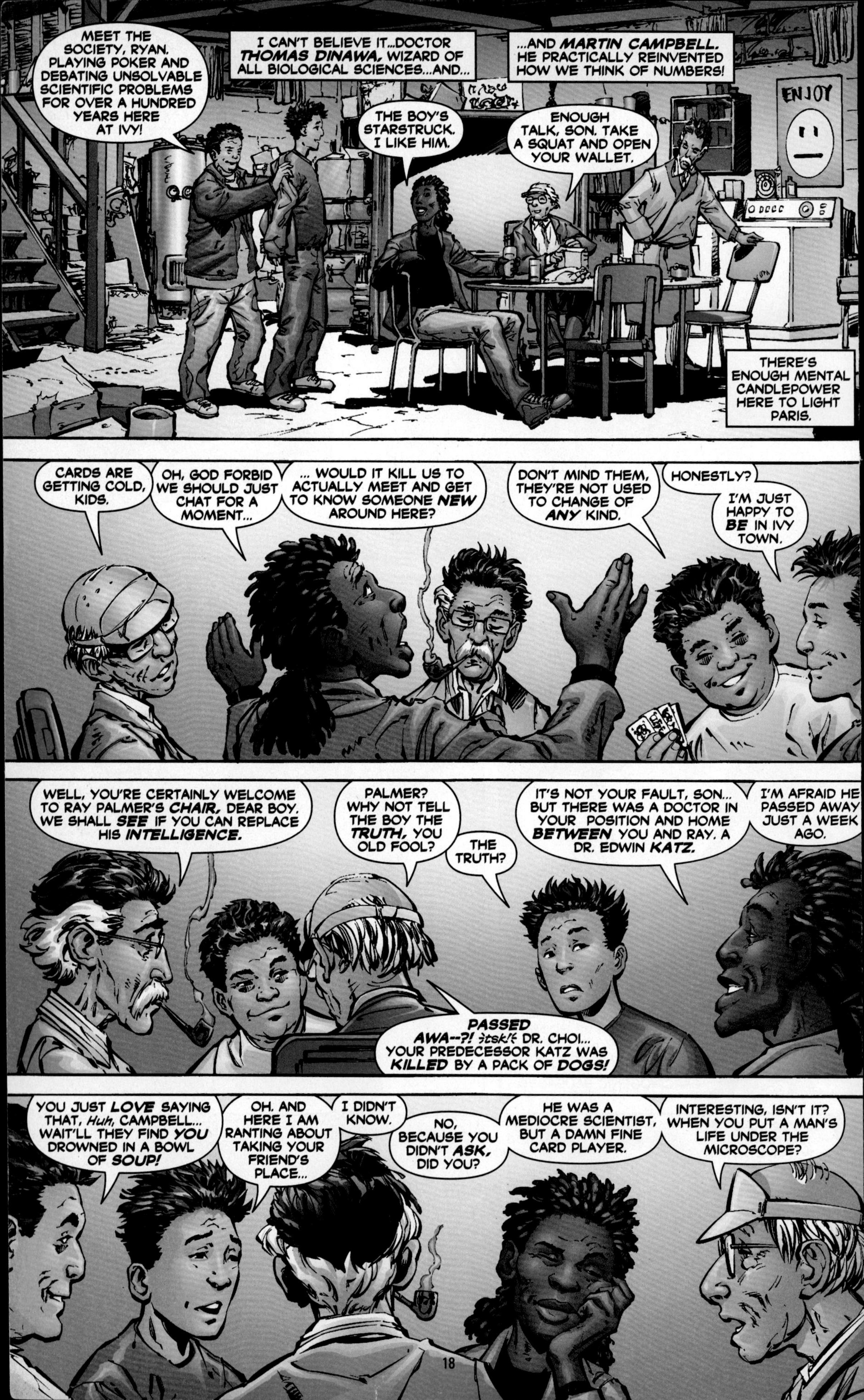

MEET THE SOCIETY, RYAN. PLAYING POKER AND DEBATING UNSOLVABLE SCIENTIFIC PROBLEMS FOR OVER A HUNDRED YEARS HERE AT IVY!
I CAN'T BELIEVE IT...DOCTOR ***THOMAS DINAWA,*** WIZARD OF ALL BIOLOGICAL SCIENCES...AND...
...AND ***MARTIN CAMPBELL.*** HE PRACTICALLY REINVENTED HOW WE THINK OF NUMBERS!
ENJOY
THE BOY'S STARSTRUCK. I LIKE HIM.
ENOUGH TALK, SON. TAKE A SQUAT AND OPEN YOUR WALLET.
THERE'S ENOUGH MENTAL CANDLEPOWER HERE TO LIGHT PARIS.
CARDS ARE GETTING COLD, KIDS.
OH, GOD FORBID WE SHOULD JUST CHAT FOR A MOMENT...
... WOULD IT KILL US TO ACTUALLY MEET AND GET TO KNOW SOMEONE ***NEW*** AROUND HERE?
DON'T MIND THEM, THEY'RE NOT USED TO CHANGE OF ***ANY*** KIND.
HONESTLY?
I'M JUST HAPPY TO ***BE*** IN IVY TOWN.
WELL, YOU'RE CERTAINLY WELCOME TO RAY PALMER'S ***CHAIR,*** DEAR BOY. WE SHALL ***SEE*** IF YOU CAN REPLACE HIS ***INTELLIGENCE.***
PALMER? WHY NOT TELL THE BOY THE ***TRUTH,*** YOU OLD FOOL?
THE TRUTH?
IT'S NOT YOUR FAULT, SON... BUT THERE WAS A DOCTOR IN YOUR POSITION AND HOME ***BETWEEN*** YOU AND RAY. A DR. EDWIN ***KATZ.***
I'M AFRAID HE PASSED AWAY JUST A WEEK AGO.
PASSED AWA--?! *tsk!* DR. CHOI... YOUR PREDECESSOR KATZ WAS ***KILLED*** BY A PACK OF ***DOGS!***
YOU JUST ***LOVE*** SAYING THAT, *Huh,* CAMPBELL... WAIT'LL THEY FIND ***YOU*** DROWNED IN A BOWL OF ***SOUP!***
OH. AND HERE I AM RANTING ABOUT TAKING YOUR FRIEND'S PLACE...
I DIDN'T KNOW.
NO, BECAUSE YOU DIDN'T ***ASK,*** DID YOU?
HE WAS A MEDIOCRE SCIENTIST, BUT A DAMN FINE CARD PLAYER.
INTERESTING, ISN'T IT? WHEN YOU PUT A MAN'S LIFE UNDER THE MICROSCOPE?

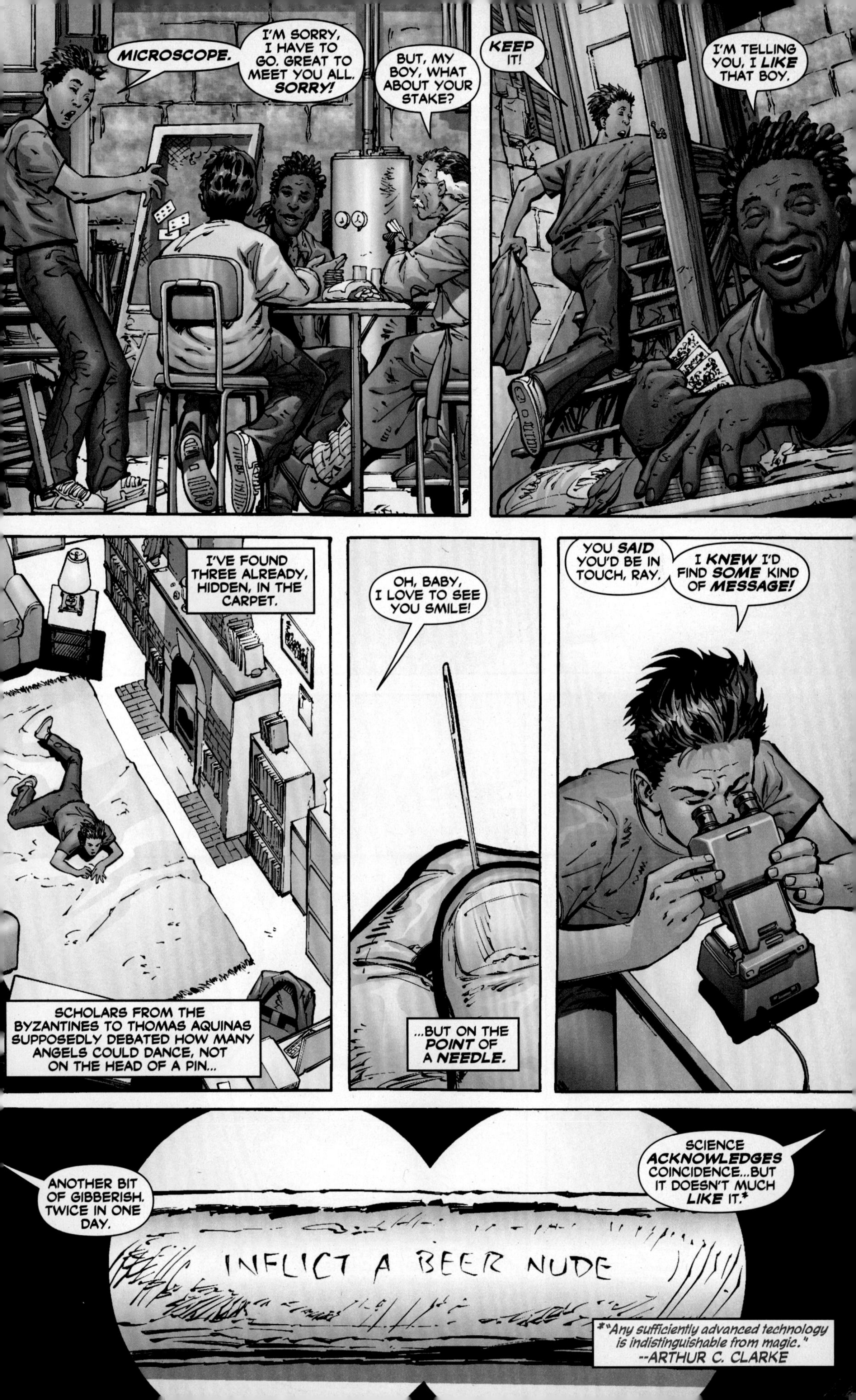
MICROSCOPE.
I'M SORRY, I HAVE TO GO. GREAT TO MEET YOU ALL. SORRY!
BUT, MY BOY, WHAT ABOUT YOUR STAKE?
KEEP IT!
I'M TELLING YOU, I LIKE THAT BOY.
I'VE FOUND THREE ALREADY, HIDDEN, IN THE CARPET.
SCHOLARS FROM THE BYZANTINES TO THOMAS AQUINAS SUPPOSEDLY DEBATED HOW MANY ANGELS COULD DANCE, NOT ON THE HEAD OF A PIN...
OH, BABY, I LOVE TO SEE YOU SMILE!
...BUT ON THE POINT OF A NEEDLE.
YOU SAID YOU'D BE IN TOUCH, RAY.
I KNEW I'D FIND SOME KIND OF MESSAGE!
ANOTHER BIT OF GIBBERISH. TWICE IN ONE DAY.
INFLICT A BEER NUDE
SCIENCE ACKNOWLEDGES COINCIDENCE...BUT IT DOESN'T MUCH LIKE IT.*
*"Any sufficiently advanced technology is indistinguishable from magic." --ARTHUR C. CLARKE

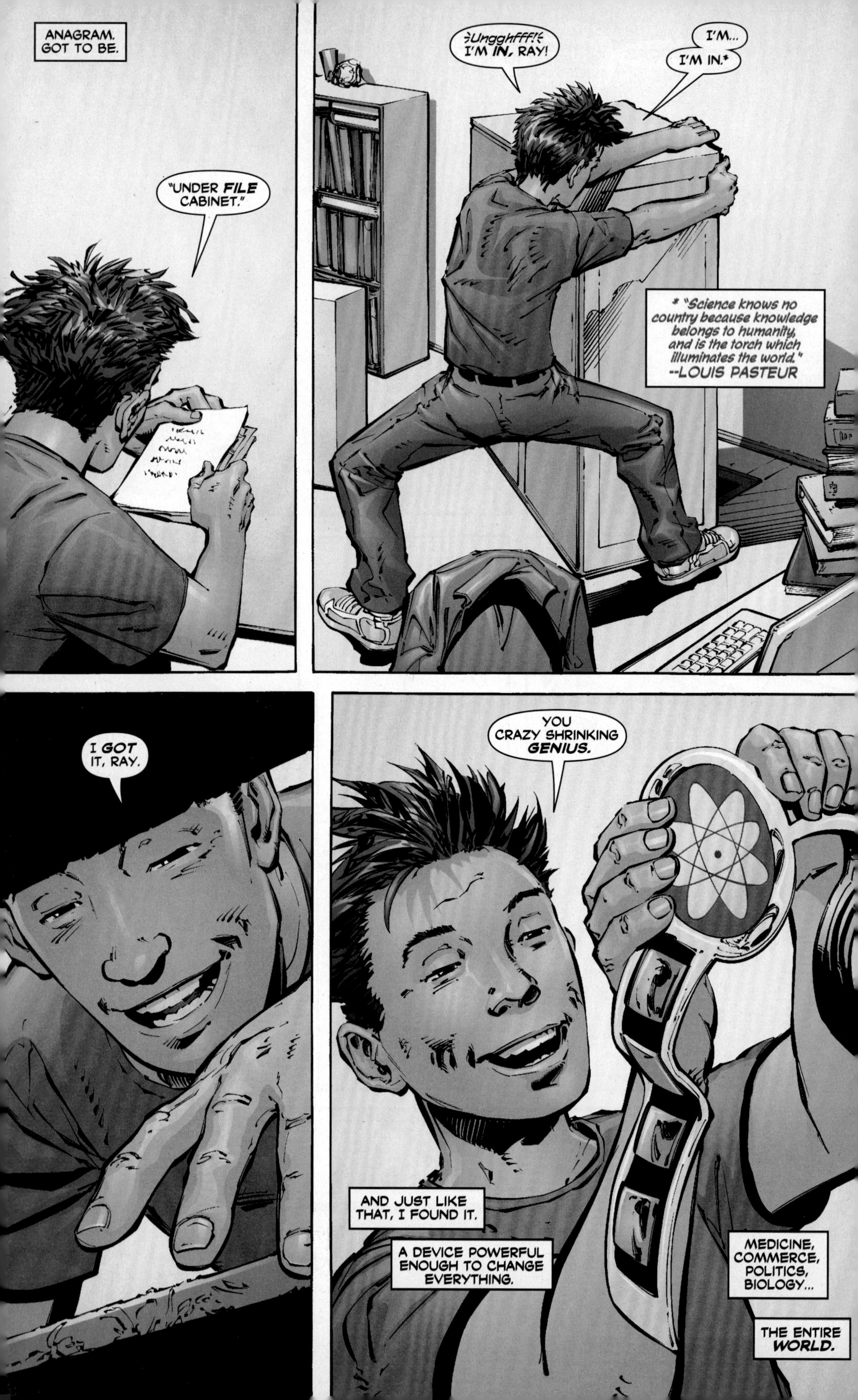
ANAGRAM. GOT TO BE.
"UNDER FILE CABINET."
UNGGHFFF!! I'M IN, RAY!
I'M...
I'M IN.*
* "Science knows no country because knowledge belongs to humanity, and is the torch which illuminates the world." --LOUIS PASTEUR
I GOT IT, RAY.
YOU CRAZY SHRINKING GENIUS.
AND JUST LIKE THAT, I FOUND IT.
A DEVICE POWERFUL ENOUGH TO CHANGE EVERYTHING.
MEDICINE, COMMERCE, POLITICS, BIOLOGY...
THE ENTIRE WORLD.

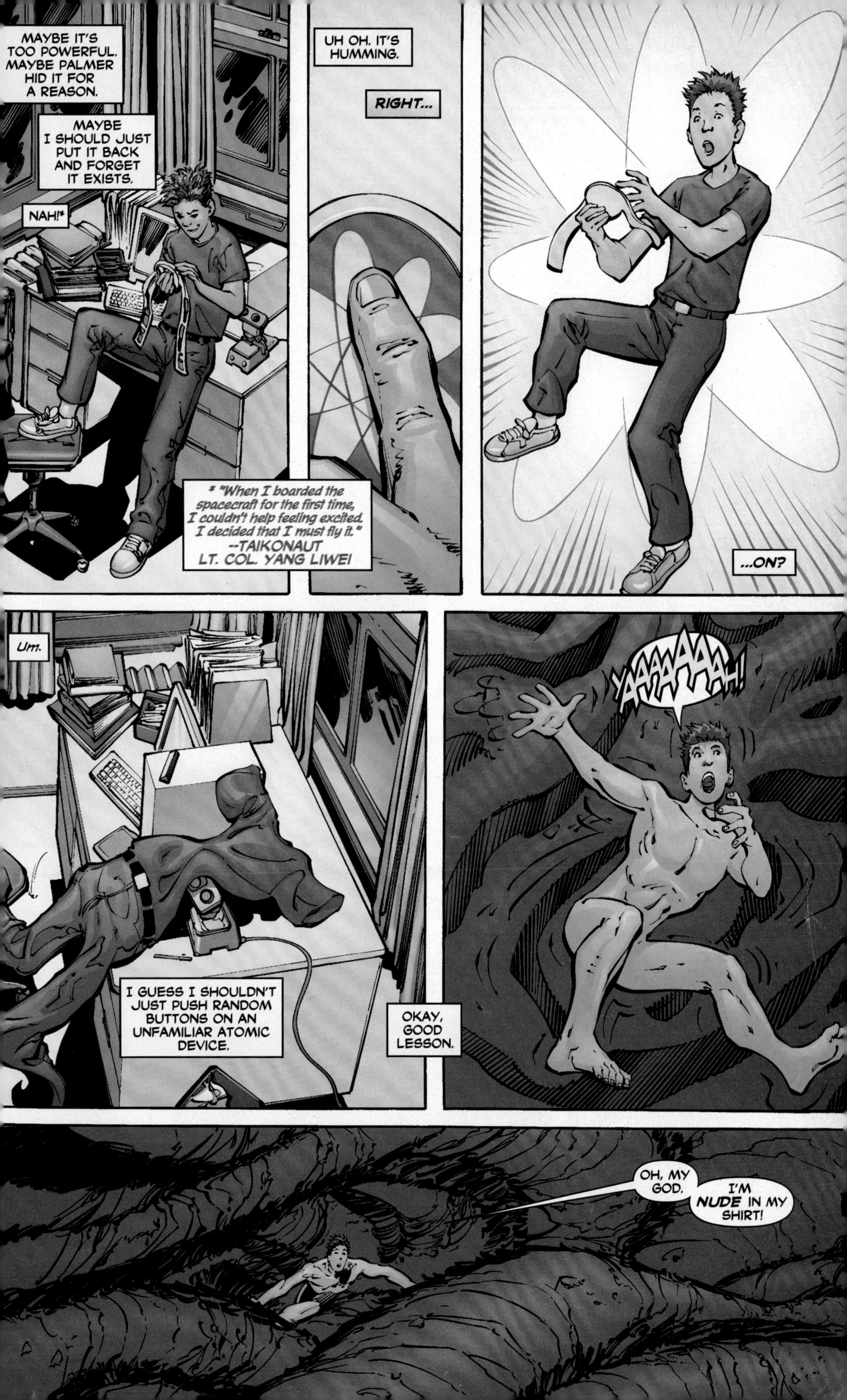
MAYBE IT'S TOO POWERFUL. MAYBE PALMER HID IT FOR A REASON.
MAYBE I SHOULD JUST PUT IT BACK AND FORGET IT EXISTS.
NAH!*
* "When I boarded the spacecraft for the first time, I couldn't help feeling excited. I decided that I must fly it." --TAIKONAUT LT. COL. YANG LIWEI
UH OH. IT'S HUMMING.
RIGHT...
...ON?
Um.
I GUESS I SHOULDN'T JUST PUSH RANDOM BUTTONS ON AN UNFAMILIAR ATOMIC DEVICE.
OKAY, GOOD LESSON.
YAAAAAAAH!
OH, MY GOD.
I'M NUDE IN MY SHIRT!

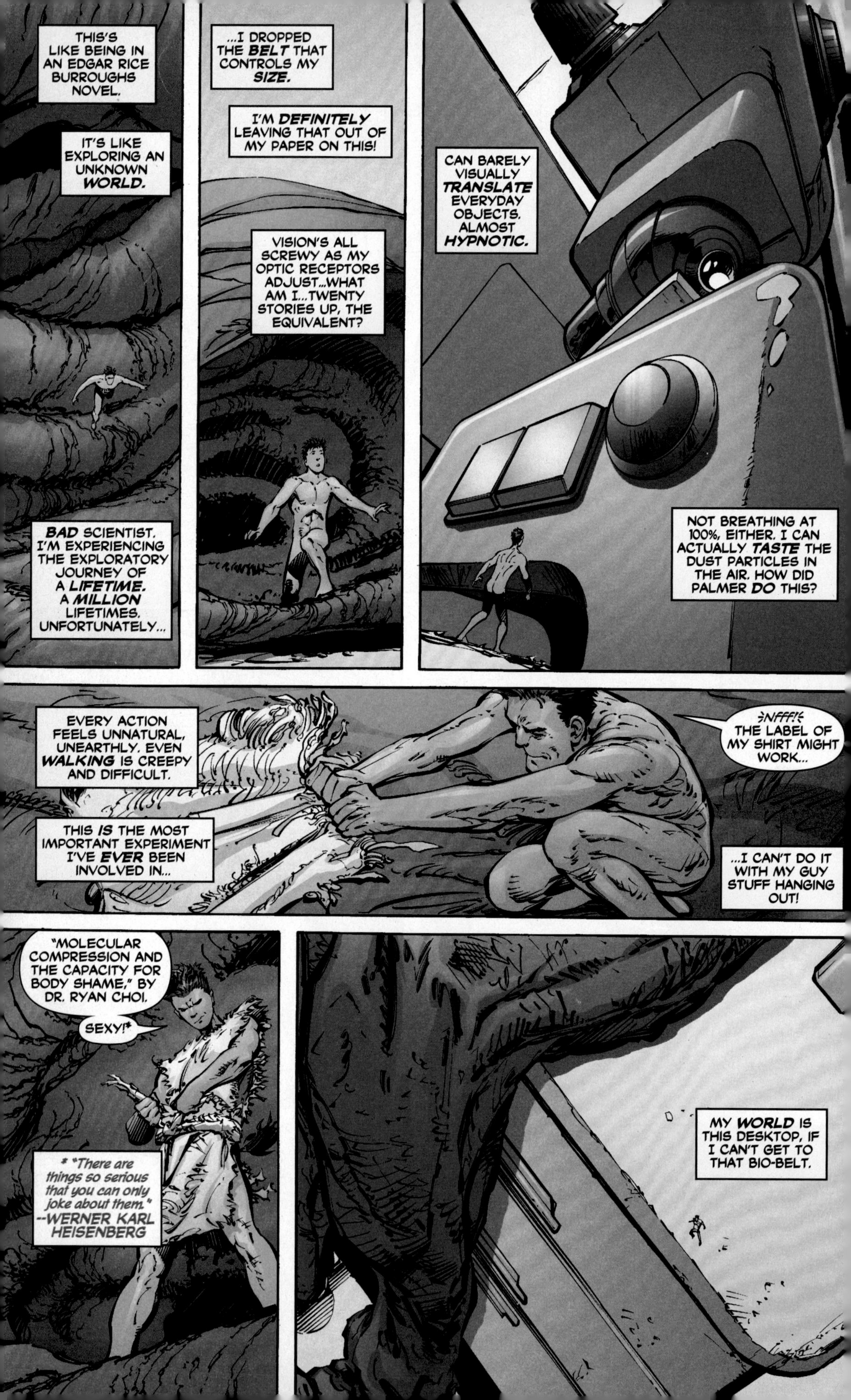

THIS'S LIKE BEING IN AN EDGAR RICE BURROUGHS NOVEL.
IT'S LIKE EXPLORING AN UNKNOWN WORLD.
BAD SCIENTIST. I'M EXPERIENCING THE EXPLORATORY JOURNEY OF A LIFETIME. A MILLION LIFETIMES. UNFORTUNATELY...
...I DROPPED THE BELT THAT CONTROLS MY SIZE.
I'M DEFINITELY LEAVING THAT OUT OF MY PAPER ON THIS!
VISION'S ALL SCREWY AS MY OPTIC RECEPTORS ADJUST...WHAT AM I...TWENTY STORIES UP, THE EQUIVALENT?
CAN BARELY VISUALLY TRANSLATE EVERYDAY OBJECTS. ALMOST HYPNOTIC.
NOT BREATHING AT 100%, EITHER. I CAN ACTUALLY TASTE THE DUST PARTICLES IN THE AIR. HOW DID PALMER DO THIS?
EVERY ACTION FEELS UNNATURAL, UNEARTHLY. EVEN WALKING IS CREEPY AND DIFFICULT.
THIS IS THE MOST IMPORTANT EXPERIMENT I'VE EVER BEEN INVOLVED IN...
...I CAN'T DO IT WITH MY GUY STUFF HANGING OUT!
NFFF! THE LABEL OF MY SHIRT MIGHT WORK...
"MOLECULAR COMPRESSION AND THE CAPACITY FOR BODY SHAME," BY DR. RYAN CHOI.
SEXY!*
* "There are things so serious that you can only joke about them." --WERNER KARL HEISENBERG
MY WORLD IS THIS DESKTOP, IF I CAN'T GET TO THAT BIO-BELT.

UH OH...I SERIOUSLY HOPE THAT GUST OF WIND ISN'T WHAT I'M *AFRAID* IT--

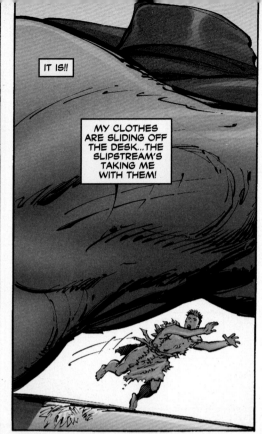

IT IS!!

MY CLOTHES ARE SLIDING OFF THE DESK...THE SLIPSTREAM'S TAKING ME WITH THEM!

YOWCH!

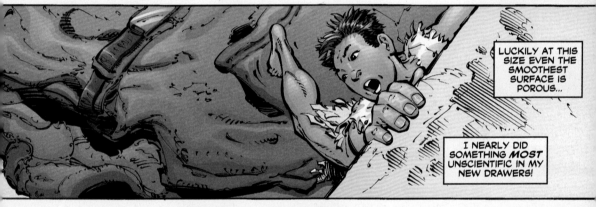

LUCKILY AT THIS SIZE EVEN THE SMOOTHEST SURFACE IS POROUS...

I NEARLY DID SOMETHING *MOST* UNSCIENTIFIC IN MY NEW DRAWERS!

HAVE TO GET DOWN TO THAT BELT, OR I COULD *DIE* UP HERE!

AHA!

OR IS THAT SUPPOSED TO BE "EUREKA!"?

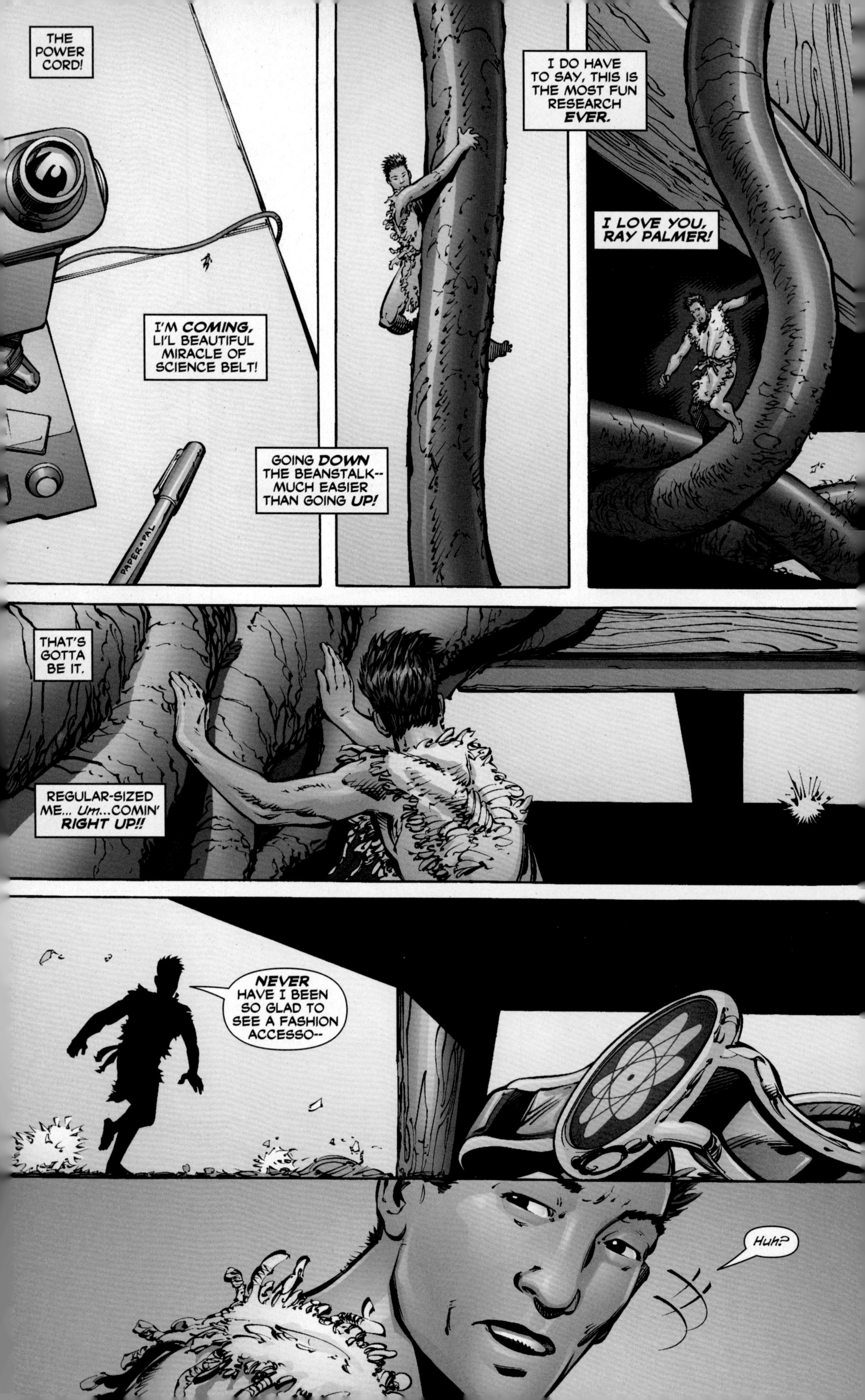

THE POWER CORD!
I'M COMING, LI'L BEAUTIFUL MIRACLE OF SCIENCE BELT!
PAPER•PAL
GOING DOWN THE BEANSTALK-- MUCH EASIER THAN GOING UP!
I DO HAVE TO SAY, THIS IS THE MOST FUN RESEARCH EVER.
I LOVE YOU, RAY PALMER!
THAT'S GOTTA BE IT.
REGULAR-SIZED ME... Um...COMIN' RIGHT UP!!
NEVER HAVE I BEEN SO GLAD TO SEE A FASHION ACCESSO--
Huh?

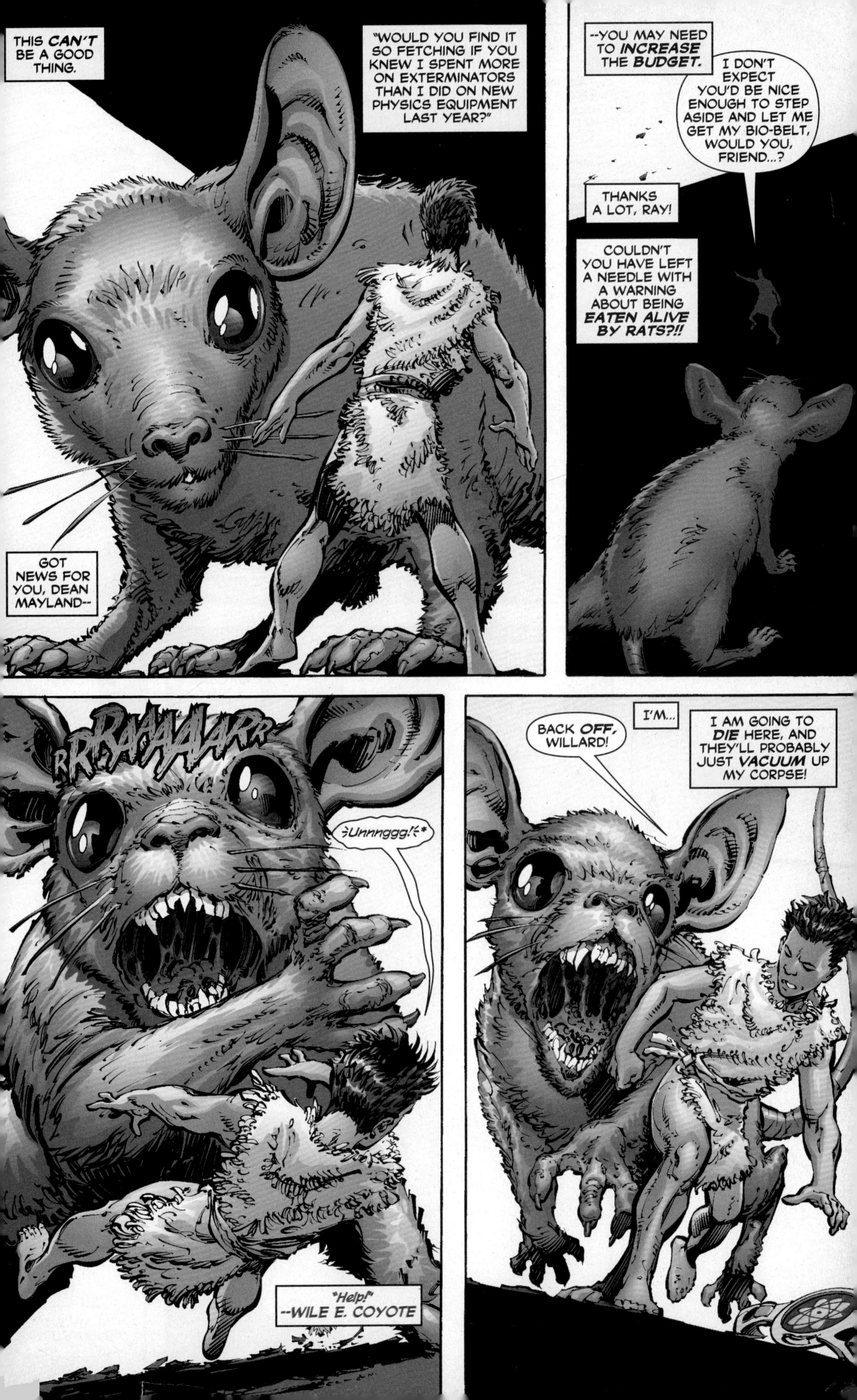
THIS CAN'T BE A GOOD THING.
"WOULD YOU FIND IT SO FETCHING IF YOU KNEW I SPENT MORE ON EXTERMINATORS THAN I DID ON NEW PHYSICS EQUIPMENT LAST YEAR?"
GOT NEWS FOR YOU, DEAN MAYLAND--
--YOU MAY NEED TO INCREASE THE BUDGET.
I DON'T EXPECT YOU'D BE NICE ENOUGH TO STEP ASIDE AND LET ME GET MY BIO-BELT, WOULD YOU, FRIEND...?
THANKS A LOT, RAY!
COULDN'T YOU HAVE LEFT A NEEDLE WITH A WARNING ABOUT BEING EATEN ALIVE BY RATS?!!
RRRAAAAARRR
Unnnggg!
"Help!" --WILE E. COYOTE
I'M...
BACK OFF, WILLARD!
I AM GOING TO DIE HERE, AND THEY'LL PROBABLY JUST VACUUM UP MY CORPSE!

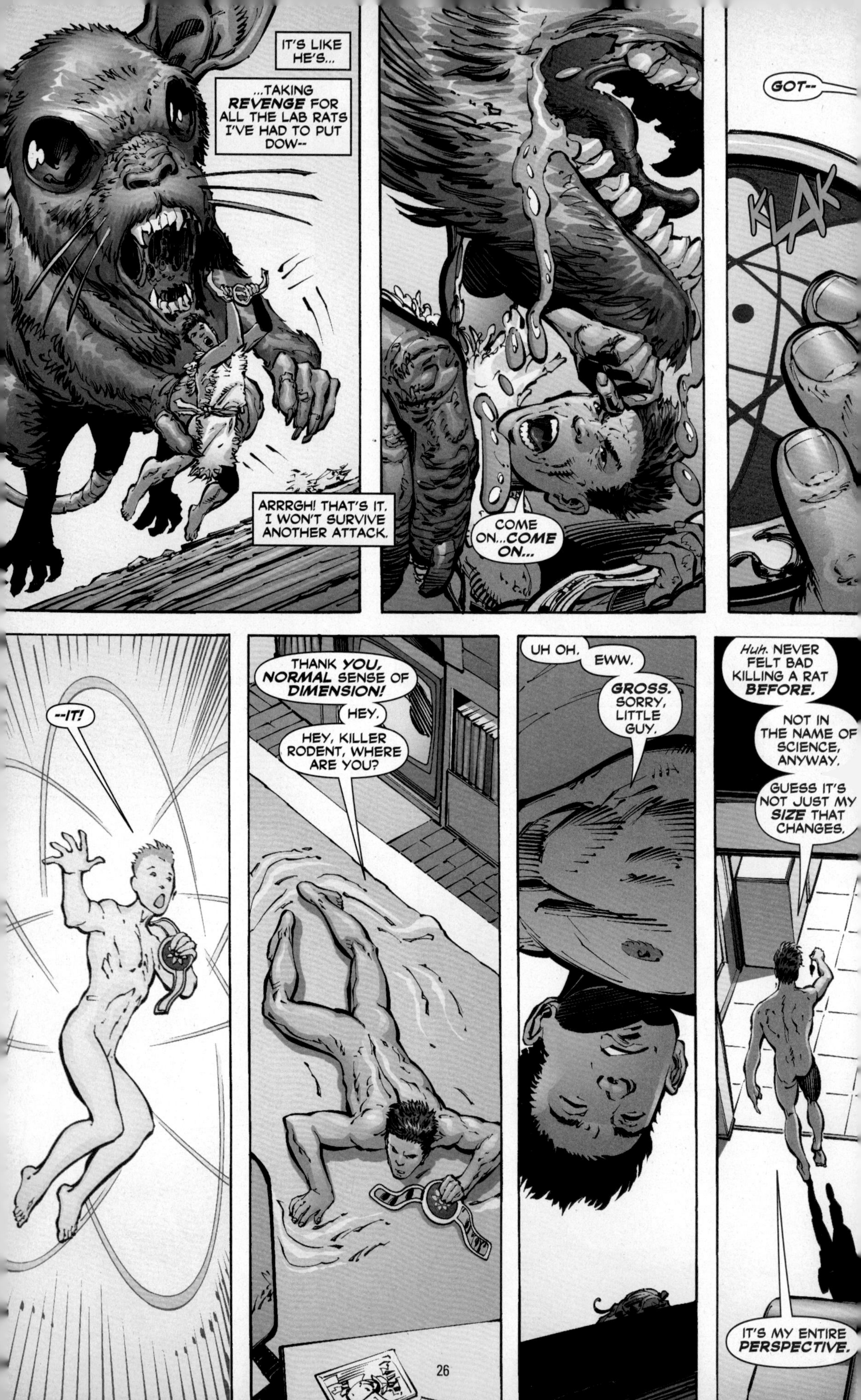

IT'S LIKE HE'S...
...TAKING REVENGE FOR ALL THE LAB RATS I'VE HAD TO PUT DOW--
ARRRGH! THAT'S IT. I WON'T SURVIVE ANOTHER ATTACK.
COME ON...COME ON...
GOT--
KLAK
--IT!
THANK YOU, NORMAL SENSE OF DIMENSION!
HEY.
HEY, KILLER RODENT, WHERE ARE YOU?
UH OH.
EWW.
GROSS. SORRY, LITTLE GUY.
Huh. NEVER FELT BAD KILLING A RAT BEFORE.
NOT IN THE NAME OF SCIENCE, ANYWAY.
GUESS IT'S NOT JUST MY SIZE THAT CHANGES.
IT'S MY ENTIRE PERSPECTIVE.

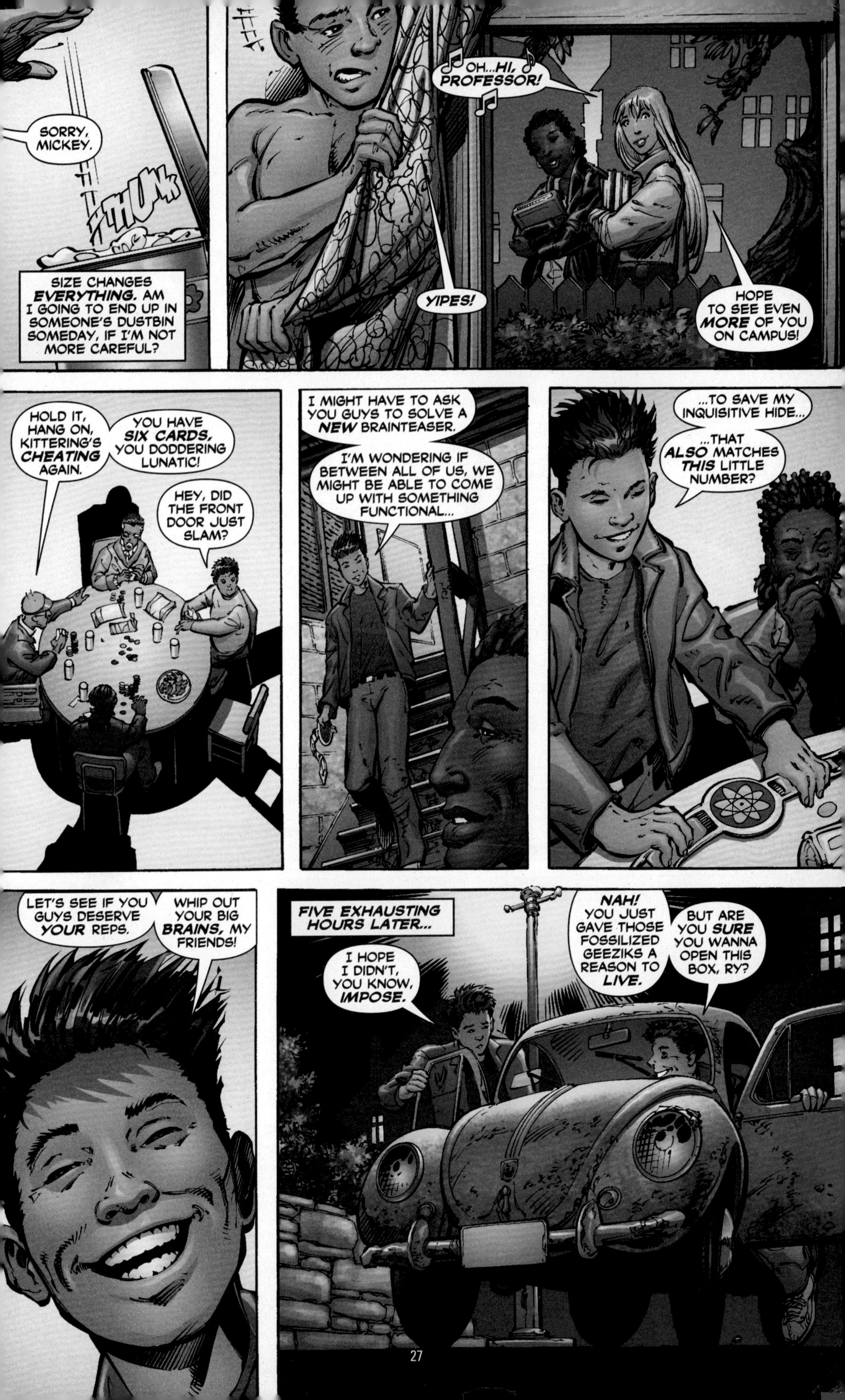
SORRY, MICKEY.
THUNK
SIZE CHANGES EVERYTHING. AM I GOING TO END UP IN SOMEONE'S DUSTBIN SOMEDAY, IF I'M NOT MORE CAREFUL?
OH...HI, PROFESSOR!
YIPES!
HOPE TO SEE EVEN MORE OF YOU ON CAMPUS!
HOLD IT, HANG ON, KITTERING'S CHEATING AGAIN.
YOU HAVE SIX CARDS, YOU DODDERING LUNATIC!
HEY, DID THE FRONT DOOR JUST SLAM?
I MIGHT HAVE TO ASK YOU GUYS TO SOLVE A NEW BRAINTEASER.
I'M WONDERING IF BETWEEN ALL OF US, WE MIGHT BE ABLE TO COME UP WITH SOMETHING FUNCTIONAL...
...TO SAVE MY INQUISITIVE HIDE...
...THAT ALSO MATCHES THIS LITTLE NUMBER?
LET'S SEE IF YOU GUYS DESERVE YOUR REPS.
WHIP OUT YOUR BIG BRAINS, MY FRIENDS!
FIVE EXHAUSTING HOURS LATER...
I HOPE I DIDN'T, YOU KNOW, IMPOSE.
NAH! YOU JUST GAVE THOSE FOSSILIZED GEEZIKS A REASON TO LIVE.
BUT ARE YOU SURE YOU WANNA OPEN THIS BOX, RY?

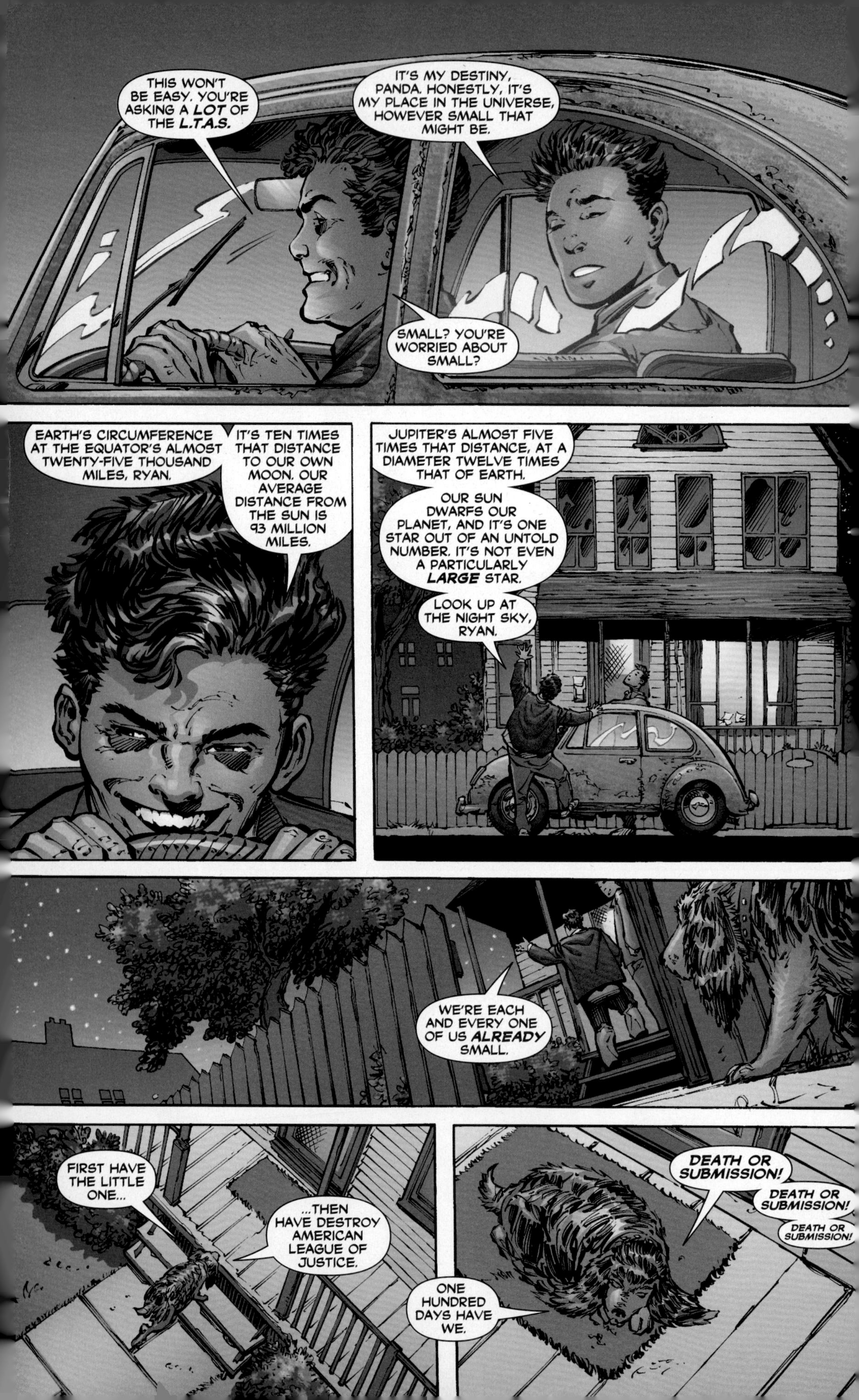
THIS WON'T BE EASY. YOU'RE ASKING A *LOT* OF THE *L.T.A.S.*
IT'S MY DESTINY, PANDA. HONESTLY, IT'S MY PLACE IN THE UNIVERSE, HOWEVER SMALL THAT MIGHT BE.
SMALL? YOU'RE WORRIED ABOUT SMALL?
EARTH'S CIRCUMFERENCE AT THE EQUATOR'S ALMOST TWENTY-FIVE THOUSAND MILES, RYAN.
IT'S TEN TIMES THAT DISTANCE TO OUR OWN MOON. OUR AVERAGE DISTANCE FROM THE SUN IS 93 MILLION MILES.
JUPITER'S ALMOST FIVE TIMES THAT DISTANCE, AT A DIAMETER TWELVE TIMES THAT OF EARTH.
OUR SUN DWARFS OUR PLANET, AND IT'S ONE STAR OUT OF AN UNTOLD NUMBER. IT'S NOT EVEN A PARTICULARLY *LARGE* STAR.
LOOK UP AT THE NIGHT SKY, RYAN.
WE'RE EACH AND EVERY ONE OF US *ALREADY* SMALL.
FIRST HAVE THE LITTLE ONE...
...THEN HAVE DESTROY AMERICAN LEAGUE OF JUSTICE.
ONE HUNDRED DAYS HAVE WE.
DEATH OR SUBMISSION!
DEATH OR SUBMISSION!
DEATH OR SUBMISSION!

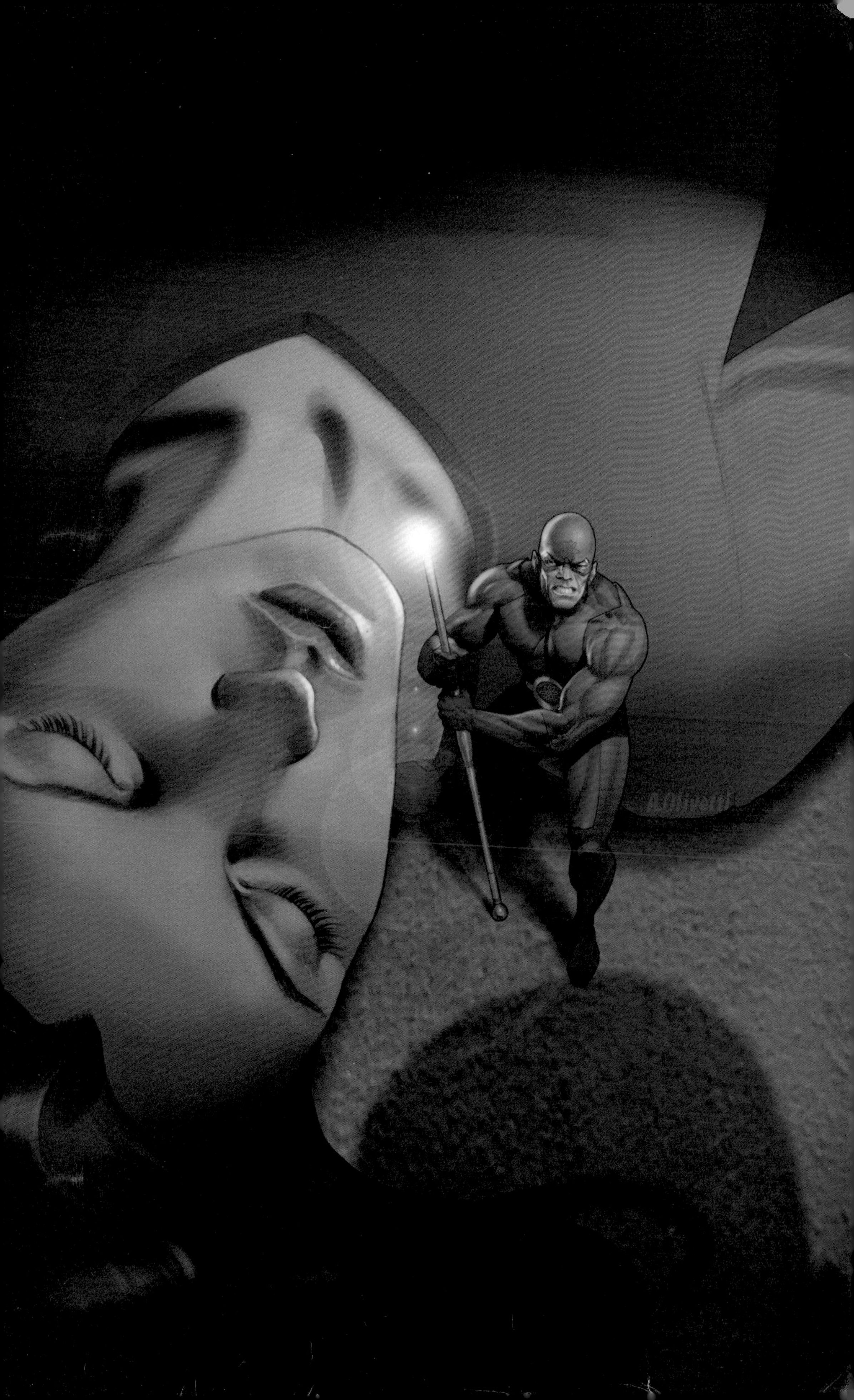

MY LIFE IN MINIATURE: PART TWO
ATOMIC SHELL

from **THE ALL NEW ATOM #2**
Cover by **Ariel Olivetti**

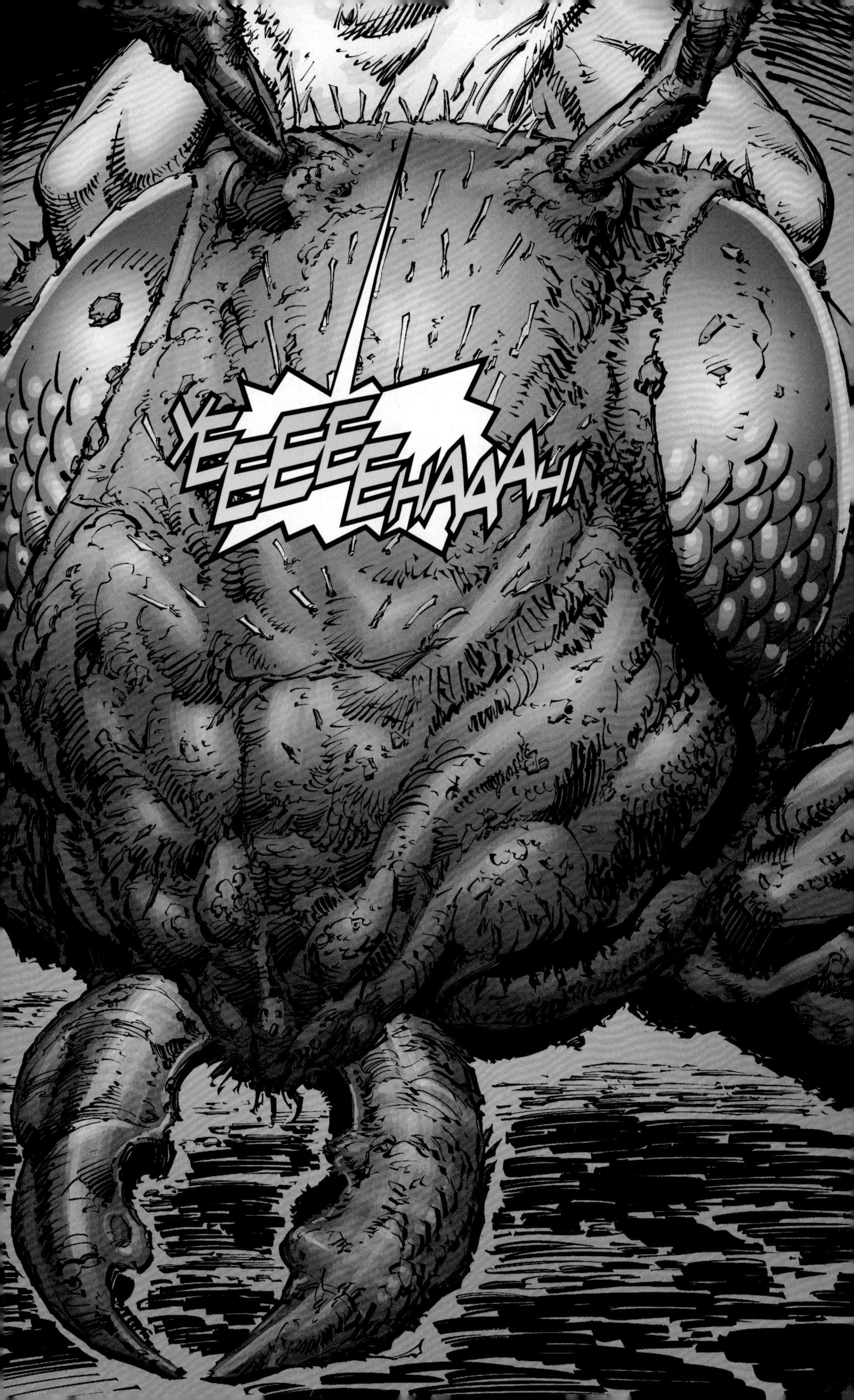
YEEEEEEHAAAH!

HAVING A GOOD TIME, RYAN?

WELL, I WOULDN'T GO THAT FAR...

COULD YOU SPEAK UP?

I SAID, "THIS IS ONE SAD RIDE, DR. DINAWA!"

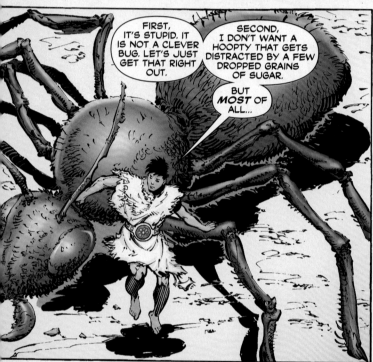

FIRST, IT'S STUPID. IT IS NOT A CLEVER BUG, LET'S JUST GET THAT RIGHT OUT.

SECOND, I DON'T WANT A HOOPTY THAT GETS DISTRACTED BY A FEW DROPPED GRAINS OF SUGAR.

BUT MOST OF ALL...

...IT SMELLS LIKE A HUGE FART.

SORRY, THAT WASN'T VERY SCIENTIFIC OF ME. *

* "An idealist is one who, on noticing that a rose smells better than a cabbage, concludes that it will also make better soup."--HENRY L. MENCKEN

THAT'S THE PHEROMONE TRAIL YOU'RE SMELLING.

THE ANT LEAVES IT ON THE TRAIL FROM THE NEST WHEN HUNTING FOR FOOD, FOR OTHER ANTS TO FOLLOW.

FASCINATING STUFF. IF YOU CRUSH AN ANT--

--IT SENDS OFF A DIFFERENT, 'ALARM' PHEROMONE, THAT SENDS THE OTHERS OF ITS COLONY INTO A FIGHTING FRENZY.

DOC, DON'T GET ME WRONG, YOU'RE A BRILLIANT MAN AND I RESPECT YOU IMMENSELY...

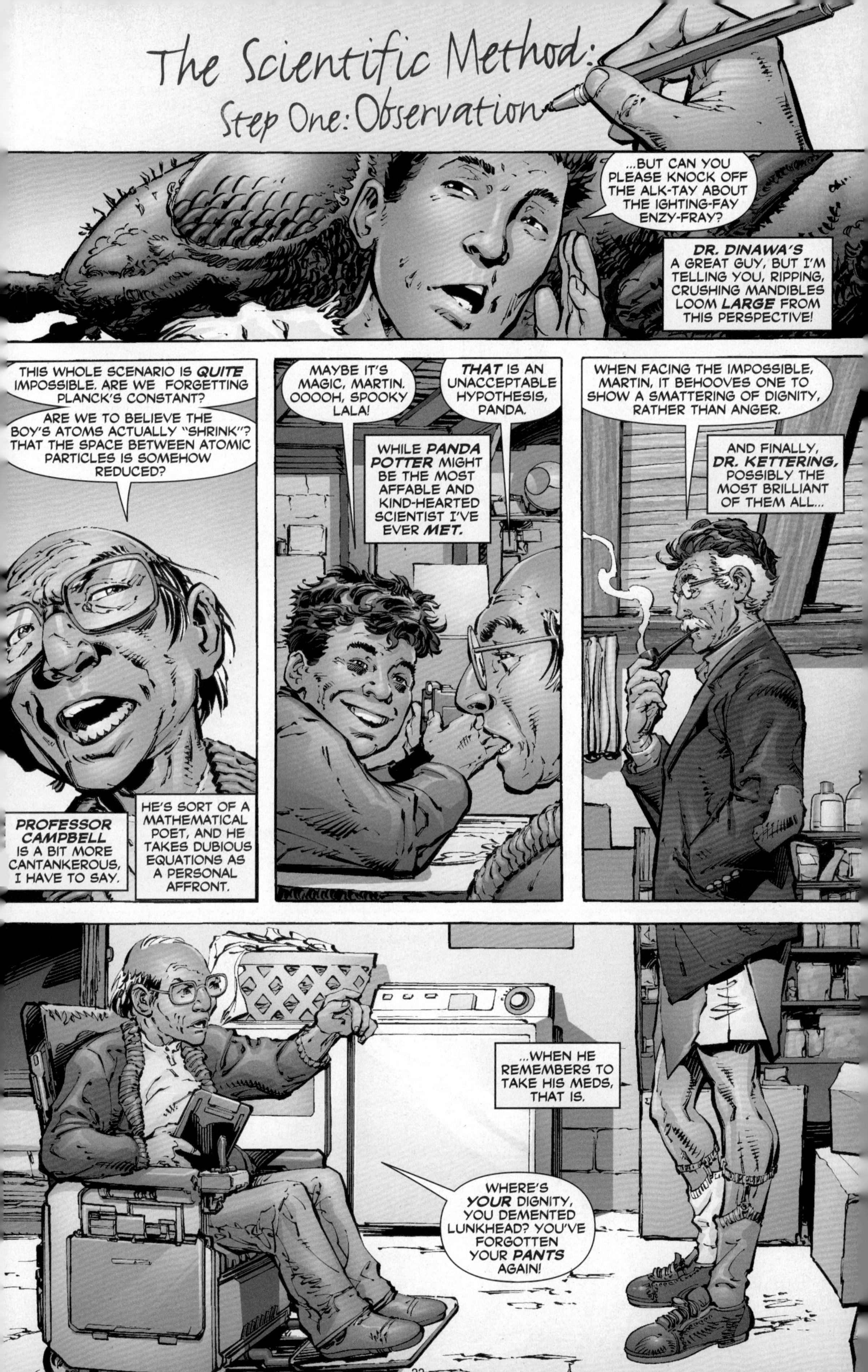
The Scientific Method:
Step One: Observation
...BUT CAN YOU PLEASE KNOCK OFF THE ALK-TAY ABOUT THE IGHTING-FAY ENZY-FRAY?
DR. DINAWA'S A GREAT GUY, BUT I'M TELLING YOU, RIPPING, CRUSHING MANDIBLES LOOM LARGE FROM THIS PERSPECTIVE!
THIS WHOLE SCENARIO IS QUITE IMPOSSIBLE. ARE WE FORGETTING PLANCK'S CONSTANT?
ARE WE TO BELIEVE THE BOY'S ATOMS ACTUALLY "SHRINK"? THAT THE SPACE BETWEEN ATOMIC PARTICLES IS SOMEHOW REDUCED?
PROFESSOR CAMPBELL IS A BIT MORE CANTANKEROUS, I HAVE TO SAY.
HE'S SORT OF A MATHEMATICAL POET, AND HE TAKES DUBIOUS EQUATIONS AS A PERSONAL AFFRONT.
MAYBE IT'S MAGIC, MARTIN. OOOOH, SPOOKY LALA!
THAT IS AN UNACCEPTABLE HYPOTHESIS, PANDA.
WHILE PANDA POTTER MIGHT BE THE MOST AFFABLE AND KIND-HEARTED SCIENTIST I'VE EVER MET.
WHEN FACING THE IMPOSSIBLE, MARTIN, IT BEHOOVES ONE TO SHOW A SMATTERING OF DIGNITY, RATHER THAN ANGER.
AND FINALLY, DR. KETTERING, POSSIBLY THE MOST BRILLIANT OF THEM ALL...
...WHEN HE REMEMBERS TO TAKE HIS MEDS, THAT IS.
WHERE'S YOUR DIGNITY, YOU DEMENTED LUNKHEAD? YOU'VE FORGOTTEN YOUR PANTS AGAIN!

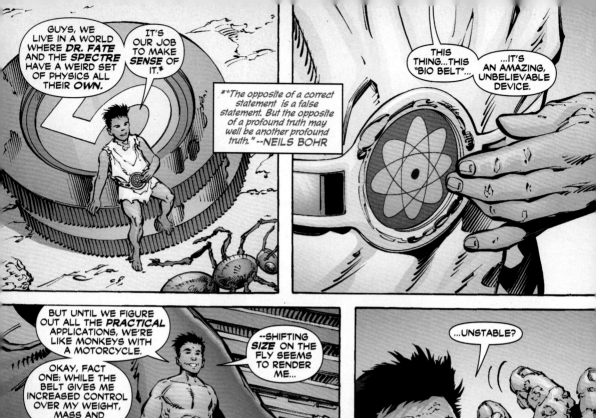

GUYS, WE LIVE IN A WORLD WHERE *DR. FATE* AND THE *SPECTRE* HAVE A WEIRD SET OF PHYSICS ALL THEIR *OWN.*

IT'S OUR JOB TO MAKE *SENSE* OF IT.*

*"The opposite of a correct statement is a false statement. But the opposite of a profound truth may well be another profound truth." --NEILS BOHR

THIS THING...THIS "BIO BELT"...

...IT'S AN AMAZING, UNBELIEVABLE DEVICE.

BUT UNTIL WE FIGURE OUT ALL THE *PRACTICAL* APPLICATIONS, WE'RE LIKE MONKEYS WITH A MOTORCYCLE.

OKAY, FACT ONE: WHILE THE BELT GIVES ME INCREASED CONTROL OVER MY WEIGHT, MASS AND DENSITY--

--SHIFTING *SIZE* ON THE FLY SEEMS TO RENDER ME...

...UNSTABLE?

OH. OW.

GWIIIIW

RYAN! HIT THE *SIZE* CONTROLS ON YOUR *BELT!*

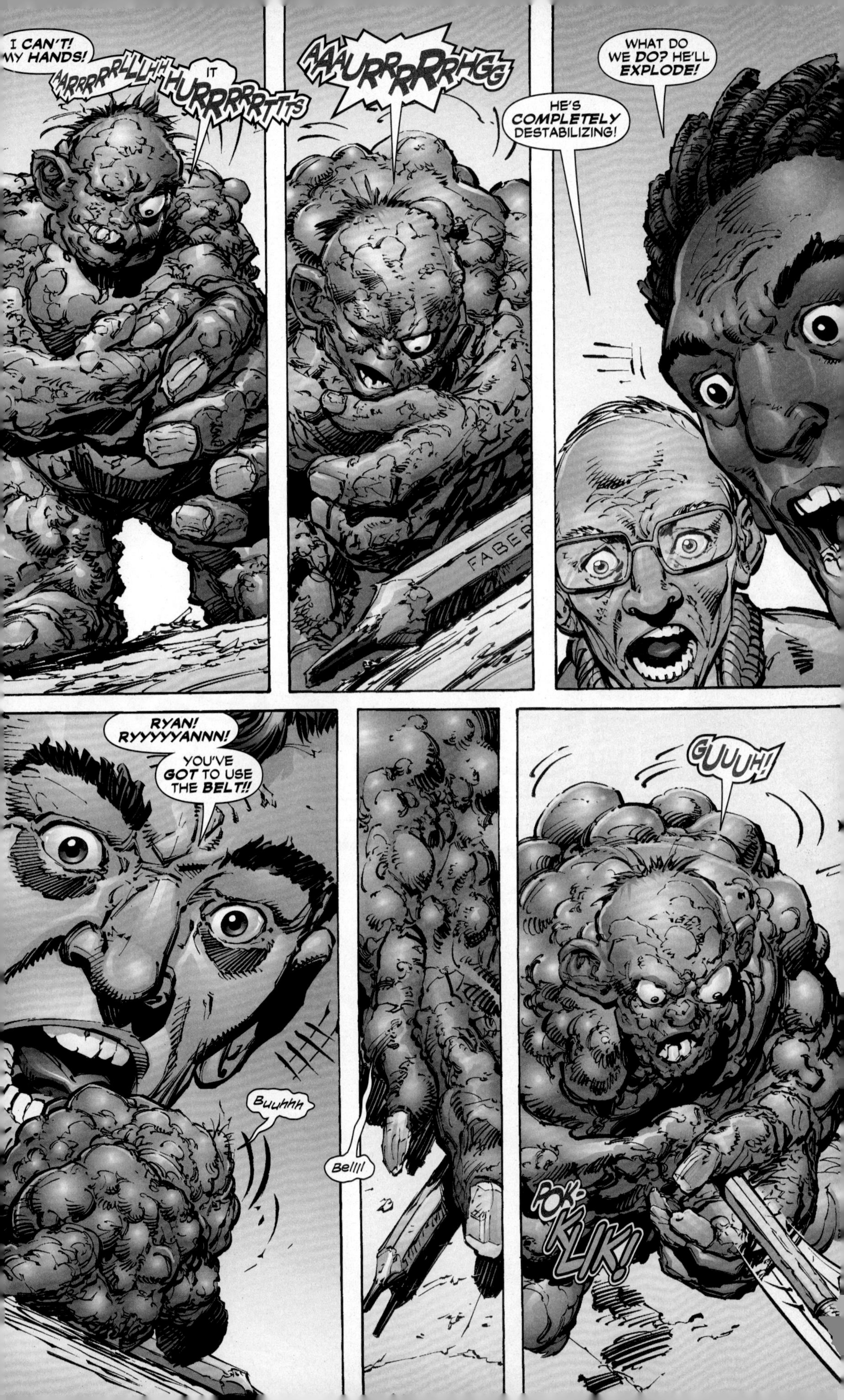
I CAN'T! MY HANDS!
AARRRRRLLLHH
IT HURRRRRRTTTS
AAAURRRRRRHGG
WHAT DO WE DO? HE'LL EXPLODE!
HE'S COMPLETELY DESTABILIZING!
FABER
RYAN! RYYYYYANNN!
YOU'VE GOT TO USE THE BELT!!
Buuhhh
Bellll
GUUUH!
POK
KLIK!

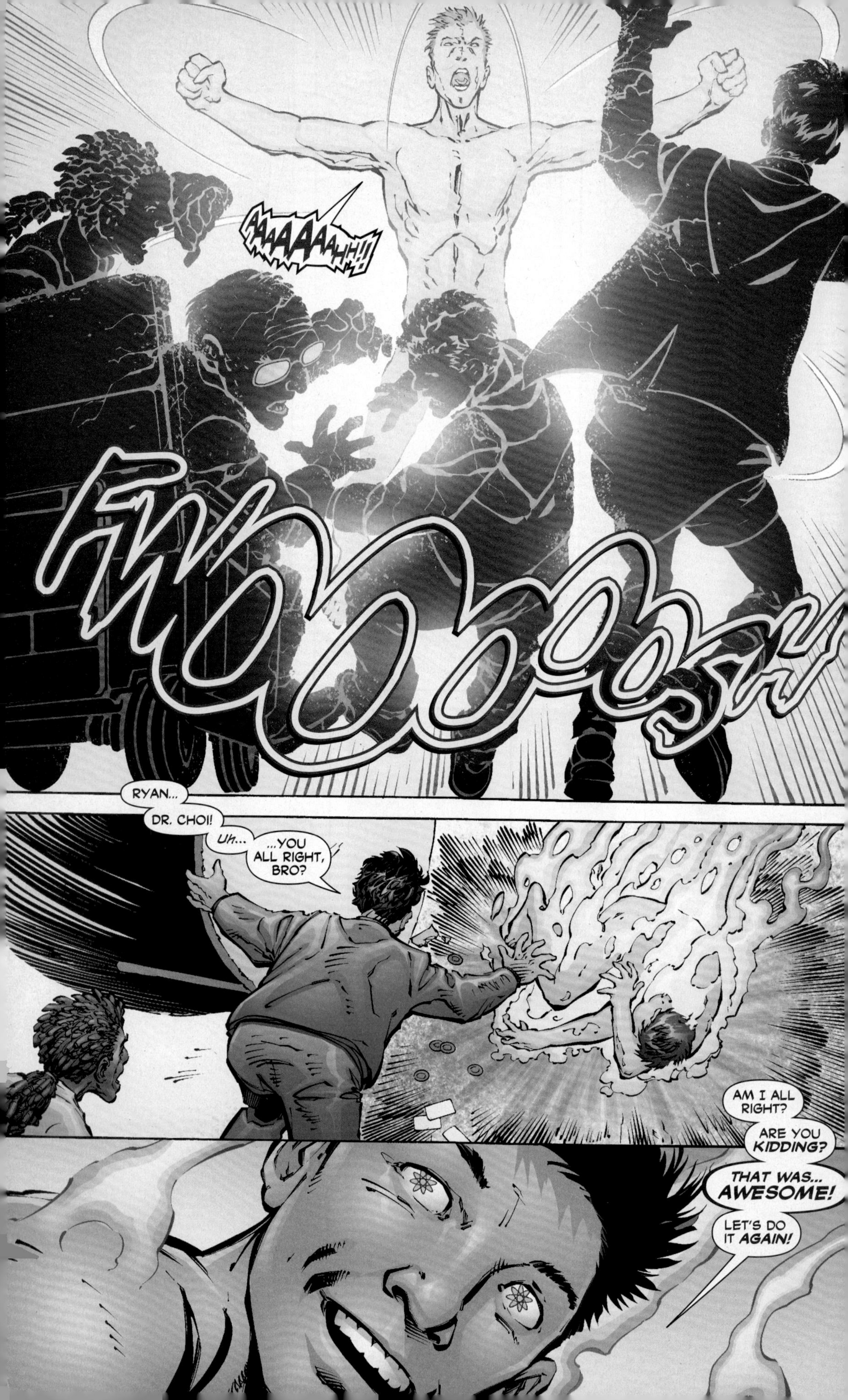
AAAAAAAHH!!!
FWOOOOOSH
RYAN...
DR. CHOI!
Uh...
...YOU ALL RIGHT, BRO?
AM I ALL RIGHT?
ARE YOU KIDDING?
THAT WAS... AWESOME!
LET'S DO IT AGAIN!

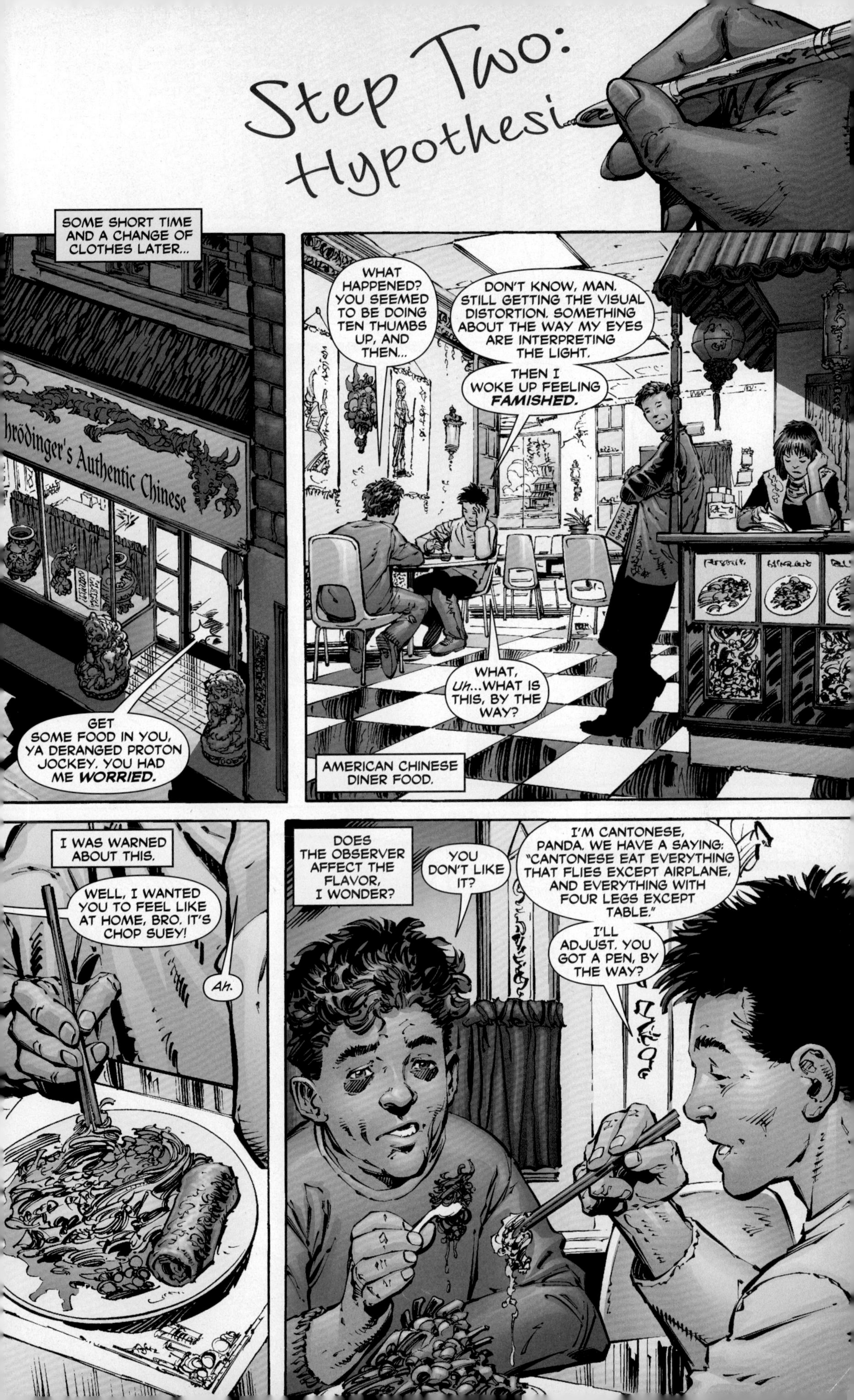
Step Two:
Hypothesi
SOME SHORT TIME AND A CHANGE OF CLOTHES LATER...
hrödinger's Authentic Chinese
GET SOME FOOD IN YOU, YA DERANGED PROTON JOCKEY. YOU HAD ME WORRIED.
WHAT HAPPENED? YOU SEEMED TO BE DOING TEN THUMBS UP, AND THEN...
DON'T KNOW, MAN. STILL GETTING THE VISUAL DISTORTION. SOMETHING ABOUT THE WAY MY EYES ARE INTERPRETING THE LIGHT.
THEN I WOKE UP FEELING FAMISHED.
WHAT, Uh...WHAT IS THIS, BY THE WAY?
AMERICAN CHINESE DINER FOOD.
I WAS WARNED ABOUT THIS.
WELL, I WANTED YOU TO FEEL LIKE AT HOME, BRO. IT'S CHOP SUEY!
Ah.
DOES THE OBSERVER AFFECT THE FLAVOR, I WONDER?
YOU DON'T LIKE IT?
I'M CANTONESE, PANDA. WE HAVE A SAYING: "CANTONESE EAT EVERYTHING THAT FLIES EXCEPT AIRPLANE, AND EVERYTHING WITH FOUR LEGS EXCEPT TABLE."
I'LL ADJUST. YOU GOT A PEN, BY THE WAY?

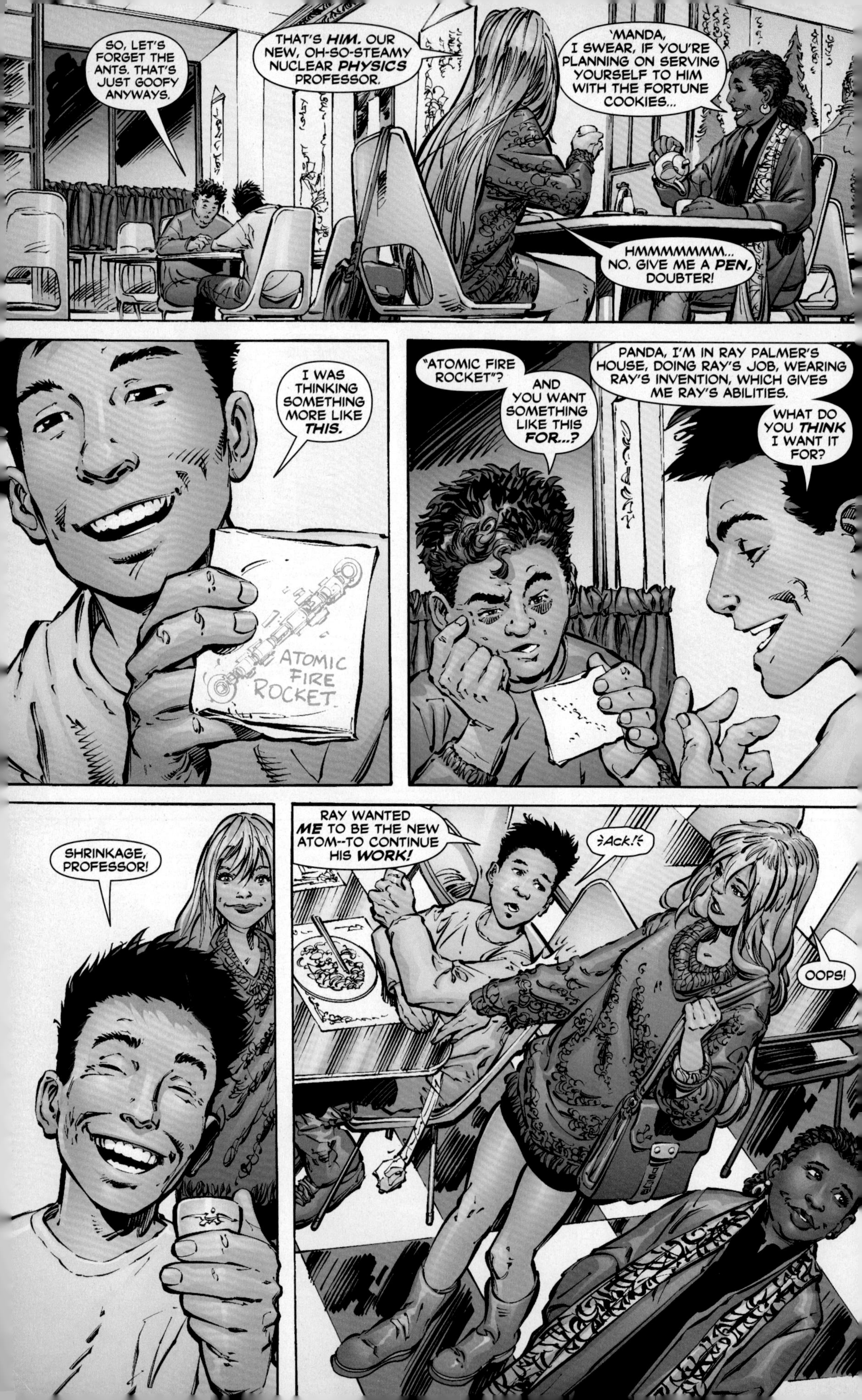
SO, LET'S FORGET THE ANTS. THAT'S JUST GOOFY ANYWAYS.
THAT'S HIM. OUR NEW, OH-SO-STEAMY NUCLEAR PHYSICS PROFESSOR.
'MANDA, I SWEAR, IF YOU'RE PLANNING ON SERVING YOURSELF TO HIM WITH THE FORTUNE COOKIES...
HMMMMMMM... NO. GIVE ME A PEN, DOUBTER!
I WAS THINKING SOMETHING MORE LIKE THIS.
ATOMIC FIRE ROCKET
"ATOMIC FIRE ROCKET"?
AND YOU WANT SOMETHING LIKE THIS FOR...?
PANDA, I'M IN RAY PALMER'S HOUSE, DOING RAY'S JOB, WEARING RAY'S INVENTION, WHICH GIVES ME RAY'S ABILITIES.
WHAT DO YOU THINK I WANT IT FOR?
SHRINKAGE, PROFESSOR!
RAY WANTED ME TO BE THE NEW ATOM--TO CONTINUE HIS WORK!
Ack!
OOPS!

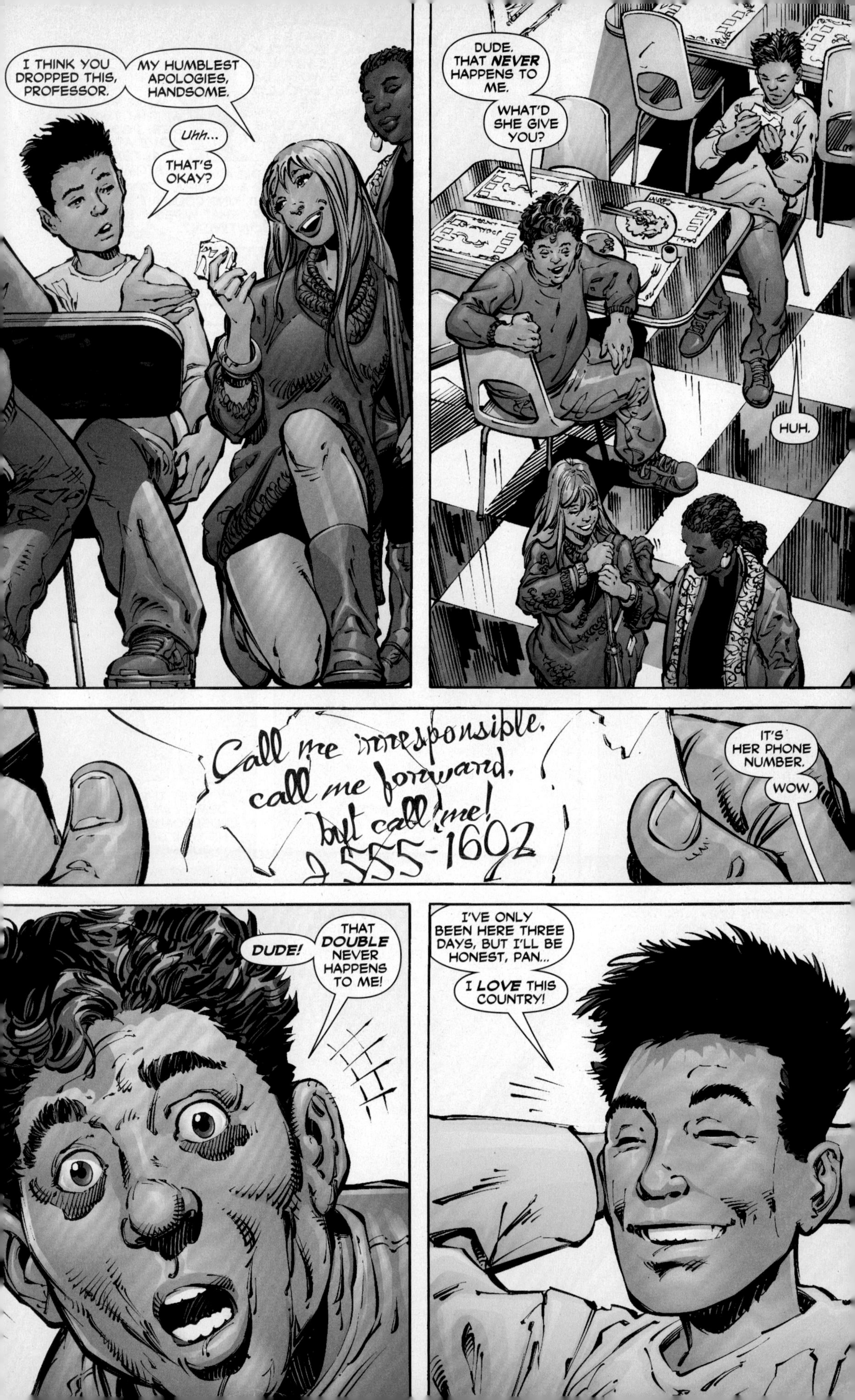
I THINK YOU DROPPED THIS, PROFESSOR.
MY HUMBLEST APOLOGIES, HANDSOME.
Uhh...
THAT'S OKAY?
DUDE. THAT NEVER HAPPENS TO ME.
WHAT'D SHE GIVE YOU?
HUH.
Call me irresponsible, call me forward, but call me! 555-1602
IT'S HER PHONE NUMBER.
WOW.
DUDE!
THAT DOUBLE NEVER HAPPENS TO ME!
I'VE ONLY BEEN HERE THREE DAYS, BUT I'LL BE HONEST, PAN...
I LOVE THIS COUNTRY!

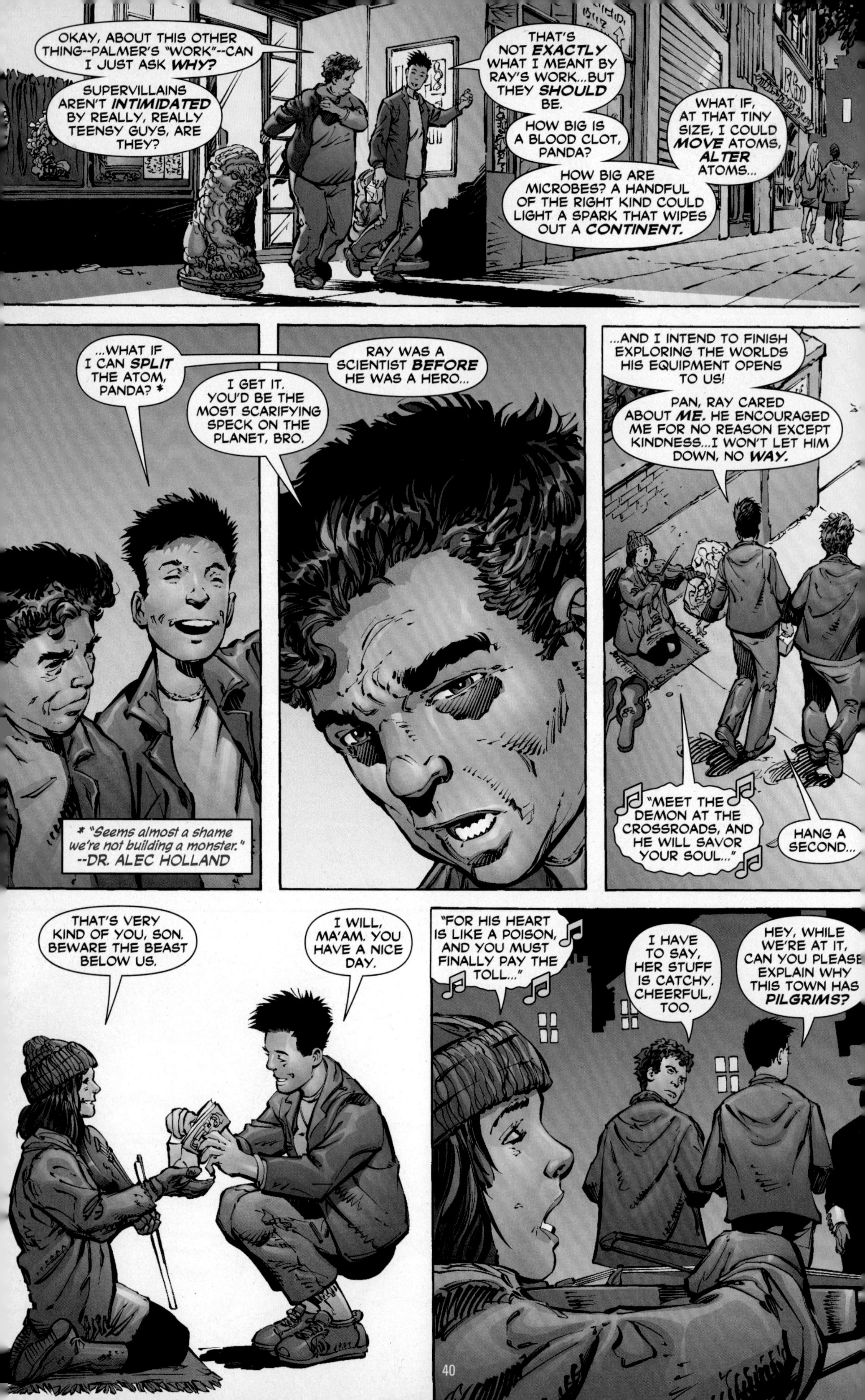
OKAY, ABOUT THIS OTHER THING--PALMER'S "WORK"--CAN I JUST ASK WHY?
SUPERVILLAINS AREN'T INTIMIDATED BY REALLY, REALLY TEENSY GUYS, ARE THEY?
THAT'S NOT EXACTLY WHAT I MEANT BY RAY'S WORK...BUT THEY SHOULD BE.
HOW BIG IS A BLOOD CLOT, PANDA?
HOW BIG ARE MICROBES? A HANDFUL OF THE RIGHT KIND COULD LIGHT A SPARK THAT WIPES OUT A CONTINENT.
WHAT IF, AT THAT TINY SIZE, I COULD MOVE ATOMS, ALTER ATOMS...
...WHAT IF I CAN SPLIT THE ATOM, PANDA? *
I GET IT. YOU'D BE THE MOST SCARIFYING SPECK ON THE PLANET, BRO.
* "Seems almost a shame we're not building a monster." --DR. ALEC HOLLAND
RAY WAS A SCIENTIST BEFORE HE WAS A HERO...
...AND I INTEND TO FINISH EXPLORING THE WORLDS HIS EQUIPMENT OPENS TO US!
PAN, RAY CARED ABOUT ME. HE ENCOURAGED ME FOR NO REASON EXCEPT KINDNESS...I WON'T LET HIM DOWN, NO WAY.
"MEET THE DEMON AT THE CROSSROADS, AND HE WILL SAVOR YOUR SOUL..."
HANG A SECOND...
THAT'S VERY KIND OF YOU, SON. BEWARE THE BEAST BELOW US.
I WILL, MA'AM. YOU HAVE A NICE DAY.
"FOR HIS HEART IS LIKE A POISON, AND YOU MUST FINALLY PAY THE TOLL..."
I HAVE TO SAY, HER STUFF IS CATCHY. CHEERFUL, TOO.
HEY, WHILE WE'RE AT IT, CAN YOU PLEASE EXPLAIN WHY THIS TOWN HAS PILGRIMS?

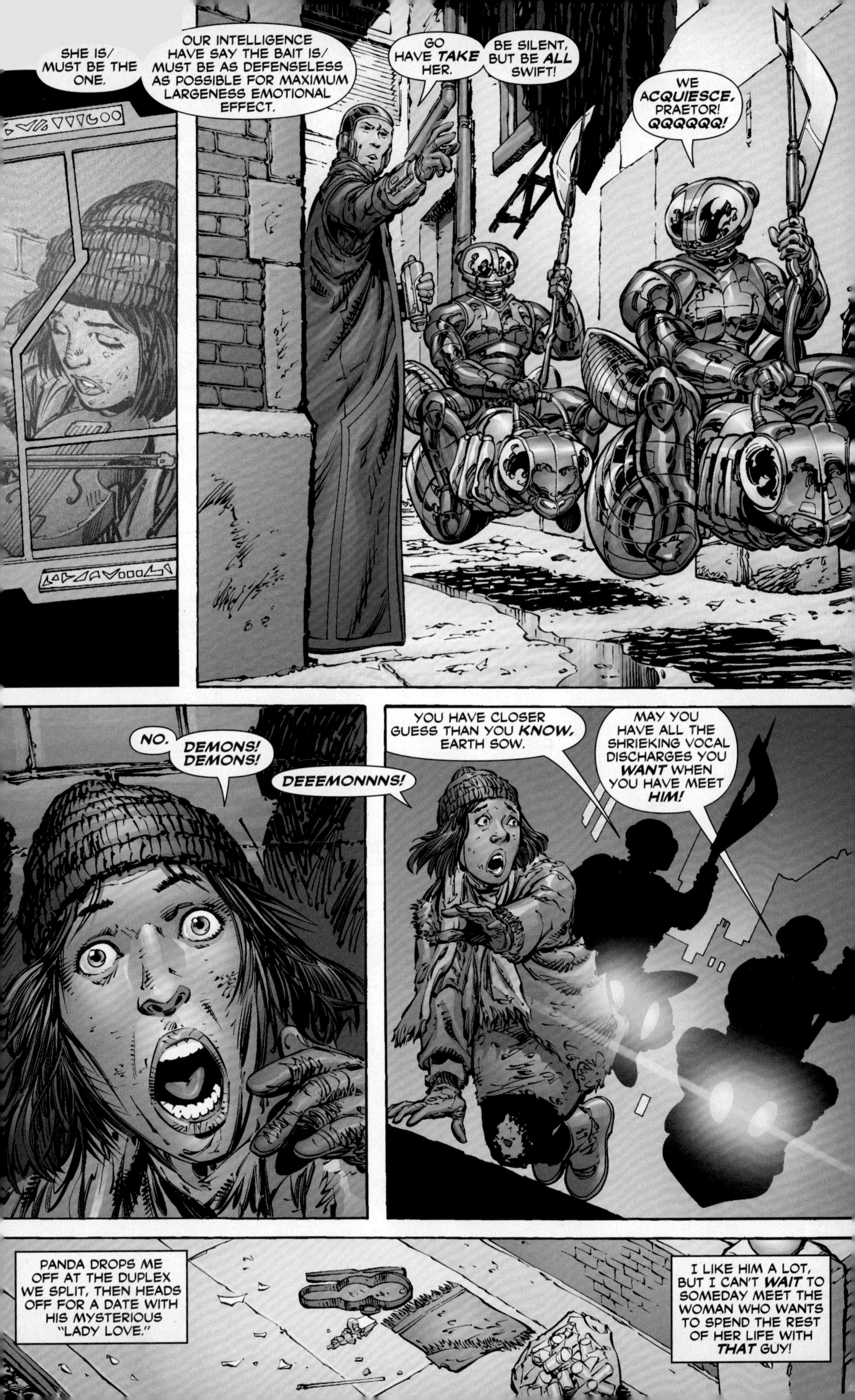

SHE IS/ MUST BE THE ONE.
OUR INTELLIGENCE HAVE SAY THE BAIT IS/ MUST BE AS DEFENSELESS AS POSSIBLE FOR MAXIMUM LARGENESS EMOTIONAL EFFECT.
GO HAVE TAKE HER.
BE SILENT, BUT BE ALL SWIFT!
WE ACQUIESCE, PRAETOR! QQQQQQ!
NO. DEMONS! DEMONS!
DEEEMONNNS!
YOU HAVE CLOSER GUESS THAN YOU KNOW, EARTH SOW.
MAY YOU HAVE ALL THE SHRIEKING VOCAL DISCHARGES YOU WANT WHEN YOU HAVE MEET HIM!
PANDA DROPS ME OFF AT THE DUPLEX WE SPLIT, THEN HEADS OFF FOR A DATE WITH HIS MYSTERIOUS "LADY LOVE."
I LIKE HIM A LOT, BUT I CAN'T WAIT TO SOMEDAY MEET THE WOMAN WHO WANTS TO SPEND THE REST OF HER LIFE WITH THAT GUY!

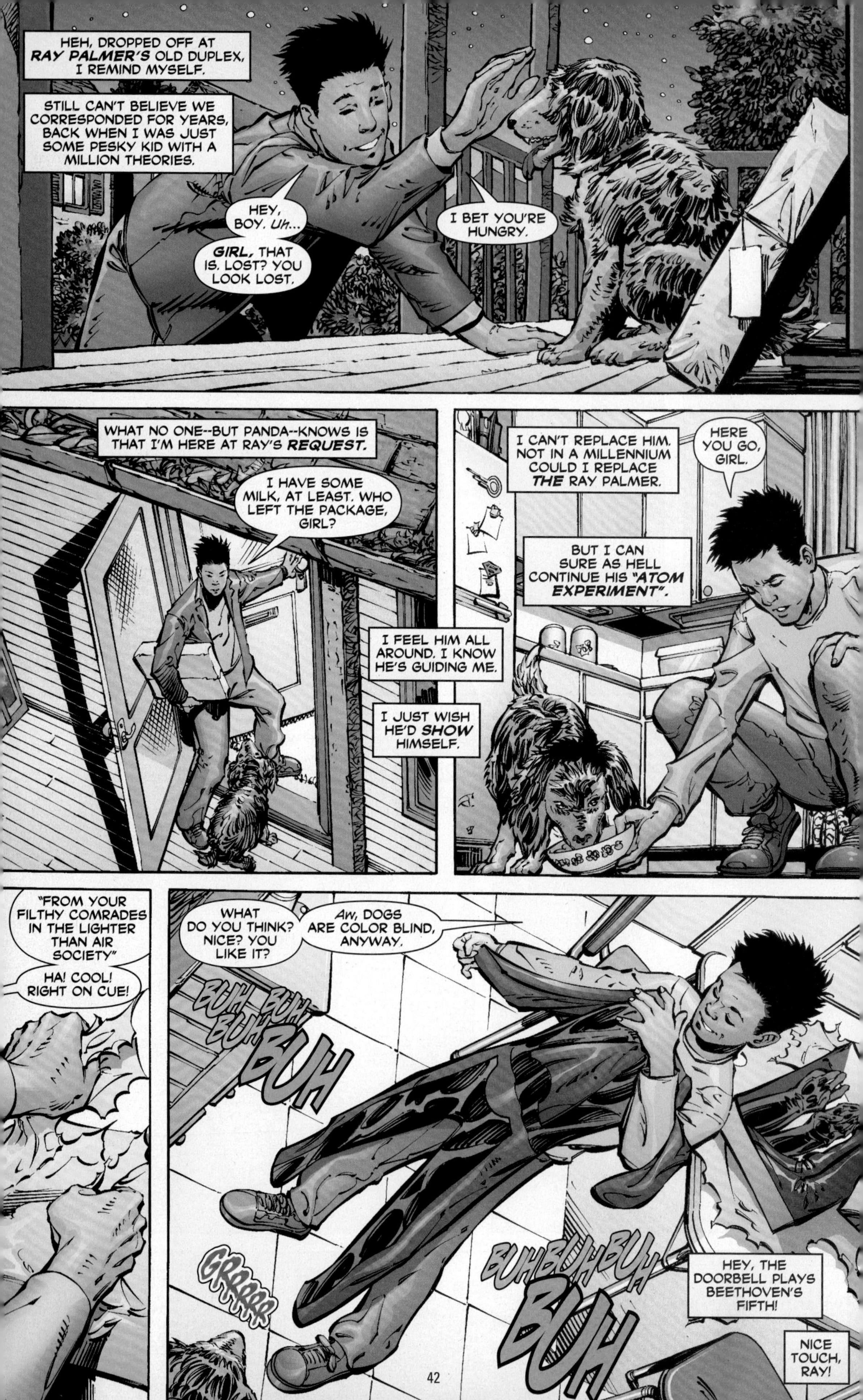
HEH, DROPPED OFF AT RAY PALMER'S OLD DUPLEX, I REMIND MYSELF.
STILL CAN'T BELIEVE WE CORRESPONDED FOR YEARS, BACK WHEN I WAS JUST SOME PESKY KID WITH A MILLION THEORIES.
HEY, BOY. Uh...
GIRL, THAT IS. LOST? YOU LOOK LOST.
I BET YOU'RE HUNGRY.
WHAT NO ONE--BUT PANDA--KNOWS IS THAT I'M HERE AT RAY'S REQUEST.
I HAVE SOME MILK, AT LEAST. WHO LEFT THE PACKAGE, GIRL?
I FEEL HIM ALL AROUND. I KNOW HE'S GUIDING ME.
I JUST WISH HE'D SHOW HIMSELF.
I CAN'T REPLACE HIM. NOT IN A MILLENNIUM COULD I REPLACE THE RAY PALMER.
HERE YOU GO, GIRL.
BUT I CAN SURE AS HELL CONTINUE HIS "ATOM EXPERIMENT".
"FROM YOUR FILTHY COMRADES IN THE LIGHTER THAN AIR SOCIETY"
HA! COOL! RIGHT ON CUE!
WHAT DO YOU THINK? NICE? YOU LIKE IT?
Aw, DOGS ARE COLOR BLIND, ANYWAY.
BUH BUH BUH BUH
GRRRRR
BUHBUHBUH BUH
HEY, THE DOORBELL PLAYS BEETHOVEN'S FIFTH!
NICE TOUCH, RAY!

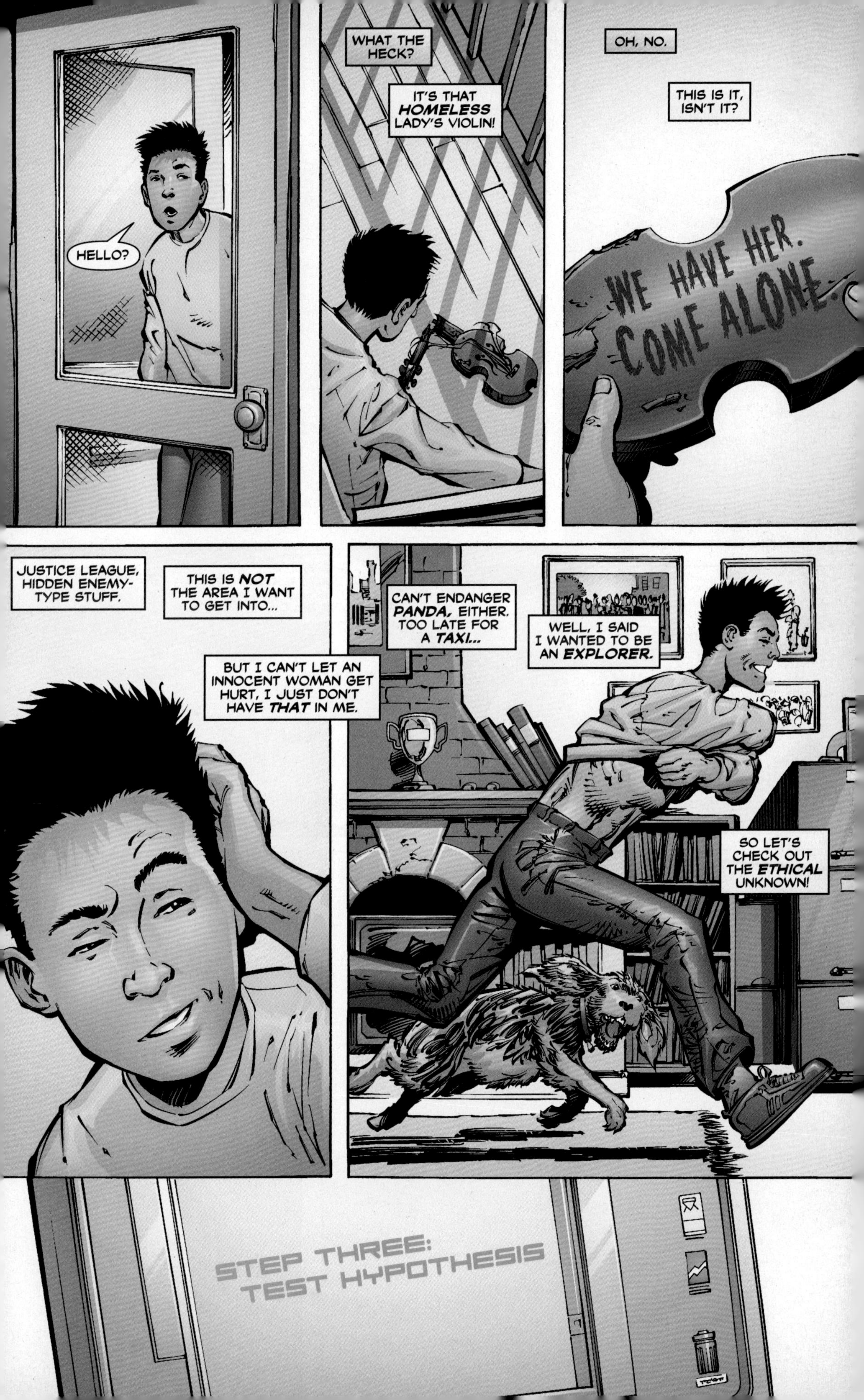
HELLO?
WHAT THE HECK?
IT'S THAT HOMELESS LADY'S VIOLIN!
OH, NO.
THIS IS IT, ISN'T IT?
WE HAVE HER. COME ALONE.
JUSTICE LEAGUE, HIDDEN ENEMY-TYPE STUFF.
THIS IS NOT THE AREA I WANT TO GET INTO...
BUT I CAN'T LET AN INNOCENT WOMAN GET HURT, I JUST DON'T HAVE THAT IN ME.
CAN'T ENDANGER PANDA, EITHER. TOO LATE FOR A TAXI...
WELL, I SAID I WANTED TO BE AN EXPLORER.
SO LET'S CHECK OUT THE ETHICAL UNKNOWN!
STEP THREE: TEST HYPOTHESIS

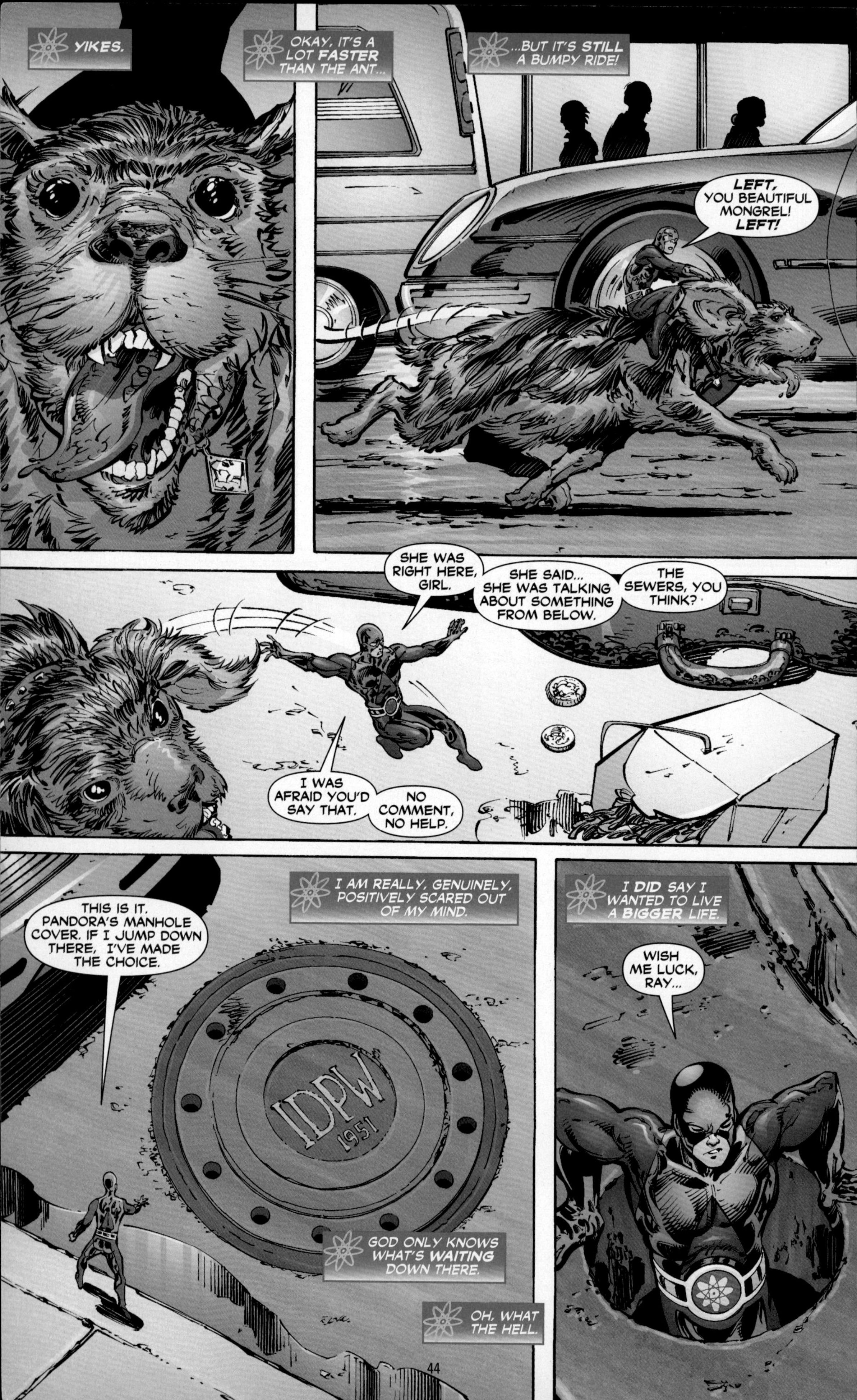
YIKES.
OKAY, IT'S A LOT FASTER THAN THE ANT...
...BUT IT'S STILL A BUMPY RIDE!
LEFT, YOU BEAUTIFUL MONGREL! LEFT!
SHE WAS RIGHT HERE, GIRL.
SHE SAID... SHE WAS TALKING ABOUT SOMETHING FROM BELOW.
THE SEWERS, YOU THINK?
I WAS AFRAID YOU'D SAY THAT.
NO COMMENT, NO HELP.
THIS IS IT. PANDORA'S MANHOLE COVER. IF I JUMP DOWN THERE, I'VE MADE THE CHOICE.
I AM REALLY, GENUINELY, POSITIVELY SCARED OUT OF MY MIND.
IDPW 1951
GOD ONLY KNOWS WHAT'S WAITING DOWN THERE.
OH, WHAT THE HELL.
I DID SAY I WANTED TO LIVE A BIGGER LIFE.
WISH ME LUCK, RAY...

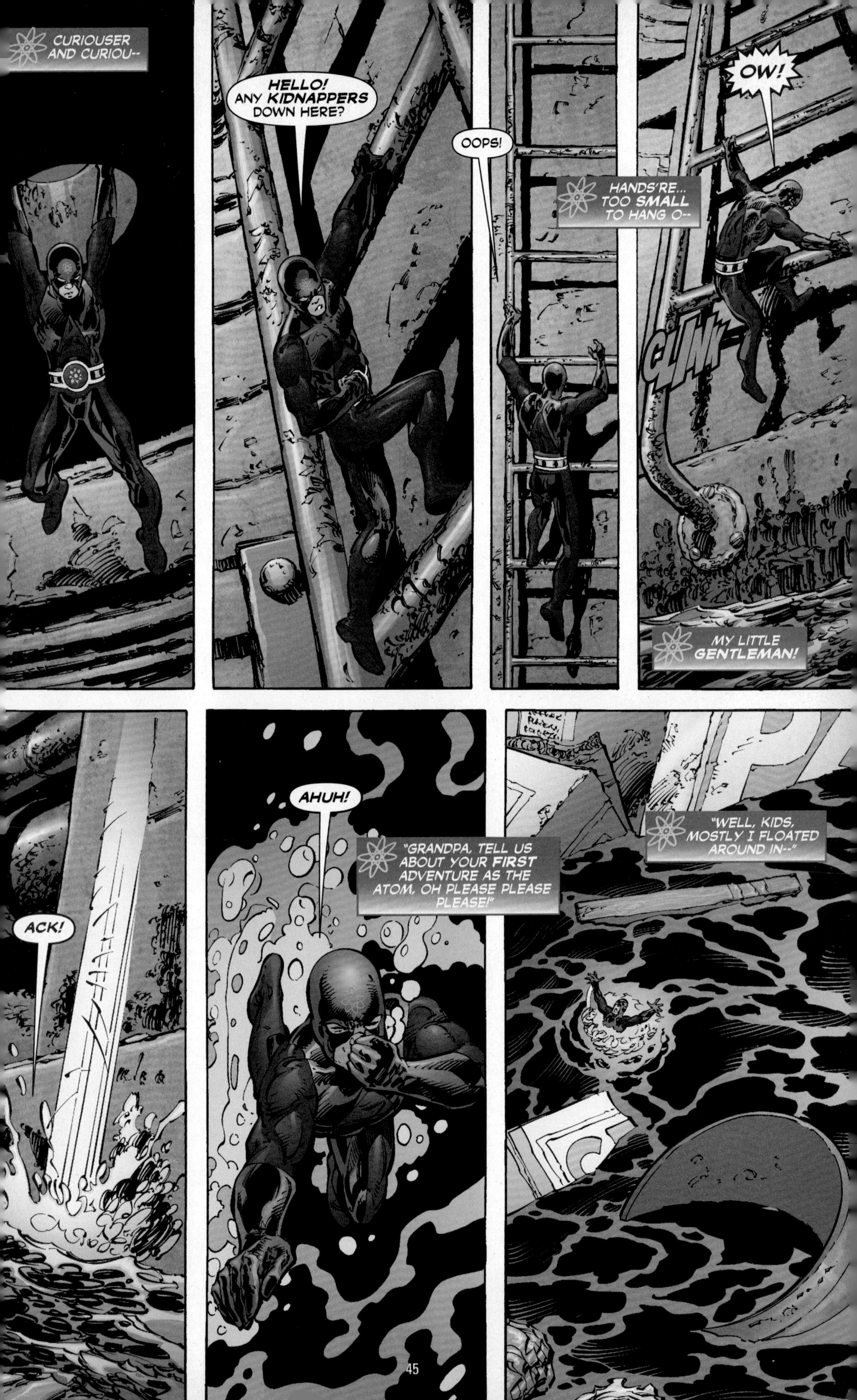
CURIOUSER AND CURIOU--
HELLO! ANY KIDNAPPERS DOWN HERE?
OOPS!
HANDS'RE... TOO SMALL TO HANG O--
OW!
CLINK
MY LITTLE GENTLEMAN!
ACK!
AHUH!
"GRANDPA, TELL US ABOUT YOUR FIRST ADVENTURE AS THE ATOM, OH PLEASE PLEASE PLEASE!"
"WELL, KIDS, MOSTLY I FLOATED AROUND IN--"

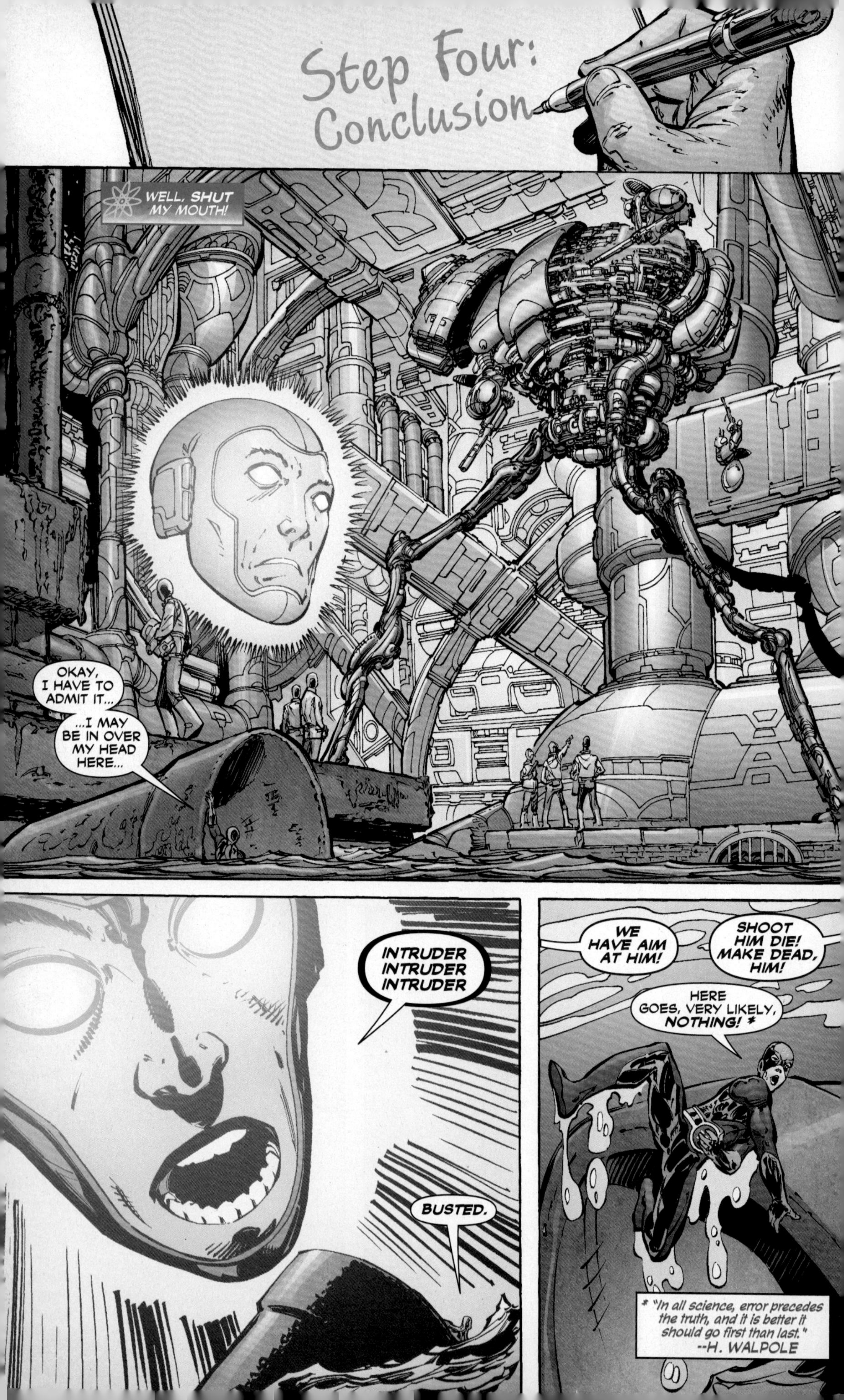

Step Four: Conclusion
WELL, SHUT MY MOUTH!
OKAY, I HAVE TO ADMIT IT...
...I MAY BE IN OVER MY HEAD HERE...
INTRUDER INTRUDER INTRUDER
BUSTED.
WE HAVE AIM AT HIM!
SHOOT HIM DIE! MAKE DEAD, HIM!
HERE GOES, VERY LIKELY, NOTHING! *
* "In all science, error precedes the truth, and it is better it should go first than last." --H. WALPOLE

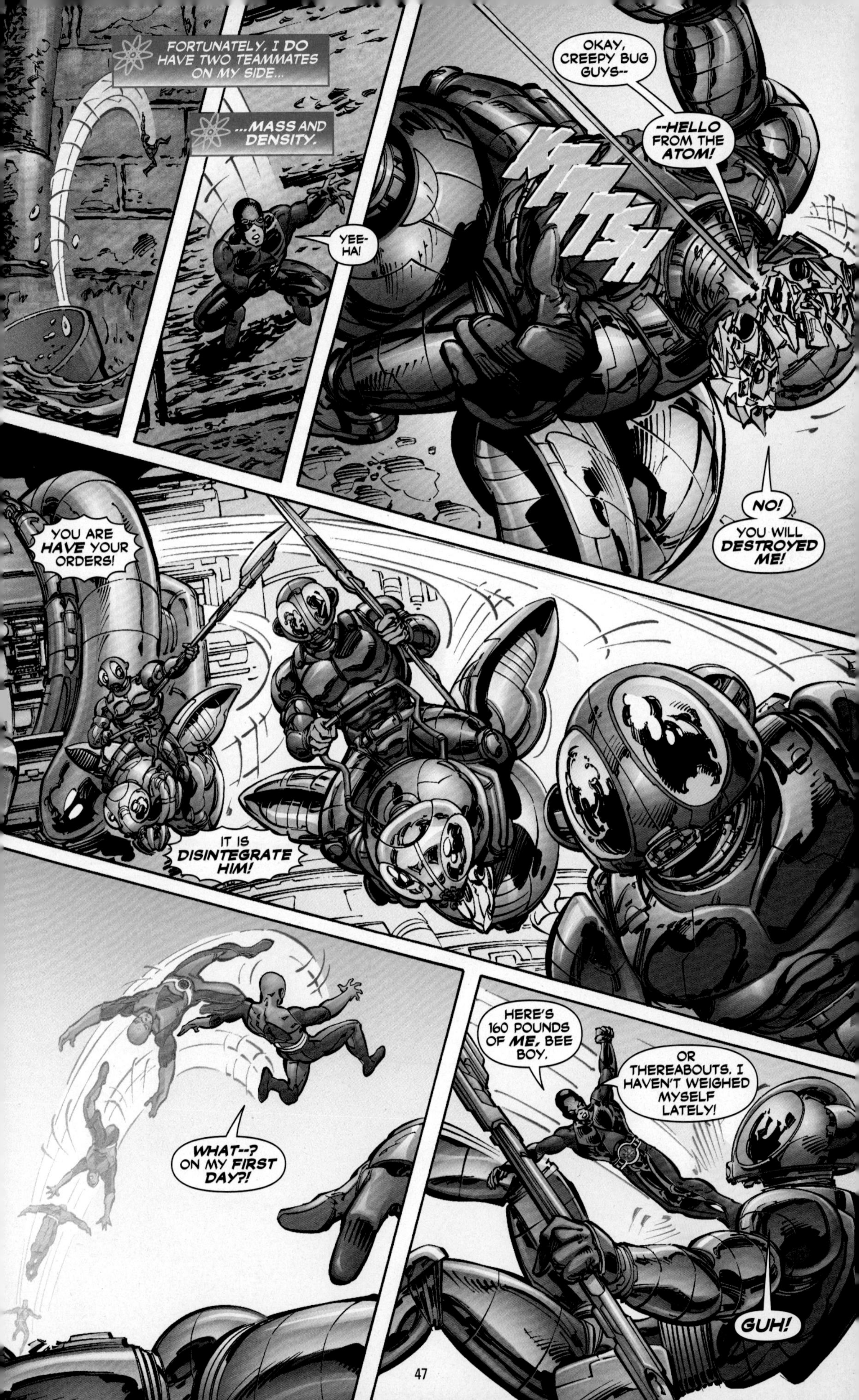
FORTUNATELY, I DO HAVE TWO TEAMMATES ON MY SIDE...
...MASS AND DENSITY.
YEE-HA!
OKAY, CREEPY BUG GUYS--
--HELLO FROM THE ATOM!
KTTTSH
NO! YOU WILL DESTROYED ME!
YOU ARE HAVE YOUR ORDERS!
IT IS DISINTEGRATE HIM!
WHAT--? ON MY FIRST DAY?!
HERE'S 160 POUNDS OF ME, BEE BOY.
OR THEREABOUTS. I HAVEN'T WEIGHED MYSELF LATELY!
GUH!

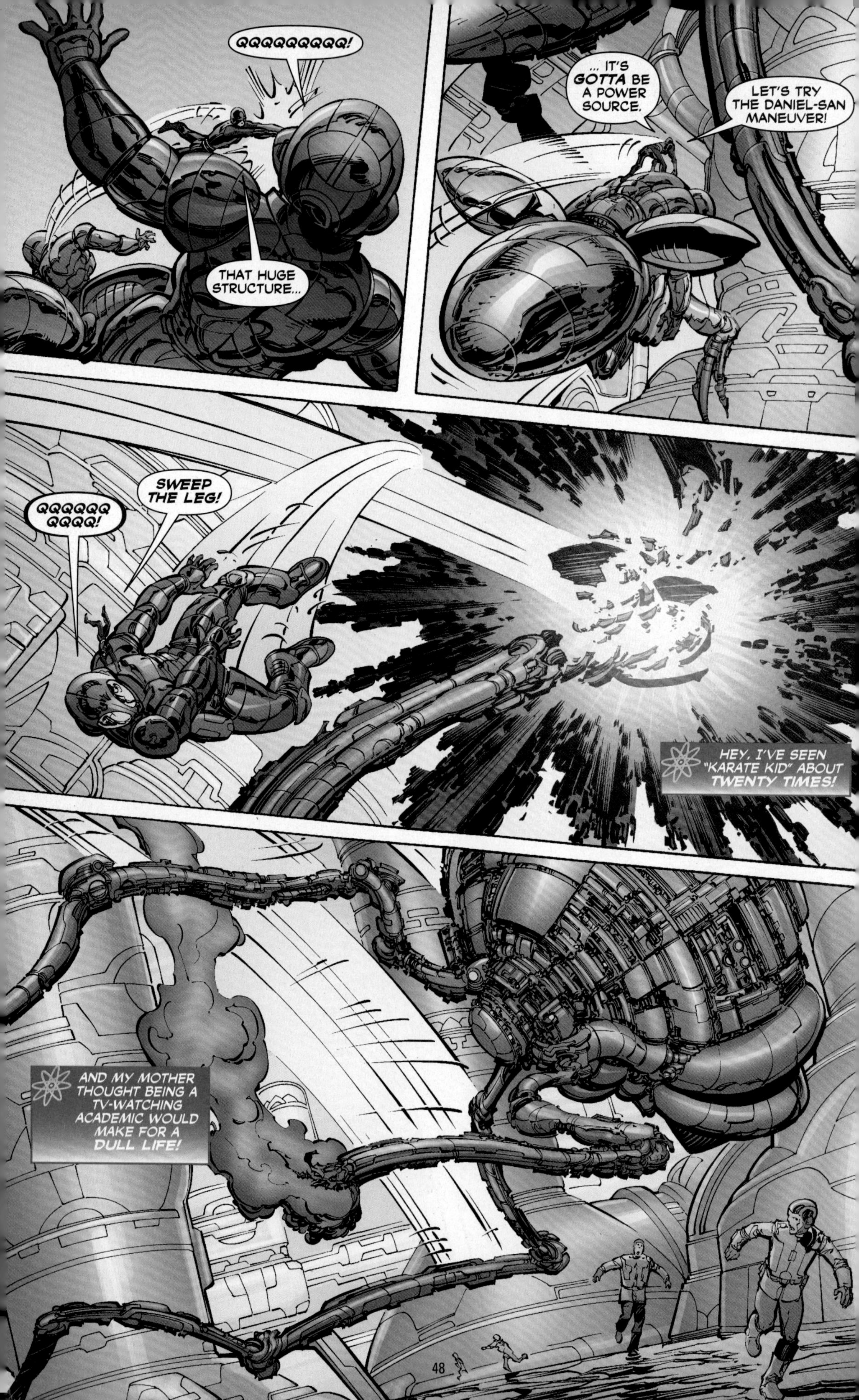
QQQQQQQQQ!
THAT HUGE STRUCTURE...
... IT'S GOTTA BE A POWER SOURCE.
LET'S TRY THE DANIEL-SAN MANEUVER!
QQQQQQ QQQQ!
SWEEP THE LEG!
HEY, I'VE SEEN "KARATE KID" ABOUT TWENTY TIMES!
AND MY MOTHER THOUGHT BEING A TV-WATCHING ACADEMIC WOULD MAKE FOR A DULL LIFE!

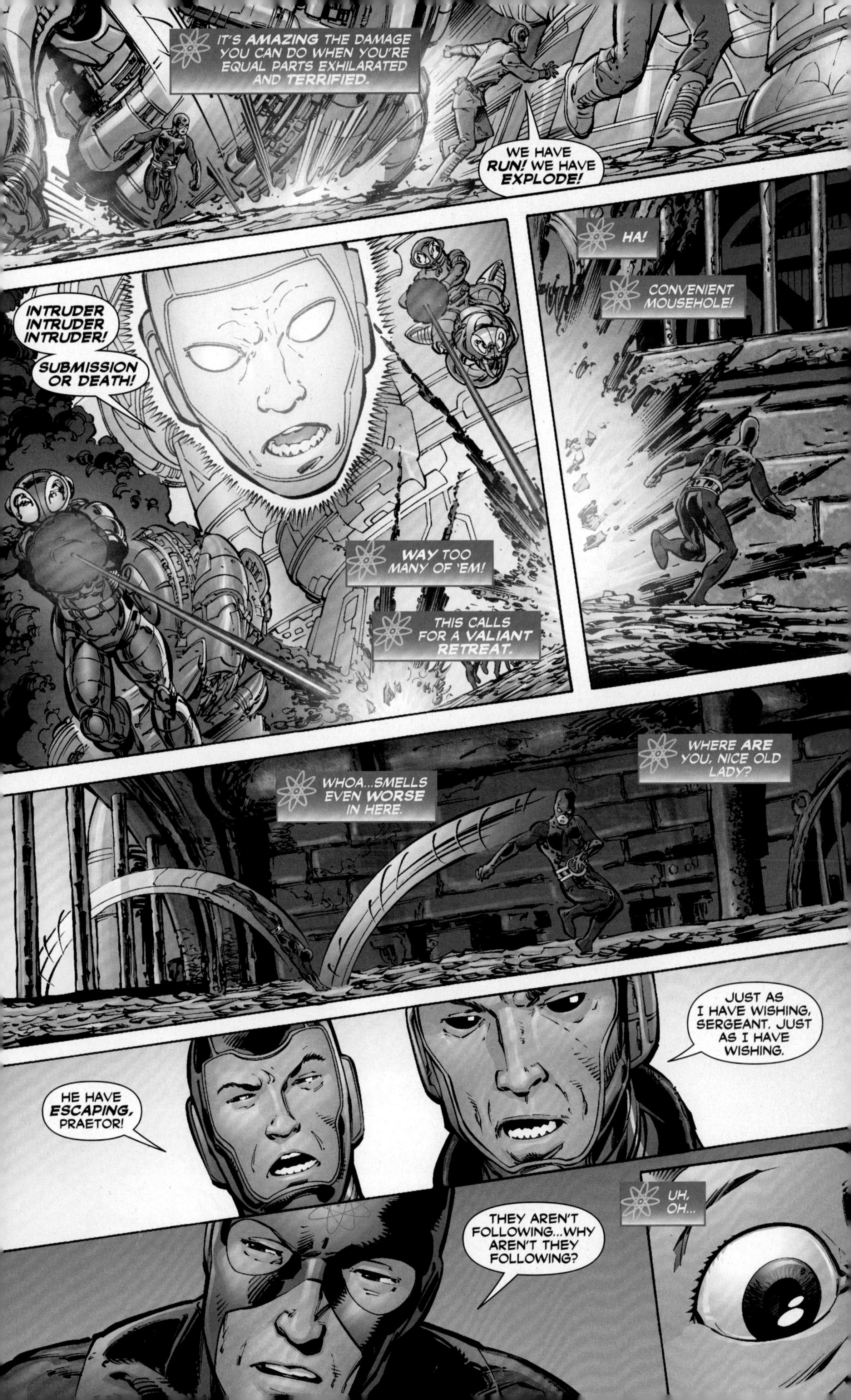
IT'S AMAZING THE DAMAGE YOU CAN DO WHEN YOU'RE EQUAL PARTS EXHILARATED AND TERRIFIED.
WE HAVE RUN! WE HAVE EXPLODE!
INTRUDER INTRUDER INTRUDER!
SUBMISSION OR DEATH!
WAY TOO MANY OF 'EM!
THIS CALLS FOR A VALIANT RETREAT.
HA!
CONVENIENT MOUSEHOLE!
WHOA...SMELLS EVEN WORSE IN HERE.
WHERE ARE YOU, NICE OLD LADY?
HE HAVE ESCAPING, PRAETOR!
JUST AS I HAVE WISHING, SERGEANT. JUST AS I HAVE WISHING.
THEY AREN'T FOLLOWING...WHY AREN'T THEY FOLLOWING?
UH, OH...

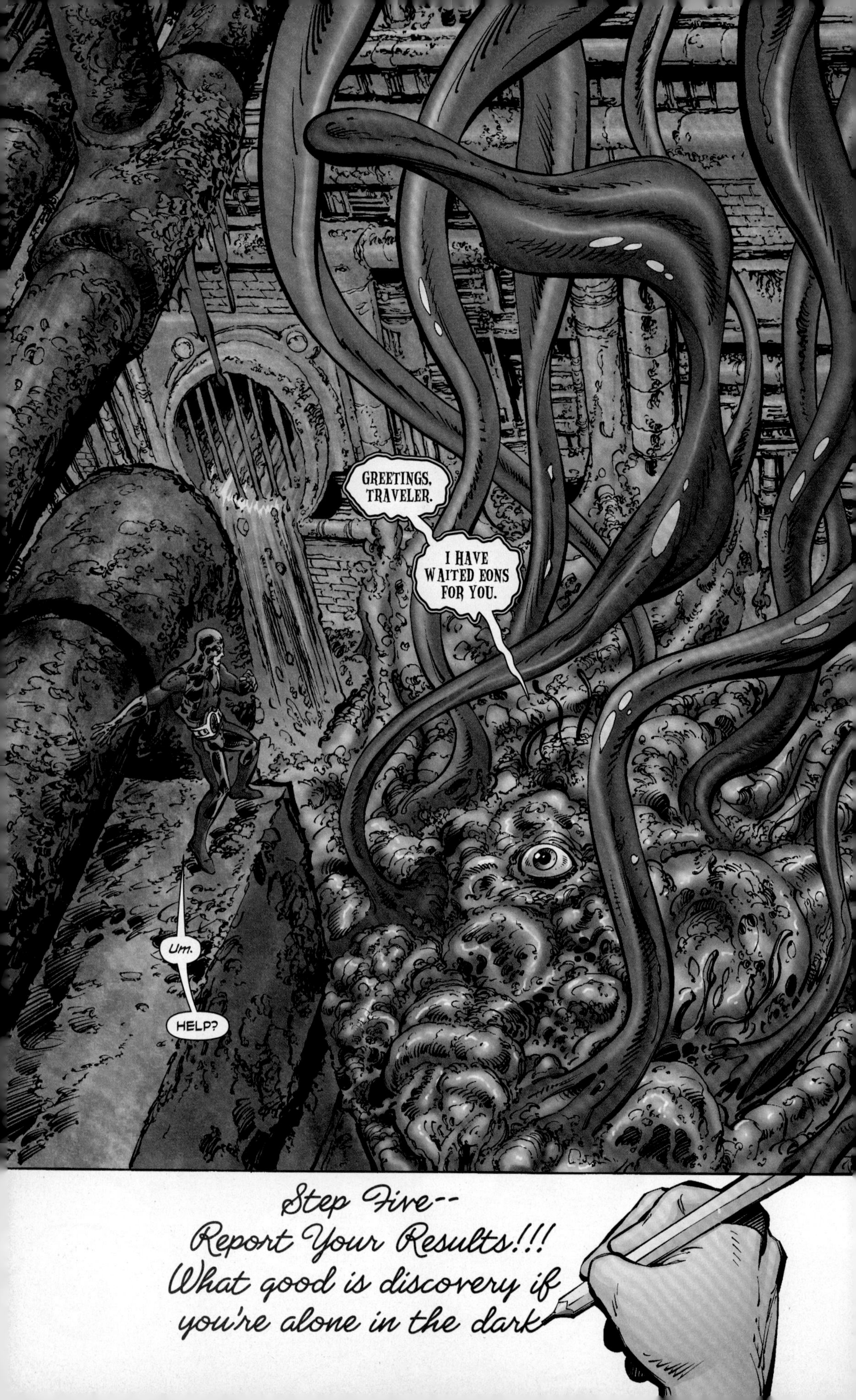
GREETINGS, TRAVELER.
I HAVE WAITED EONS FOR YOU.
Um.
HELP?
Step Five-- Report Your Results!!! What good is discovery if you're alone in the dark

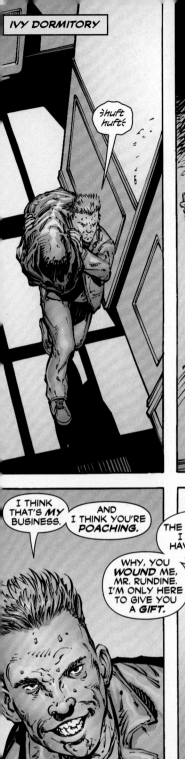

ఃhuftః
huftః

HELLO, SYLBERT. I SEE YOU'VE BEEN *SHOPPING.*

LET ME INTRODUCE MYSELF.

I KNOW WHO YOU ARE. HOW'D YOU GET IN MY ROOM?

I HAVE MY WAYS. AND FRANKLY, MR. RUNDINE...

...I'D SAY THAT'S THE LEAST OF YOUR WORRIES.

WHAT DO YOU PLAN TO DO WITH WHAT'S IN THE BAG, SYLBERT? YOU *KNOW* THERE'S NO COOKING IN THE DORMITORIES.

I THINK THAT'S *MY* BUSINESS.

AND I THINK YOU'RE *POACHING.*

WHY, YOU *WOUND* ME, MR. RUNDINE. I'M ONLY HERE TO GIVE YOU A *GIFT.*

I'M AFRAID THE FIRST GENTLEMAN I CHOSE DOESN'T HAVE YOUR LEVEL OF *MOTIVATION.*

SO I'M CHOOSING *YOU* AS HIS REPLACEMENT.

I DON'T KNOW WHAT THE HELL YOU'RE TALKIN' ABOUT, MISTER.

OH, I THINK YOU'LL LIKE IT.

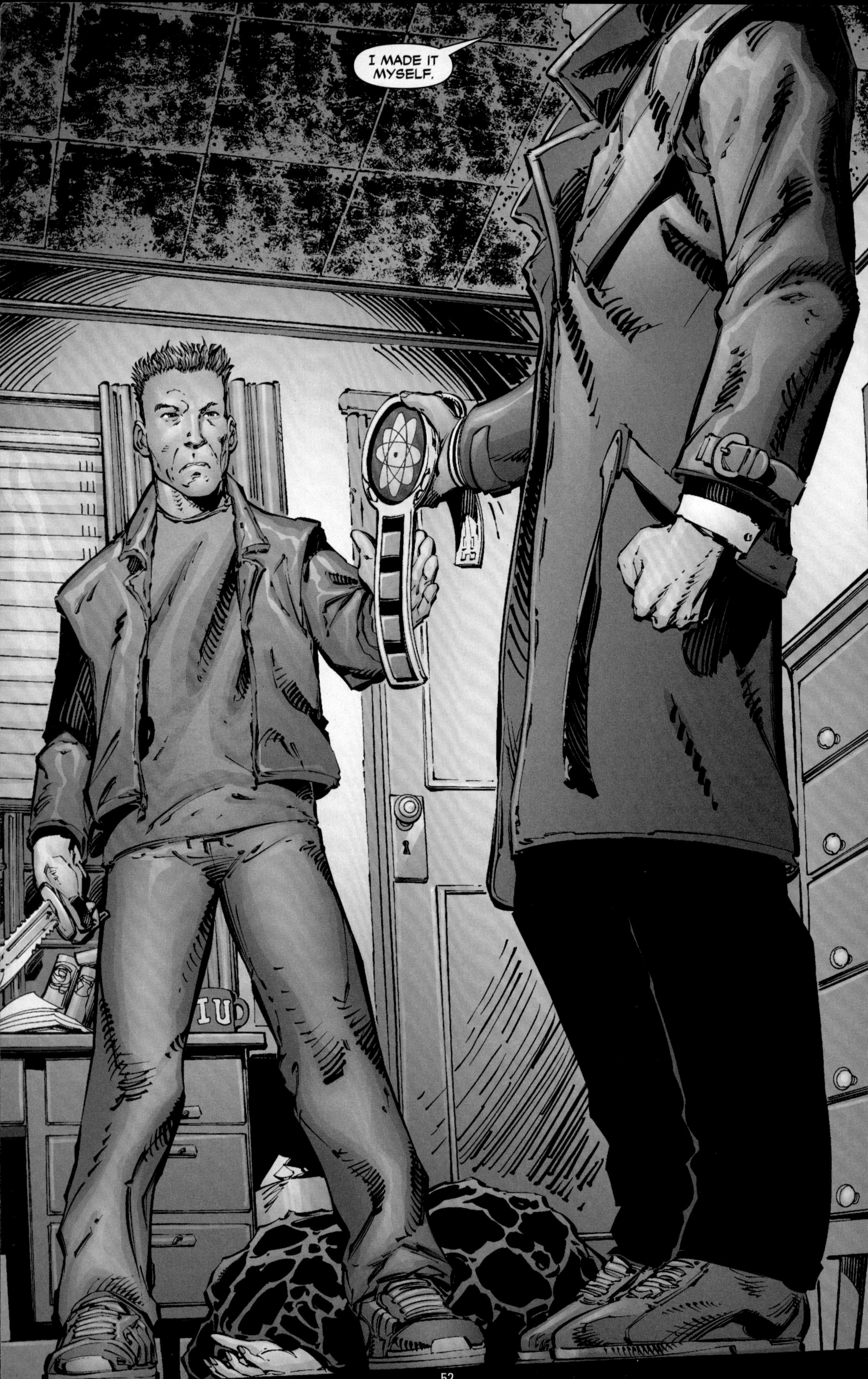
I MADE IT MYSELF.

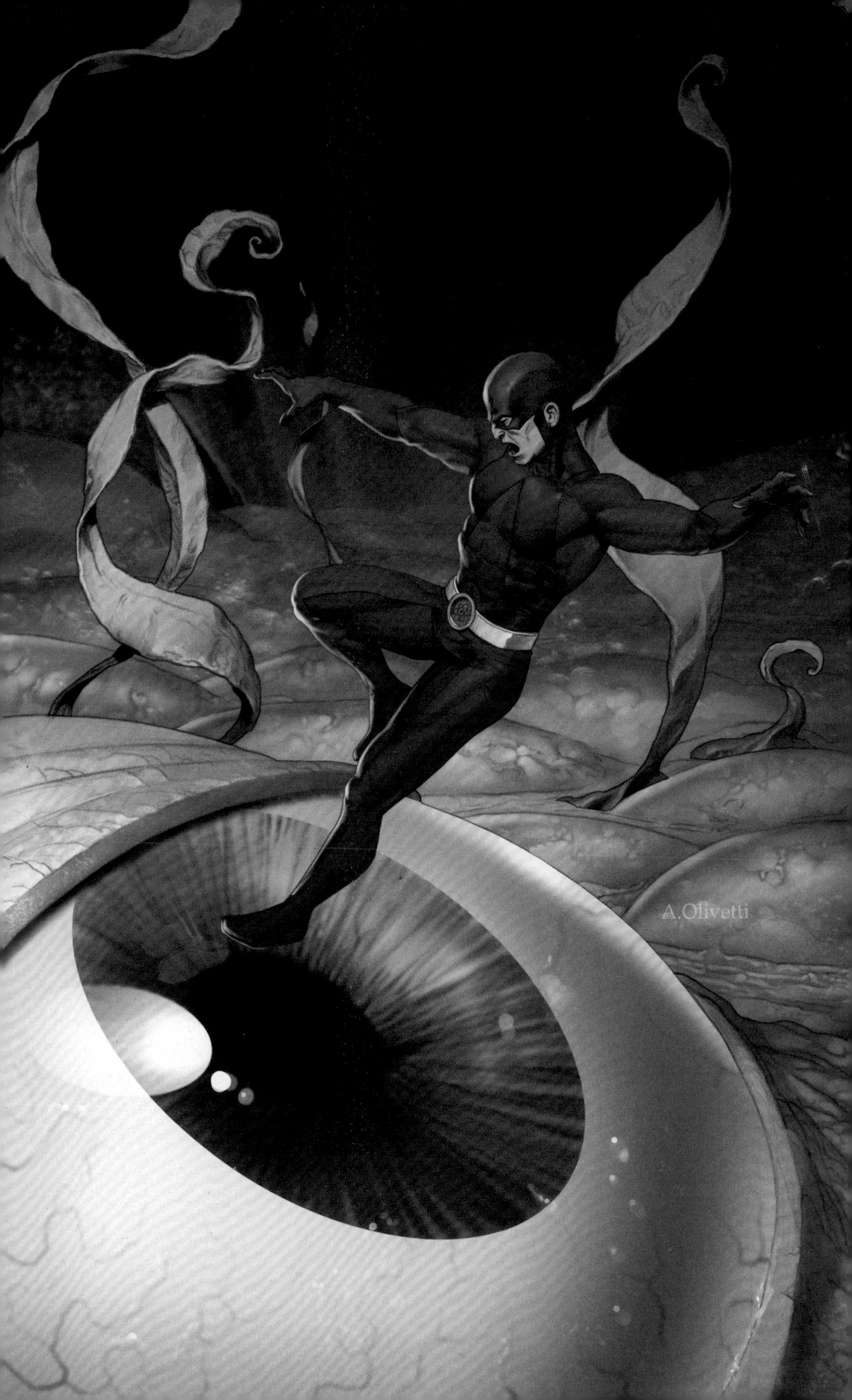
A.Olivetti

MY LIFE IN MINIATURE: PART THREE
BINDING ENERGIES

from **THE ALL NEW ATOM #3**
Cover by **Ariel Olivetti**

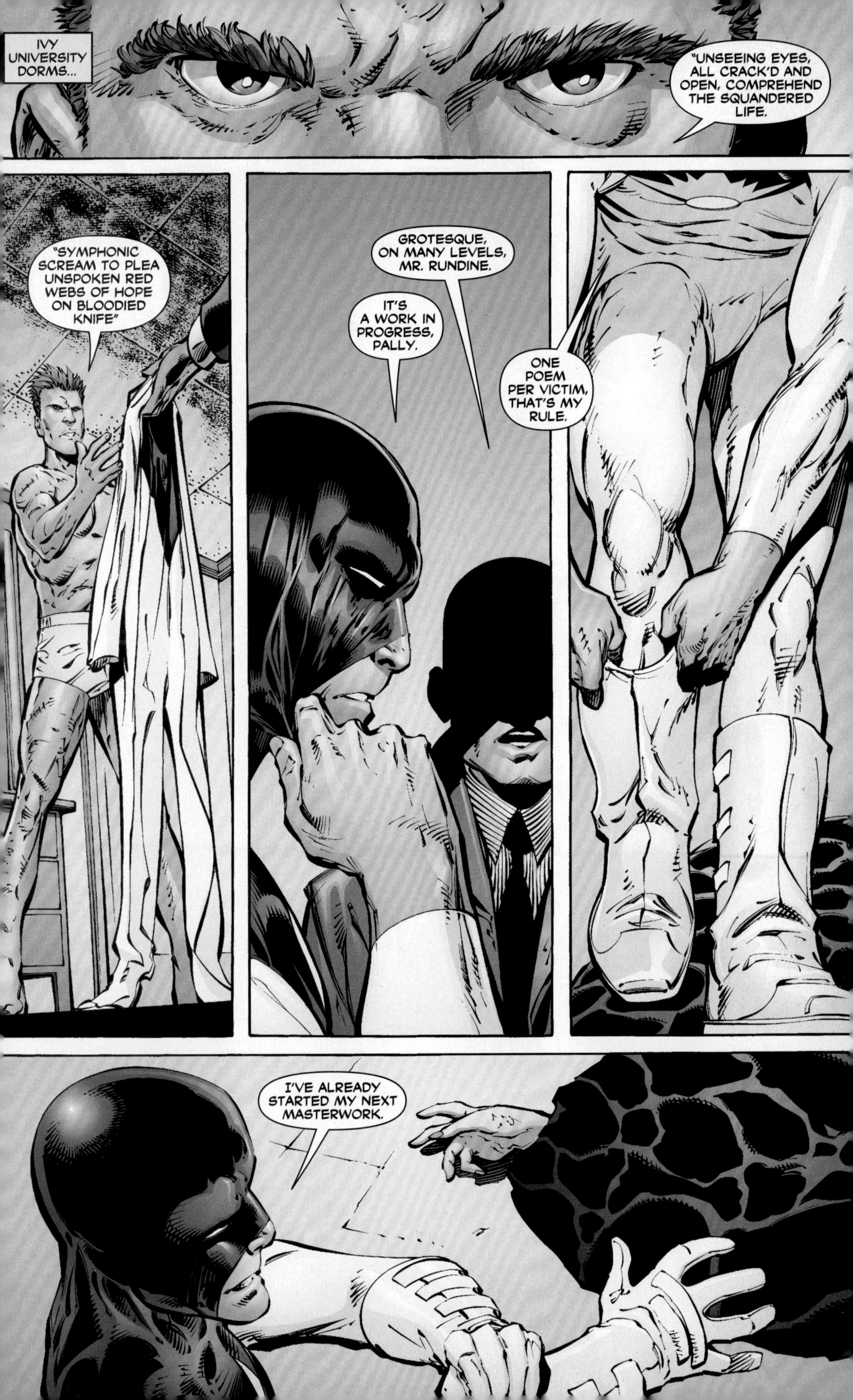
IVY UNIVERSITY DORMS...
"UNSEEING EYES, ALL CRACK'D AND OPEN, COMPREHEND THE SQUANDERED LIFE.
"SYMPHONIC SCREAM TO PLEA UNSPOKEN RED WEBS OF HOPE ON BLOODIED KNIFE"
GROTESQUE, ON MANY LEVELS, MR. RUNDINE.
IT'S A WORK IN PROGRESS, PALLY.
ONE POEM PER VICTIM, THAT'S MY RULE.
I'VE ALREADY STARTED MY NEXT MASTERWORK.

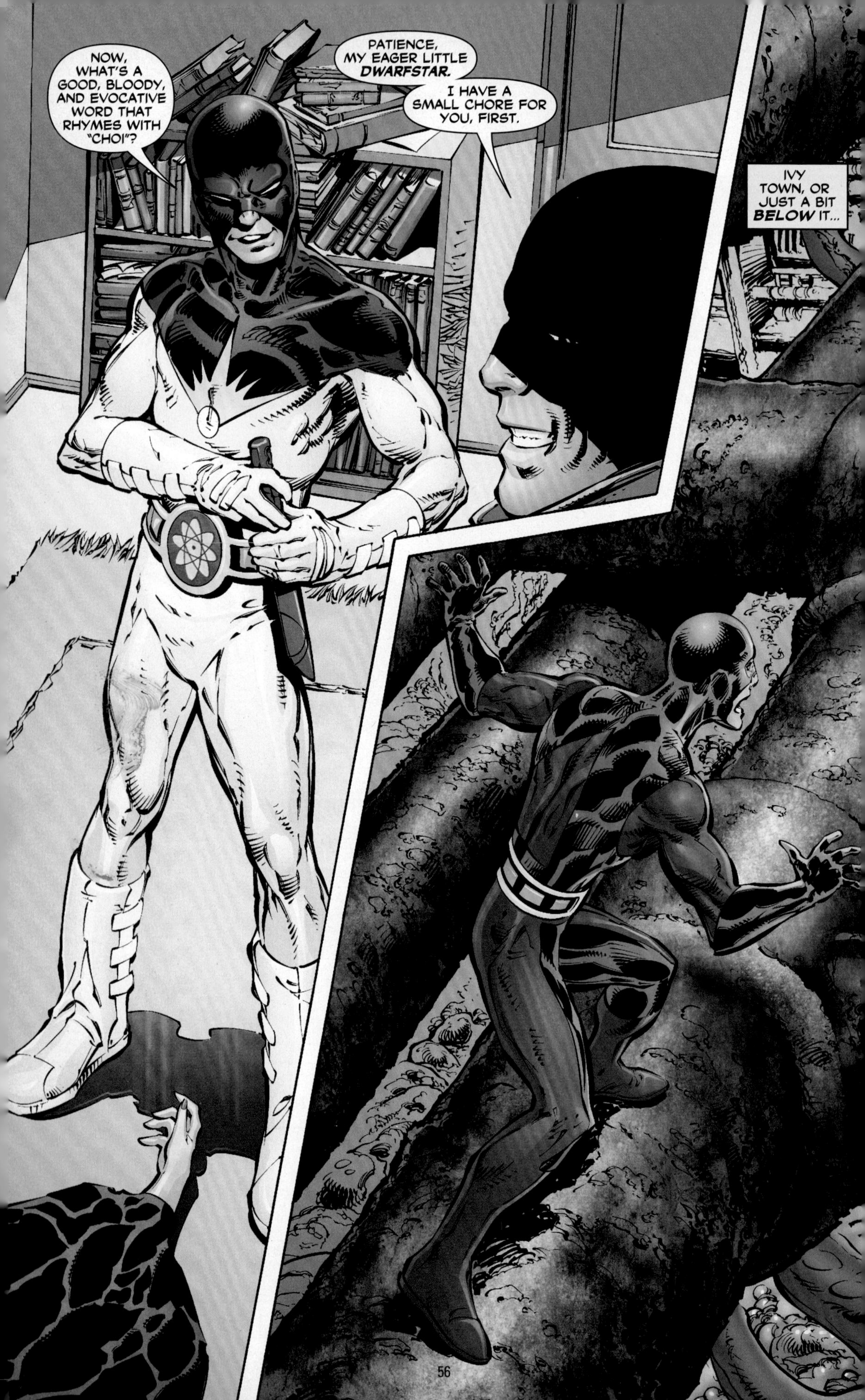

NOW, WHAT'S A GOOD, BLOODY, AND EVOCATIVE WORD THAT RHYMES WITH "CHOI"?
PATIENCE, MY EAGER LITTLE DWARFSTAR.
I HAVE A SMALL CHORE FOR YOU, FIRST.
IVY TOWN, OR JUST A BIT BELOW IT...

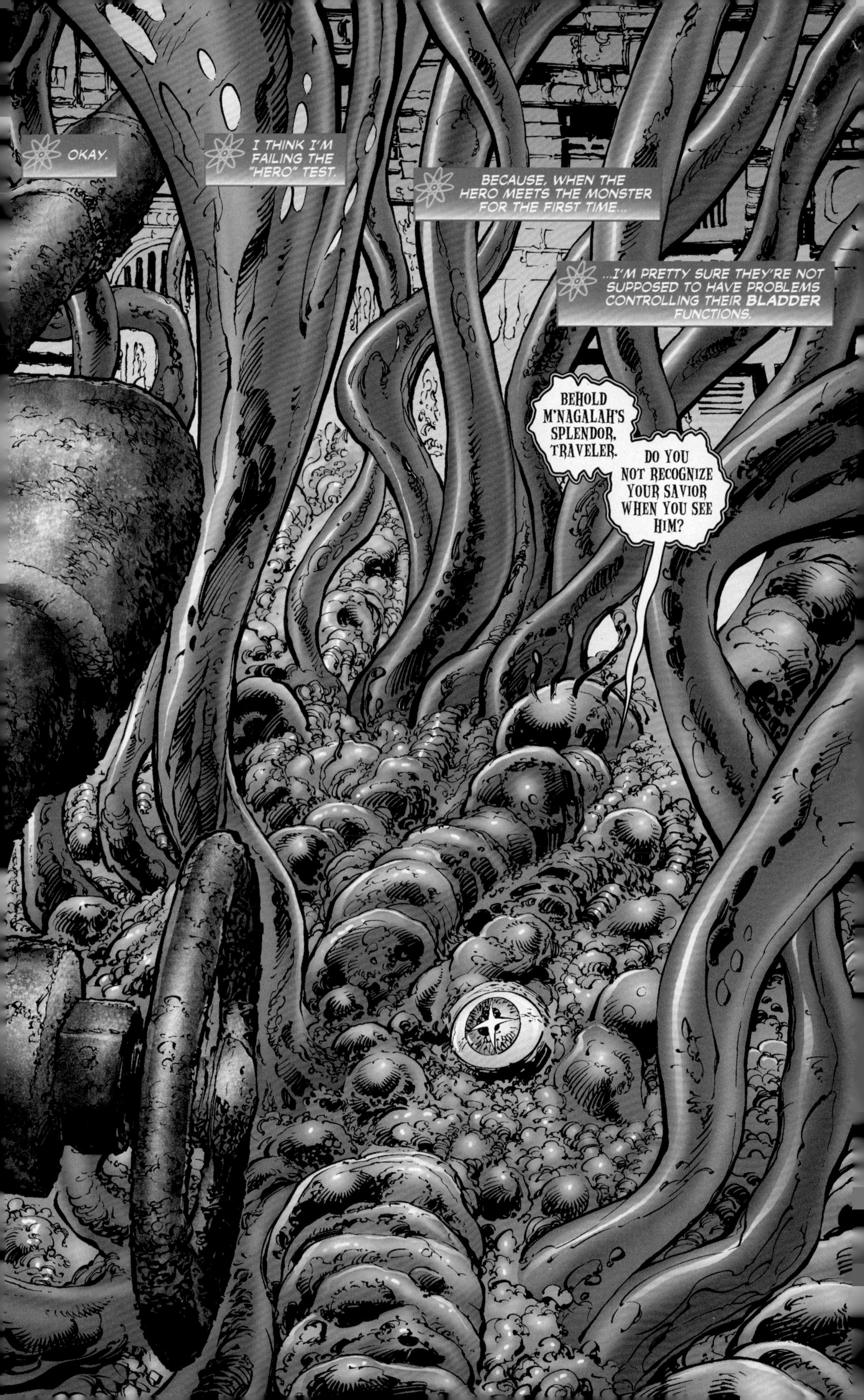
OKAY.
I THINK I'M FAILING THE "HERO" TEST.
BECAUSE, WHEN THE HERO MEETS THE MONSTER FOR THE FIRST TIME...
...I'M PRETTY SURE THEY'RE NOT SUPPOSED TO HAVE PROBLEMS CONTROLLING THEIR **BLADDER** FUNCTIONS.
BEHOLD M'NAGALAH'S SPLENDOR, TRAVELER.
DO YOU NOT RECOGNIZE YOUR SAVIOR WHEN YOU SEE HIM?

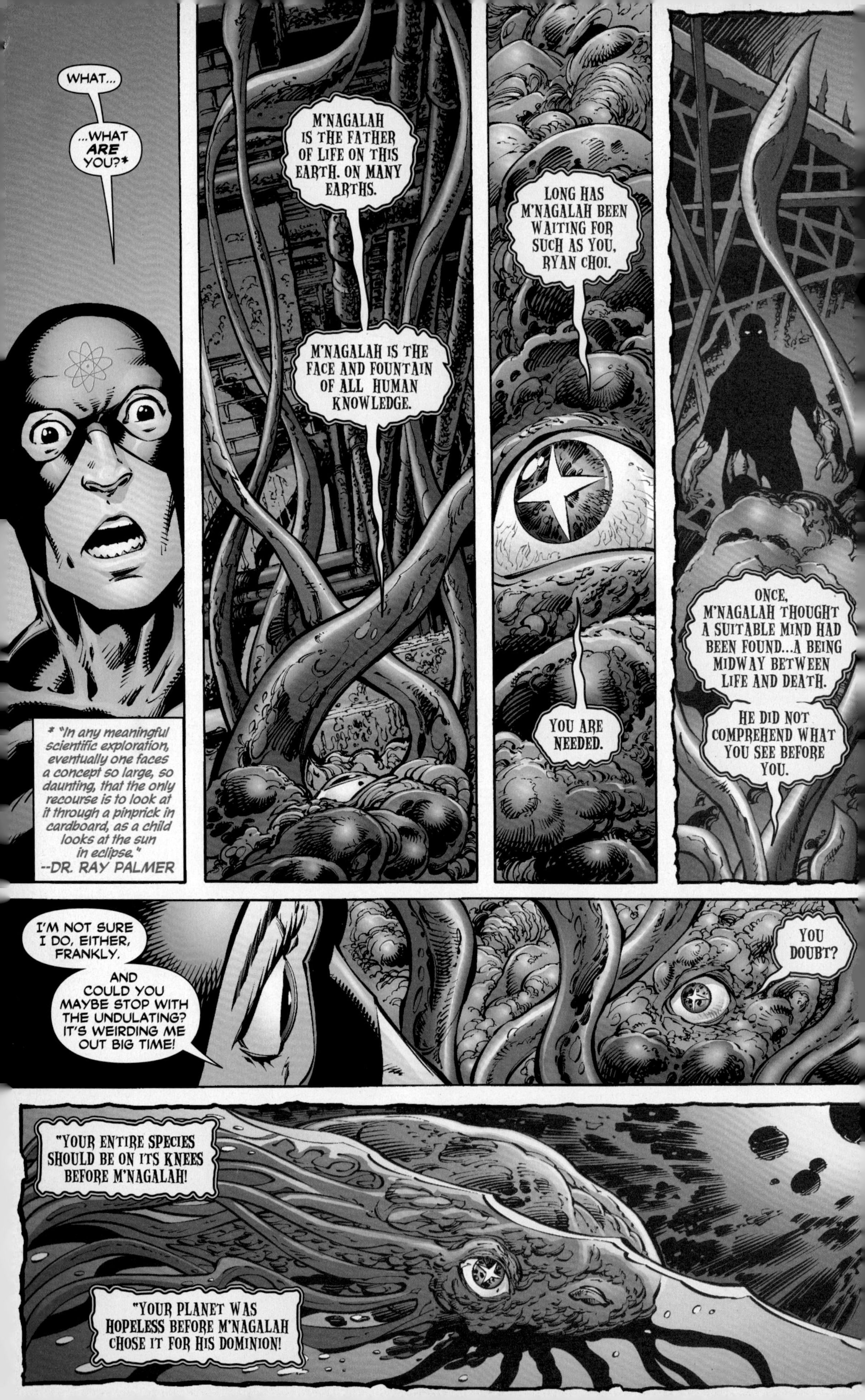
WHAT...
...WHAT ARE YOU?*
* "In any meaningful scientific exploration, eventually one faces a concept so large, so daunting, that the only recourse is to look at it through a pinprick in cardboard, as a child looks at the sun in eclipse." --DR. RAY PALMER
M'NAGALAH IS THE FATHER OF LIFE ON THIS EARTH. ON MANY EARTHS.
M'NAGALAH IS THE FACE AND FOUNTAIN OF ALL HUMAN KNOWLEDGE.
LONG HAS M'NAGALAH BEEN WAITING FOR SUCH AS YOU, RYAN CHOI.
YOU ARE NEEDED.
ONCE, M'NAGALAH THOUGHT A SUITABLE MIND HAD BEEN FOUND...A BEING MIDWAY BETWEEN LIFE AND DEATH.
HE DID NOT COMPREHEND WHAT YOU SEE BEFORE YOU.
I'M NOT SURE I DO, EITHER, FRANKLY.
AND COULD YOU MAYBE STOP WITH THE UNDULATING? IT'S WEIRDING ME OUT BIG TIME!
YOU DOUBT?
"YOUR ENTIRE SPECIES SHOULD BE ON ITS KNEES BEFORE M'NAGALAH!
"YOUR PLANET WAS HOPELESS BEFORE M'NAGALAH CHOSE IT FOR HIS DOMINION!

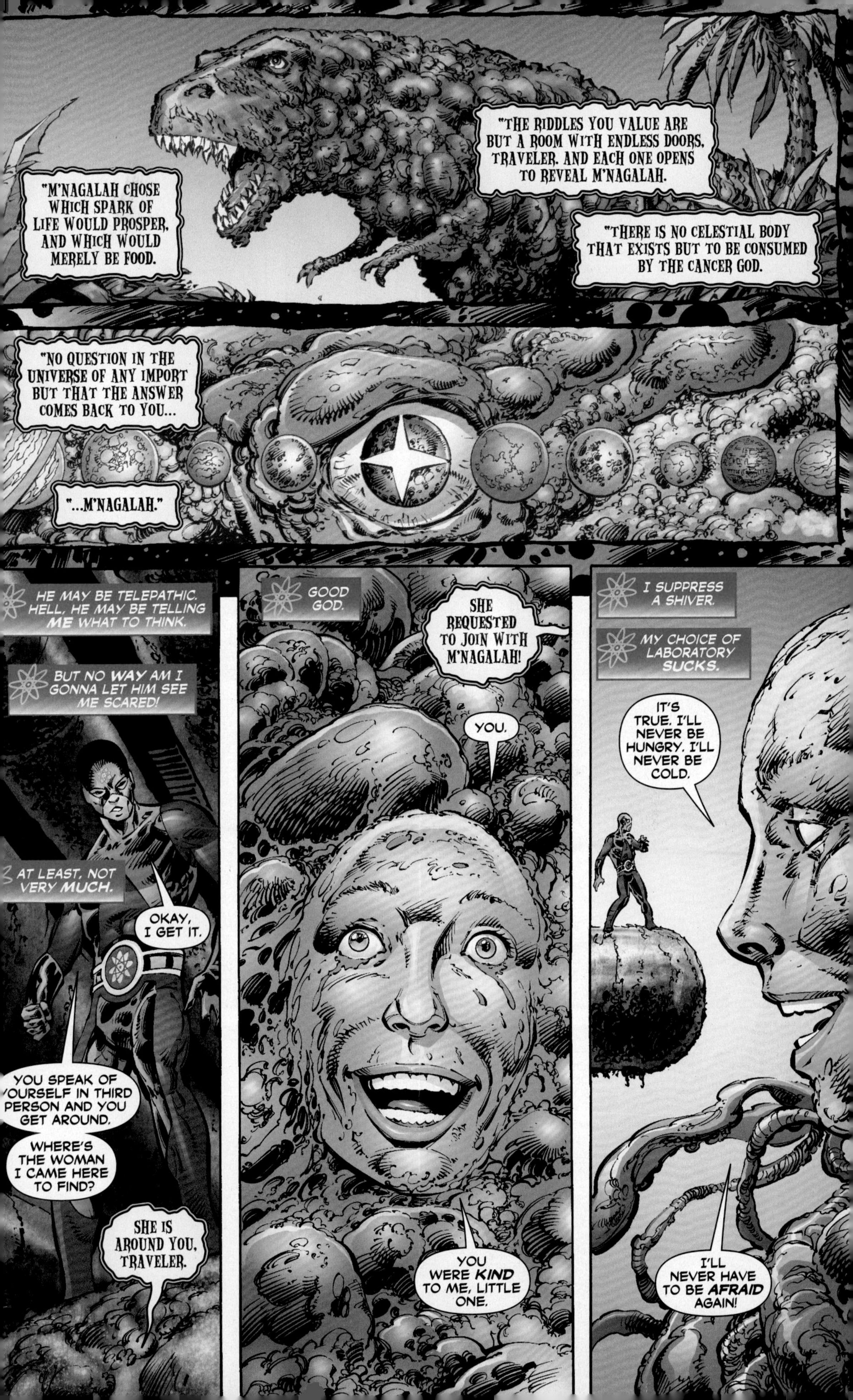
"M'NAGALAH CHOSE WHICH SPARK OF LIFE WOULD PROSPER, AND WHICH WOULD MERELY BE FOOD.
"THE RIDDLES YOU VALUE ARE BUT A ROOM WITH ENDLESS DOORS, TRAVELER. AND EACH ONE OPENS TO REVEAL M'NAGALAH.
"THERE IS NO CELESTIAL BODY THAT EXISTS BUT TO BE CONSUMED BY THE CANCER GOD.
"NO QUESTION IN THE UNIVERSE OF ANY IMPORT BUT THAT THE ANSWER COMES BACK TO YOU...
"...M'NAGALAH."
HE MAY BE TELEPATHIC. HELL, HE MAY BE TELLING ME WHAT TO THINK.
BUT NO WAY AM I GONNA LET HIM SEE ME SCARED!
AT LEAST, NOT VERY MUCH.
OKAY, I GET IT.
YOU SPEAK OF YOURSELF IN THIRD PERSON AND YOU GET AROUND.
WHERE'S THE WOMAN I CAME HERE TO FIND?
SHE IS AROUND YOU, TRAVELER.
GOOD GOD.
SHE REQUESTED TO JOIN WITH M'NAGALAH!
YOU.
YOU WERE KIND TO ME, LITTLE ONE.
I SUPPRESS A SHIVER.
MY CHOICE OF LABORATORY SUCKS.
IT'S TRUE. I'LL NEVER BE HUNGRY. I'LL NEVER BE COLD.
I'LL NEVER HAVE TO BE AFRAID AGAIN!

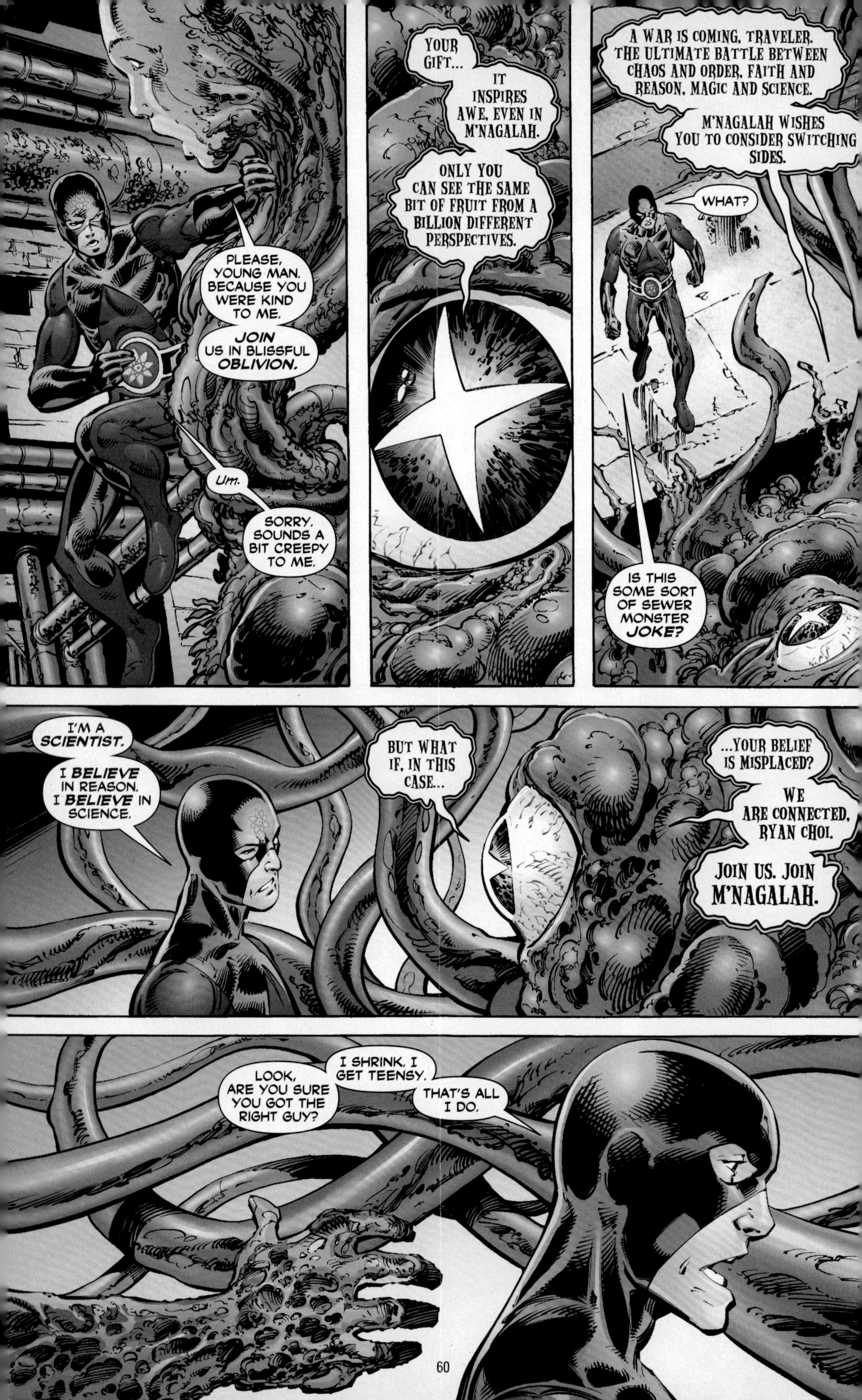

PLEASE, YOUNG MAN. BECAUSE YOU WERE KIND TO ME.
JOIN US IN BLISSFUL OBLIVION.
Um.
SORRY. SOUNDS A BIT CREEPY TO ME.
YOUR GIFT...
IT INSPIRES AWE, EVEN IN M'NAGALAH.
ONLY YOU CAN SEE THE SAME BIT OF FRUIT FROM A BILLION DIFFERENT PERSPECTIVES.
A WAR IS COMING, TRAVELER. THE ULTIMATE BATTLE BETWEEN CHAOS AND ORDER, FAITH AND REASON, MAGIC AND SCIENCE.
M'NAGALAH WISHES YOU TO CONSIDER SWITCHING SIDES.
WHAT?
IS THIS SOME SORT OF SEWER MONSTER JOKE?
I'M A SCIENTIST.
I BELIEVE IN REASON. I BELIEVE IN SCIENCE.
BUT WHAT IF, IN THIS CASE...
...YOUR BELIEF IS MISPLACED?
WE ARE CONNECTED, RYAN CHOI.
JOIN US. JOIN M'NAGALAH.
LOOK, ARE YOU SURE YOU GOT THE RIGHT GUY?
I SHRINK. I GET TEENSY.
THAT'S ALL I DO.

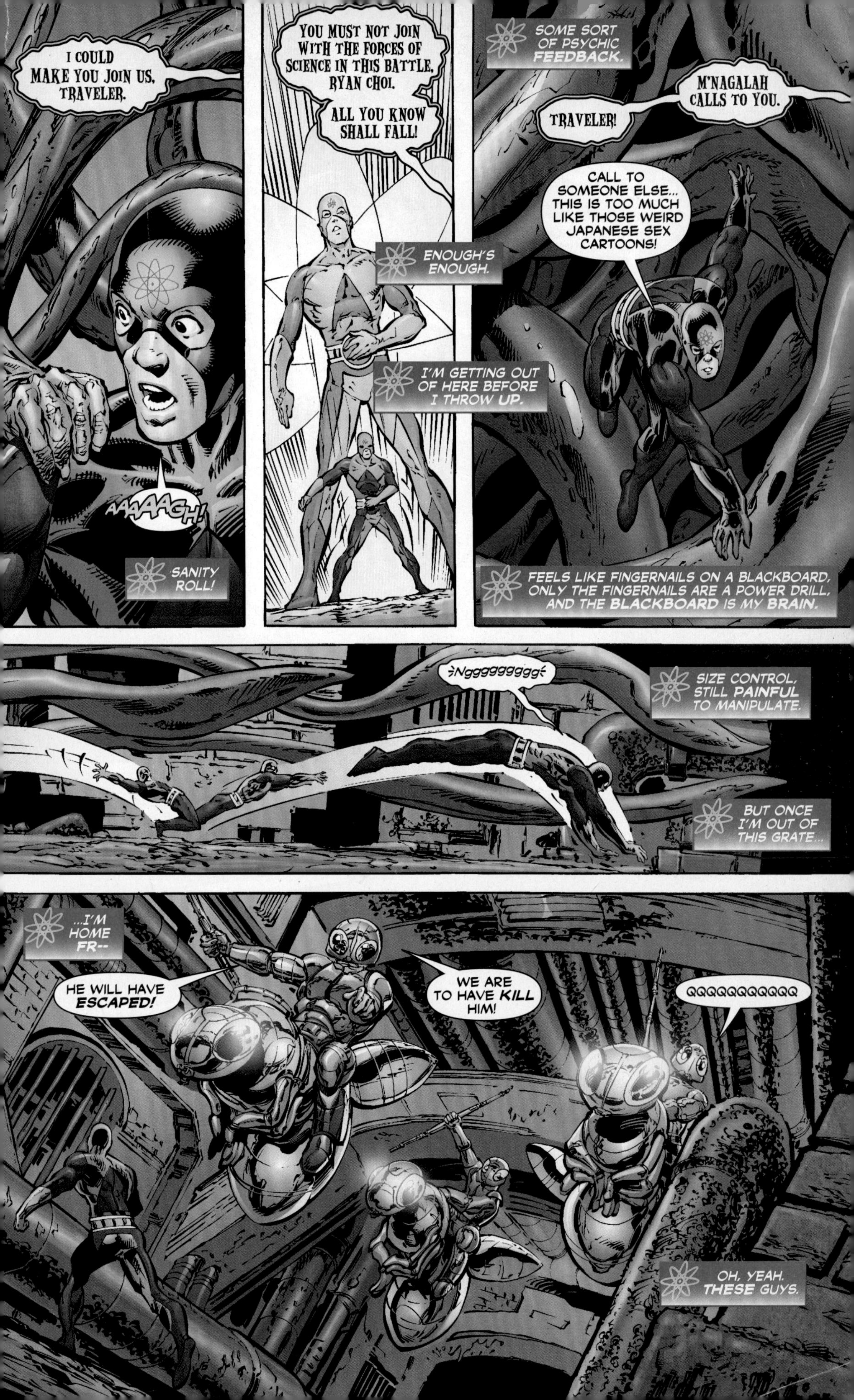
I COULD MAKE YOU JOIN US, TRAVELER.
AAAAAGH!
SANITY ROLL!
YOU MUST NOT JOIN WITH THE FORCES OF SCIENCE IN THIS BATTLE, RYAN CHOI.
ALL YOU KNOW SHALL FALL!
ENOUGH'S ENOUGH.
I'M GETTING OUT OF HERE BEFORE I THROW UP.
SOME SORT OF PSYCHIC FEEDBACK.
TRAVELER!
M'NAGALAH CALLS TO YOU.
CALL TO SOMEONE ELSE... THIS IS TOO MUCH LIKE THOSE WEIRD JAPANESE SEX CARTOONS!
FEELS LIKE FINGERNAILS ON A BLACKBOARD, ONLY THE FINGERNAILS ARE A POWER DRILL, AND THE BLACKBOARD IS MY BRAIN.
Nggggggggg
SIZE CONTROL, STILL PAINFUL TO MANIPULATE.
BUT ONCE I'M OUT OF THIS GRATE...
...I'M HOME FR--
HE WILL HAVE ESCAPED!
WE ARE TO HAVE KILL HIM!
QQQQQQQQQQ
OH, YEAH. THESE GUYS.

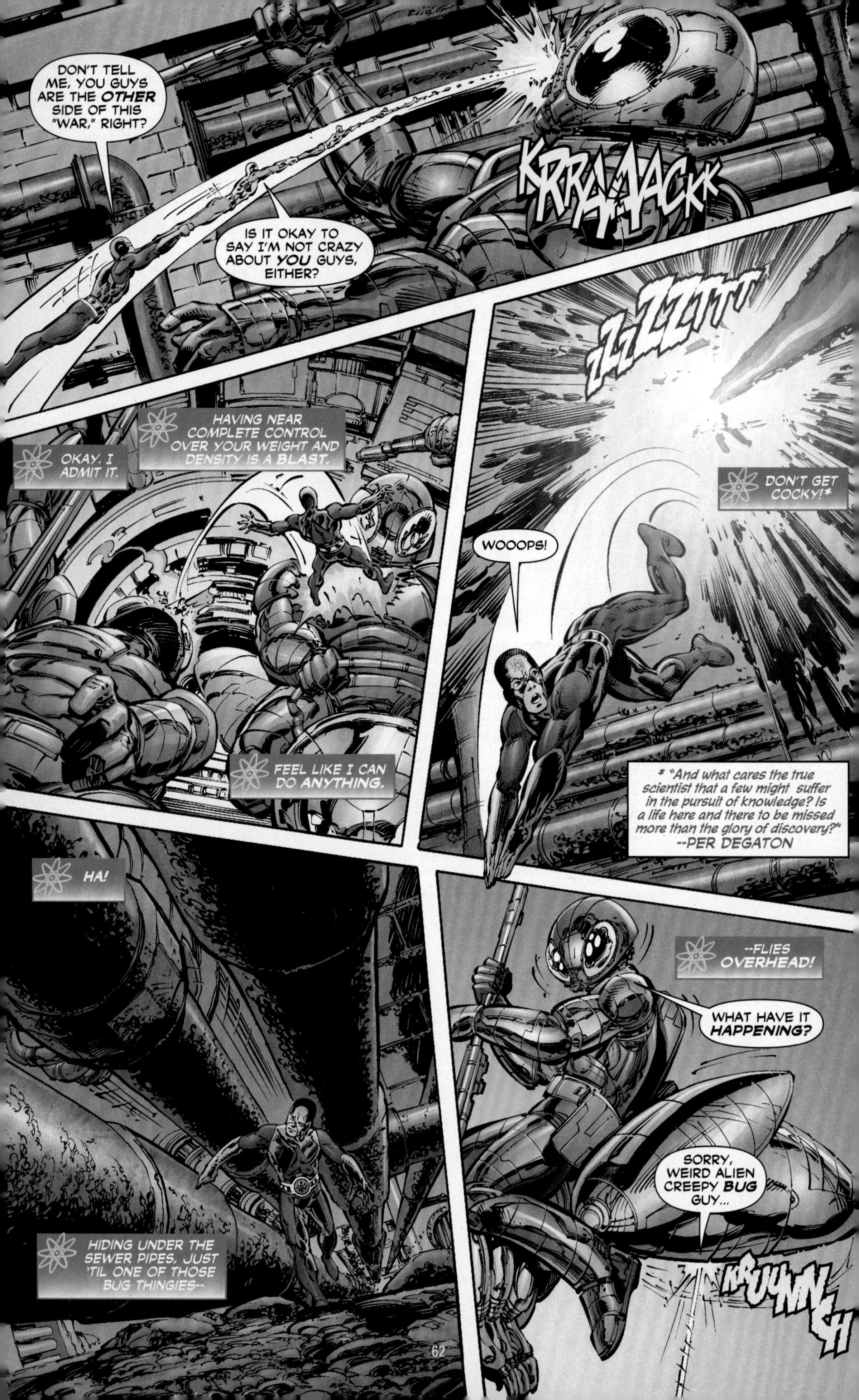

DON'T TELL ME, YOU GUYS ARE THE OTHER SIDE OF THIS "WAR," RIGHT?
IS IT OKAY TO SAY I'M NOT CRAZY ABOUT YOU GUYS, EITHER?
KRRAAACKK
OKAY. I ADMIT IT.
HAVING NEAR COMPLETE CONTROL OVER YOUR WEIGHT AND DENSITY IS A BLAST.
FEEL LIKE I CAN DO ANYTHING.
ZZZZZTTTT
DON'T GET COCKY!*
WOOOPS!
* "And what cares the true scientist that a few might suffer in the pursuit of knowledge? Is a life here and there to be missed more than the glory of discovery?" --PER DEGATON
HA!
HIDING UNDER THE SEWER PIPES, JUST 'TIL ONE OF THOSE BUG THINGIES--
--FLIES OVERHEAD!
WHAT HAVE IT HAPPENING?
SORRY, WEIRD ALIEN CREEPY BUG GUY...
KRUUNNCH

I WILL BE DEFEATING!

...DON'T YOU KNOW THAT BAD GRAMMAR STUNTS YOUR *GROWTH*?

WE ARE TO BE *REVENGEFUL!*

I ALWAYS SAY REVENGEFUL IS A DISH BEST SERVED COLDY.

LIKE SALADISH.

QQQQQQQ QQQQQ!

OH... HANG ON A SEC.

IN THE WRECKAGE--

--WHAT HAVE WE HERE? *

* "And it all began with some ancients who questioned how far we could divide matter. It shows what asking the right questions can bring about."
--DR. ISAAC ASIMOV

DR. HELMOND KETTERING'S BASEMENT.

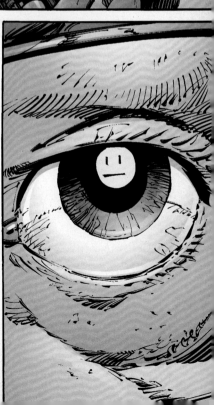

ENJOY

DR. *KETTERING!*

SORRY TO INTERRUPT... *Uh...* ...YOUR *STARING,* BUT I THINK YOU'RE GONNA WANNA *SEE* THIS!

OKAY, I WAS DOWN IN THE SEWER, RIGHT?

DON'T LOOK AT *ME,* I JUST CAME FOR THE STALE CHIPS.

AND I WAS ATTACKED AGAIN... BY *ALIENS.*

CREEPY, NASTY, *SMELLY* LITTLE SIZE-CHANGING ALIENS, TOO.

LOOK, I KNOW THIS SOUNDS STUPID, BUT IT'S SOMETHING ABOUT IVY TOWN. IT'S A NEXUS OF SOME SORT...

...A CLASH POINT OF *MAGIC* AND *SCIENCE.*

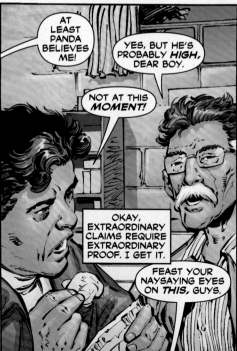

AT LEAST PANDA BELIEVES ME!

YES, BUT HE'S PROBABLY *HIGH,* DEAR BOY.

NOT AT THIS *MOMENT!*

OKAY, EXTRAORDINARY CLAIMS REQUIRE EXTRAORDINARY PROOF. I GET IT.

FEAST YOUR NAYSAYING EYES ON *THIS,* GUYS.

IT'S A *PARTICLE DRIVE* YOU CAN HOLD WITH ONE *HAND.*

STILL THINK I'M NUTS?

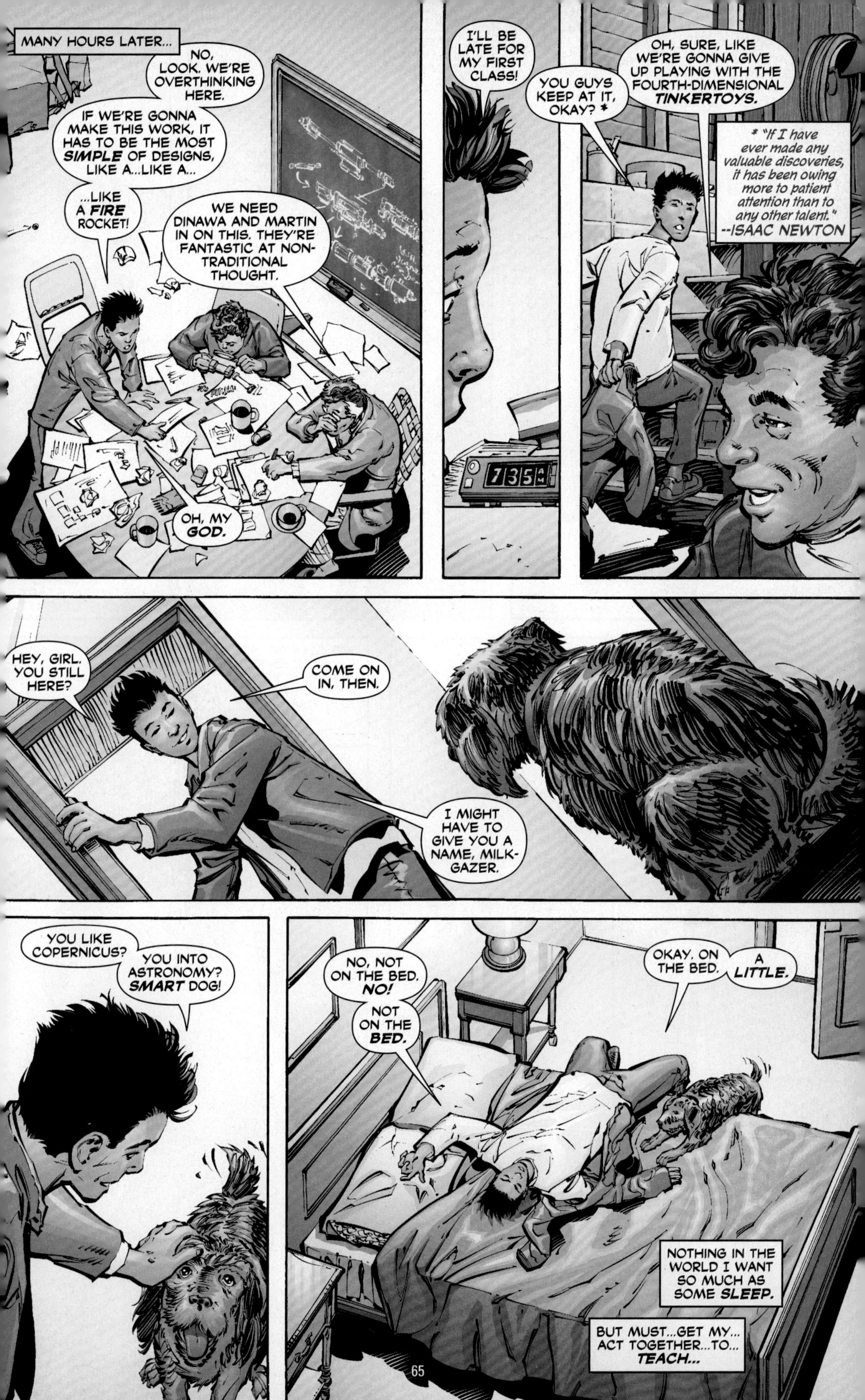
MANY HOURS LATER...
NO, LOOK. WE'RE OVERTHINKING HERE.
IF WE'RE GONNA MAKE THIS WORK, IT HAS TO BE THE MOST SIMPLE OF DESIGNS, LIKE A...LIKE A...
...LIKE A FIRE ROCKET!
WE NEED DINAWA AND MARTIN IN ON THIS. THEY'RE FANTASTIC AT NON-TRADITIONAL THOUGHT.
OH, MY GOD.
I'LL BE LATE FOR MY FIRST CLASS!
YOU GUYS KEEP AT IT, OKAY? *
OH, SURE, LIKE WE'RE GONNA GIVE UP PLAYING WITH THE FOURTH-DIMENSIONAL TINKERTOYS.
* "If I have ever made any valuable discoveries, it has been owing more to patient attention than to any other talent." --ISAAC NEWTON
7:35 AM
HEY, GIRL. YOU STILL HERE?
COME ON IN, THEN.
I MIGHT HAVE TO GIVE YOU A NAME, MILK-GAZER.
YOU LIKE COPERNICUS?
YOU INTO ASTRONOMY? SMART DOG!
NO, NOT ON THE BED. NO!
NOT ON THE BED.
OKAY. ON THE BED.
A LITTLE.
NOTHING IN THE WORLD I WANT SO MUCH AS SOME SLEEP.
BUT MUST...GET MY... ACT TOGETHER...TO... TEACH...

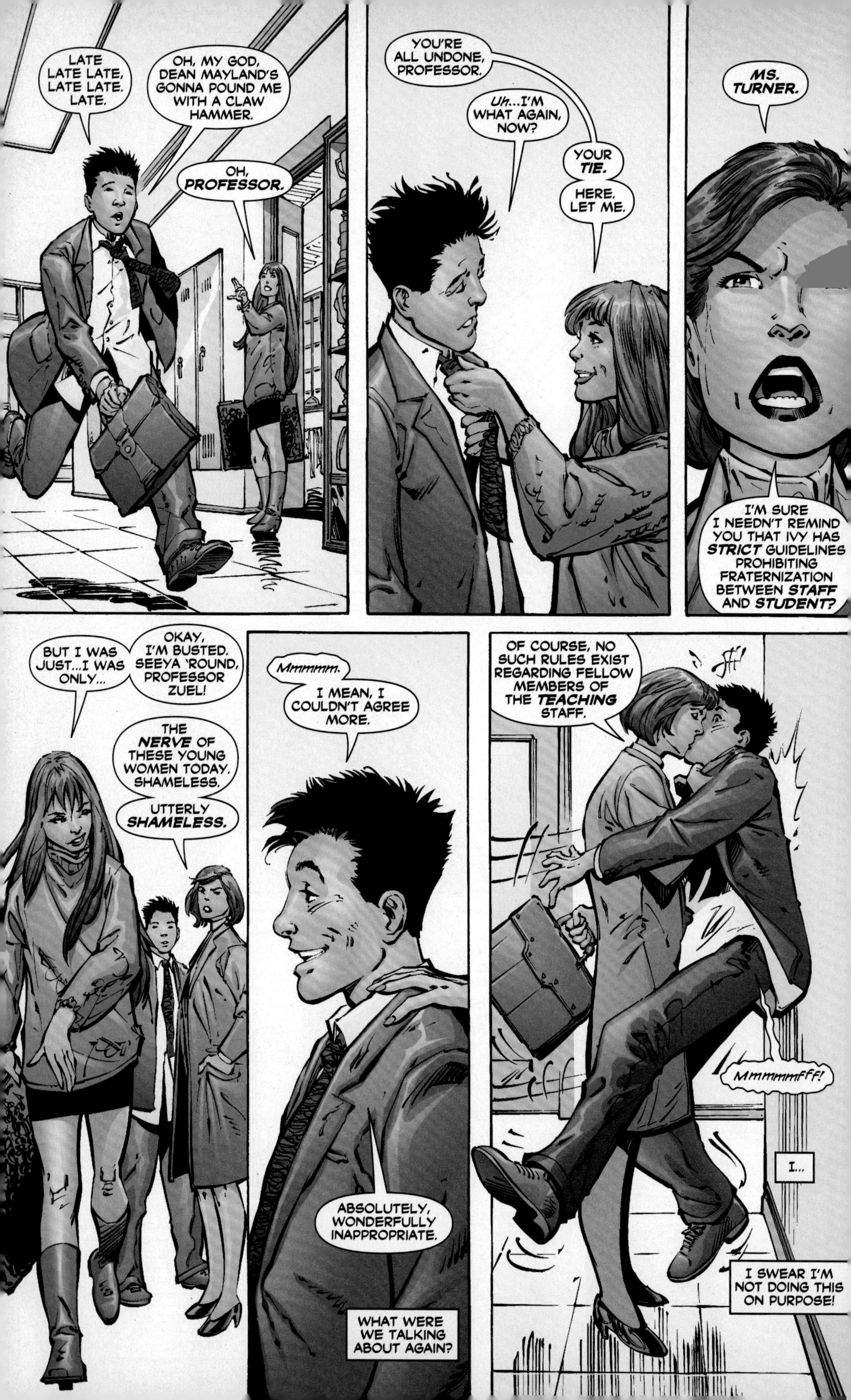
LATE LATE LATE, LATE LATE. LATE.
OH, MY GOD, DEAN MAYLAND'S GONNA POUND ME WITH A CLAW HAMMER.
OH, PROFESSOR.
YOU'RE ALL UNDONE, PROFESSOR.
Uh...I'M WHAT AGAIN, NOW?
YOUR TIE.
HERE. LET ME.
MS. TURNER.
I'M SURE I NEEDN'T REMIND YOU THAT IVY HAS STRICT GUIDELINES PROHIBITING FRATERNIZATION BETWEEN STAFF AND STUDENT?
BUT I WAS JUST...I WAS ONLY...
OKAY, I'M BUSTED. SEEYA 'ROUND, PROFESSOR ZUEL!
THE NERVE OF THESE YOUNG WOMEN TODAY. SHAMELESS.
UTTERLY SHAMELESS.
Mmmmmm.
I MEAN, I COULDN'T AGREE MORE.
ABSOLUTELY, WONDERFULLY INAPPROPRIATE.
WHAT WERE WE TALKING ABOUT AGAIN?
OF COURSE, NO SUCH RULES EXIST REGARDING FELLOW MEMBERS OF THE TEACHING STAFF.
Mmmmmmfff!
I...
I SWEAR I'M NOT DOING THIS ON PURPOSE!

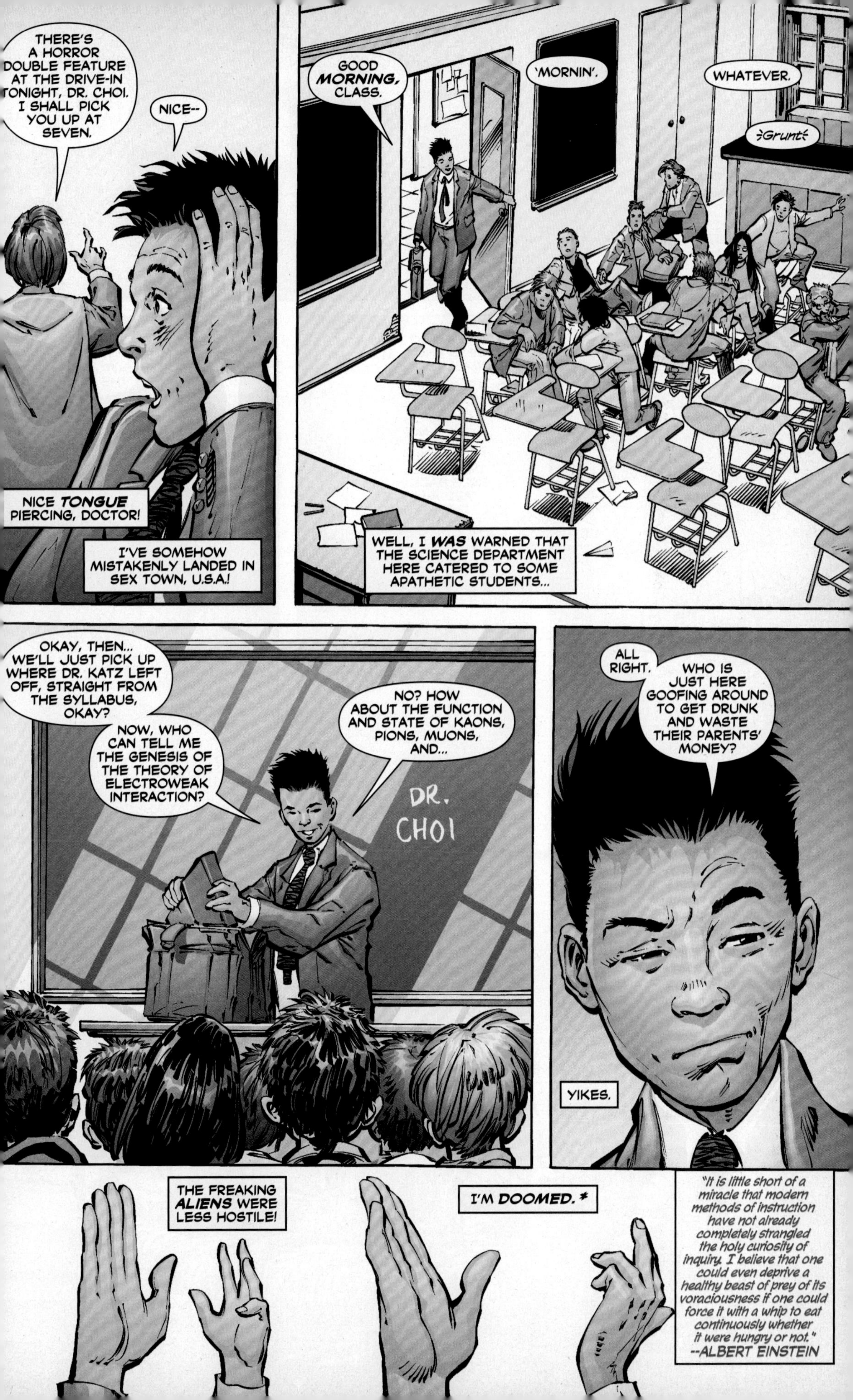

THERE'S A HORROR DOUBLE FEATURE AT THE DRIVE-IN TONIGHT, DR. CHOI. I SHALL PICK YOU UP AT SEVEN.
NICE--
NICE TONGUE PIERCING, DOCTOR!
I'VE SOMEHOW MISTAKENLY LANDED IN SEX TOWN, U.S.A.!
GOOD MORNING, CLASS.
'MORNIN'.
WHATEVER.
Grunt
WELL, I WAS WARNED THAT THE SCIENCE DEPARTMENT HERE CATERED TO SOME APATHETIC STUDENTS...
OKAY, THEN... WE'LL JUST PICK UP WHERE DR. KATZ LEFT OFF, STRAIGHT FROM THE SYLLABUS, OKAY?
NOW, WHO CAN TELL ME THE GENESIS OF THE THEORY OF ELECTROWEAK INTERACTION?
NO? HOW ABOUT THE FUNCTION AND STATE OF KAONS, PIONS, MUONS, AND...
DR. CHOI
ALL RIGHT.
WHO IS JUST HERE GOOFING AROUND TO GET DRUNK AND WASTE THEIR PARENTS' MONEY?
YIKES.
THE FREAKING ALIENS WERE LESS HOSTILE!
I'M DOOMED.*
"It is little short of a miracle that modern methods of instruction have not already completely strangled the holy curiosity of inquiry. I believe that one could even deprive a healthy beast of prey of its voraciousness if one could force it with a whip to eat continuously whether it were hungry or not."
--ALBERT EINSTEIN

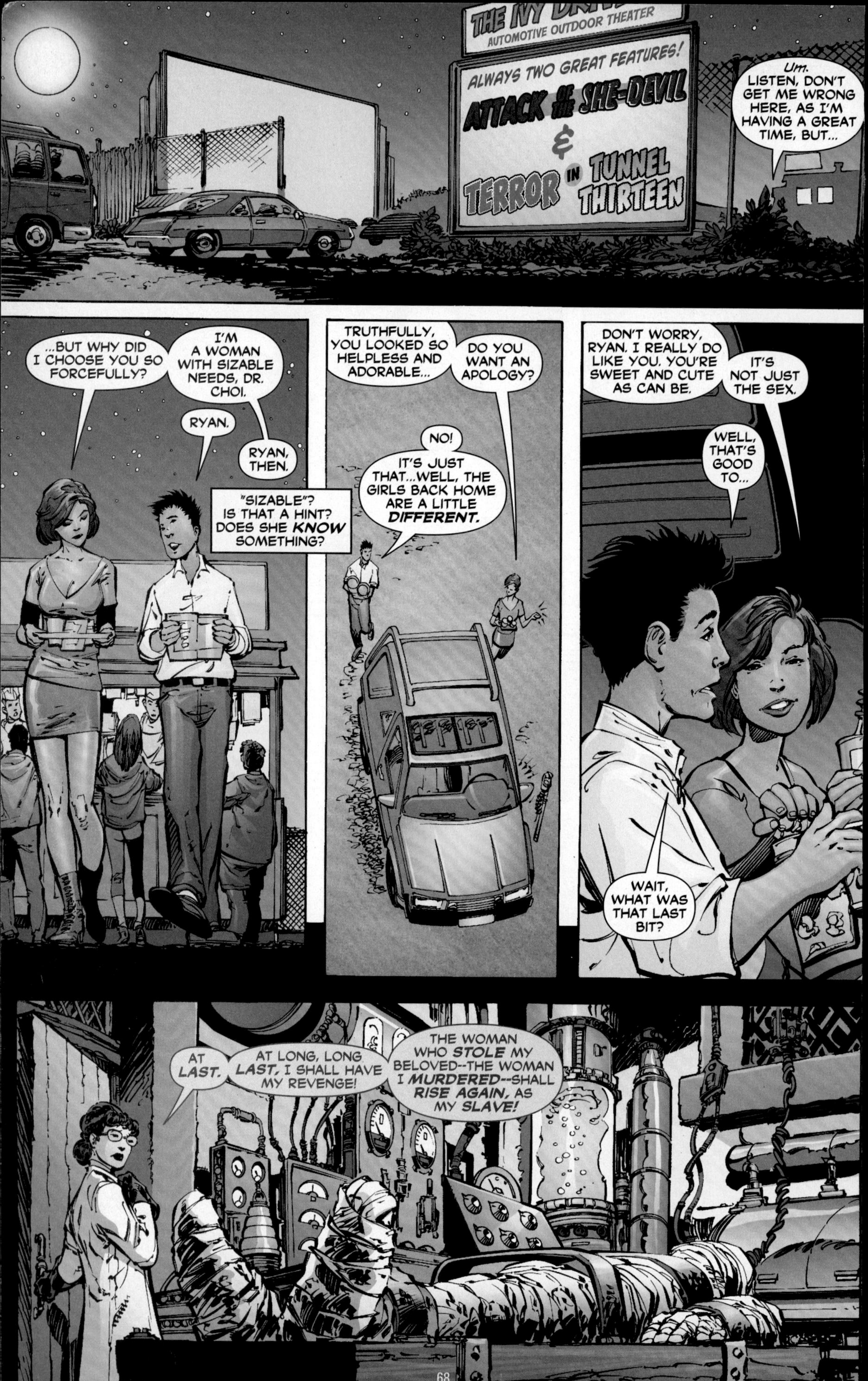
AUTOMOTIVE OUTDOOR THEATER
ALWAYS TWO GREAT FEATURES!
ATTACK OF THE SHE-DEVIL
&
TERROR IN TUNNEL THIRTEEN
Um. LISTEN, DON'T GET ME WRONG HERE, AS I'M HAVING A GREAT TIME, BUT...
...BUT WHY DID I CHOOSE YOU SO FORCEFULLY?
I'M A WOMAN WITH SIZABLE NEEDS, DR. CHOI.
RYAN.
RYAN, THEN.
"SIZABLE"? IS THAT A HINT? DOES SHE KNOW SOMETHING?
TRUTHFULLY, YOU LOOKED SO HELPLESS AND ADORABLE...
DO YOU WANT AN APOLOGY?
NO!
IT'S JUST THAT...WELL, THE GIRLS BACK HOME ARE A LITTLE DIFFERENT.
DON'T WORRY, RYAN. I REALLY DO LIKE YOU. YOU'RE SWEET AND CUTE AS CAN BE.
IT'S NOT JUST THE SEX.
WELL, THAT'S GOOD TO...
WAIT, WHAT WAS THAT LAST BIT?
AT LAST.
AT LONG, LONG LAST, I SHALL HAVE MY REVENGE!
THE WOMAN WHO STOLE MY BELOVED--THE WOMAN I MURDERED--SHALL RISE AGAIN, AS MY SLAVE!

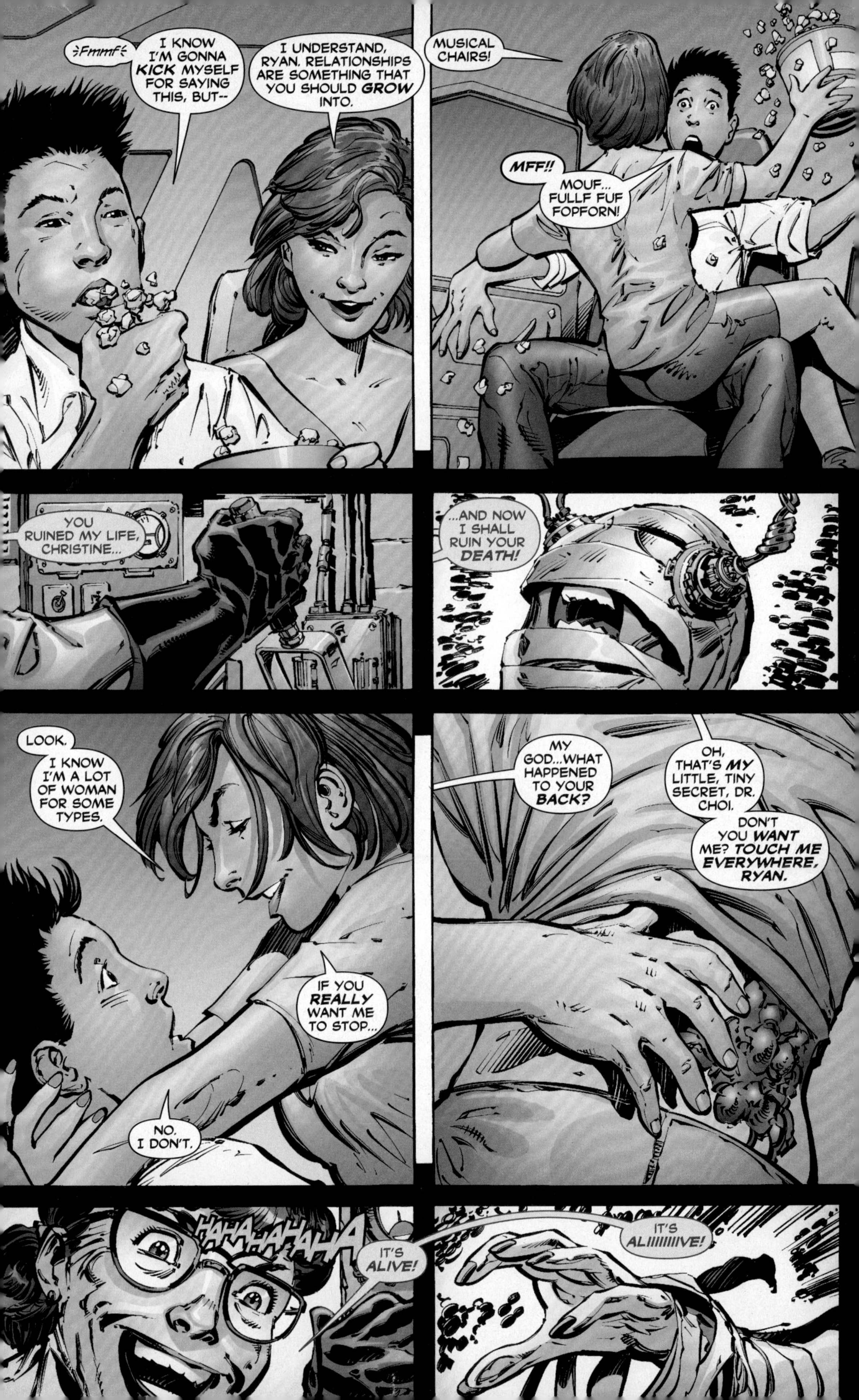

Fmmf
I KNOW I'M GONNA KICK MYSELF FOR SAYING THIS, BUT--
I UNDERSTAND, RYAN. RELATIONSHIPS ARE SOMETHING THAT YOU SHOULD GROW INTO.
MUSICAL CHAIRS!
MFF!!
MOUF... FULLF FUF FOPFORN!
YOU RUINED MY LIFE, CHRISTINE...
...AND NOW I SHALL RUIN YOUR DEATH!
LOOK.
I KNOW I'M A LOT OF WOMAN FOR SOME TYPES.
IF YOU REALLY WANT ME TO STOP...
NO. I DON'T.
MY GOD...WHAT HAPPENED TO YOUR BACK?
OH, THAT'S MY LITTLE, TINY SECRET, DR. CHOI.
DON'T YOU WANT ME? TOUCH ME EVERYWHERE, RYAN.
HAHAHAHAHAHA
IT'S ALIVE!
IT'S ALIIIIIIIIVE!

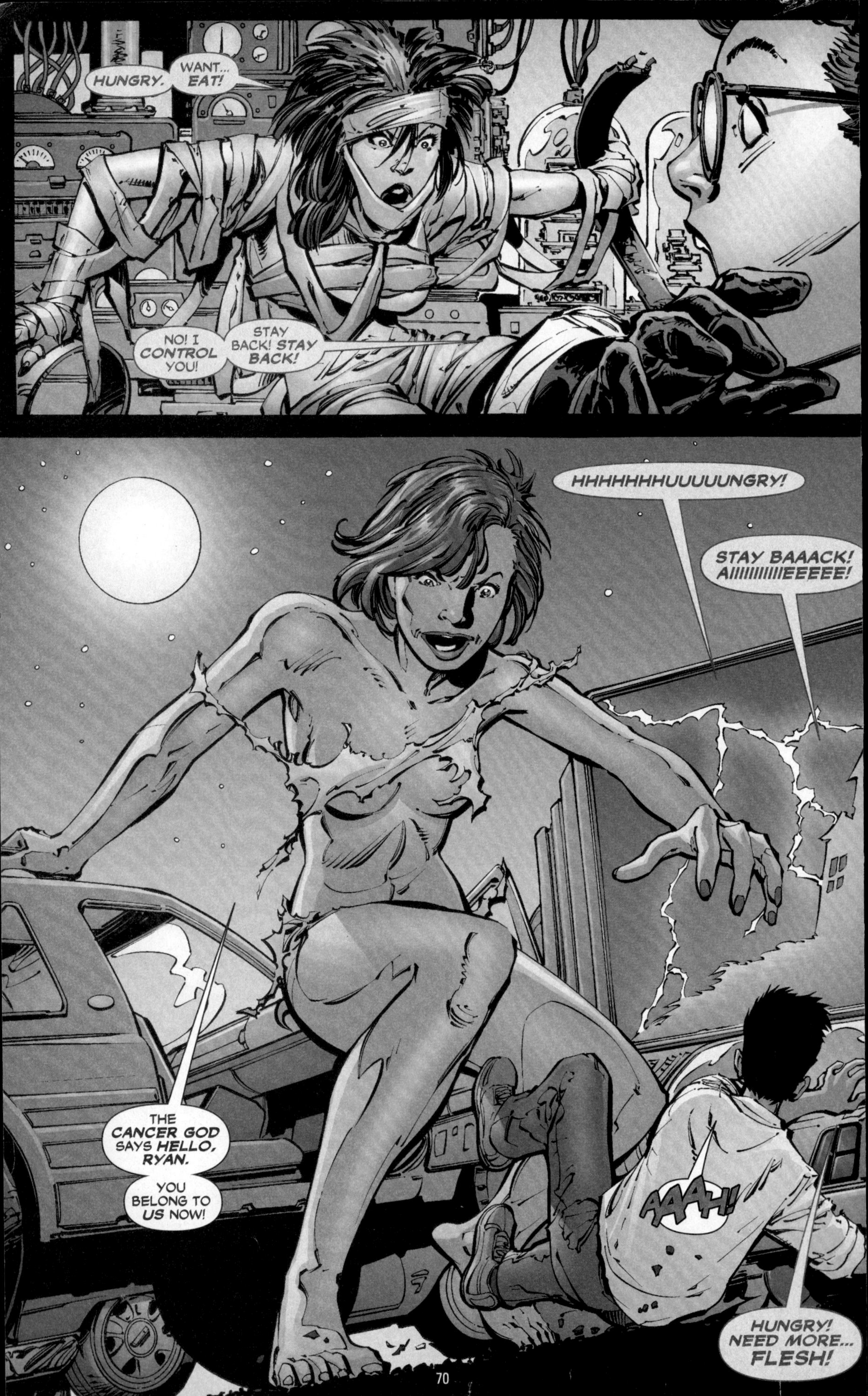
HUNGRY.
WANT... EAT!
NO! I CONTROL YOU!
STAY BACK! STAY BACK!
HHHHHHHUUUUUNGRY!
STAY BAAACK! AIIIIIIIIIEEEEE!
THE CANCER GOD SAYS HELLO, RYAN.
YOU BELONG TO US NOW!
AAAH!
HUNGRY! NEED MORE... FLESH!

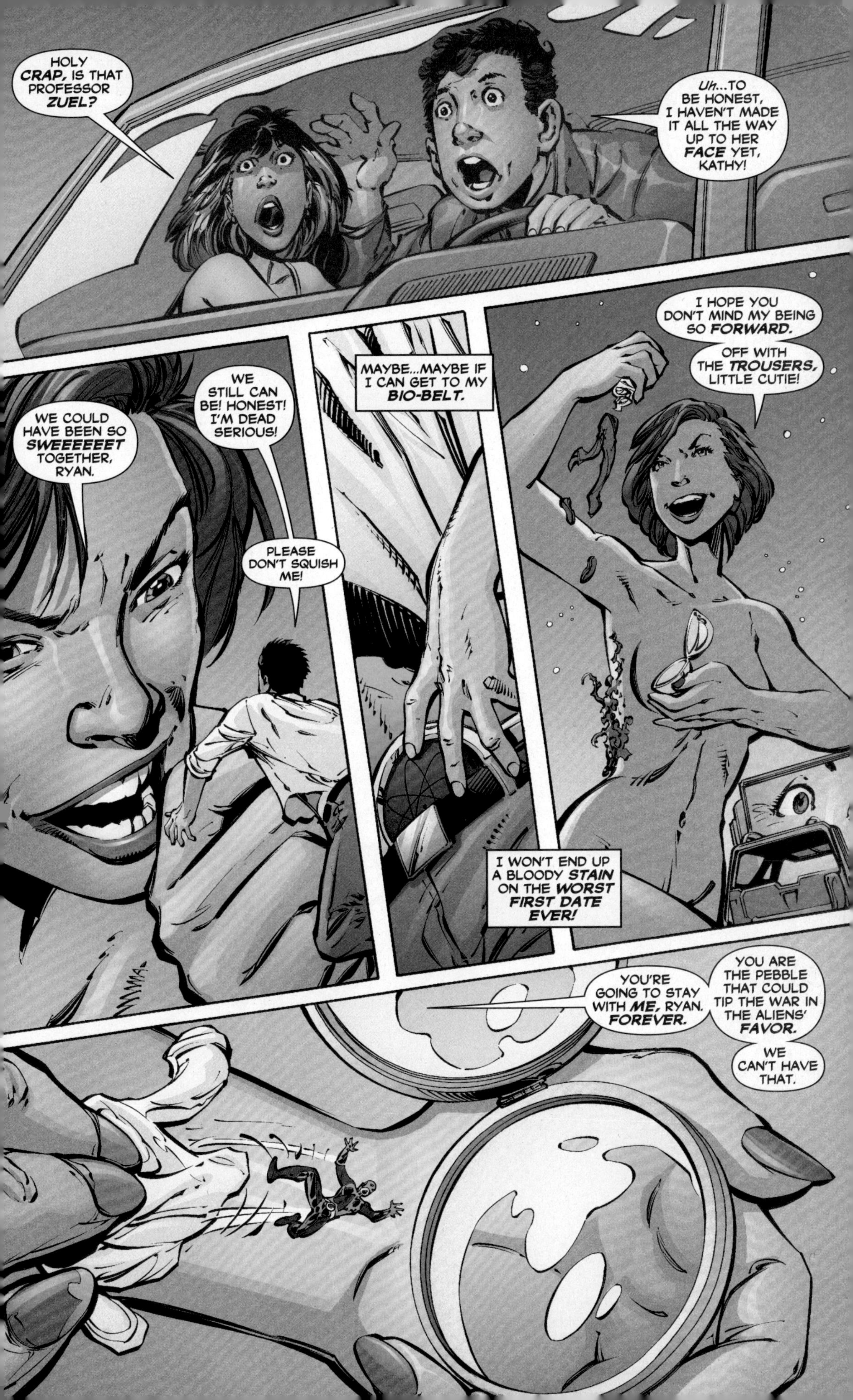
HOLY CRAP, IS THAT PROFESSOR ZUEL?
Uh...TO BE HONEST, I HAVEN'T MADE IT ALL THE WAY UP TO HER FACE YET, KATHY!
WE COULD HAVE BEEN SO SWEEEEEET TOGETHER, RYAN.
WE STILL CAN BE! HONEST! I'M DEAD SERIOUS!
PLEASE DON'T SQUISH ME!
MAYBE...MAYBE IF I CAN GET TO MY BIO-BELT.
I WON'T END UP A BLOODY STAIN ON THE WORST FIRST DATE EVER!
I HOPE YOU DON'T MIND MY BEING SO FORWARD.
OFF WITH THE TROUSERS, LITTLE CUTIE!
YOU'RE GOING TO STAY WITH ME, RYAN. FOREVER.
YOU ARE THE PEBBLE THAT COULD TIP THE WAR IN THE ALIENS' FAVOR.
WE CAN'T HAVE THAT.

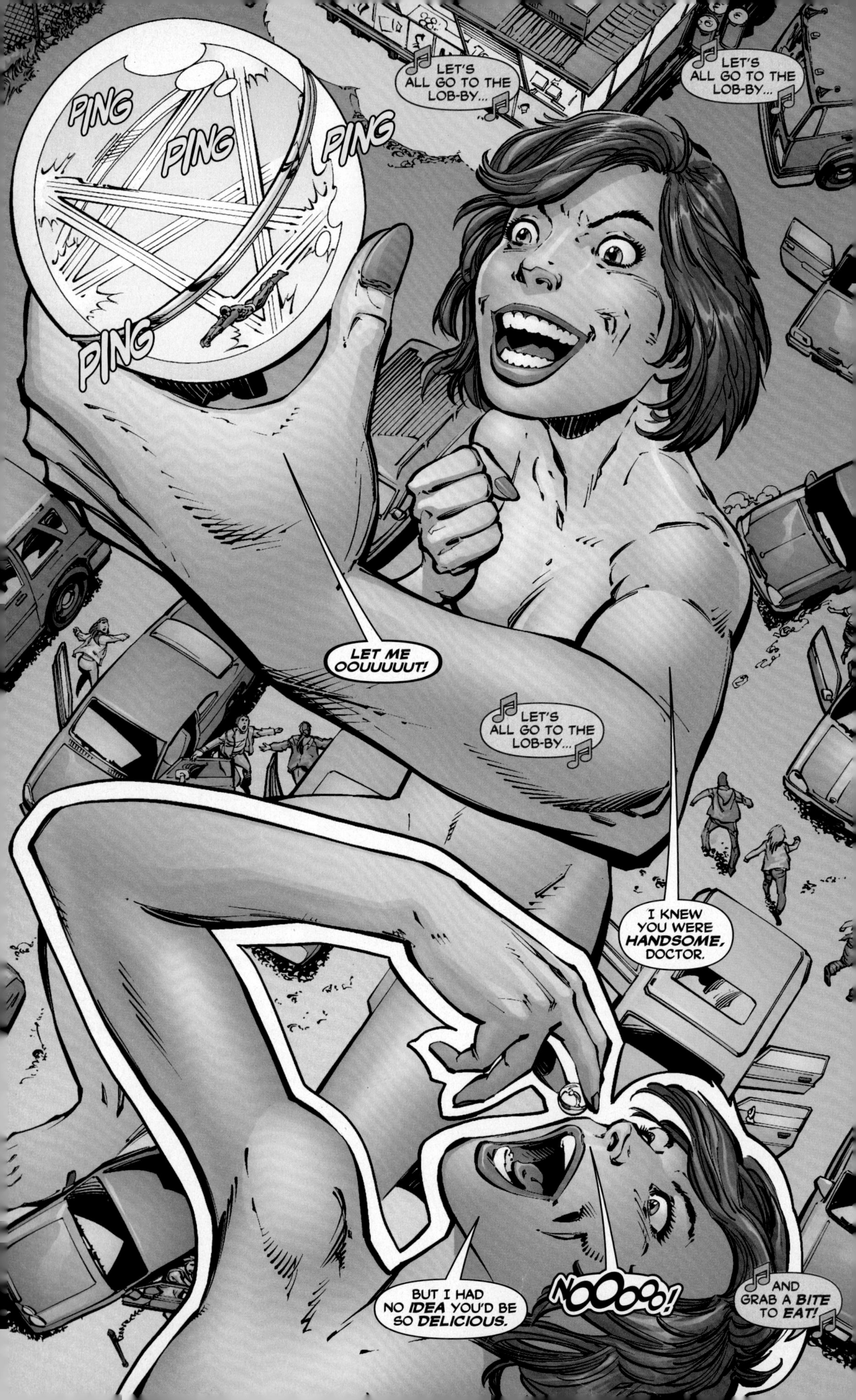
LET'S ALL GO TO THE LOB-BY...
LET'S ALL GO TO THE LOB-BY...
PING
PING
PING
PING
LET ME OOUUUUUT!
LET'S ALL GO TO THE LOB-BY...
I KNEW YOU WERE HANDSOME, DOCTOR.
BUT I HAD NO IDEA YOU'D BE SO DELICIOUS.
NOOOOO!
AND GRAB A BITE TO EAT!

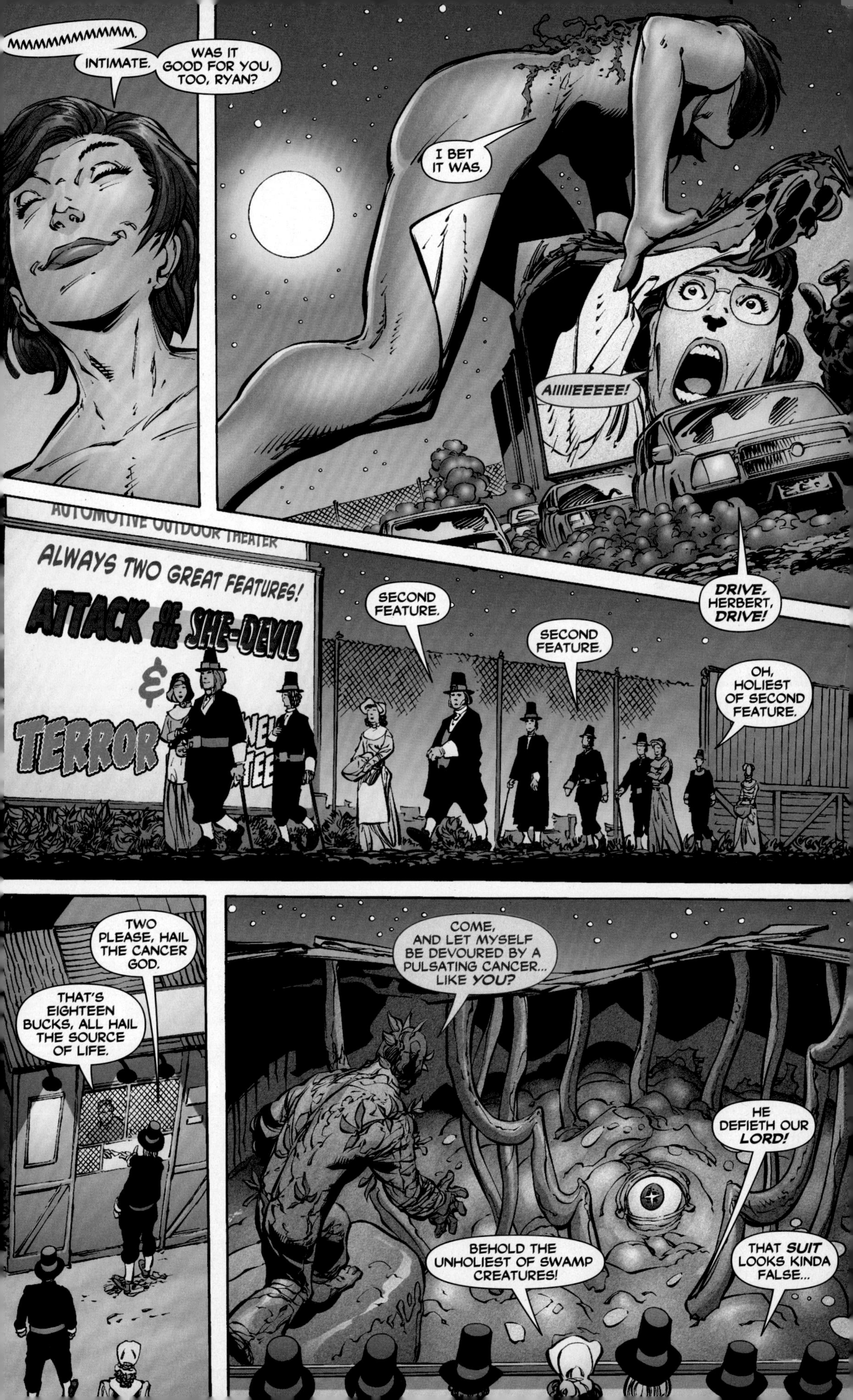
MMMMMMMMMMM.
INTIMATE.
WAS IT GOOD FOR YOU, TOO, RYAN?
I BET IT WAS.
AIIIIEEEEE!
DRIVE, HERBERT, DRIVE!
AUTOMOTIVE OUTDOOR THEATER
ALWAYS TWO GREAT FEATURES!
ATTACK OF THE SHE-DEVIL
&
TERROR
SECOND FEATURE.
SECOND FEATURE.
OH, HOLIEST OF SECOND FEATURE.
TWO PLEASE, HAIL THE CANCER GOD.
THAT'S EIGHTEEN BUCKS, ALL HAIL THE SOURCE OF LIFE.
COME, AND LET MYSELF BE DEVOURED BY A PULSATING CANCER... LIKE YOU?
HE DEFIETH OUR LORD!
BEHOLD THE UNHOLIEST OF SWAMP CREATURES!
THAT SUIT LOOKS KINDA FALSE...

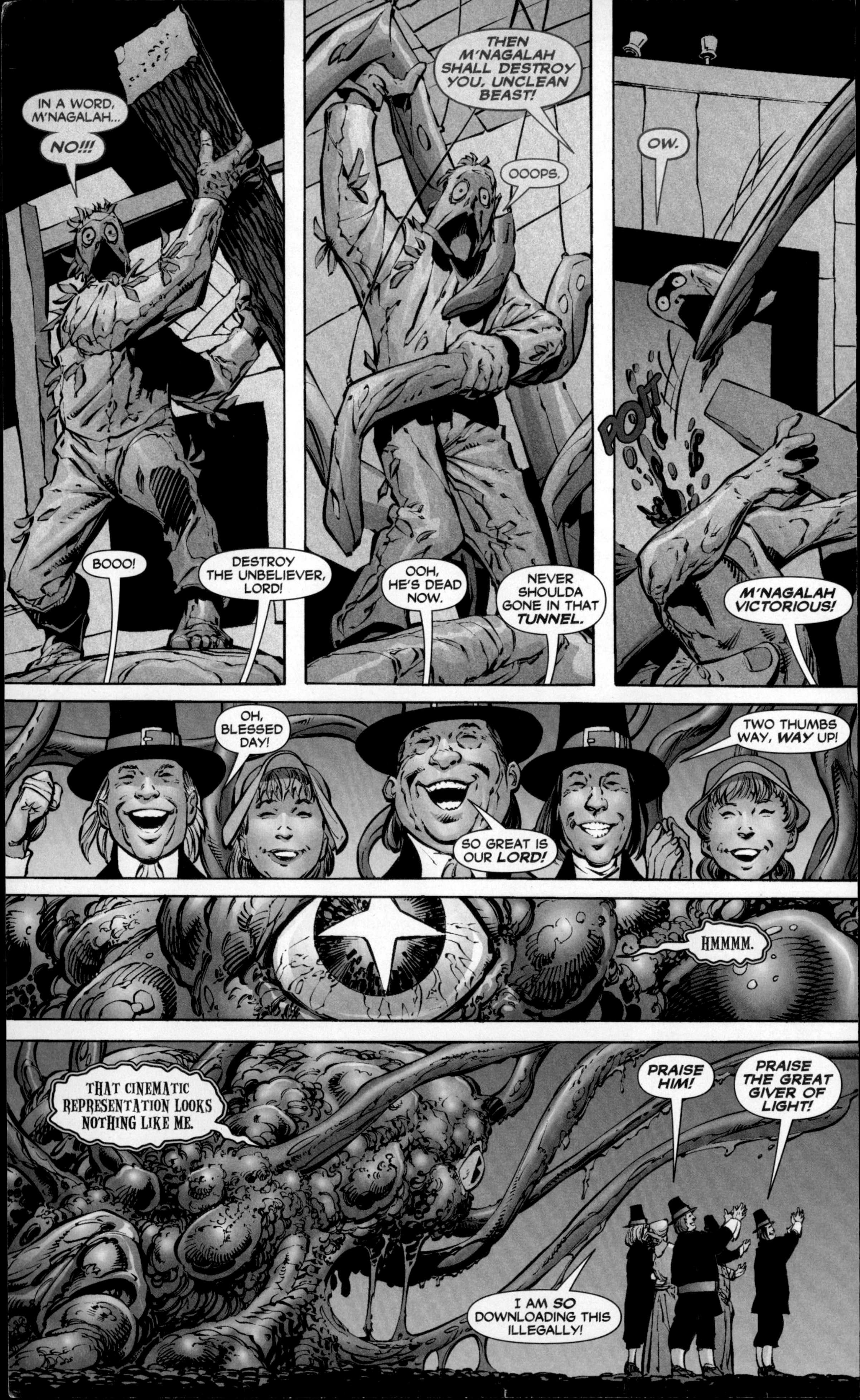
IN A WORD, M'NAGALAH...
NO!!!
THEN M'NAGALAH SHALL DESTROY YOU, UNCLEAN BEAST!
OOOPS.
OW.
POIT
BOOO!
DESTROY THE UNBELIEVER, LORD!
OOH, HE'S DEAD NOW.
NEVER SHOULDA GONE IN THAT TUNNEL.
M'NAGALAH VICTORIOUS!
OH, BLESSED DAY!
TWO THUMBS WAY, WAY UP!
SO GREAT IS OUR LORD!
HMMMM.
THAT CINEMATIC REPRESENTATION LOOKS NOTHING LIKE ME.
PRAISE HIM!
PRAISE THE GREAT GIVER OF LIGHT!
I AM SO DOWNLOADING THIS ILLEGALLY!

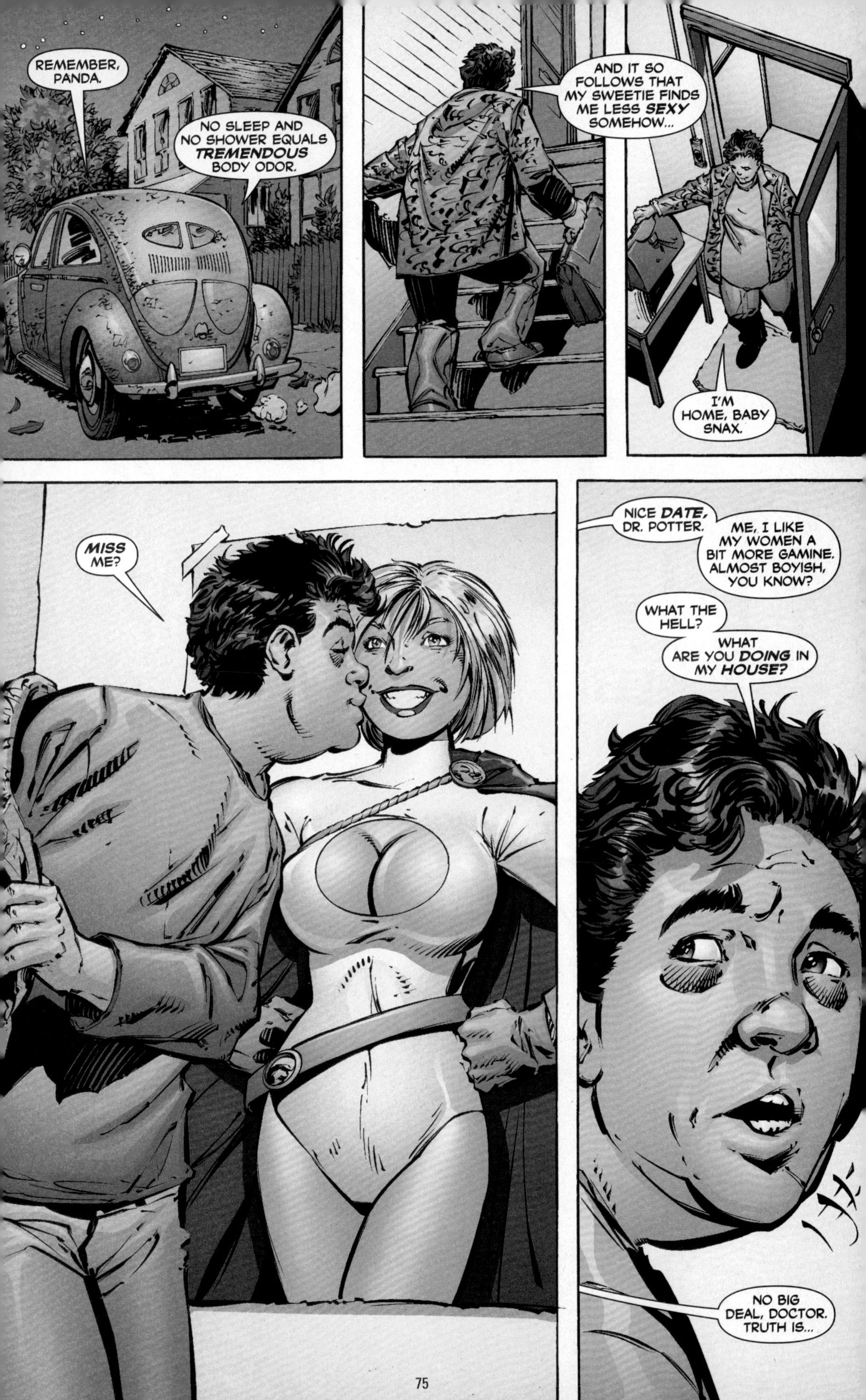
REMEMBER, PANDA.
NO SLEEP AND NO SHOWER EQUALS TREMENDOUS BODY ODOR.
AND IT SO FOLLOWS THAT MY SWEETIE FINDS ME LESS SEXY SOMEHOW...
I'M HOME, BABY SNAX.
MISS ME?
NICE DATE, DR. POTTER.
ME, I LIKE MY WOMEN A BIT MORE GAMINE. ALMOST BOYISH, YOU KNOW?
WHAT THE HELL?
WHAT ARE YOU DOING IN MY HOUSE?
NO BIG DEAL, DOCTOR. TRUTH IS...

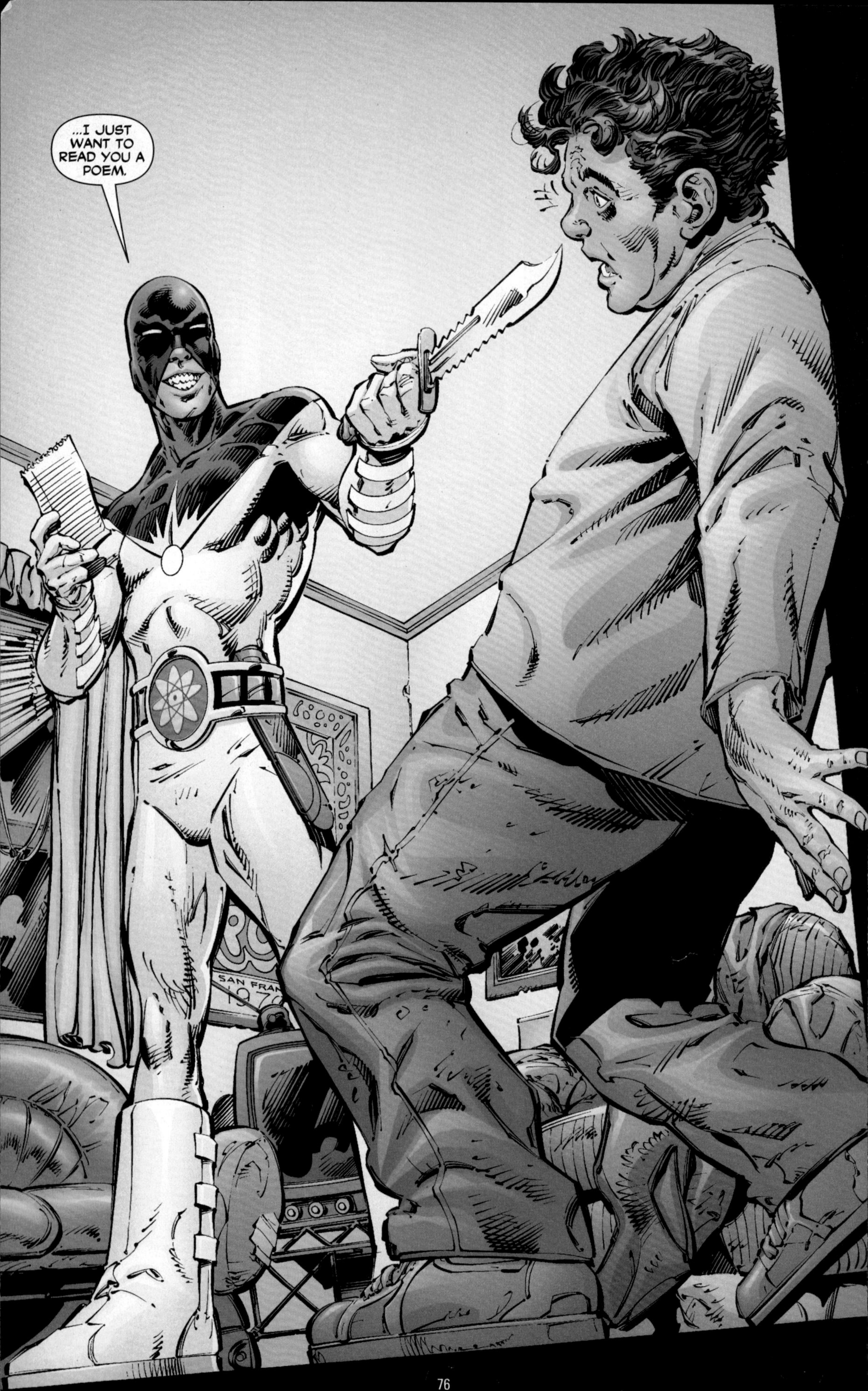
...I JUST WANT TO READ YOU A POEM.

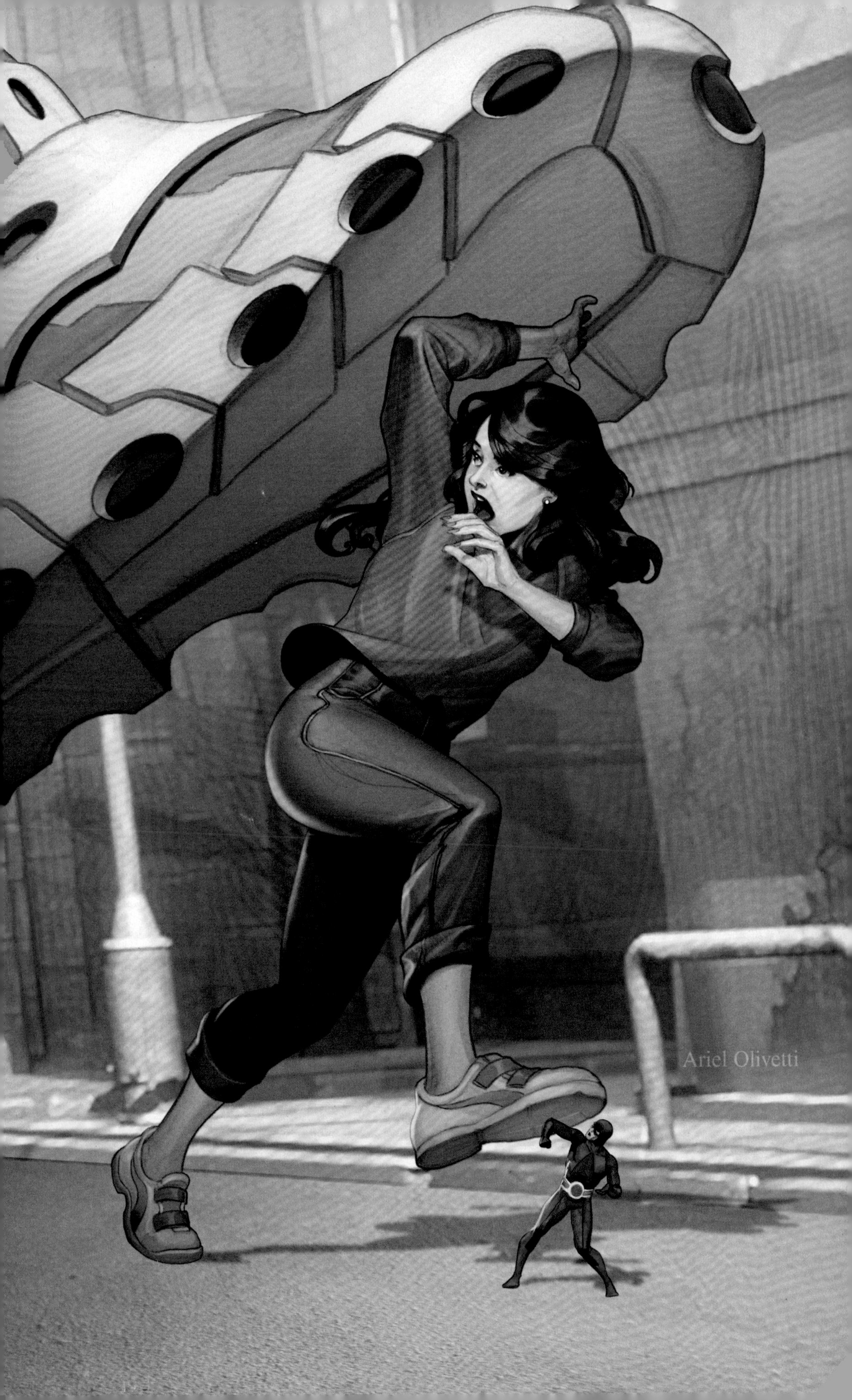
Ariel Olivetti

MY LIFE IN MINIATURE: PART FOUR
AGGRESSIVE IDEOLOGIES

from **THE ALL NEW ATOM #4**
Cover by **Ariel Olivetti**

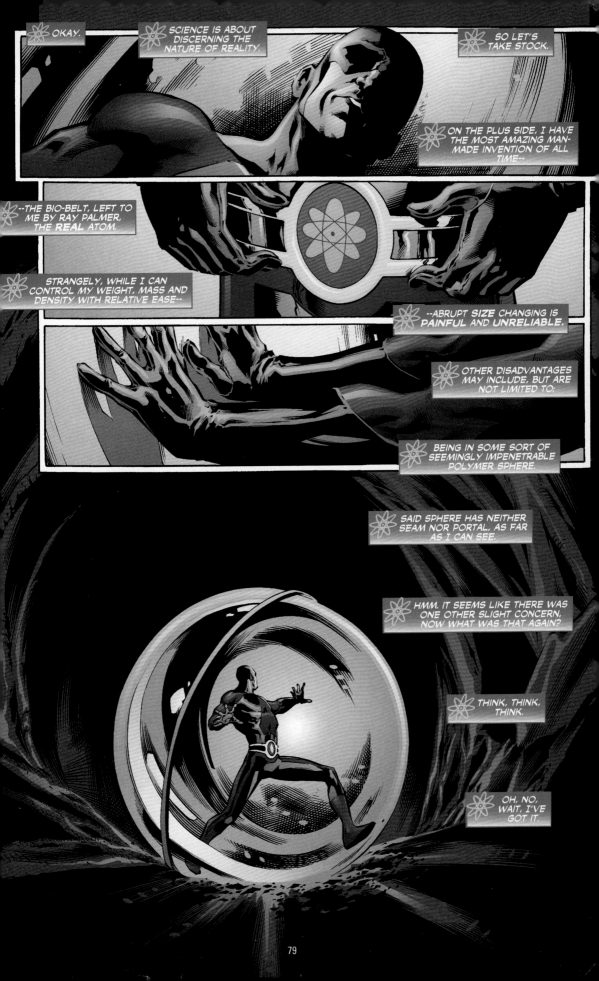

OKAY.

SCIENCE IS ABOUT DISCERNING THE NATURE OF REALITY.

SO LET'S TAKE STOCK.

ON THE PLUS SIDE, I HAVE THE MOST AMAZING MAN-MADE INVENTION OF ALL TIME--

--THE BIO-BELT, LEFT TO ME BY RAY PALMER, THE *REAL* ATOM.

STRANGELY, WHILE I CAN CONTROL MY WEIGHT, MASS AND DENSITY WITH RELATIVE EASE--

--ABRUPT *SIZE* CHANGING IS PAINFUL AND UNRELIABLE.

OTHER DISADVANTAGES MAY INCLUDE, BUT ARE NOT LIMITED TO:

BEING IN SOME SORT OF SEEMINGLY IMPENETRABLE POLYMER SPHERE.

SAID SPHERE HAS NEITHER SEAM NOR PORTAL, AS FAR AS I CAN SEE.

HMM. IT SEEMS LIKE THERE WAS ONE OTHER SLIGHT CONCERN, NOW WHAT WAS THAT AGAIN?

THINK, THINK, THINK.

OH, NO, WAIT, I'VE GOT IT.

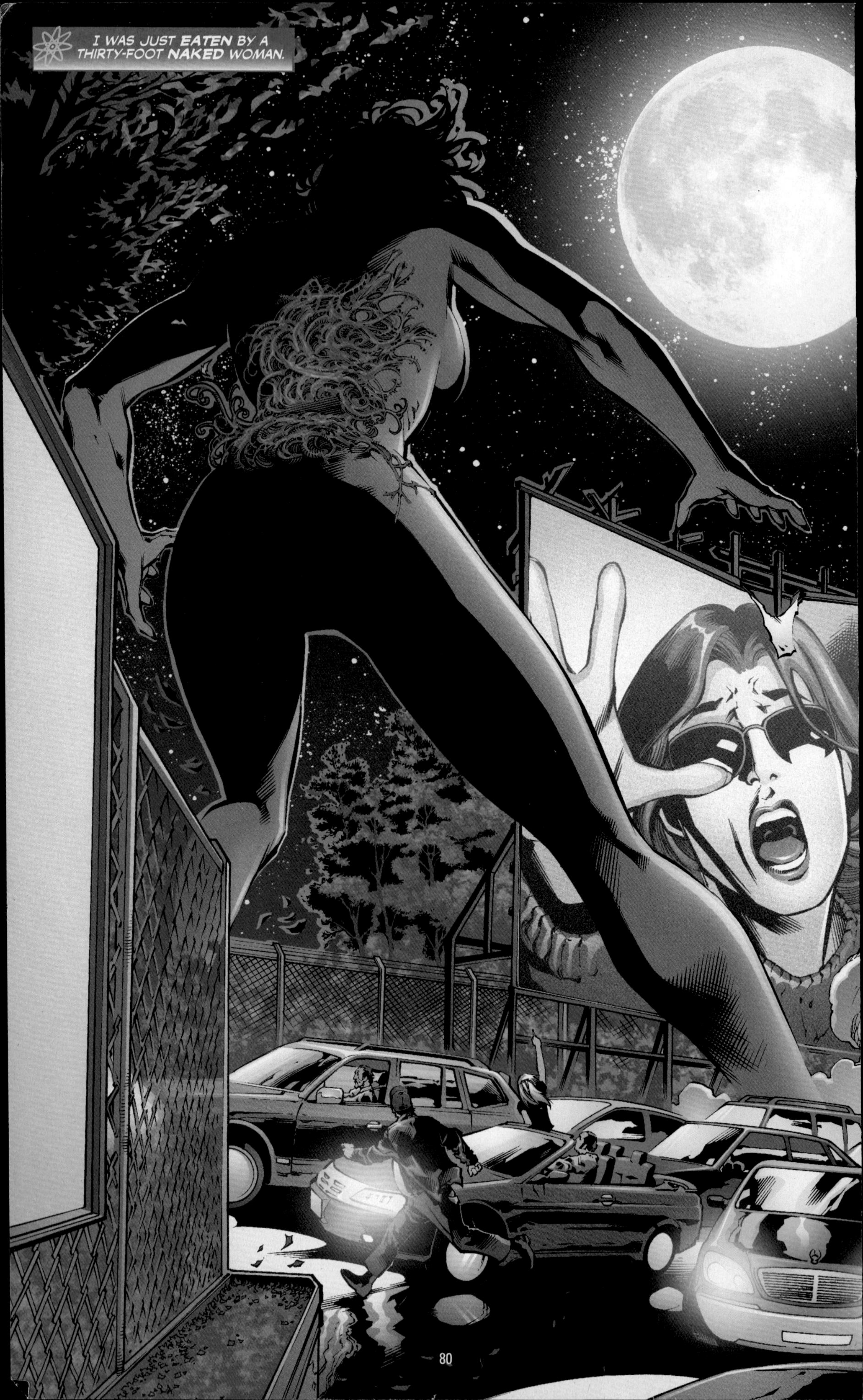
I WAS JUST **EATEN** BY A THIRTY-FOOT **NAKED** WOMAN.

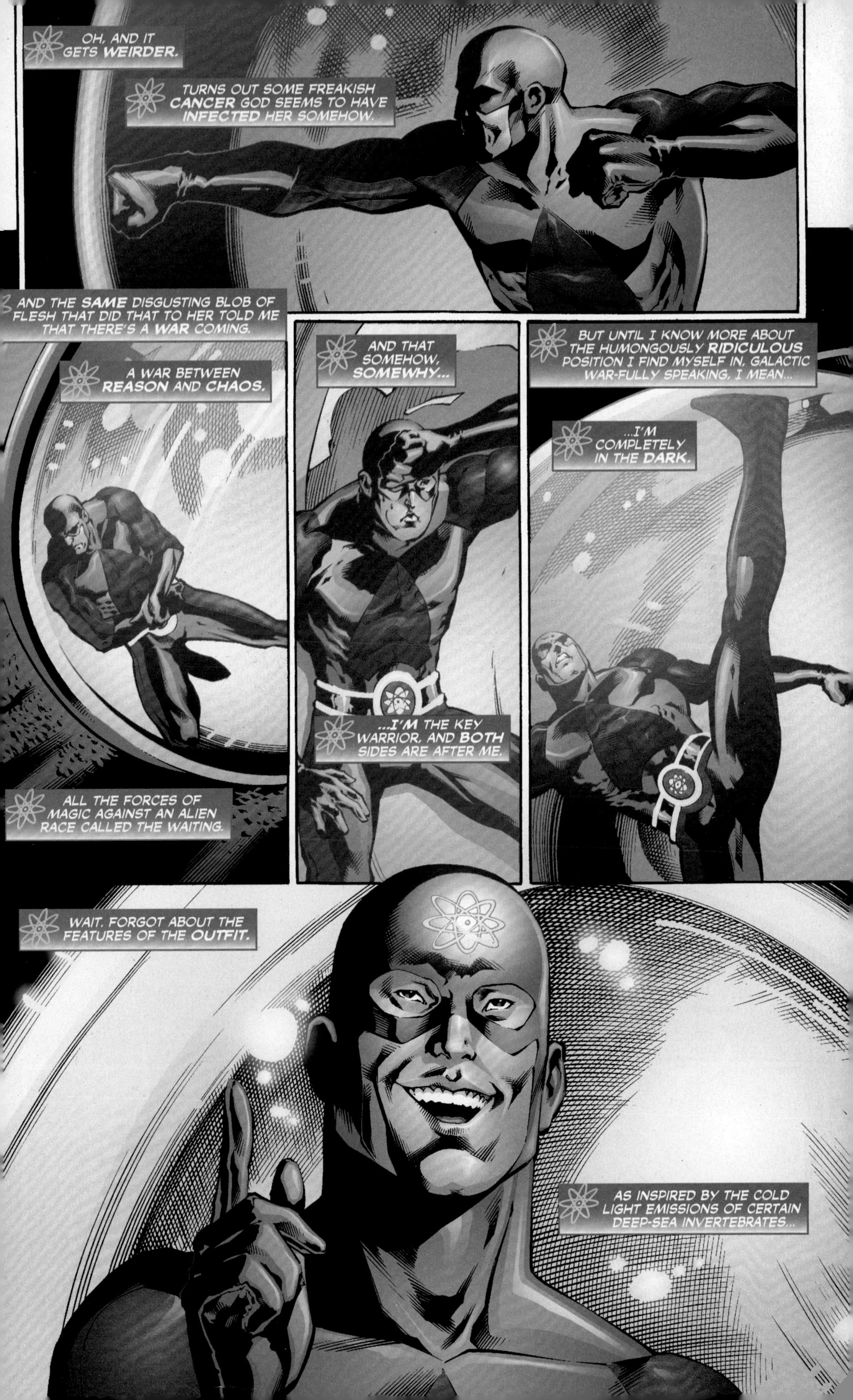
OH, AND IT GETS **WEIRDER.**
TURNS OUT SOME FREAKISH **CANCER** GOD SEEMS TO HAVE **INFECTED** HER SOMEHOW.
AND THE **SAME** DISGUSTING BLOB OF FLESH THAT DID THAT TO HER TOLD ME THAT THERE'S A **WAR** COMING.
A WAR BETWEEN **REASON** AND **CHAOS.**
ALL THE FORCES OF MAGIC AGAINST AN ALIEN RACE CALLED THE WAITING.
AND THAT SOMEHOW, **SOMEWHY...**
...I'M THE KEY WARRIOR, AND **BOTH** SIDES ARE AFTER ME.
BUT UNTIL I KNOW MORE ABOUT THE HUMONGOUSLY **RIDICULOUS** POSITION I FIND MYSELF IN, GALACTIC WAR-FULLY SPEAKING, I MEAN...
...I'M COMPLETELY IN THE **DARK.**
WAIT. FORGOT ABOUT THE FEATURES OF THE **OUTFIT.**
AS INSPIRED BY THE COLD LIGHT EMISSIONS OF CERTAIN DEEP-SEA INVERTEBRATES...

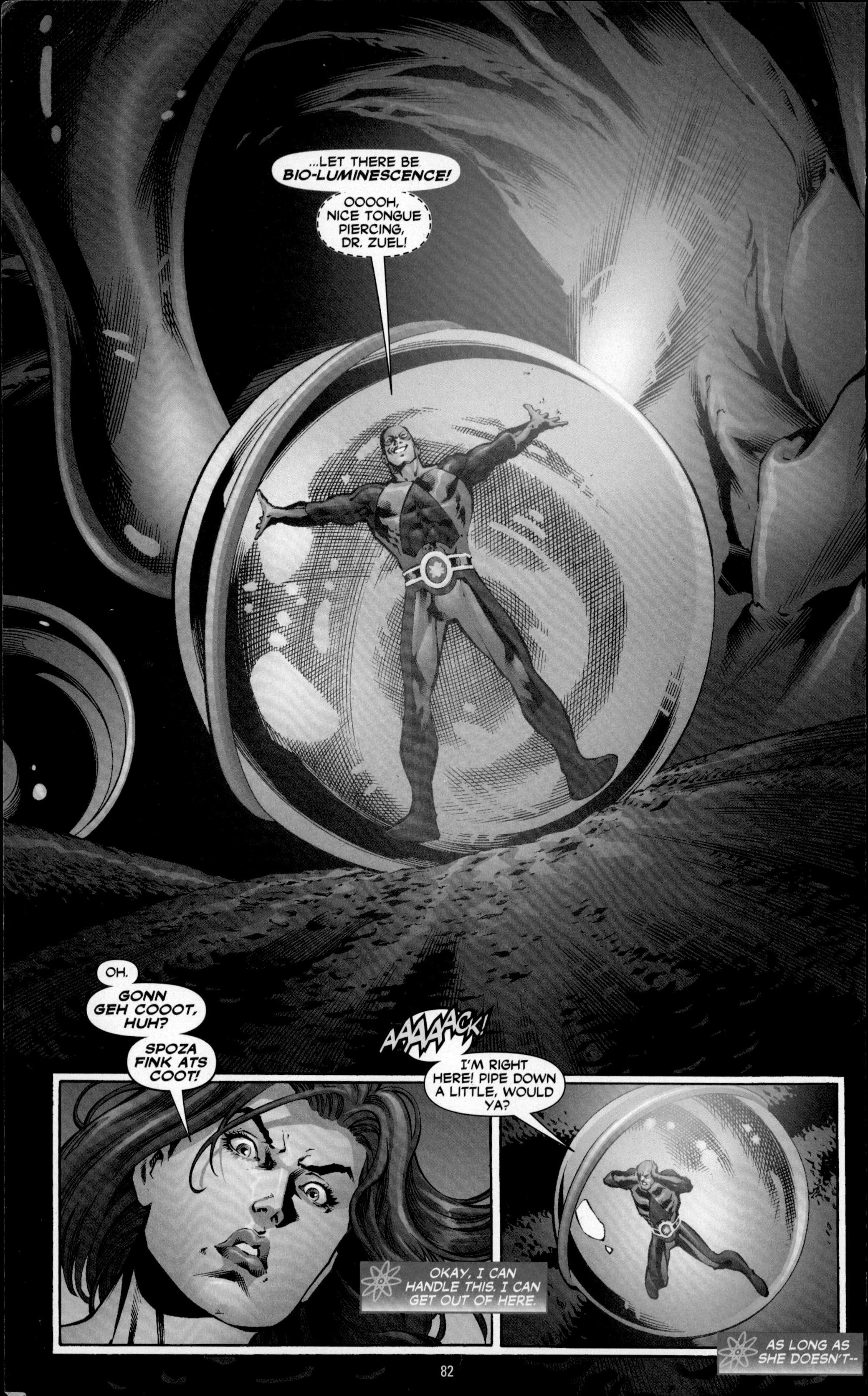
...LET THERE BE BIO-LUMINESCENCE!
OOOOH, NICE TONGUE PIERCING, DR. ZUEL!
OH.
GONN GEH COOOT, HUH?
SPOZA FINK ATS COOT!
AAAAAACK!
I'M RIGHT HERE! PIPE DOWN A LITTLE, WOULD YA?
OKAY, I CAN HANDLE THIS. I CAN GET OUT OF HERE.
AS LONG AS SHE DOESN'T--

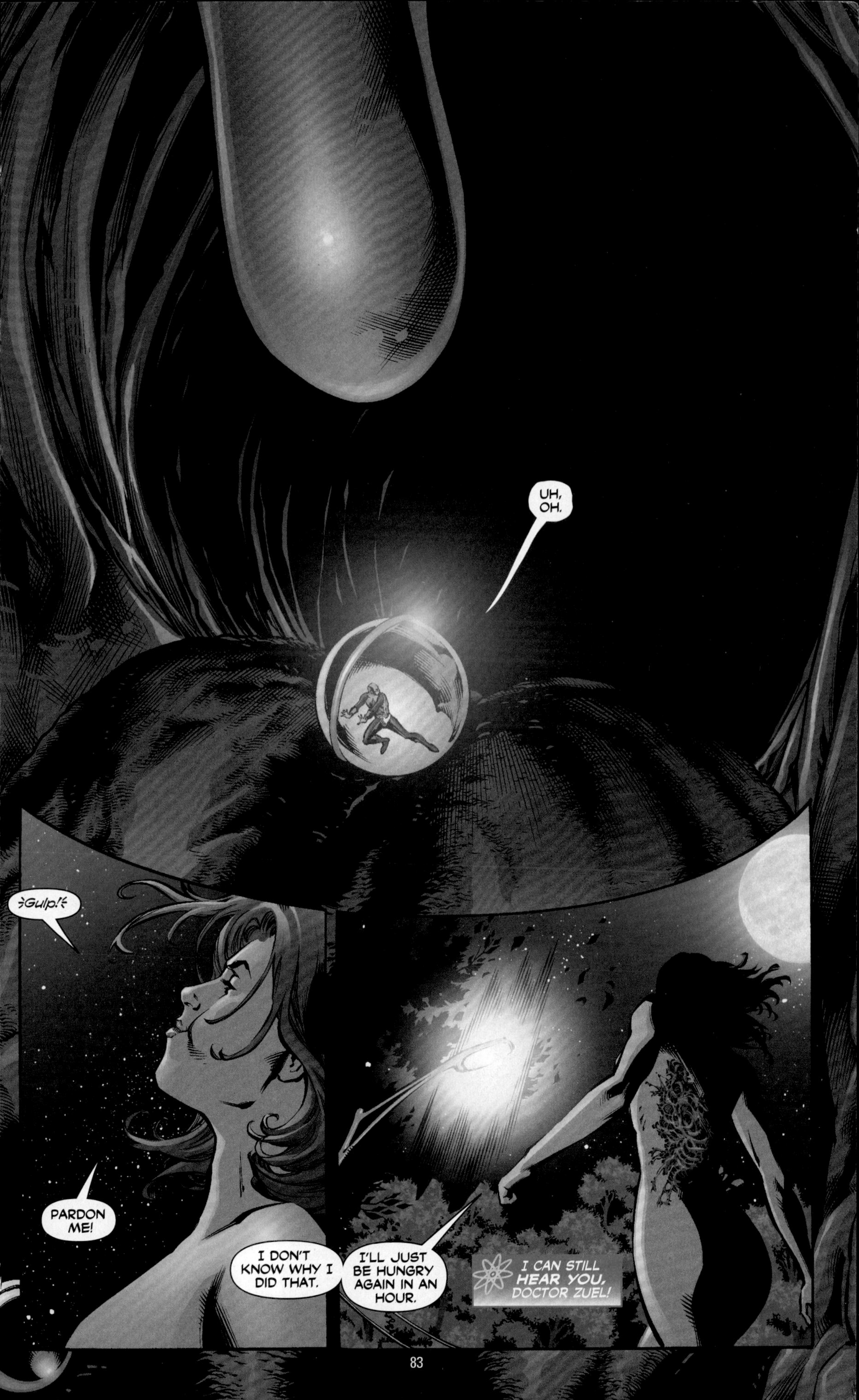
UH, OH.
GULP!
PARDON ME!
I DON'T KNOW WHY I DID THAT.
I'LL JUST BE HUNGRY AGAIN IN AN HOUR.
I CAN STILL HEAR YOU, DOCTOR ZUEL!

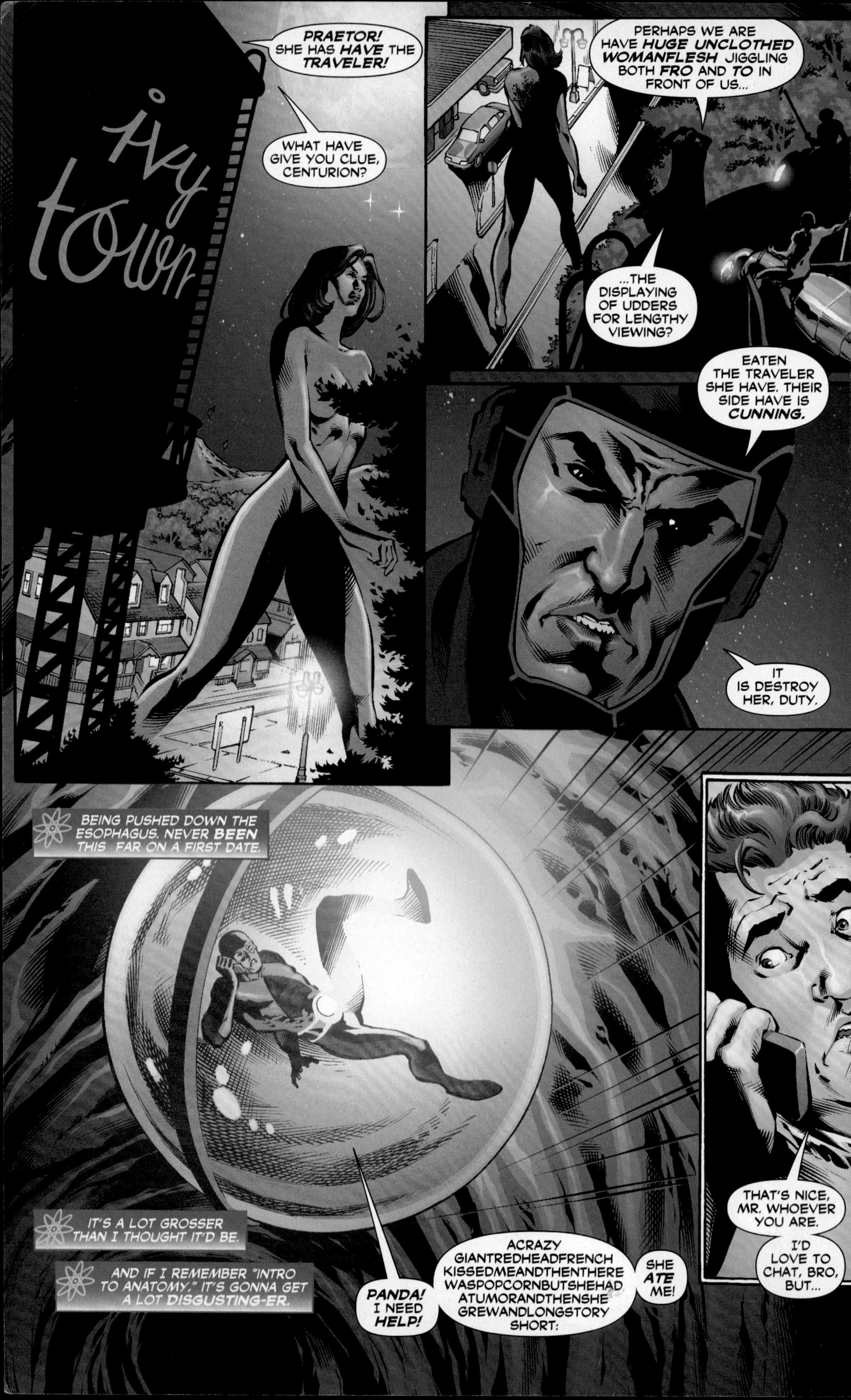
ivy town
PRAETOR! SHE HAS HAVE THE TRAVELER!
WHAT HAVE GIVE YOU CLUE, CENTURION?
PERHAPS WE ARE HAVE HUGE UNCLOTHED WOMANFLESH JIGGLING BOTH FRO AND TO IN FRONT OF US...
...THE DISPLAYING OF UDDERS FOR LENGTHY VIEWING?
EATEN THE TRAVELER SHE HAVE. THEIR SIDE HAVE IS CUNNING.
IT IS DESTROY HER, DUTY.
BEING PUSHED DOWN THE ESOPHAGUS. NEVER BEEN THIS FAR ON A FIRST DATE.
IT'S A LOT GROSSER THAN I THOUGHT IT'D BE.
AND IF I REMEMBER "INTRO TO ANATOMY," IT'S GONNA GET A LOT DISGUSTING-ER.
PANDA! I NEED HELP!
ACRAZY GIANTREDHEADFRENCH KISSEDMEANDTHENTHERE WASPOPCORNBUTSHEHAD ATUMORANDTHENSHE GREWANDLONGSTORY SHORT:
SHE ATE ME!
THAT'S NICE, MR. WHOEVER YOU ARE.
I'D LOVE TO CHAT, BRO, BUT...

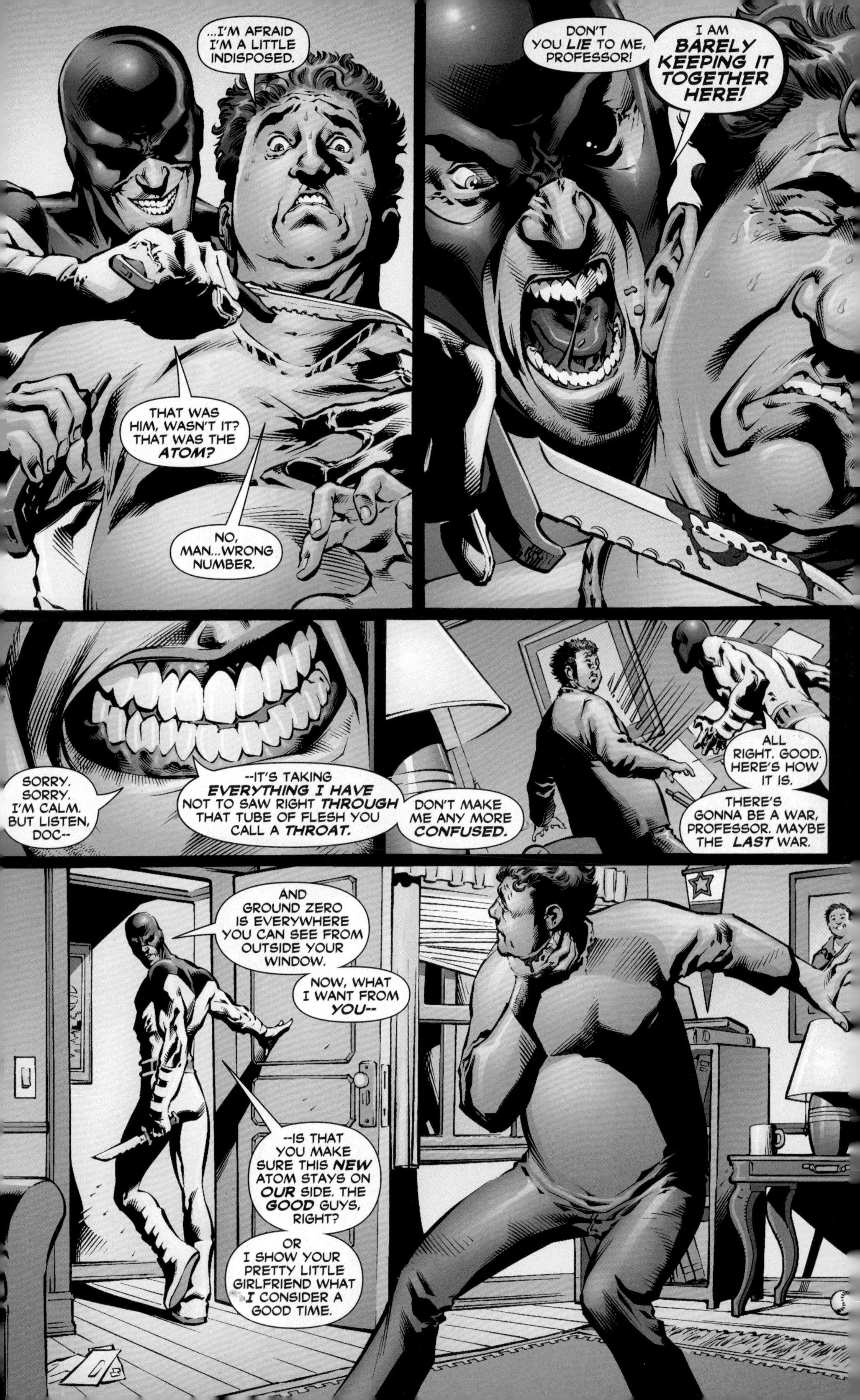

...I'M AFRAID I'M A LITTLE INDISPOSED.
THAT WAS HIM, WASN'T IT? THAT WAS THE *ATOM?*
NO, MAN...WRONG NUMBER.
DON'T YOU *LIE* TO ME, PROFESSOR!
I AM *BARELY KEEPING IT TOGETHER HERE!*
SORRY. SORRY. I'M CALM. BUT LISTEN, DOC--
--IT'S TAKING *EVERYTHING I HAVE* NOT TO SAW RIGHT *THROUGH* THAT TUBE OF FLESH YOU CALL A *THROAT.*
DON'T MAKE ME ANY MORE *CONFUSED.*
ALL RIGHT. GOOD. HERE'S HOW IT IS.
THERE'S GONNA BE A WAR, PROFESSOR. MAYBE THE *LAST* WAR.
AND GROUND ZERO IS EVERYWHERE YOU CAN SEE FROM OUTSIDE YOUR WINDOW.
NOW, WHAT I WANT FROM *YOU--*
--IS THAT YOU MAKE SURE THIS *NEW* ATOM STAYS ON *OUR* SIDE. THE *GOOD* GUYS, RIGHT?
OR I SHOW YOUR PRETTY LITTLE GIRLFRIEND WHAT *I* CONSIDER A GOOD TIME.

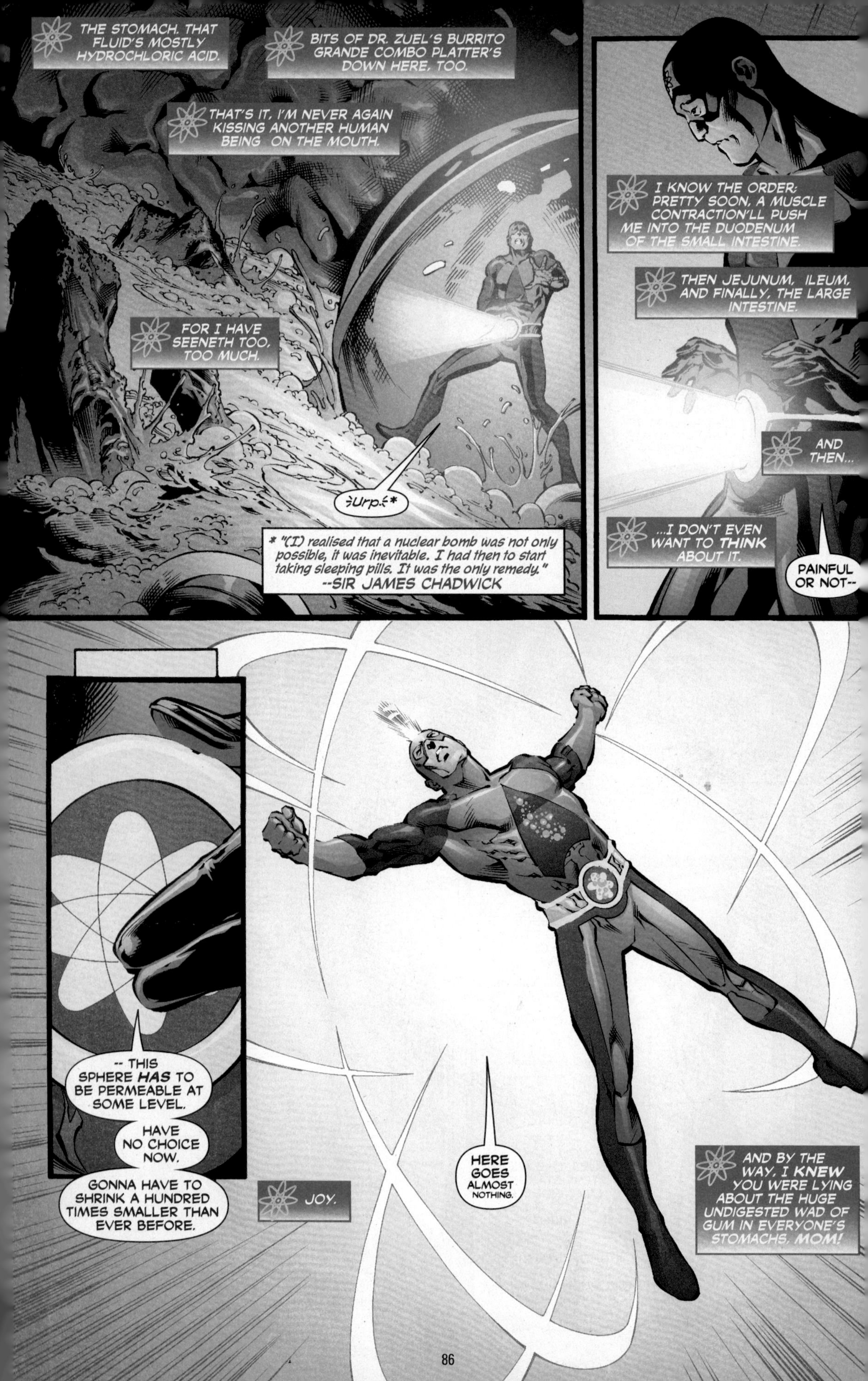
THE STOMACH. THAT FLUID'S MOSTLY HYDROCHLORIC ACID.
BITS OF DR. ZUEL'S BURRITO GRANDE COMBO PLATTER'S DOWN HERE, TOO.
THAT'S IT, I'M NEVER AGAIN KISSING ANOTHER HUMAN BEING ON THE MOUTH.
FOR I HAVE SEENETH TOO, TOO MUCH.
Urp.
* "(I) realised that a nuclear bomb was not only possible, it was inevitable. I had then to start taking sleeping pills. It was the only remedy."
--SIR JAMES CHADWICK
I KNOW THE ORDER: PRETTY SOON, A MUSCLE CONTRACTION'LL PUSH ME INTO THE DUODENUM OF THE SMALL INTESTINE.
THEN JEJUNUM, ILEUM, AND FINALLY, THE LARGE INTESTINE.
AND THEN...
...I DON'T EVEN WANT TO THINK ABOUT IT.
PAINFUL OR NOT--
-- THIS SPHERE HAS TO BE PERMEABLE AT SOME LEVEL.
HAVE NO CHOICE NOW.
GONNA HAVE TO SHRINK A HUNDRED TIMES SMALLER THAN EVER BEFORE.
JOY.
HERE GOES ALMOST NOTHING.
AND BY THE WAY, I KNEW YOU WERE LYING ABOUT THE HUGE UNDIGESTED WAD OF GUM IN EVERYONE'S STOMACHS, MOM!

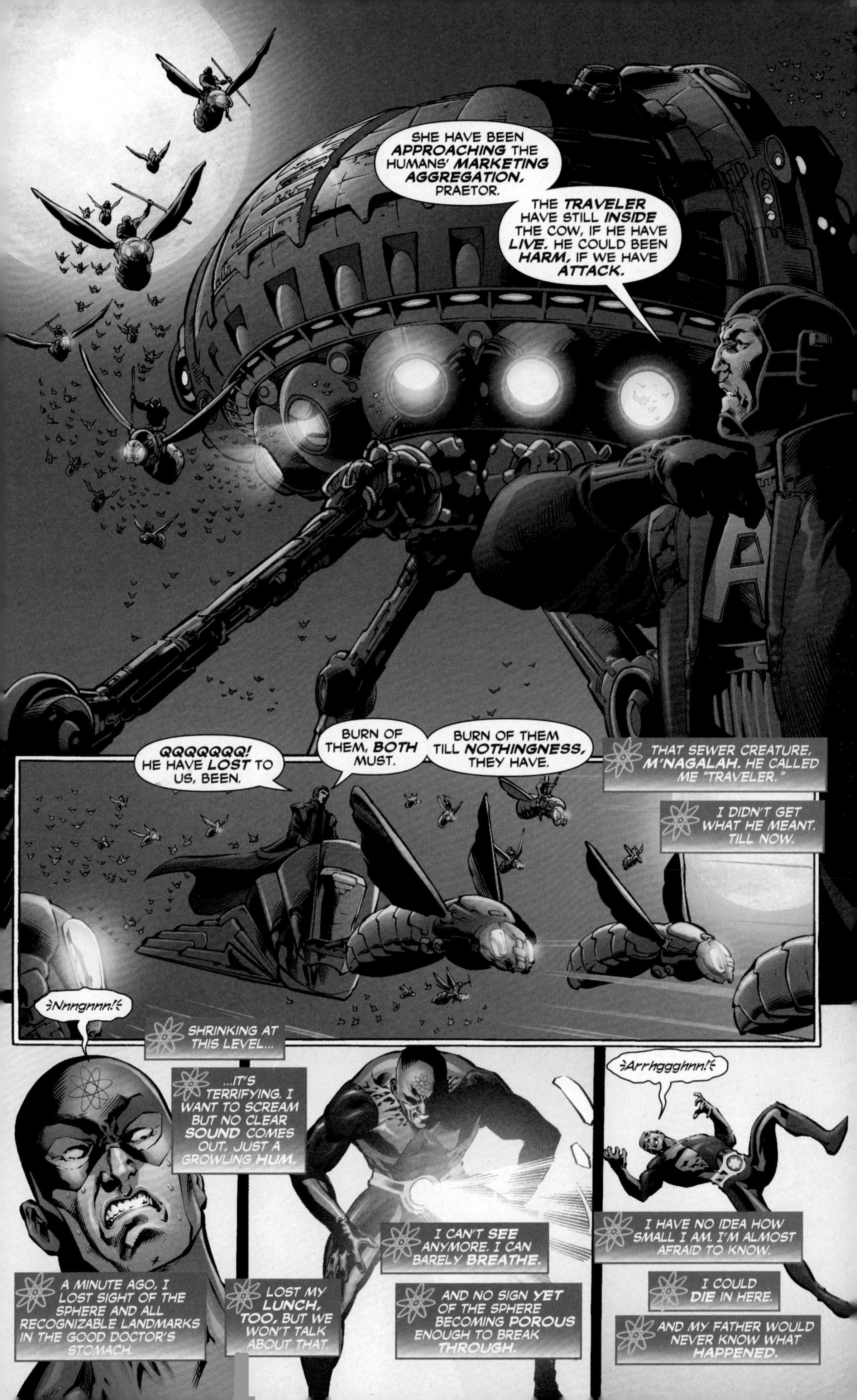

SHE HAVE BEEN APPROACHING THE HUMANS' MARKETING AGGREGATION, PRAETOR.
THE TRAVELER HAVE STILL INSIDE THE COW, IF HE HAVE LIVE. HE COULD BEEN HARM, IF WE HAVE ATTACK.
QQQQQQQ! HE HAVE LOST TO US, BEEN.
BURN OF THEM, BOTH MUST.
BURN OF THEM TILL NOTHINGNESS, THEY HAVE.
THAT SEWER CREATURE, M'NAGALAH. HE CALLED ME "TRAVELER."
I DIDN'T GET WHAT HE MEANT. TILL NOW.
‹Nnngnnn!›
SHRINKING AT THIS LEVEL...
...IT'S TERRIFYING. I WANT TO SCREAM BUT NO CLEAR SOUND COMES OUT. JUST A GROWLING HUM.
A MINUTE AGO, I LOST SIGHT OF THE SPHERE AND ALL RECOGNIZABLE LANDMARKS IN THE GOOD DOCTOR'S STOMACH.
LOST MY LUNCH, TOO, BUT WE WON'T TALK ABOUT THAT.
I CAN'T SEE ANYMORE. I CAN BARELY BREATHE.
AND NO SIGN YET OF THE SPHERE BECOMING POROUS ENOUGH TO BREAK THROUGH.
‹Arrhgggh nn!›
I HAVE NO IDEA HOW SMALL I AM. I'M ALMOST AFRAID TO KNOW.
I COULD DIE IN HERE.
AND MY FATHER WOULD NEVER KNOW WHAT HAPPENED.

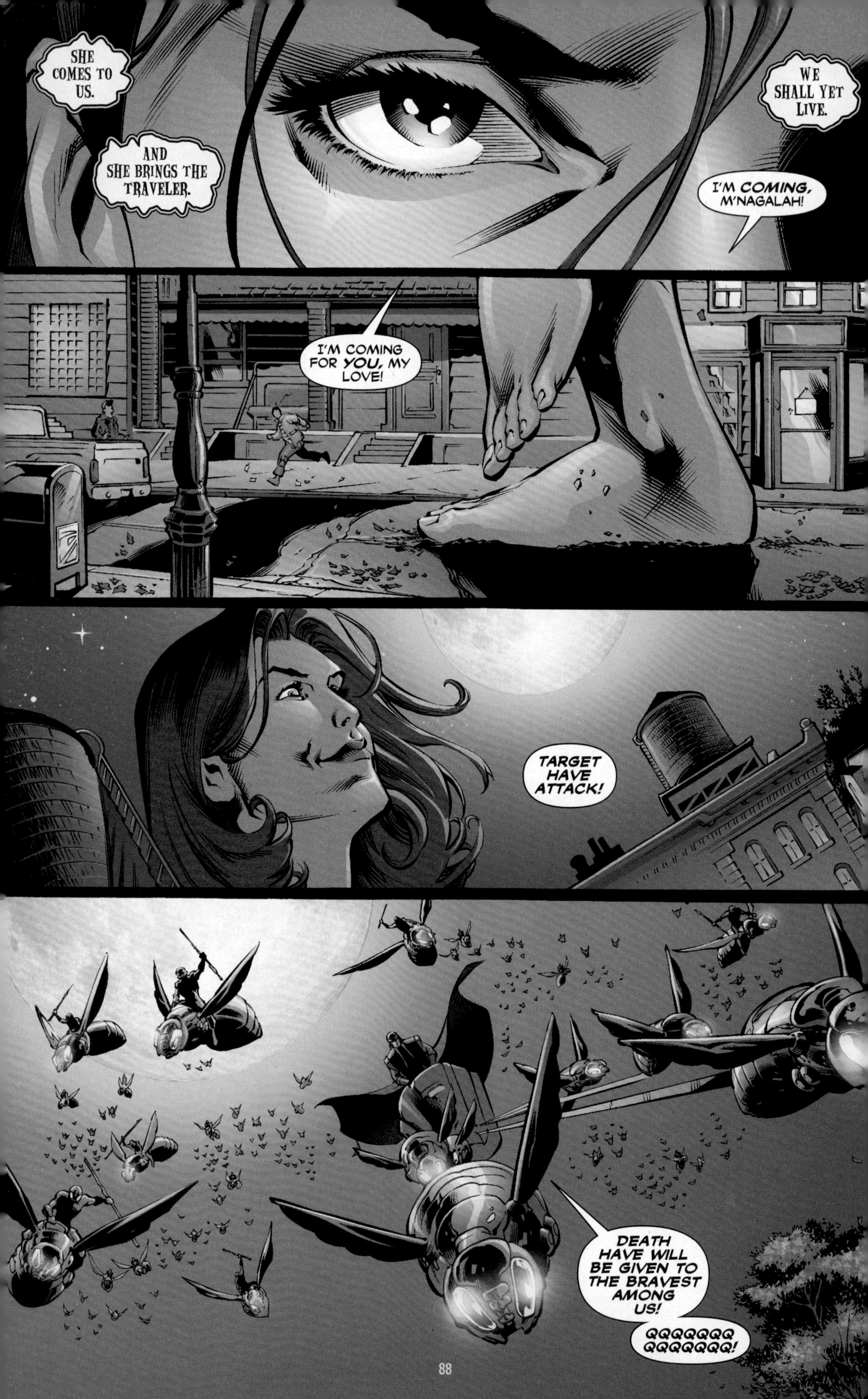
SHE COMES TO US.
AND SHE BRINGS THE TRAVELER.
WE SHALL YET LIVE.
I'M COMING, M'NAGALAH!
I'M COMING FOR YOU, MY LOVE!
TARGET HAVE ATTACK!
DEATH HAVE WILL BE GIVEN TO THE BRAVEST AMONG US!
QQQQQQQ QQQQQQQ!

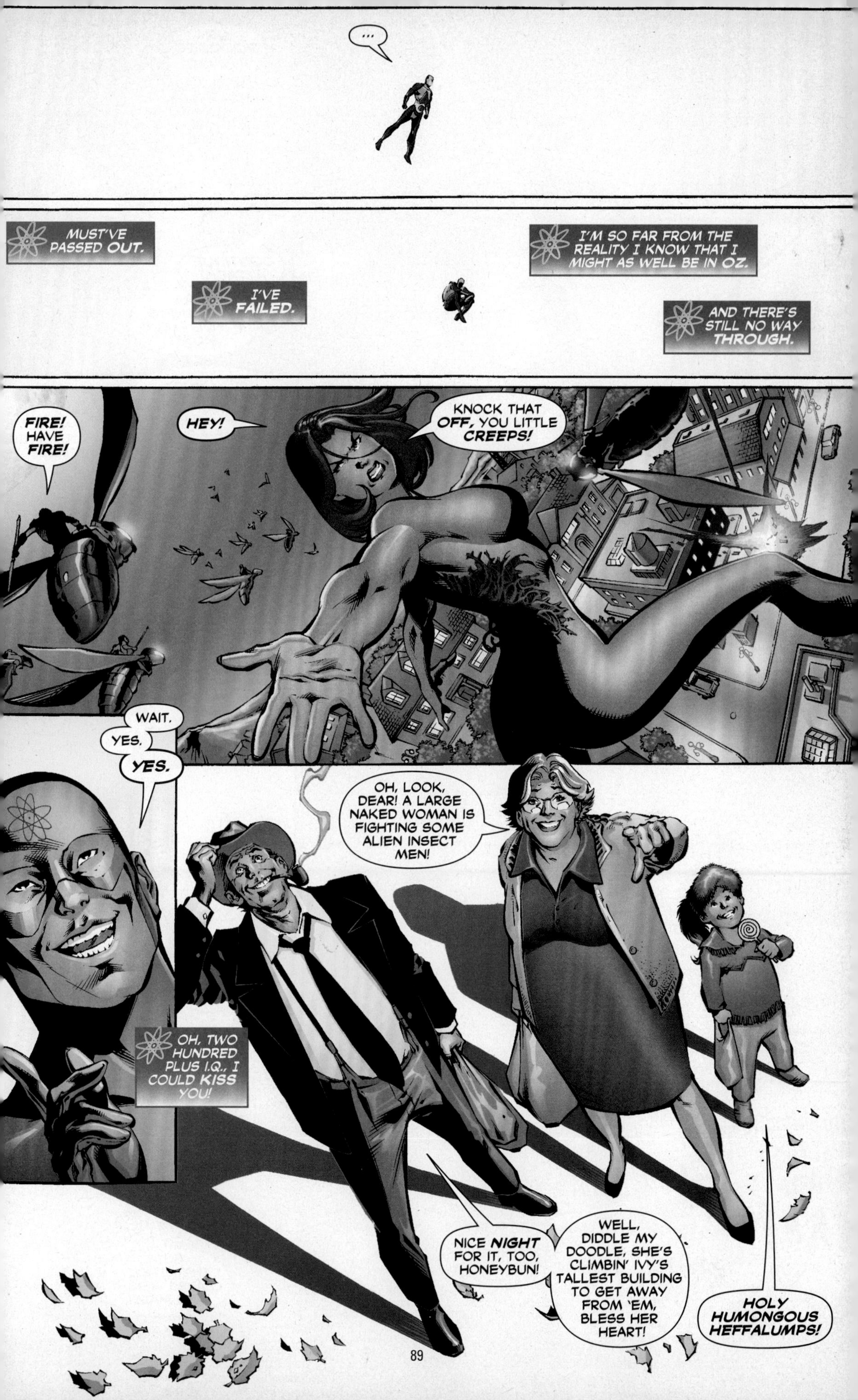
...
MUST'VE PASSED OUT.
I'VE FAILED.
I'M SO FAR FROM THE REALITY I KNOW THAT I MIGHT AS WELL BE IN OZ.
AND THERE'S STILL NO WAY THROUGH.
FIRE! HAVE FIRE!
HEY!
KNOCK THAT OFF, YOU LITTLE CREEPS!
WAIT.
YES.
YES.
OH, LOOK, DEAR! A LARGE NAKED WOMAN IS FIGHTING SOME ALIEN INSECT MEN!
OH, TWO HUNDRED PLUS I.Q., I COULD KISS YOU!
NICE NIGHT FOR IT, TOO, HONEYBUN!
WELL, DIDDLE MY DOODLE, SHE'S CLIMBIN' IVY'S TALLEST BUILDING TO GET AWAY FROM 'EM, BLESS HER HEART!
HOLY HUMONGOUS HEFFALUMPS!

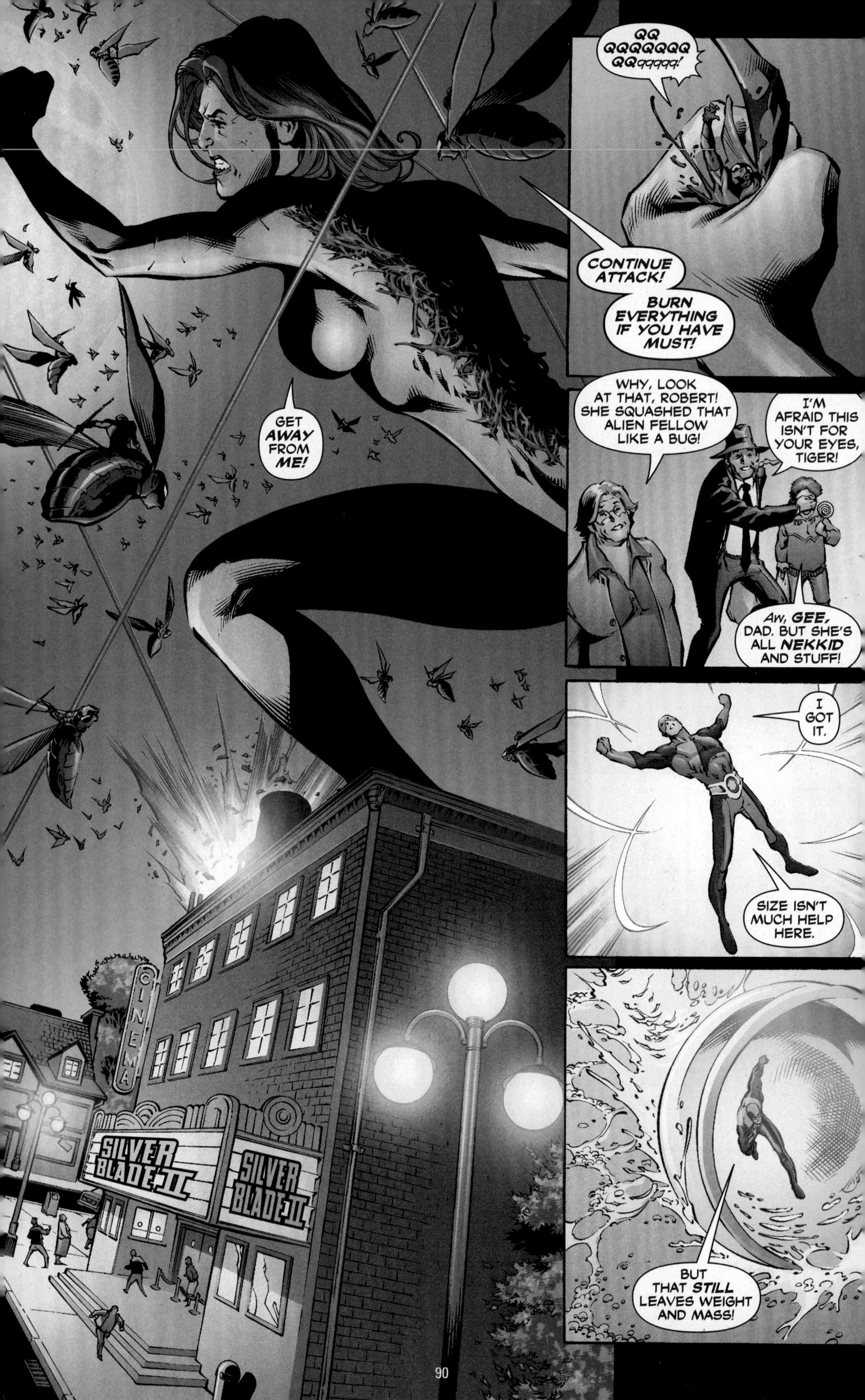
QQ QQQQQQQ QQqqqqq!
CONTINUE ATTACK!
BURN EVERYTHING IF YOU HAVE MUST!
GET AWAY FROM ME!
WHY, LOOK AT THAT, ROBERT! SHE SQUASHED THAT ALIEN FELLOW LIKE A BUG!
I'M AFRAID THIS ISN'T FOR YOUR EYES, TIGER!
AW, GEE, DAD. BUT SHE'S ALL NEKKID AND STUFF!
I GOT IT.
SIZE ISN'T MUCH HELP HERE.
BUT THAT STILL LEAVES WEIGHT AND MASS!
CINEMA
SILVER BLADE II
SILVER BLADE II

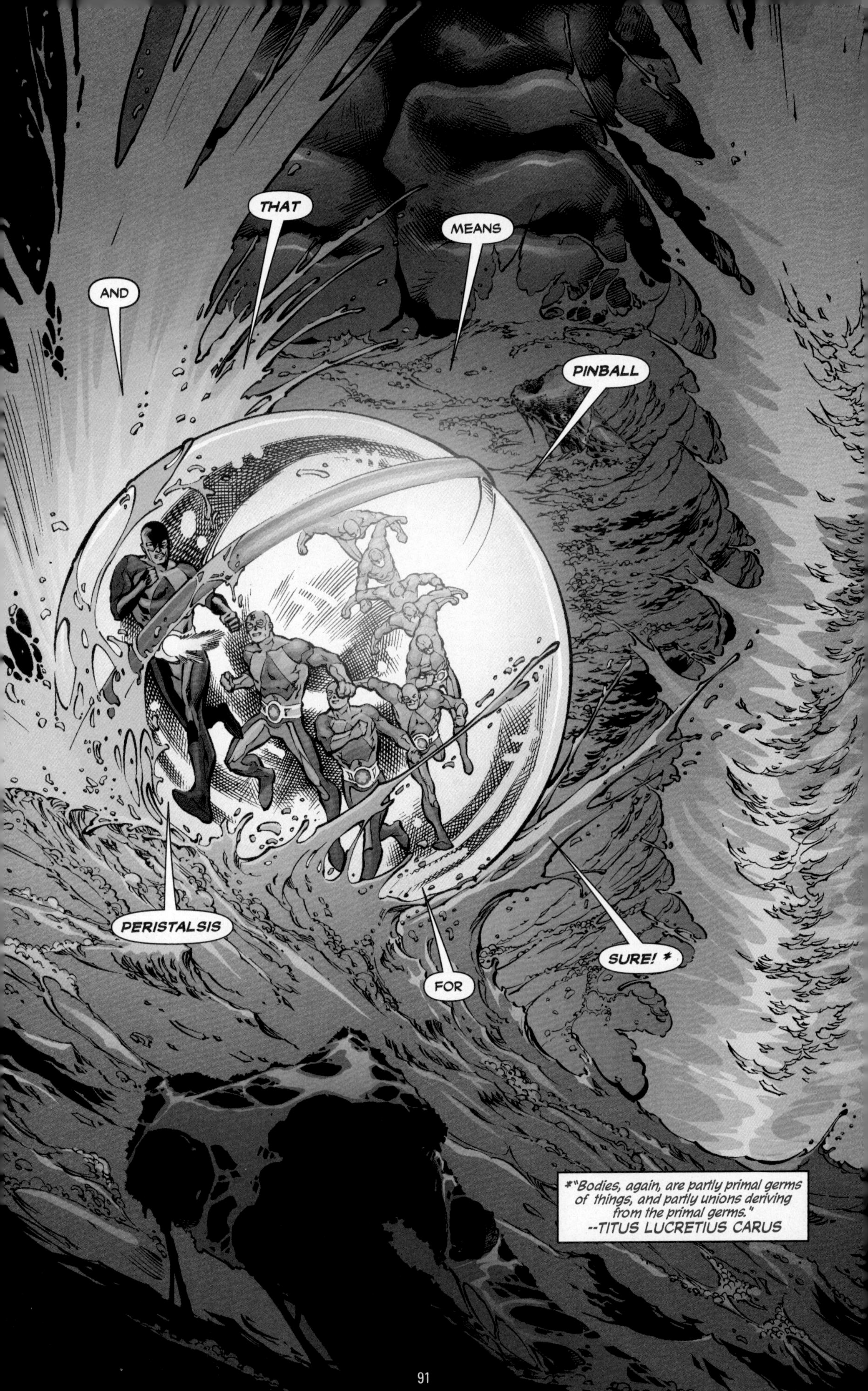
AND
THAT
MEANS
PINBALL
PERISTALSIS
FOR
SURE! *
*"Bodies, again, are partly primal germs of things, and partly unions deriving from the primal germs."
--TITUS LUCRETIUS CARUS

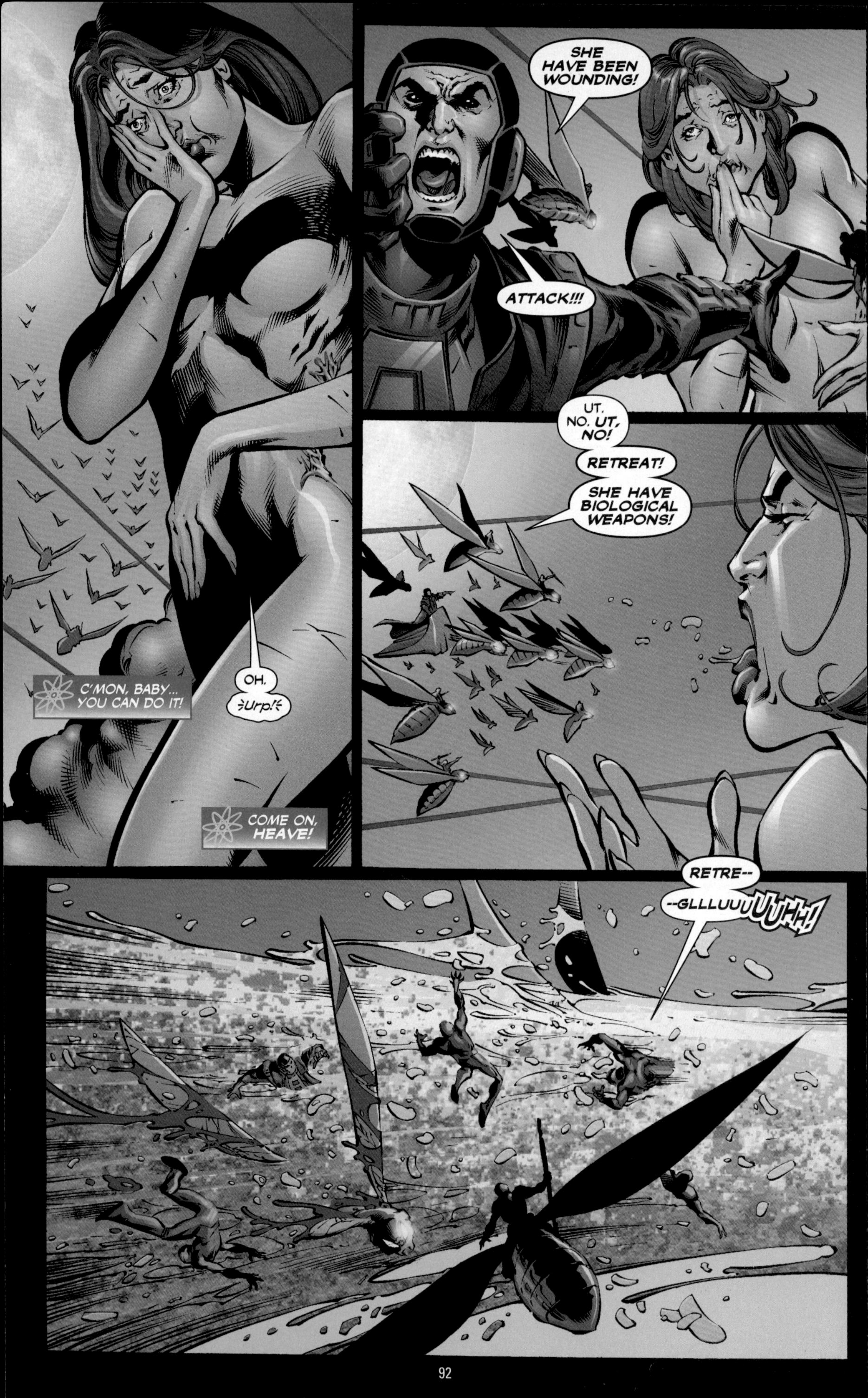

C'MON, BABY... YOU CAN DO IT!
OH.
Urp!
COME ON, HEAVE!
SHE HAVE BEEN WOUNDING!
ATTACK!!!
UT. NO. UT, NO!
RETREAT!
SHE HAVE BIOLOGICAL WEAPONS!
RETRE--
--GLLLUUUUUHH!

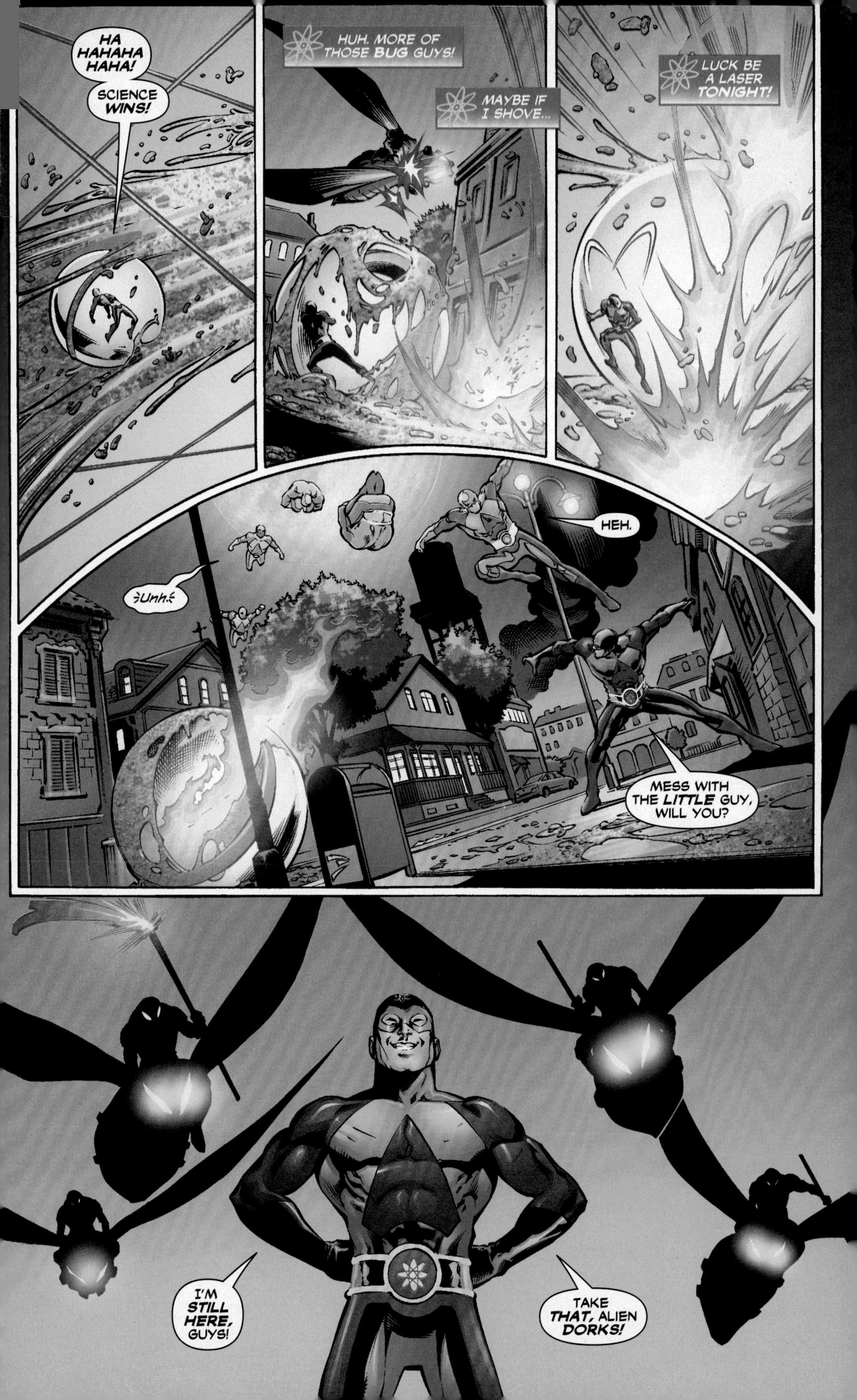
HA HAHAHA HAHA!
SCIENCE WINS!
HUH. MORE OF THOSE BUG GUYS!
MAYBE IF I SHOVE...
LUCK BE A LASER TONIGHT!
HEH.
UNH.
MESS WITH THE LITTLE GUY, WILL YOU?
I'M STILL HERE, GUYS!
TAKE THAT, ALIEN DORKS!

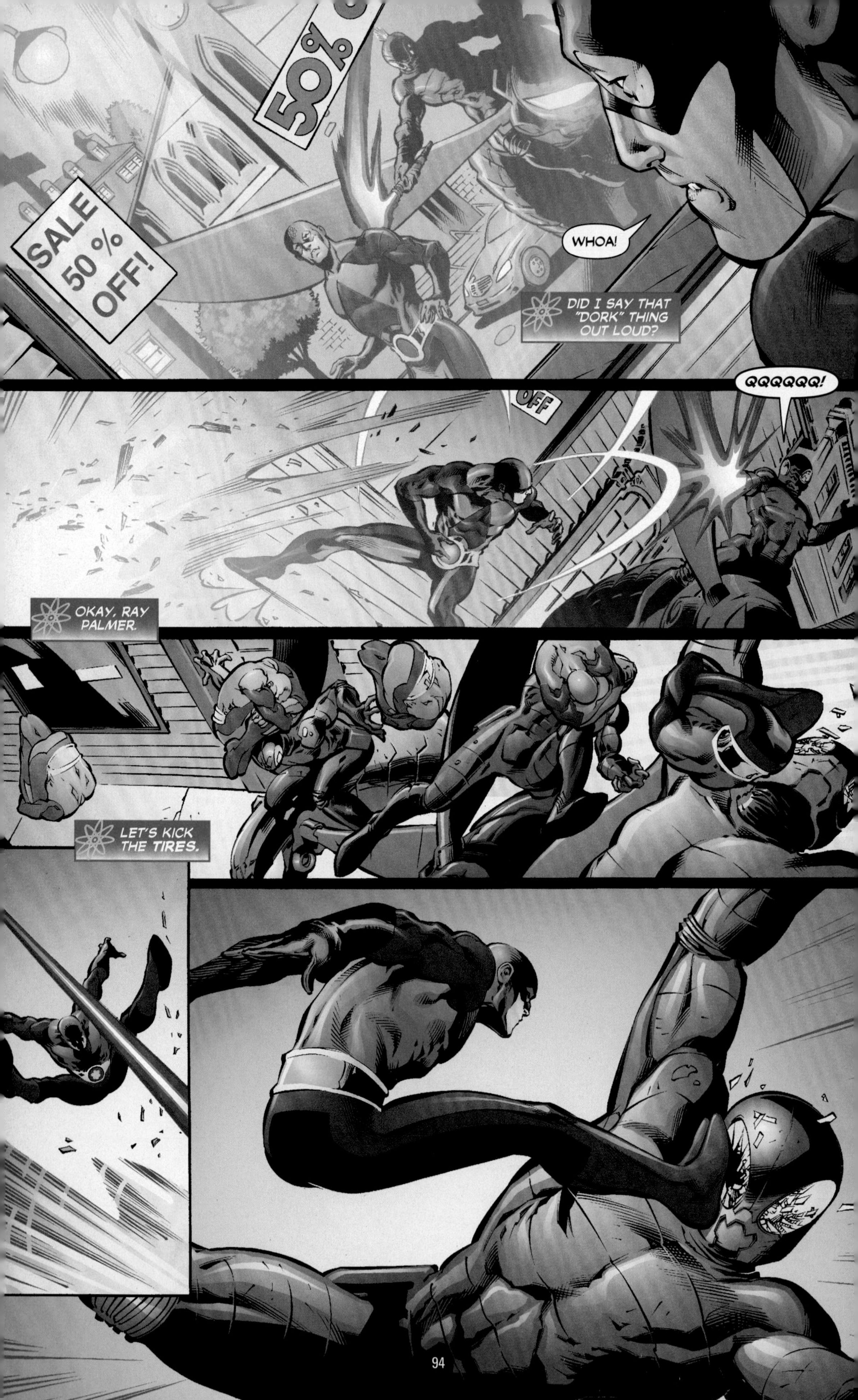
50% O
SALE 50 % OFF!
WHOA!
DID I SAY THAT "DORK" THING OUT LOUD?
QQQQQQ!
OFF
OKAY, RAY PALMER.
LET'S KICK THE TIRES.

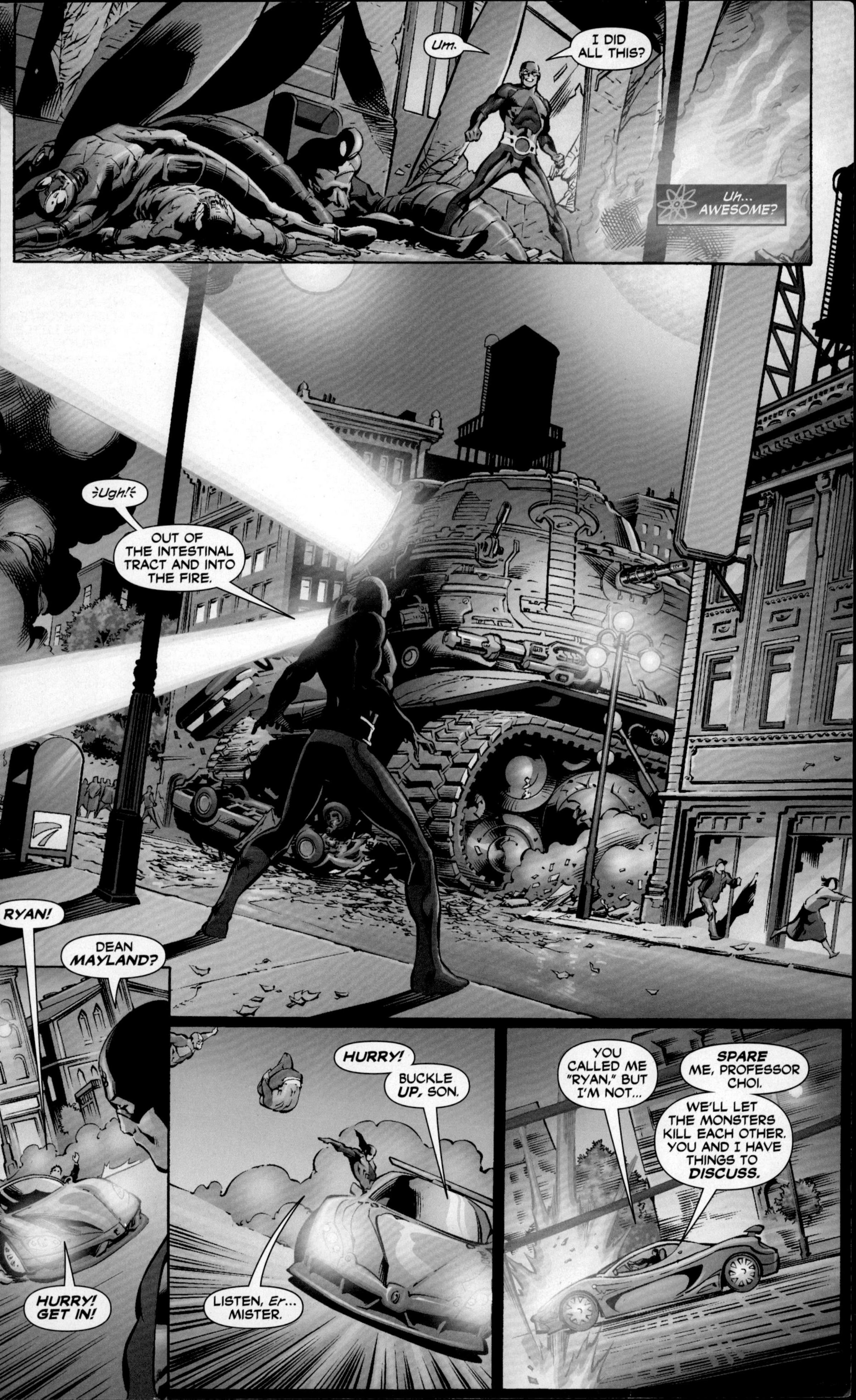
Um.
I DID ALL THIS?
Uh... AWESOME?
Ugh!
OUT OF THE INTESTINAL TRACT AND INTO THE FIRE.
RYAN!
DEAN MAYLAND?
HURRY! GET IN!
HURRY!
BUCKLE UP, SON.
LISTEN, Er... MISTER.
YOU CALLED ME "RYAN," BUT I'M NOT...
SPARE ME, PROFESSOR CHOI.
WE'LL LET THE MONSTERS KILL EACH OTHER. YOU AND I HAVE THINGS TO DISCUSS.

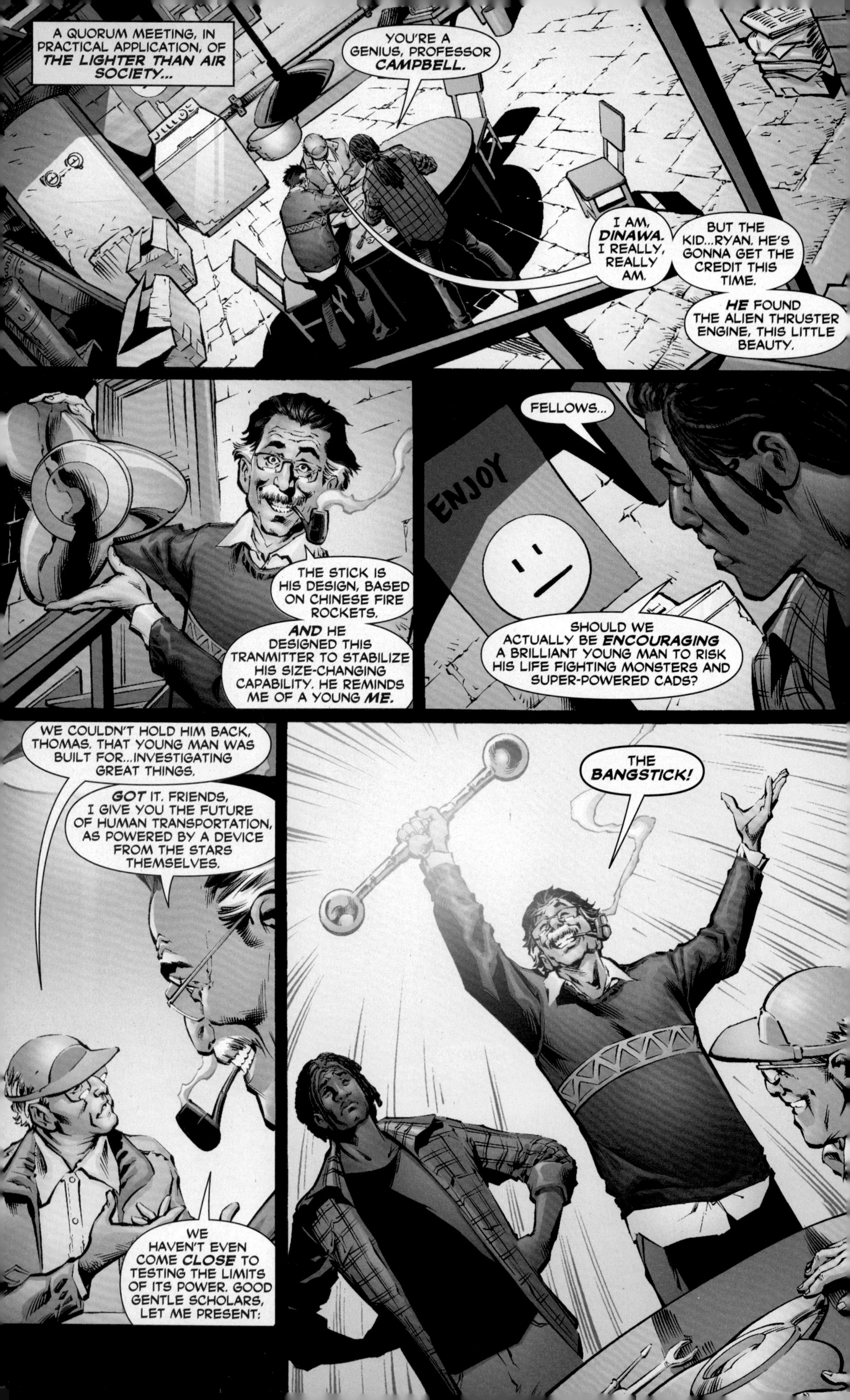
A QUORUM MEETING, IN PRACTICAL APPLICATION, OF THE LIGHTER THAN AIR SOCIETY...
YOU'RE A GENIUS, PROFESSOR CAMPBELL.
I AM, DINAWA. I REALLY, REALLY AM.
BUT THE KID...RYAN. HE'S GONNA GET THE CREDIT THIS TIME.
HE FOUND THE ALIEN THRUSTER ENGINE, THIS LITTLE BEAUTY.
THE STICK IS HIS DESIGN, BASED ON CHINESE FIRE ROCKETS.
AND HE DESIGNED THIS TRANMITTER TO STABILIZE HIS SIZE-CHANGING CAPABILITY. HE REMINDS ME OF A YOUNG ME.
FELLOWS...
ENJOY
SHOULD WE ACTUALLY BE ENCOURAGING A BRILLIANT YOUNG MAN TO RISK HIS LIFE FIGHTING MONSTERS AND SUPER-POWERED CADS?
WE COULDN'T HOLD HIM BACK, THOMAS. THAT YOUNG MAN WAS BUILT FOR...INVESTIGATING GREAT THINGS.
GOT IT. FRIENDS, I GIVE YOU THE FUTURE OF HUMAN TRANSPORTATION, AS POWERED BY A DEVICE FROM THE STARS THEMSELVES.
WE HAVEN'T EVEN COME CLOSE TO TESTING THE LIMITS OF ITS POWER. GOOD GENTLE SCHOLARS, LET ME PRESENT:
THE BANGSTICK!

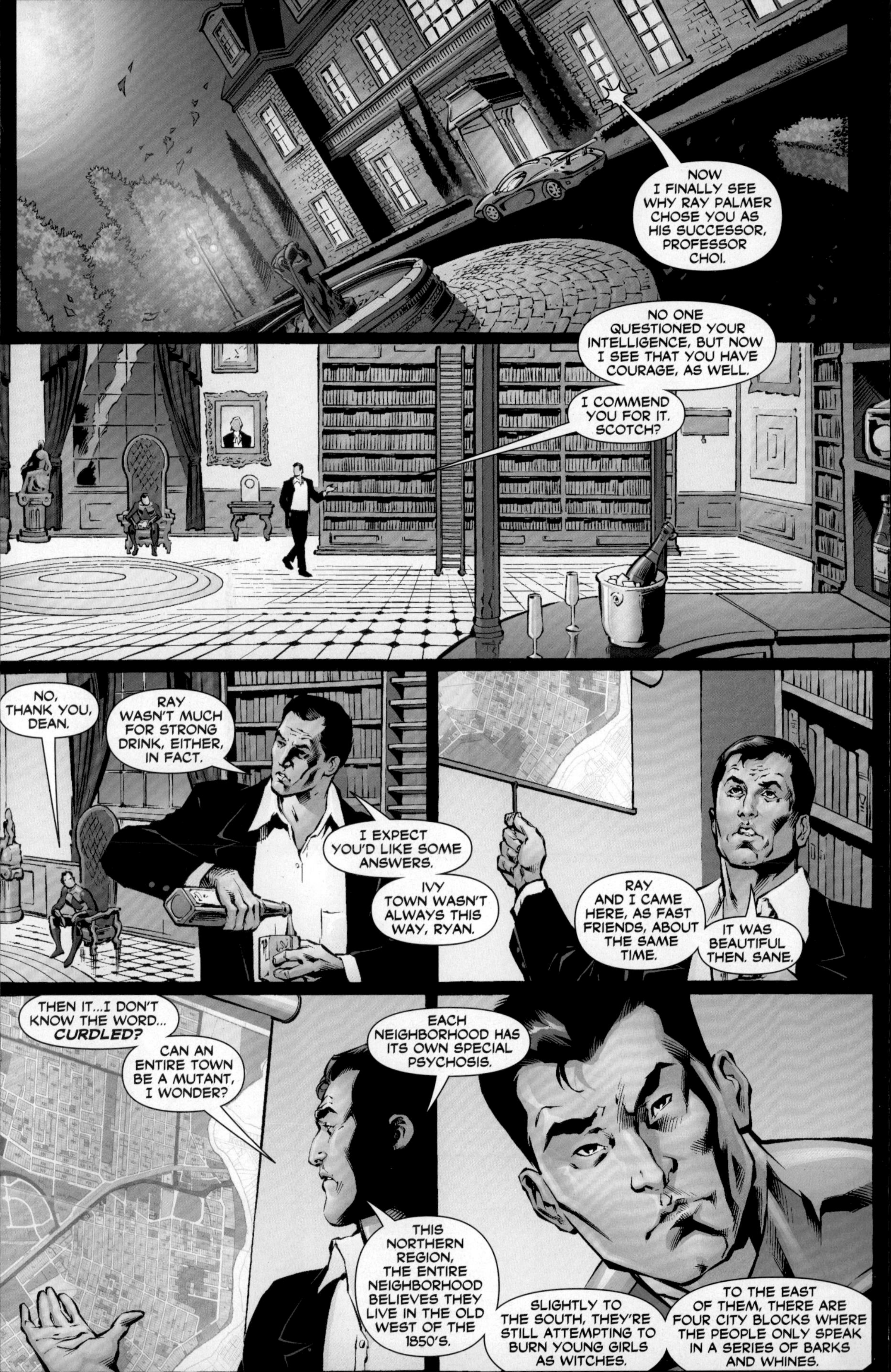
NOW I FINALLY SEE WHY RAY PALMER CHOSE YOU AS HIS SUCCESSOR, PROFESSOR CHOI.
NO ONE QUESTIONED YOUR INTELLIGENCE, BUT NOW I SEE THAT YOU HAVE COURAGE, AS WELL.
I COMMEND YOU FOR IT. SCOTCH?
NO, THANK YOU, DEAN.
RAY WASN'T MUCH FOR STRONG DRINK, EITHER, IN FACT.
I EXPECT YOU'D LIKE SOME ANSWERS.
IVY TOWN WASN'T ALWAYS THIS WAY, RYAN.
RAY AND I CAME HERE, AS FAST FRIENDS, ABOUT THE SAME TIME.
IT WAS BEAUTIFUL THEN. SANE.
THEN IT...I DON'T KNOW THE WORD... *CURDLED?*
CAN AN ENTIRE TOWN BE A MUTANT, I WONDER?
EACH NEIGHBORHOOD HAS ITS OWN SPECIAL PSYCHOSIS.
THIS NORTHERN REGION, THE ENTIRE NEIGHBORHOOD BELIEVES THEY LIVE IN THE OLD WEST OF THE 1850'S.
SLIGHTLY TO THE SOUTH, THEY'RE STILL ATTEMPTING TO BURN YOUNG GIRLS AS WITCHES.
TO THE EAST OF THEM, THERE ARE FOUR CITY BLOCKS WHERE THE PEOPLE ONLY SPEAK IN A SERIES OF BARKS AND WHINES.

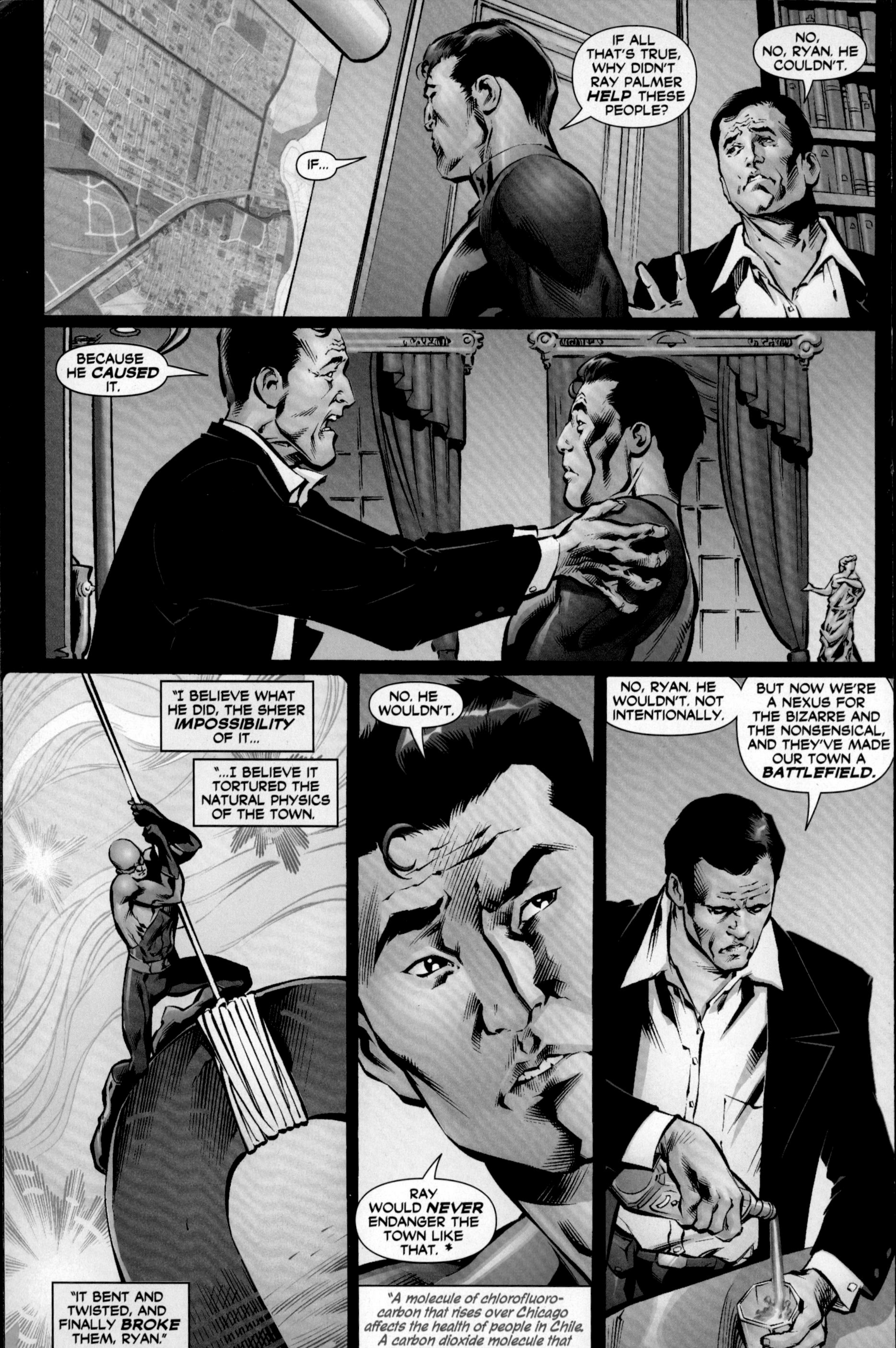
IF...
IF ALL THAT'S TRUE, WHY DIDN'T RAY PALMER HELP THESE PEOPLE?
NO, NO, RYAN. HE COULDN'T.
BECAUSE HE CAUSED IT.
"I BELIEVE WHAT HE DID, THE SHEER IMPOSSIBILITY OF IT...
"...I BELIEVE IT TORTURED THE NATURAL PHYSICS OF THE TOWN.
"IT BENT AND TWISTED, AND FINALLY BROKE THEM, RYAN."
NO. HE WOULDN'T.
RAY WOULD NEVER ENDANGER THE TOWN LIKE THAT. *
"A molecule of chlorofluorocarbon that rises over Chicago affects the health of people in Chile. A carbon dioxide molecule that rises into the atmosphere over China affects the climate in Europe." --CARL SAGAN
NO, RYAN. HE WOULDN'T. NOT INTENTIONALLY.
BUT NOW WE'RE A NEXUS FOR THE BIZARRE AND THE NONSENSICAL, AND THEY'VE MADE OUR TOWN A BATTLEFIELD.

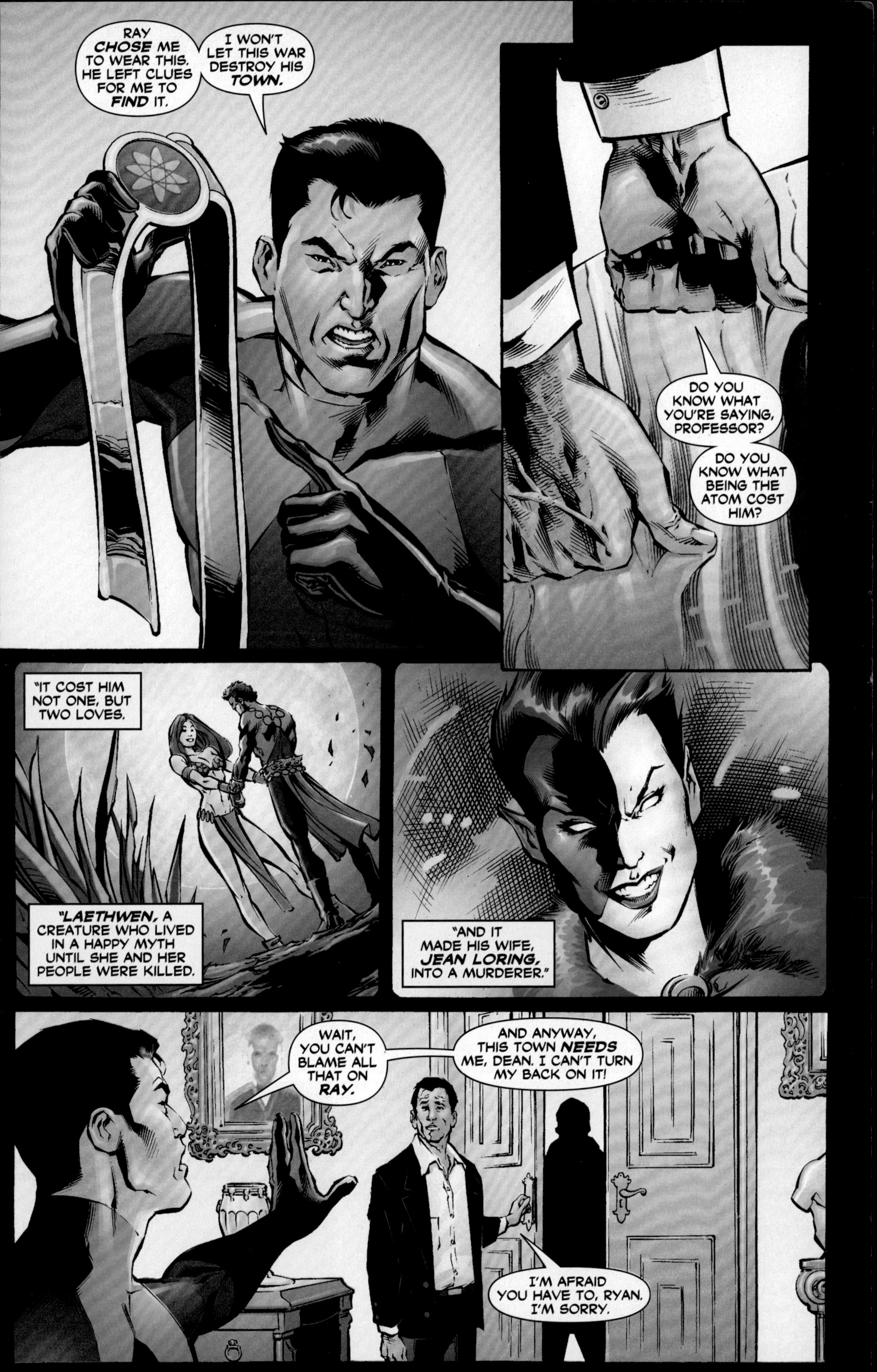
RAY CHOSE ME TO WEAR THIS. HE LEFT CLUES FOR ME TO FIND IT.
I WON'T LET THIS WAR DESTROY HIS TOWN.
DO YOU KNOW WHAT YOU'RE SAYING, PROFESSOR?
DO YOU KNOW WHAT BEING THE ATOM COST HIM?
"IT COST HIM NOT ONE, BUT TWO LOVES.
"LAETHWEN, A CREATURE WHO LIVED IN A HAPPY MYTH UNTIL SHE AND HER PEOPLE WERE KILLED.
"AND IT MADE HIS WIFE, JEAN LORING, INTO A MURDERER."
WAIT, YOU CAN'T BLAME ALL THAT ON RAY.
AND ANYWAY, THIS TOWN NEEDS ME, DEAN. I CAN'T TURN MY BACK ON IT!
I'M AFRAID YOU HAVE TO, RYAN. I'M SORRY.

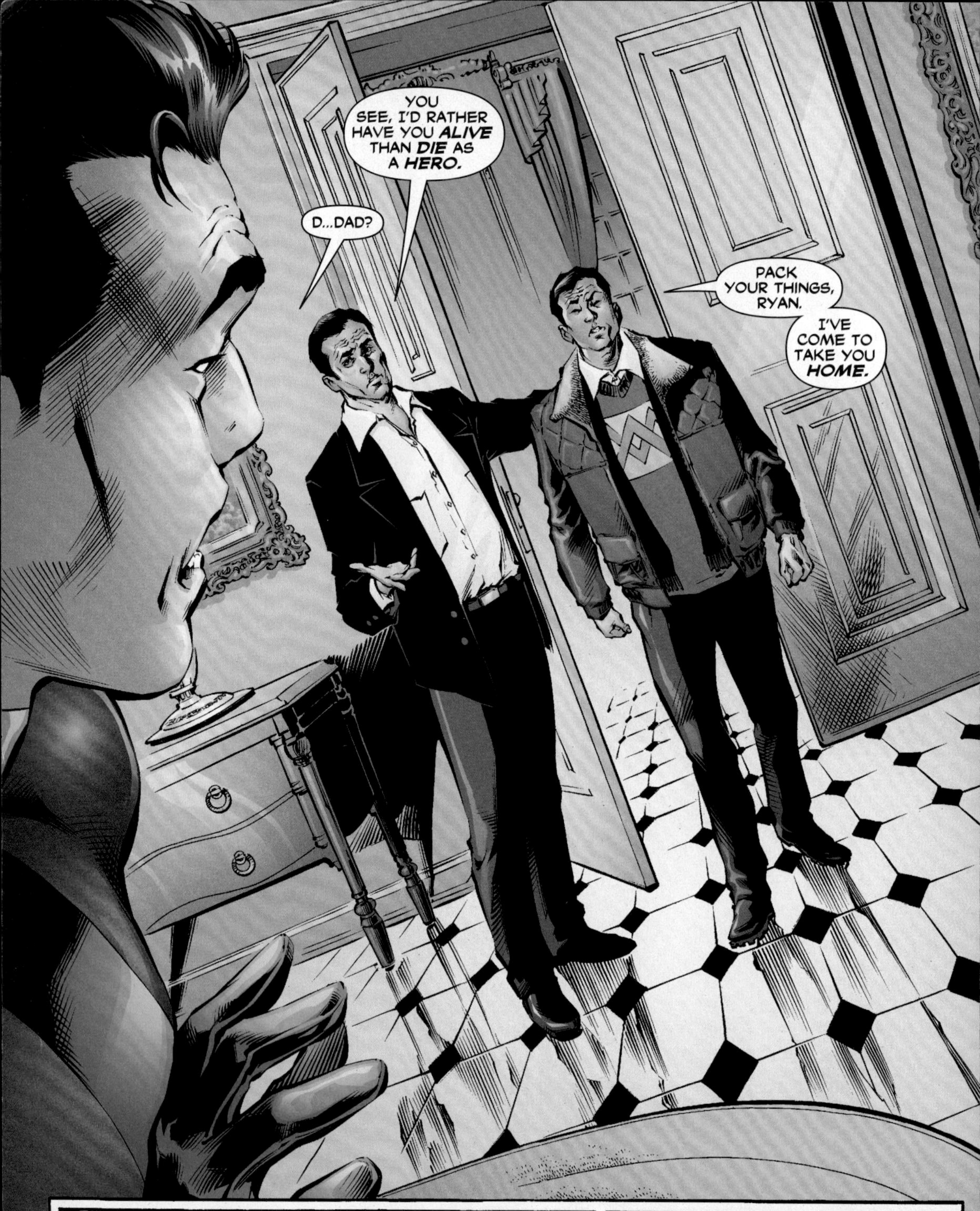
D...DAD?
YOU SEE, I'D RATHER HAVE YOU ALIVE THAN DIE AS A HERO.
PACK YOUR THINGS, RYAN.
I'VE COME TO TAKE YOU HOME.

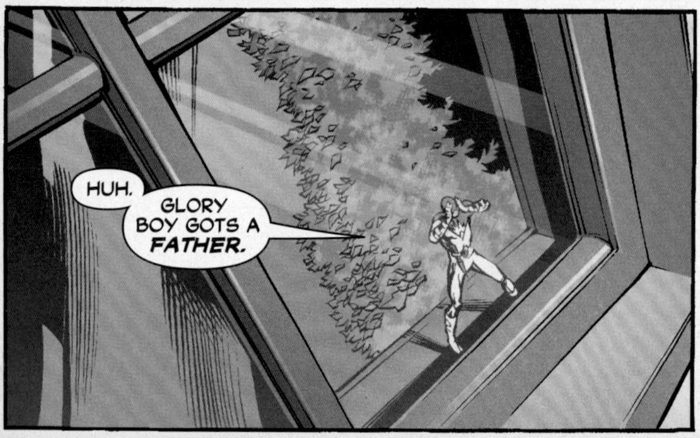
HUH.
GLORY BOY GOTS A FATHER.

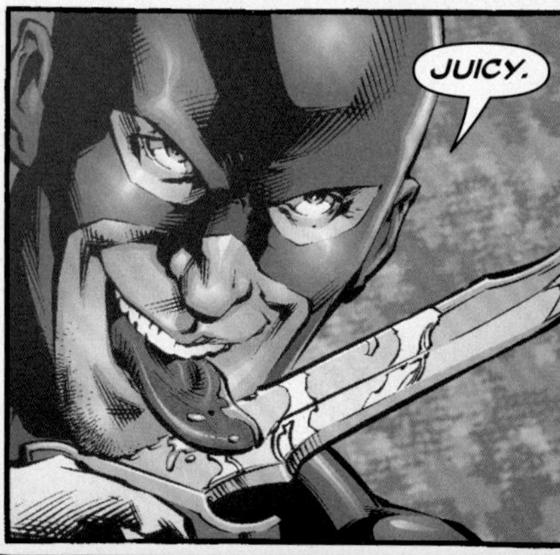
JUICY.

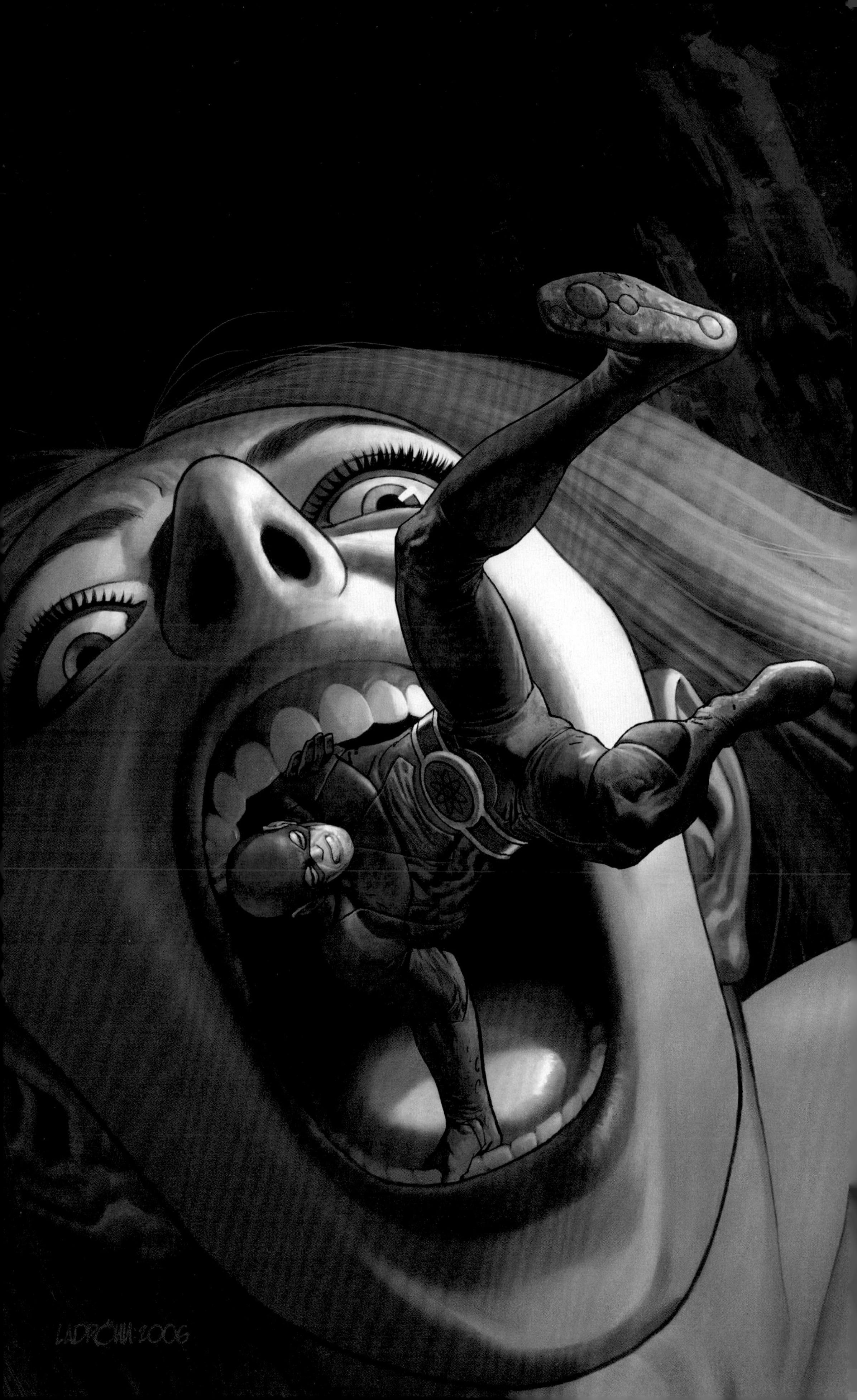
LADRÖNN·2006

MY LIFE IN MINIATURE: PART FIVE
REDLINE SHIFT

from **THE ALL NEW ATOM #5**
Cover by **Ladronn**

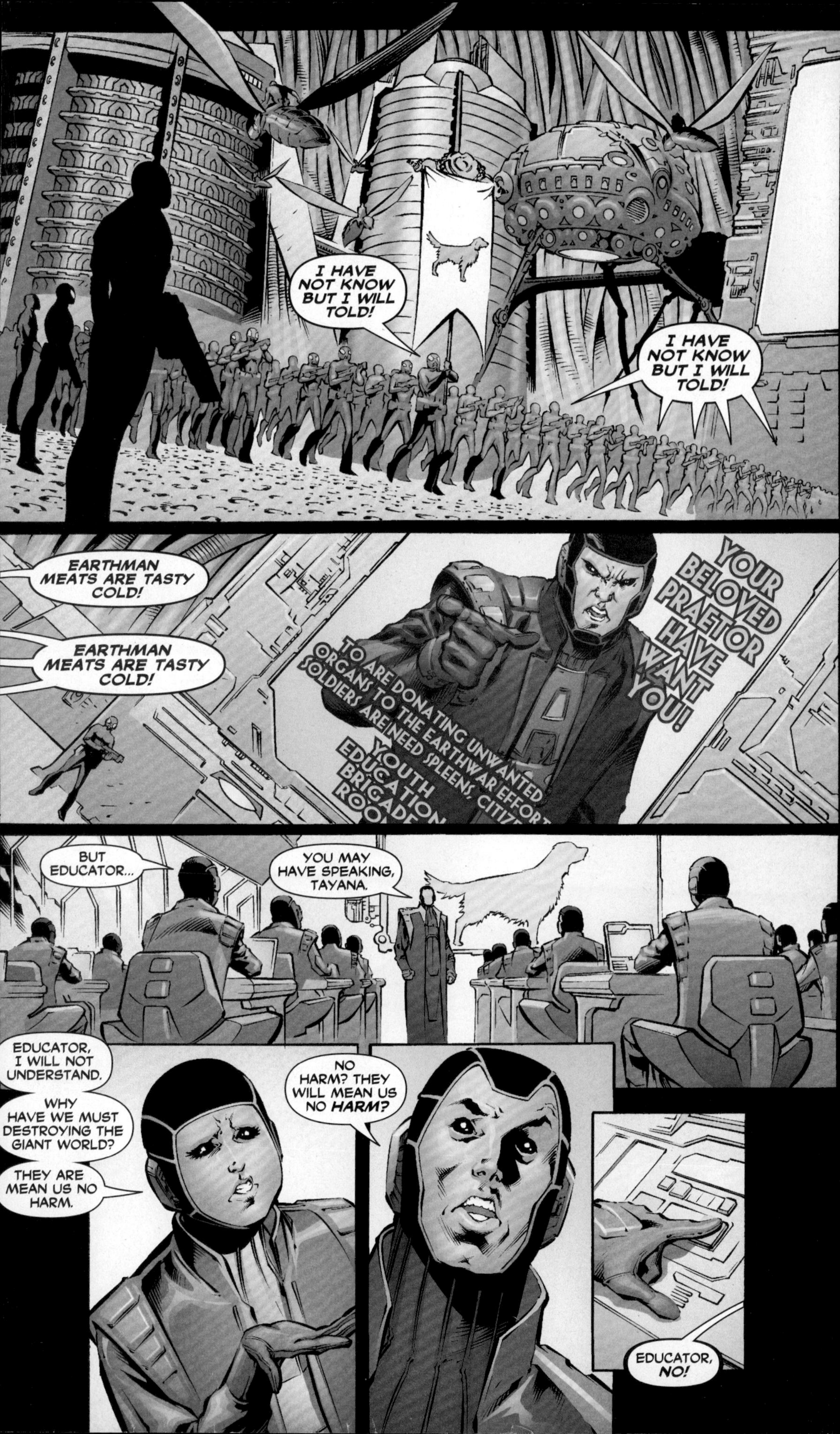
I HAVE NOT KNOW BUT I WILL TOLD!
I HAVE NOT KNOW BUT I WILL TOLD!
EARTHMAN MEATS ARE TASTY COLD!
EARTHMAN MEATS ARE TASTY COLD!
YOUR BELOVED PRAETOR HAVE WANT YOU!
TO ARE DONATING UNWANTED ORGANS TO THE EARTHWAR EFFORT
SOLDIERS ARE NEED SPLEENS,
YOUTH
BUT EDUCATOR...
YOU MAY HAVE SPEAKING, TAYANA.
EDUCATOR, I WILL NOT UNDERSTAND.
WHY HAVE WE MUST DESTROYING THE GIANT WORLD?
THEY ARE MEAN US NO HARM.
NO HARM? THEY WILL MEAN US NO HARM?
EDUCATOR, NO!

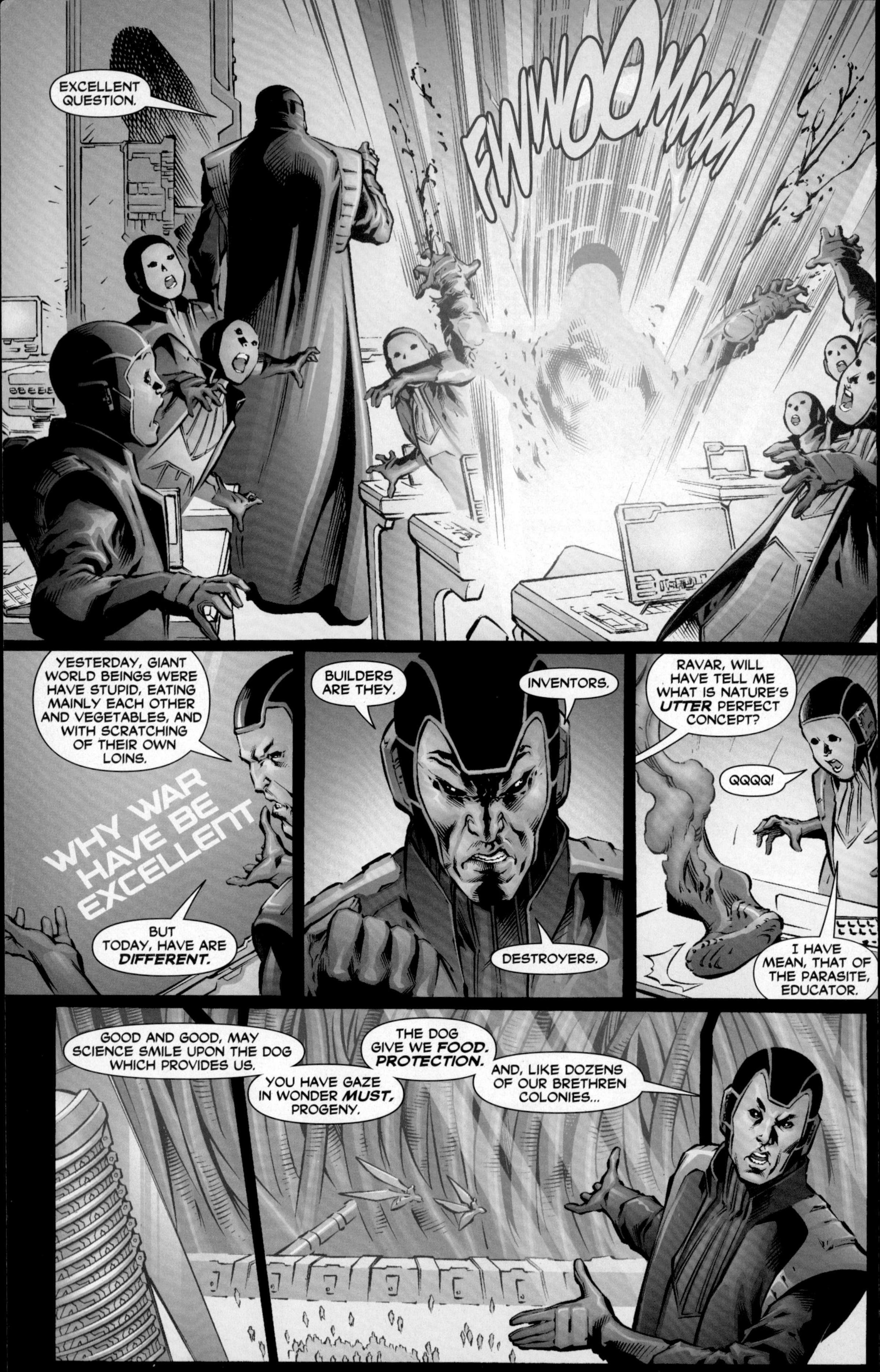
EXCELLENT QUESTION.
FWWOOMMM
YESTERDAY, GIANT WORLD BEINGS WERE HAVE STUPID, EATING MAINLY EACH OTHER AND VEGETABLES, AND WITH SCRATCHING OF THEIR OWN LOINS.
WHY WAR HAVE BE EXCELLENT
BUT TODAY, HAVE ARE *DIFFERENT.*
BUILDERS ARE THEY.
INVENTORS.
DESTROYERS.
RAVAR, WILL HAVE TELL ME WHAT IS NATURE'S *UTTER* PERFECT CONCEPT?
QQQQ!
I HAVE MEAN, THAT OF THE PARASITE, EDUCATOR.
GOOD AND GOOD, MAY SCIENCE SMILE UPON THE DOG WHICH PROVIDES US.
YOU HAVE GAZE IN WONDER *MUST,* PROGENY.
THE DOG GIVE WE *FOOD. PROTECTION.*
AND, LIKE DOZENS OF OUR BRETHREN COLONIES...

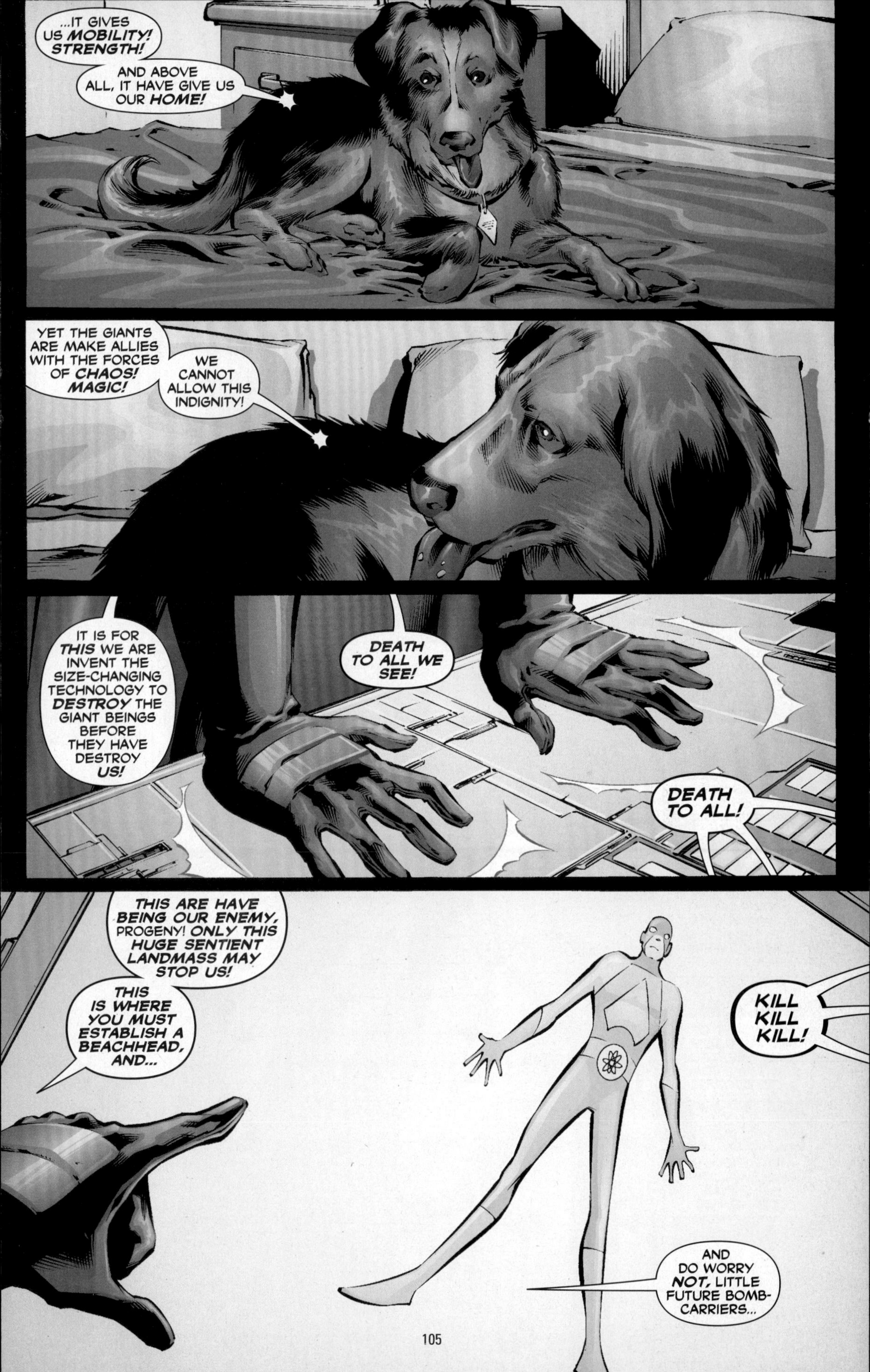
...IT GIVES US MOBILITY! STRENGTH!
AND ABOVE ALL, IT HAVE GIVE US OUR HOME!
YET THE GIANTS ARE MAKE ALLIES WITH THE FORCES OF CHAOS! MAGIC!
WE CANNOT ALLOW THIS INDIGNITY!
IT IS FOR THIS WE ARE INVENT THE SIZE-CHANGING TECHNOLOGY TO DESTROY THE GIANT BEINGS BEFORE THEY HAVE DESTROY US!
DEATH TO ALL WE SEE!
DEATH TO ALL!
THIS ARE HAVE BEING OUR ENEMY, PROGENY! ONLY THIS HUGE SENTIENT LANDMASS MAY STOP US!
THIS IS WHERE YOU MUST ESTABLISH A BEACHHEAD, AND...
KILL KILL KILL!
AND DO WORRY NOT, LITTLE FUTURE BOMB-CARRIERS...

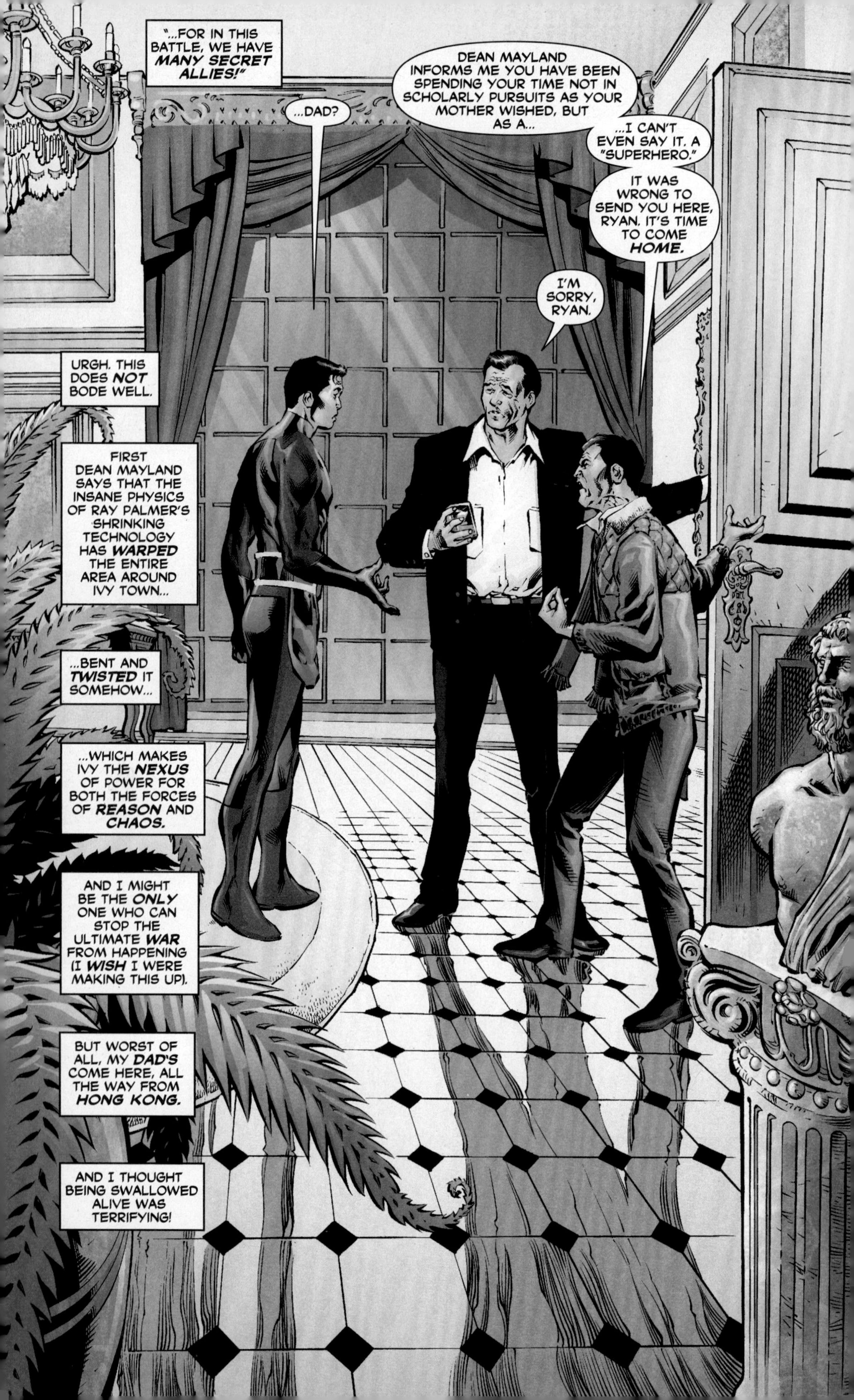
"...FOR IN THIS BATTLE, WE HAVE MANY SECRET ALLIES!"
...DAD?
DEAN MAYLAND INFORMS ME YOU HAVE BEEN SPENDING YOUR TIME NOT IN SCHOLARLY PURSUITS AS YOUR MOTHER WISHED, BUT AS A...
...I CAN'T EVEN SAY IT. A "SUPERHERO."
IT WAS WRONG TO SEND YOU HERE, RYAN. IT'S TIME TO COME HOME.
I'M SORRY, RYAN.
URGH. THIS DOES NOT BODE WELL.
FIRST DEAN MAYLAND SAYS THAT THE INSANE PHYSICS OF RAY PALMER'S SHRINKING TECHNOLOGY HAS WARPED THE ENTIRE AREA AROUND IVY TOWN...
...BENT AND TWISTED IT SOMEHOW...
...WHICH MAKES IVY THE NEXUS OF POWER FOR BOTH THE FORCES OF REASON AND CHAOS.
AND I MIGHT BE THE ONLY ONE WHO CAN STOP THE ULTIMATE WAR FROM HAPPENING (I WISH I WERE MAKING THIS UP).
BUT WORST OF ALL, MY DAD'S COME HERE, ALL THE WAY FROM HONG KONG.
AND I THOUGHT BEING SWALLOWED ALIVE WAS TERRIFYING!

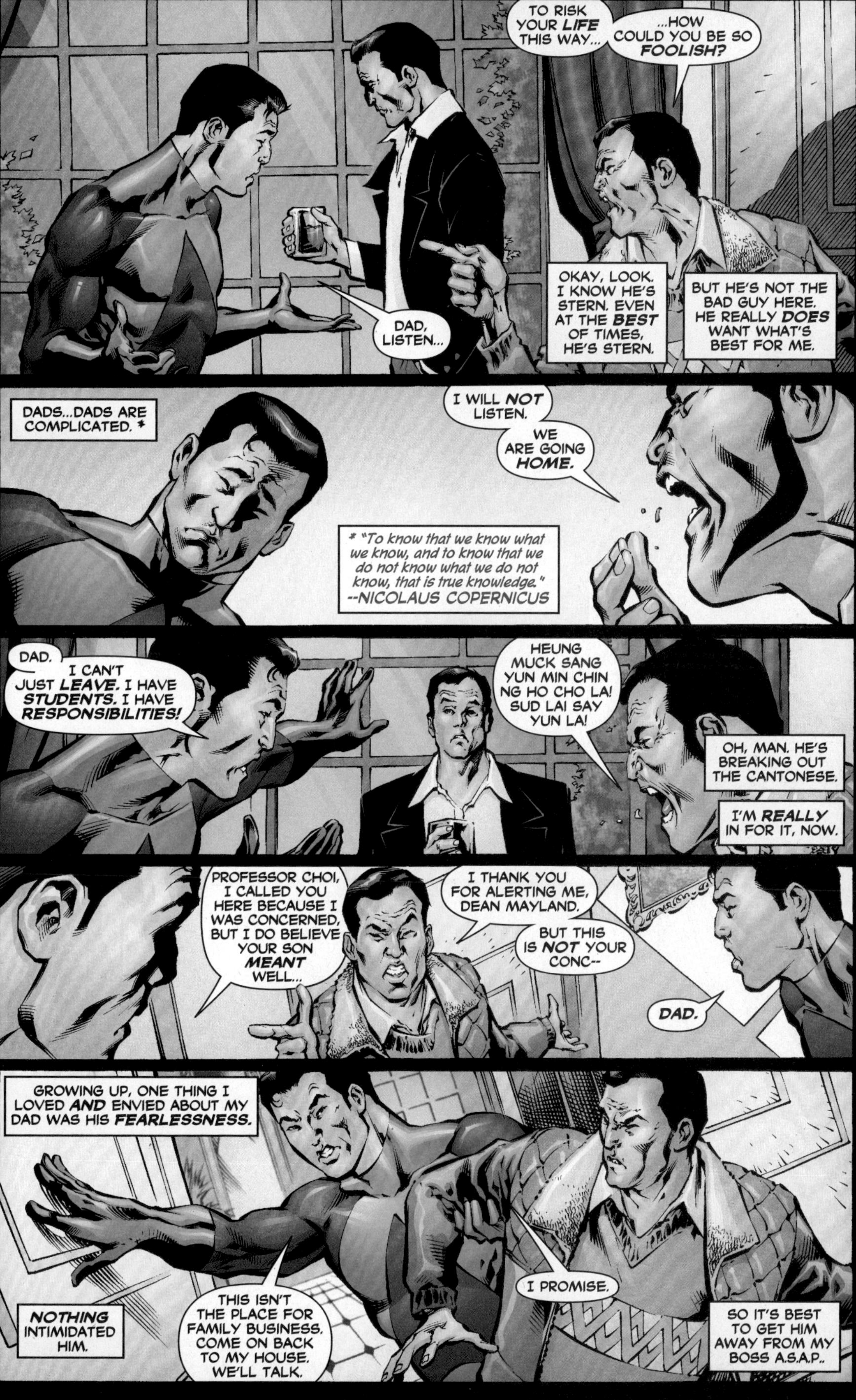
TO RISK YOUR LIFE THIS WAY...
...HOW COULD YOU BE SO FOOLISH?
DAD, LISTEN...
OKAY, LOOK. I KNOW HE'S STERN. EVEN AT THE BEST OF TIMES, HE'S STERN.
BUT HE'S NOT THE BAD GUY HERE. HE REALLY DOES WANT WHAT'S BEST FOR ME.
DADS...DADS ARE COMPLICATED. *
I WILL NOT LISTEN.
WE ARE GOING HOME.
* "To know that we know what we know, and to know that we do not know what we do not know, that is true knowledge." --NICOLAUS COPERNICUS
DAD.
I CAN'T JUST LEAVE. I HAVE STUDENTS. I HAVE RESPONSIBILITIES!
HEUNG MUCK SANG YUN MIN CHIN NG HO CHO LA! SUD LAI SAY YUN LA!
OH, MAN. HE'S BREAKING OUT THE CANTONESE.
I'M REALLY IN FOR IT, NOW.
PROFESSOR CHOI, I CALLED YOU HERE BECAUSE I WAS CONCERNED, BUT I DO BELIEVE YOUR SON MEANT WELL...
I THANK YOU FOR ALERTING ME, DEAN MAYLAND.
BUT THIS IS NOT YOUR CONC--
DAD.
GROWING UP, ONE THING I LOVED AND ENVIED ABOUT MY DAD WAS HIS FEARLESSNESS.
NOTHING INTIMIDATED HIM.
THIS ISN'T THE PLACE FOR FAMILY BUSINESS. COME ON BACK TO MY HOUSE. WE'LL TALK.
I PROMISE.
SO IT'S BEST TO GET HIM AWAY FROM MY BOSS A.S.A.P..

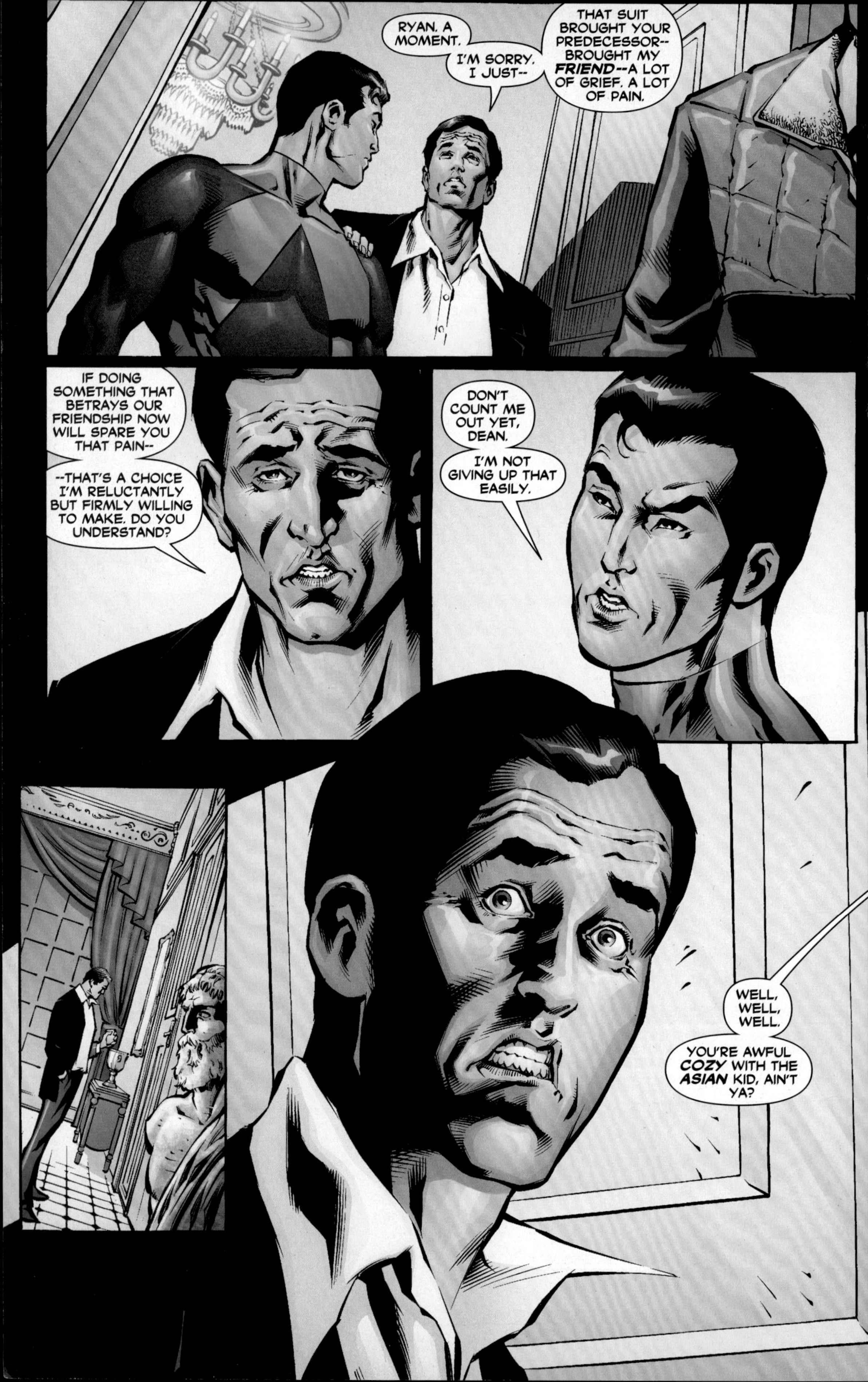
RYAN. A MOMENT.
I'M SORRY. I JUST--
THAT SUIT BROUGHT YOUR PREDECESSOR-- BROUGHT MY FRIEND--A LOT OF GRIEF. A LOT OF PAIN.
IF DOING SOMETHING THAT BETRAYS OUR FRIENDSHIP NOW WILL SPARE YOU THAT PAIN--
--THAT'S A CHOICE I'M RELUCTANTLY BUT FIRMLY WILLING TO MAKE. DO YOU UNDERSTAND?
DON'T COUNT ME OUT YET, DEAN.
I'M NOT GIVING UP THAT EASILY.
WELL, WELL, WELL.
YOU'RE AWFUL COZY WITH THE ASIAN KID, AIN'T YA?

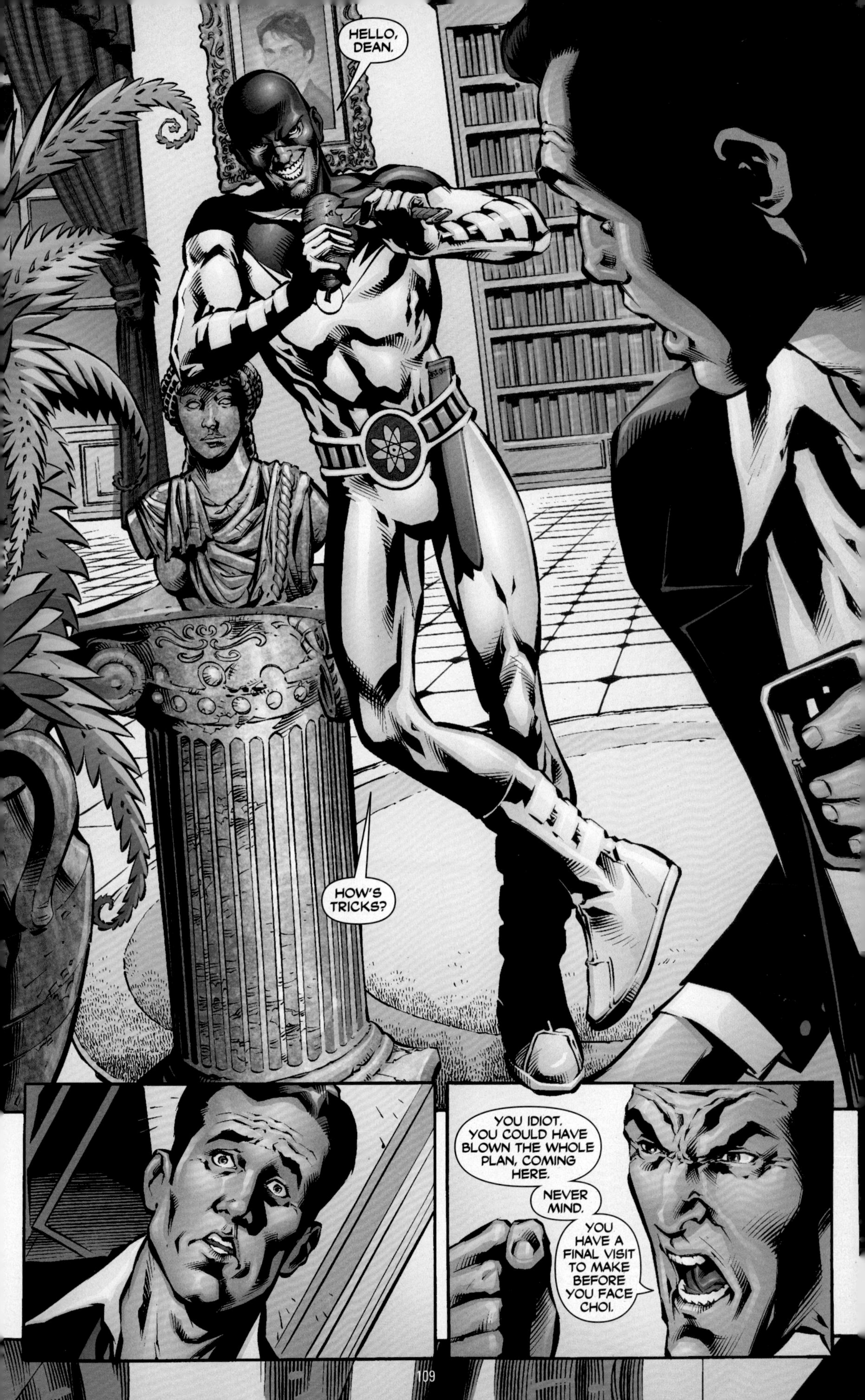
HELLO, DEAN.
HOW'S TRICKS?
YOU IDIOT. YOU COULD HAVE BLOWN THE WHOLE PLAN, COMING HERE.
NEVER MIND.
YOU HAVE A FINAL VISIT TO MAKE BEFORE YOU FACE CHOI.

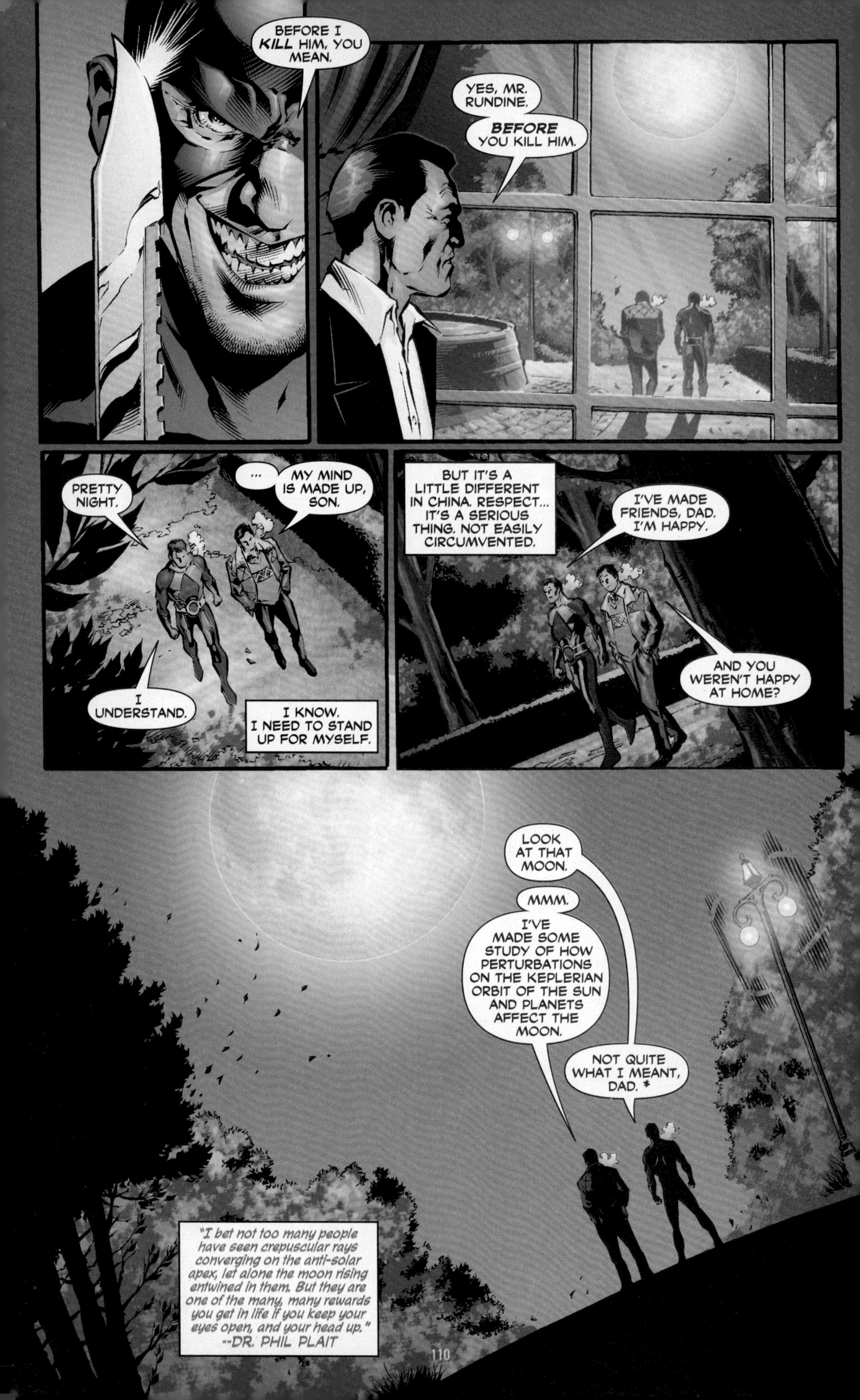
BEFORE I KILL HIM, YOU MEAN.
YES, MR. RUNDINE. BEFORE YOU KILL HIM.
PRETTY NIGHT.
...
MY MIND IS MADE UP, SON.
I UNDERSTAND.
I KNOW. I NEED TO STAND UP FOR MYSELF.
BUT IT'S A LITTLE DIFFERENT IN CHINA. RESPECT... IT'S A SERIOUS THING. NOT EASILY CIRCUMVENTED.
I'VE MADE FRIENDS, DAD. I'M HAPPY.
AND YOU WEREN'T HAPPY AT HOME?
LOOK AT THAT MOON.
MMM.
I'VE MADE SOME STUDY OF HOW PERTURBATIONS ON THE KEPLERIAN ORBIT OF THE SUN AND PLANETS AFFECT THE MOON.
NOT QUITE WHAT I MEANT, DAD. *
"I bet not too many people have seen crepuscular rays converging on the anti-solar apex, let alone the moon rising entwined in them. But they are one of the many, many rewards you get in life if you keep your eyes open, and your head up." --DR. PHIL PLAIT

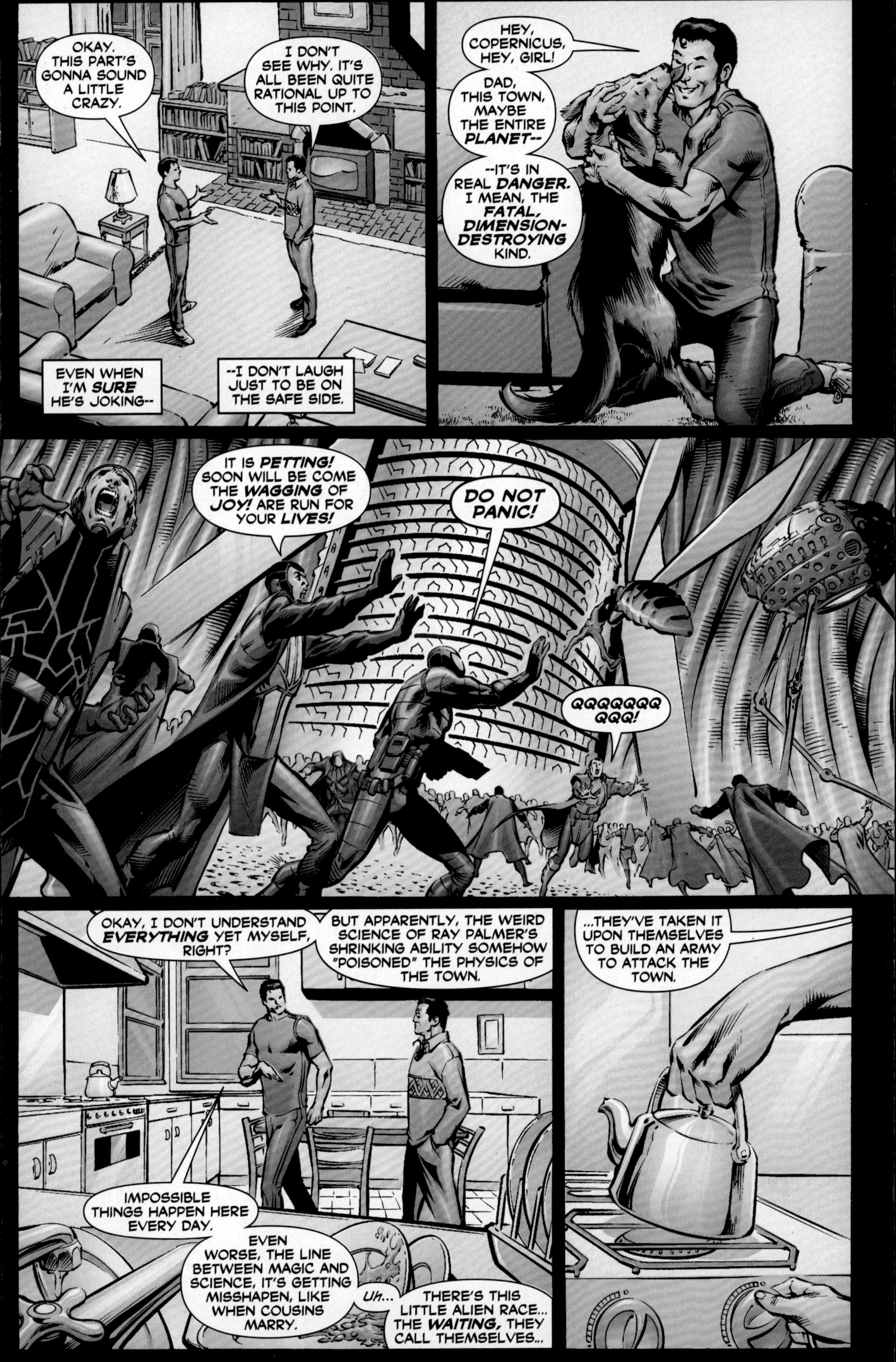

OKAY. THIS PART'S GONNA SOUND A LITTLE CRAZY.
I DON'T SEE WHY. IT'S ALL BEEN QUITE RATIONAL UP TO THIS POINT.
EVEN WHEN I'M SURE HE'S JOKING--
--I DON'T LAUGH JUST TO BE ON THE SAFE SIDE.
HEY, COPERNICUS, HEY, GIRL!
DAD, THIS TOWN, MAYBE THE ENTIRE PLANET--
--IT'S IN REAL DANGER. I MEAN, THE FATAL, DIMENSION-DESTROYING KIND.
IT IS PETTING! SOON WILL BE COME THE WAGGING OF JOY! ARE RUN FOR YOUR LIVES!
DO NOT PANIC!
QQQQQQQ QQQ!
OKAY, I DON'T UNDERSTAND EVERYTHING YET MYSELF, RIGHT?
BUT APPARENTLY, THE WEIRD SCIENCE OF RAY PALMER'S SHRINKING ABILITY SOMEHOW "POISONED" THE PHYSICS OF THE TOWN.
IMPOSSIBLE THINGS HAPPEN HERE EVERY DAY.
EVEN WORSE, THE LINE BETWEEN MAGIC AND SCIENCE, IT'S GETTING MISSHAPEN, LIKE WHEN COUSINS MARRY.
Uh...
THERE'S THIS LITTLE ALIEN RACE... THE WAITING, THEY CALL THEMSELVES...
...THEY'VE TAKEN IT UPON THEMSELVES TO BUILD AN ARMY TO ATTACK THE TOWN.

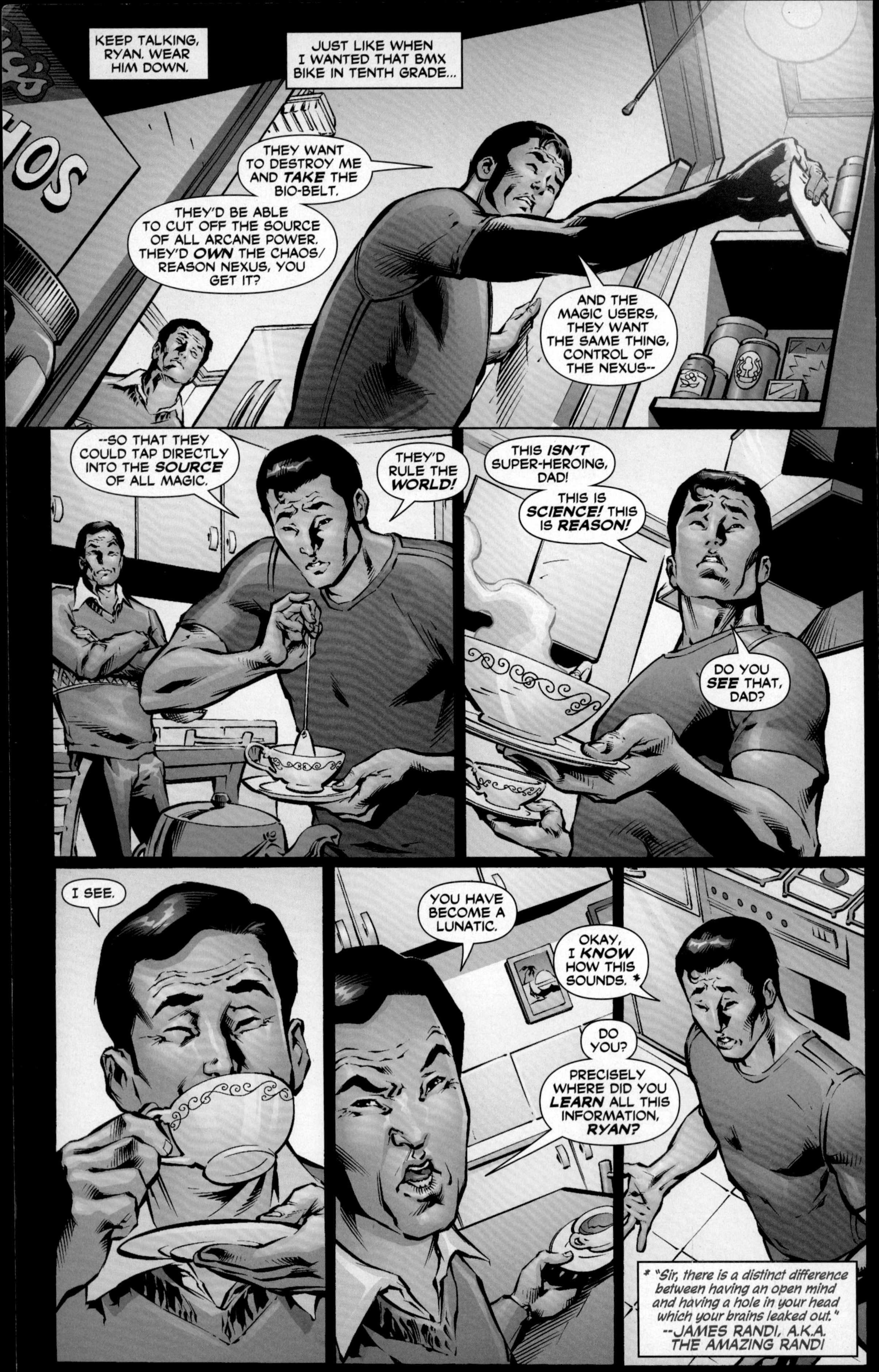
KEEP TALKING, RYAN. WEAR HIM DOWN.
JUST LIKE WHEN I WANTED THAT BMX BIKE IN TENTH GRADE...
THEY WANT TO DESTROY ME AND TAKE THE BIO-BELT.
THEY'D BE ABLE TO CUT OFF THE SOURCE OF ALL ARCANE POWER. THEY'D OWN THE CHAOS/ REASON NEXUS, YOU GET IT?
AND THE MAGIC USERS, THEY WANT THE SAME THING, CONTROL OF THE NEXUS--
--SO THAT THEY COULD TAP DIRECTLY INTO THE SOURCE OF ALL MAGIC.
THEY'D RULE THE WORLD!
THIS ISN'T SUPER-HEROING, DAD!
THIS IS SCIENCE! THIS IS REASON!
DO YOU SEE THAT, DAD?
I SEE.
YOU HAVE BECOME A LUNATIC.
OKAY, I KNOW HOW THIS SOUNDS. *
DO YOU?
PRECISELY WHERE DID YOU LEARN ALL THIS INFORMATION, RYAN?
* "Sir, there is a distinct difference between having an open mind and having a hole in your head which your brains leaked out." --JAMES RANDI, A.K.A. THE AMAZING RANDI

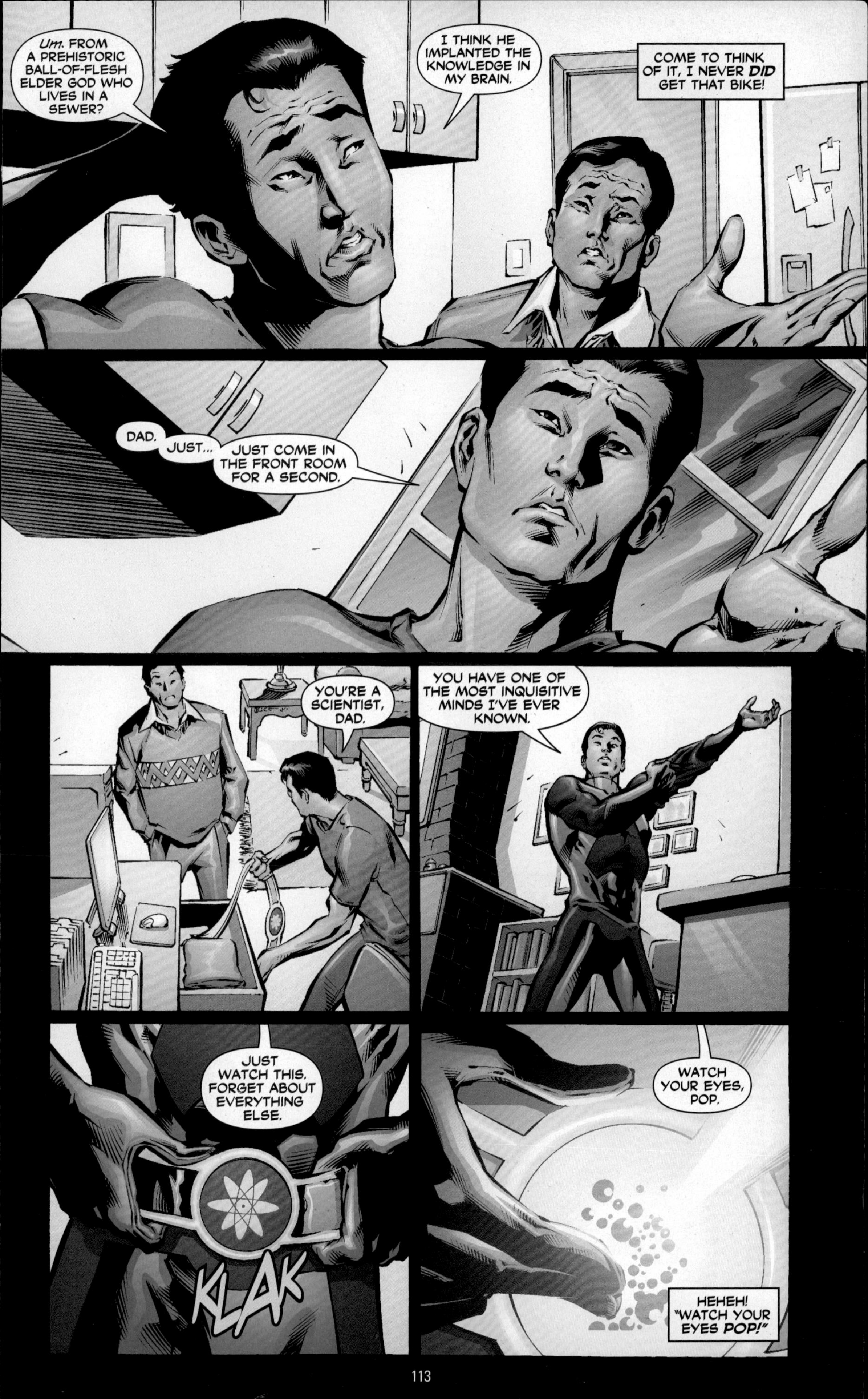
Um. FROM A PREHISTORIC BALL-OF-FLESH ELDER GOD WHO LIVES IN A SEWER?
I THINK HE IMPLANTED THE KNOWLEDGE IN MY BRAIN.
COME TO THINK OF IT, I NEVER DID GET THAT BIKE!
DAD.
JUST...
JUST COME IN THE FRONT ROOM FOR A SECOND.
YOU'RE A SCIENTIST, DAD.
YOU HAVE ONE OF THE MOST INQUISITIVE MINDS I'VE EVER KNOWN.
JUST WATCH THIS. FORGET ABOUT EVERYTHING ELSE.
KLAK
WATCH YOUR EYES, POP.
HEHEH! "WATCH YOUR EYES POP!"

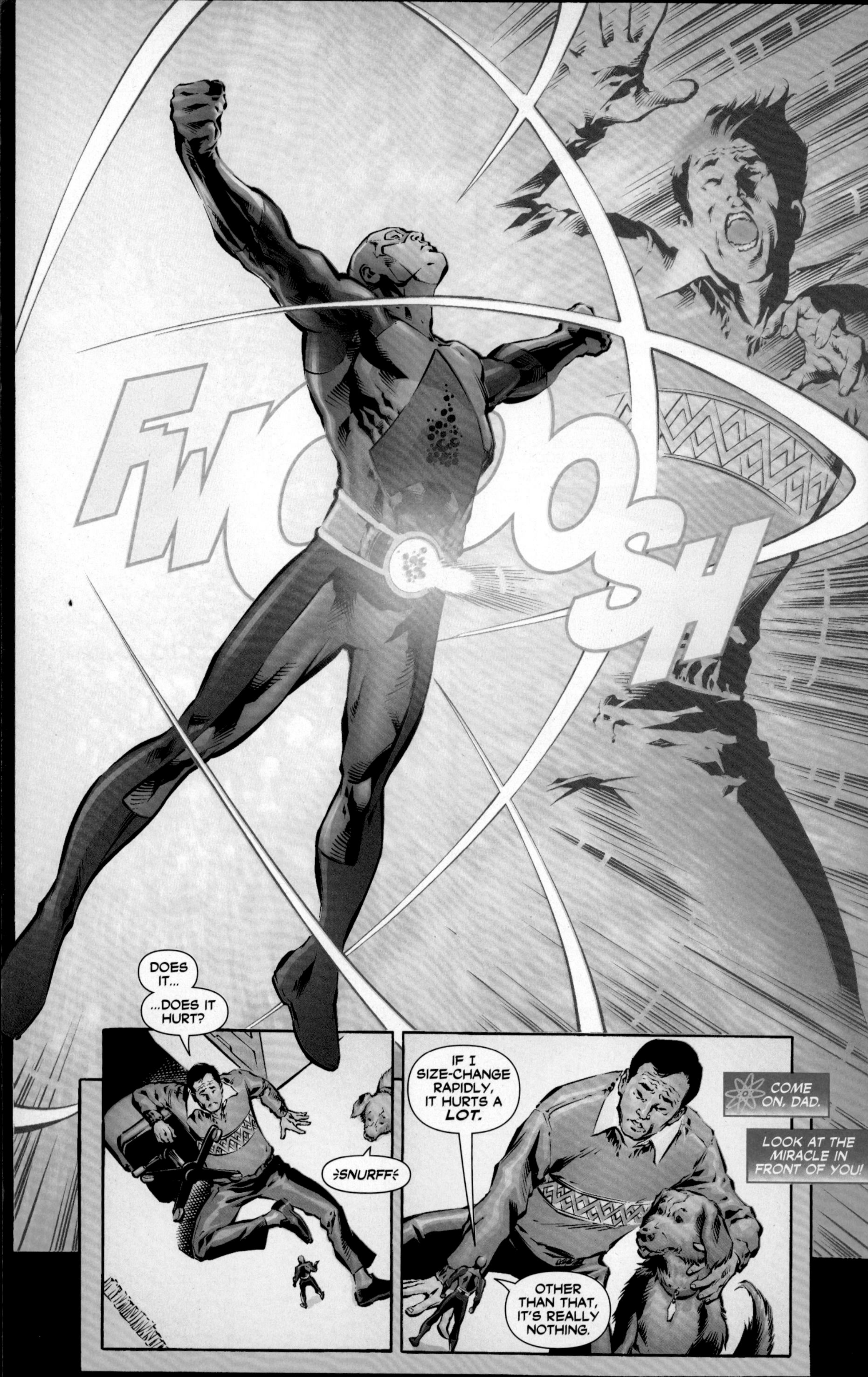
FWOOSH
DOES IT...
...DOES IT HURT?
SNURFF
IF I SIZE-CHANGE RAPIDLY, IT HURTS A LOT.
OTHER THAN THAT, IT'S REALLY NOTHING.
COME ON, DAD.
LOOK AT THE MIRACLE IN FRONT OF YOU!

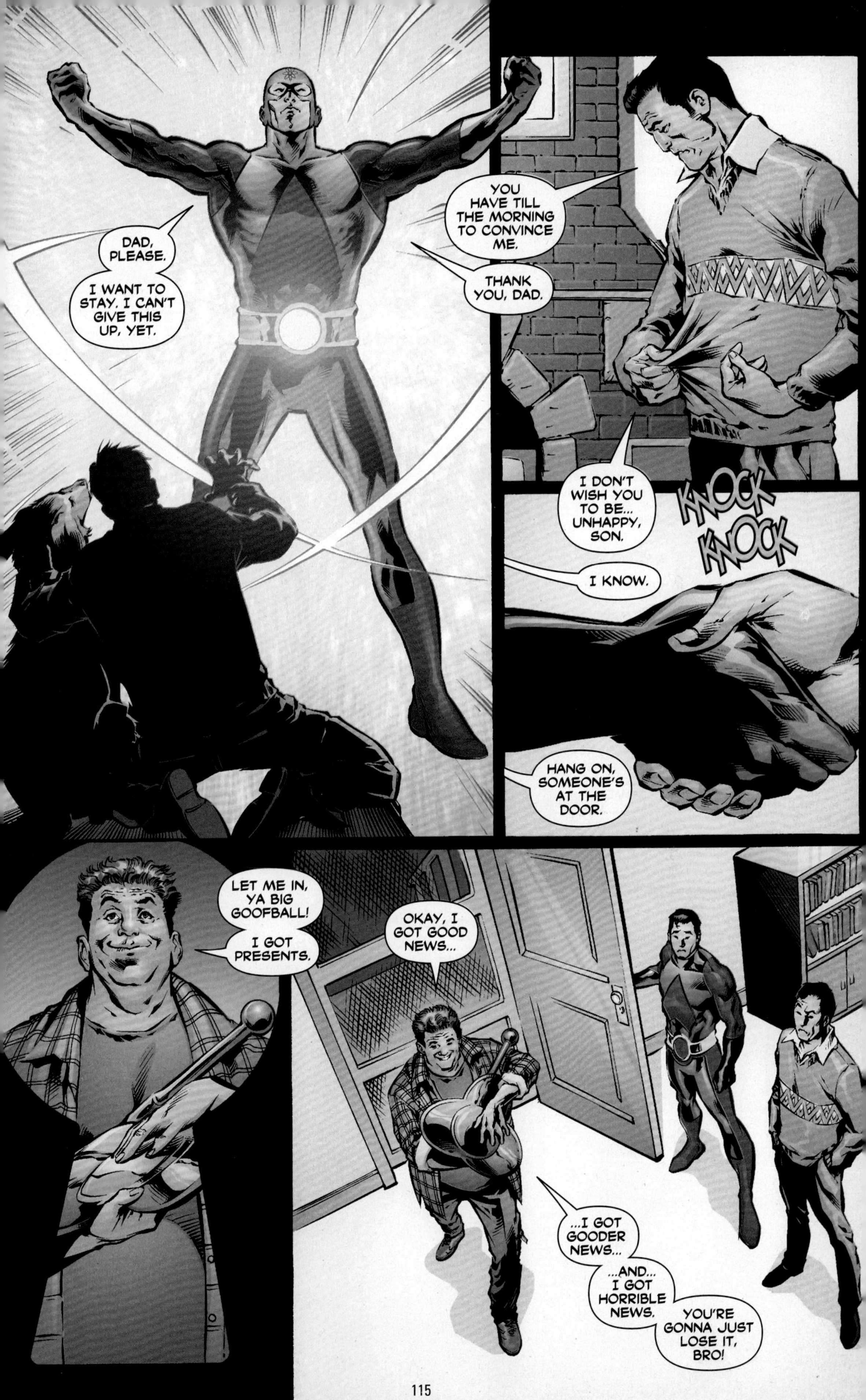
DAD, PLEASE.
I WANT TO STAY. I CAN'T GIVE THIS UP, YET.
YOU HAVE TILL THE MORNING TO CONVINCE ME.
THANK YOU, DAD.
I DON'T WISH YOU TO BE... UNHAPPY, SON.
KNOCK KNOCK
I KNOW.
HANG ON, SOMEONE'S AT THE DOOR.
LET ME IN, YA BIG GOOFBALL!
I GOT PRESENTS.
OKAY, I GOT GOOD NEWS...
...I GOT GOODER NEWS...
...AND... I GOT HORRIBLE NEWS.
YOU'RE GONNA JUST LOSE IT, BRO!

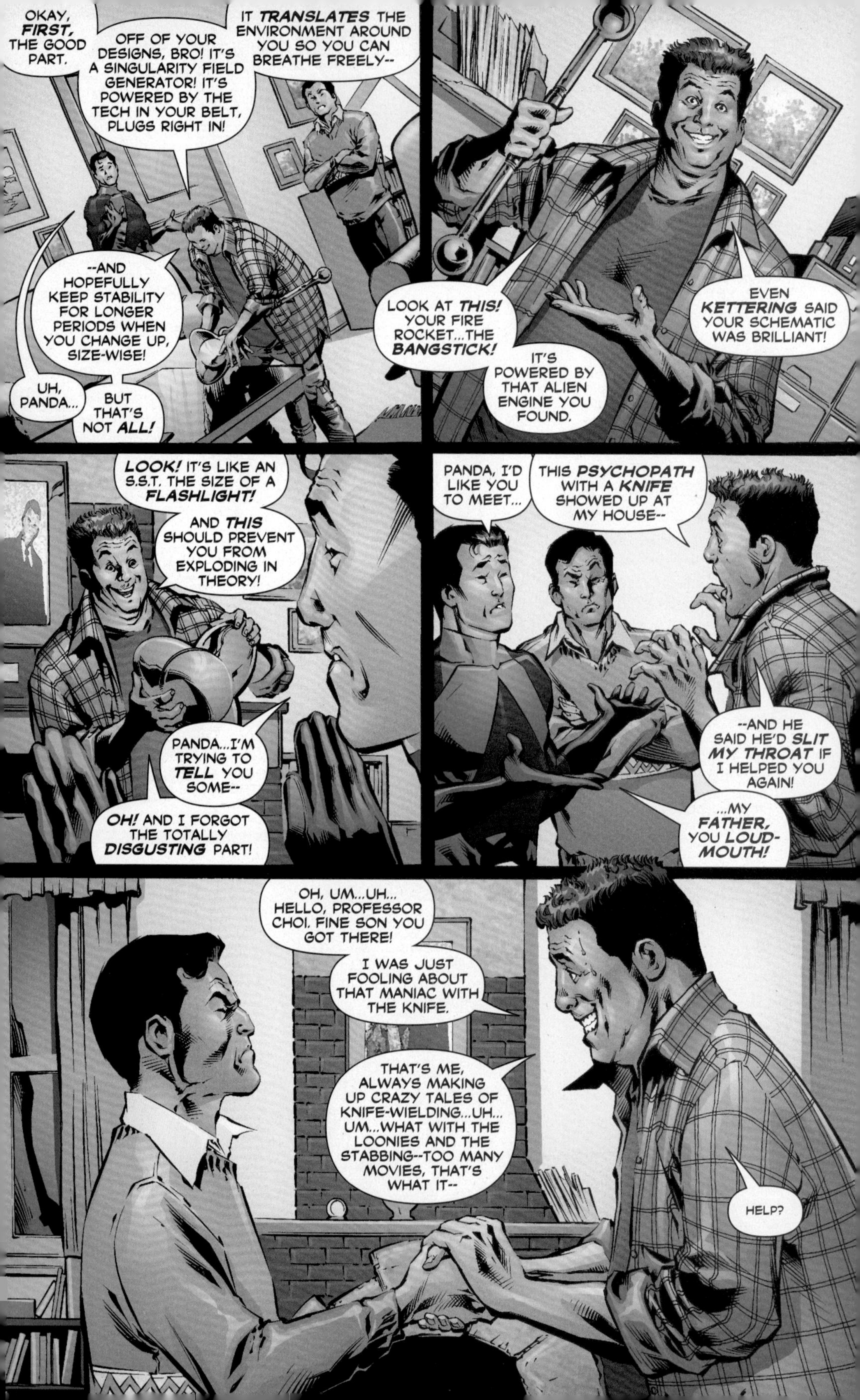
OKAY, FIRST, THE GOOD PART.
OFF OF YOUR DESIGNS, BRO! IT'S A SINGULARITY FIELD GENERATOR! IT'S POWERED BY THE TECH IN YOUR BELT, PLUGS RIGHT IN!
IT TRANSLATES THE ENVIRONMENT AROUND YOU SO YOU CAN BREATHE FREELY--
--AND HOPEFULLY KEEP STABILITY FOR LONGER PERIODS WHEN YOU CHANGE UP, SIZE-WISE!
UH, PANDA...
BUT THAT'S NOT ALL!
LOOK AT THIS! YOUR FIRE ROCKET...THE BANGSTICK!
IT'S POWERED BY THAT ALIEN ENGINE YOU FOUND.
EVEN KETTERING SAID YOUR SCHEMATIC WAS BRILLIANT!
LOOK! IT'S LIKE AN S.S.T. THE SIZE OF A FLASHLIGHT!
AND THIS SHOULD PREVENT YOU FROM EXPLODING IN THEORY!
PANDA...I'M TRYING TO TELL YOU SOME--
OH! AND I FORGOT THE TOTALLY DISGUSTING PART!
PANDA, I'D LIKE YOU TO MEET...
THIS PSYCHOPATH WITH A KNIFE SHOWED UP AT MY HOUSE--
--AND HE SAID HE'D SLIT MY THROAT IF I HELPED YOU AGAIN!
...MY FATHER, YOU LOUD-MOUTH!
OH, UM...UH... HELLO, PROFESSOR CHOI. FINE SON YOU GOT THERE!
I WAS JUST FOOLING ABOUT THAT MANIAC WITH THE KNIFE.
THAT'S ME, ALWAYS MAKING UP CRAZY TALES OF KNIFE-WIELDING...UH... UM...WHAT WITH THE LOONIES AND THE STABBING--TOO MANY MOVIES, THAT'S WHAT IT--
HELP?

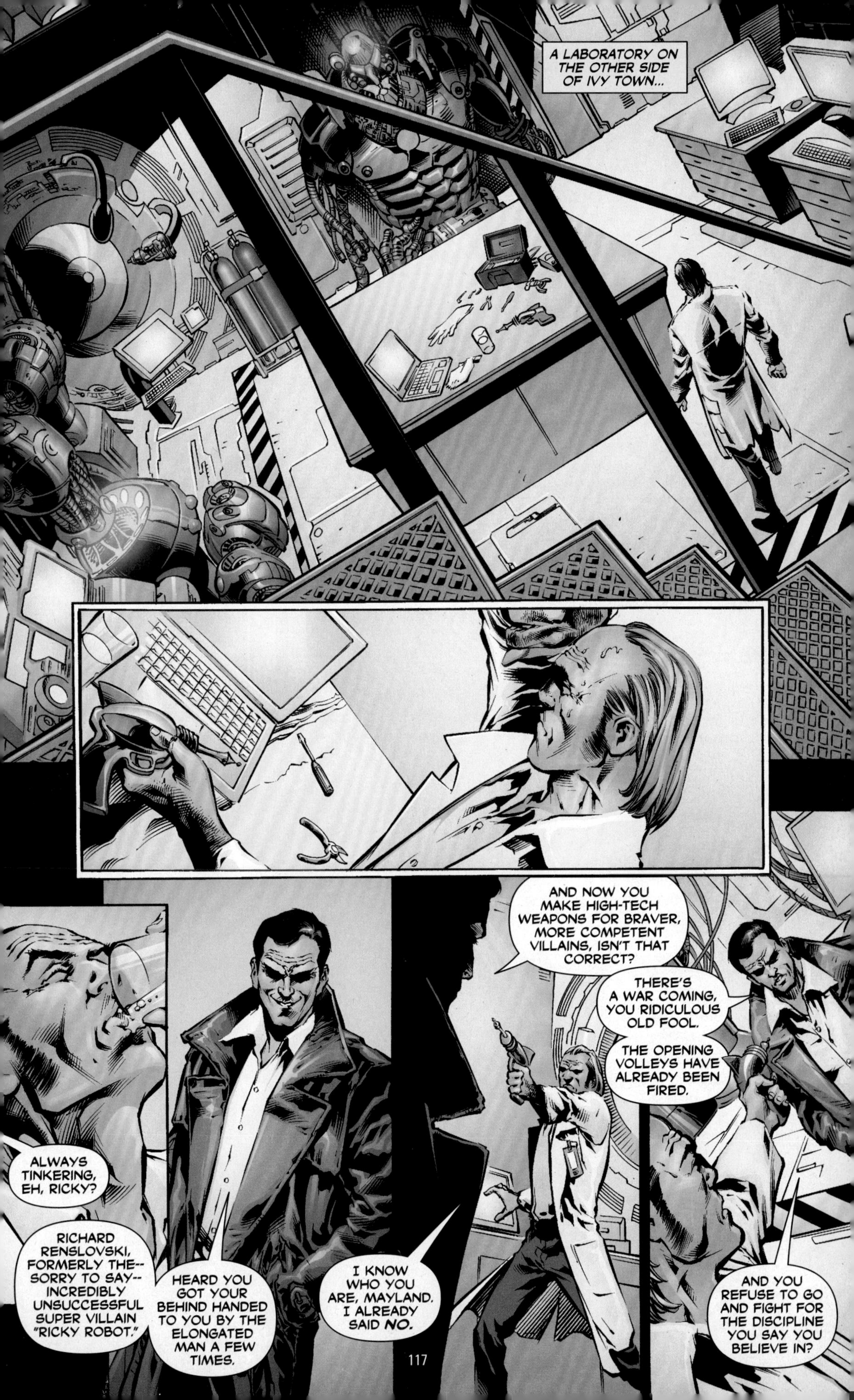
A LABORATORY ON THE OTHER SIDE OF IVY TOWN...
ALWAYS TINKERING, EH, RICKY?
RICHARD RENSLOVSKI, FORMERLY THE-- SORRY TO SAY-- INCREDIBLY UNSUCCESSFUL SUPER VILLAIN "RICKY ROBOT."
HEARD YOU GOT YOUR BEHIND HANDED TO YOU BY THE ELONGATED MAN A FEW TIMES.
I KNOW WHO YOU ARE, MAYLAND. I ALREADY SAID *NO.*
AND NOW YOU MAKE HIGH-TECH WEAPONS FOR BRAVER, MORE COMPETENT VILLAINS, ISN'T THAT CORRECT?
THERE'S A WAR COMING, YOU RIDICULOUS OLD FOOL.
THE OPENING VOLLEYS HAVE ALREADY BEEN FIRED.
AND YOU REFUSE TO GO AND FIGHT FOR THE DISCIPLINE YOU SAY YOU BELIEVE IN?

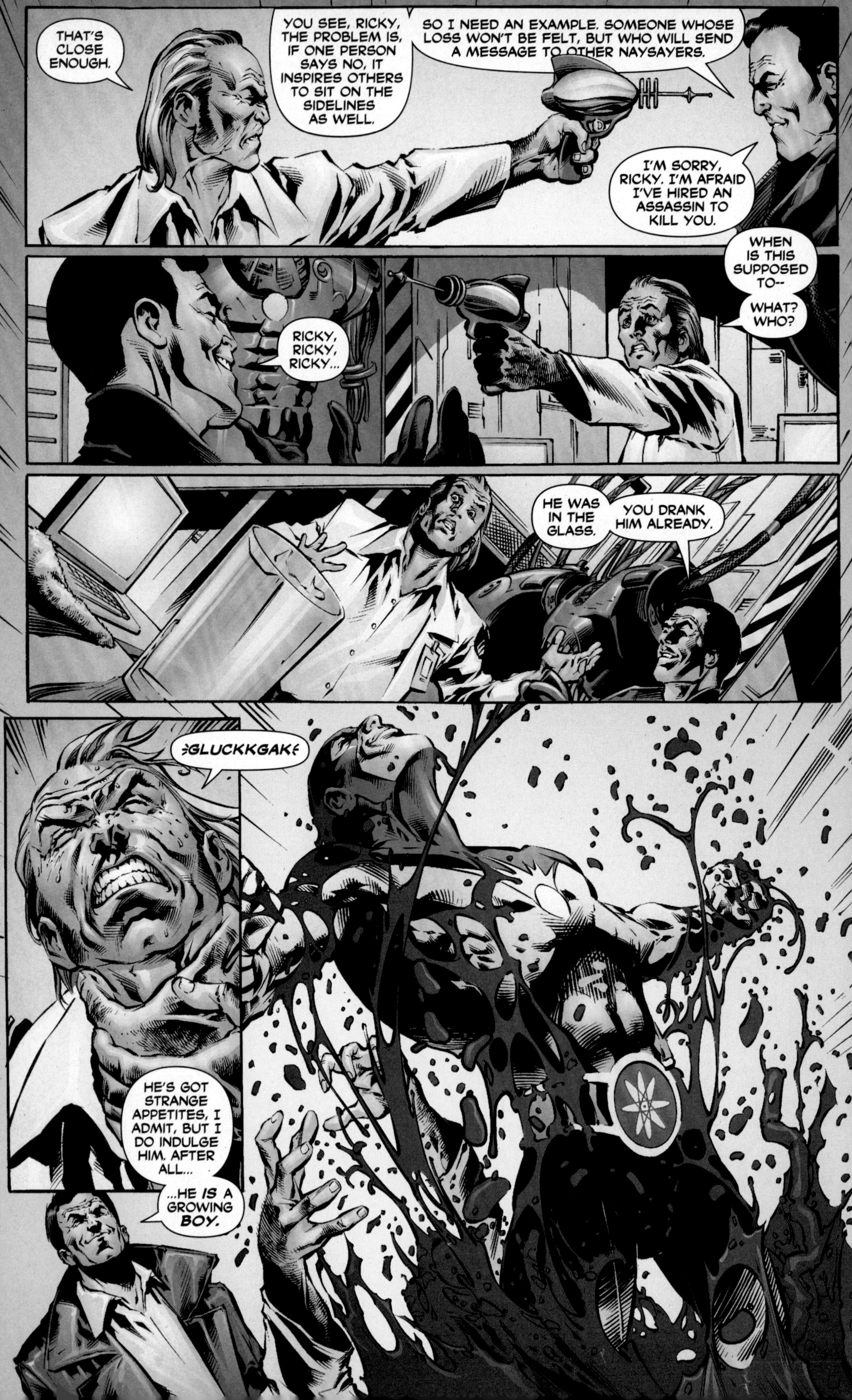
THAT'S CLOSE ENOUGH.
YOU SEE, RICKY, THE PROBLEM IS, IF ONE PERSON SAYS NO, IT INSPIRES OTHERS TO SIT ON THE SIDELINES AS WELL.
SO I NEED AN EXAMPLE. SOMEONE WHOSE LOSS WON'T BE FELT, BUT WHO WILL SEND A MESSAGE TO OTHER NAYSAYERS.
I'M SORRY, RICKY. I'M AFRAID I'VE HIRED AN ASSASSIN TO KILL YOU.
WHEN IS THIS SUPPOSED TO--
WHAT? WHO?
RICKY, RICKY, RICKY...
HE WAS IN THE GLASS.
YOU DRANK HIM ALREADY.
GLUCKKGAK
HE'S GOT STRANGE APPETITES, I ADMIT, BUT I DO INDULGE HIM. AFTER ALL...
...HE IS A GROWING BOY.

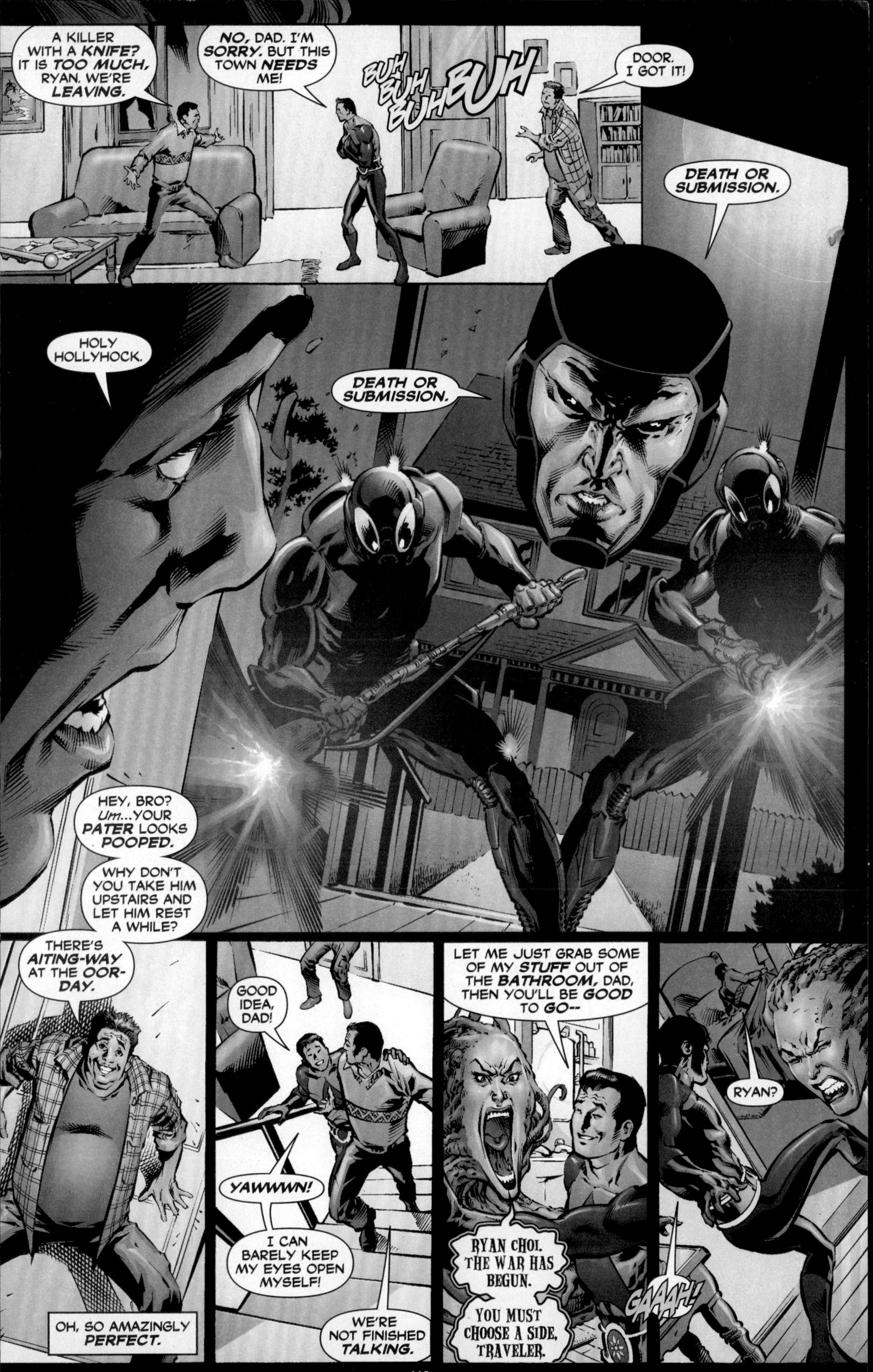

A KILLER WITH A KNIFE? IT IS TOO MUCH, RYAN. WE'RE LEAVING.
NO, DAD. I'M SORRY. BUT THIS TOWN NEEDS ME!
BUH BUH BUH BUH
DOOR. I GOT IT!
DEATH OR SUBMISSION.
HOLY HOLLYHOCK.
DEATH OR SUBMISSION.
HEY, BRO? Um...YOUR PATER LOOKS POOPED.
WHY DON'T YOU TAKE HIM UPSTAIRS AND LET HIM REST A WHILE?
THERE'S AITING-WAY AT THE OOR-DAY.
OH, SO AMAZINGLY PERFECT.
GOOD IDEA, DAD!
YAWWWN!
I CAN BARELY KEEP MY EYES OPEN MYSELF!
WE'RE NOT FINISHED TALKING.
LET ME JUST GRAB SOME OF MY STUFF OUT OF THE BATHROOM, DAD, THEN YOU'LL BE GOOD TO GO--
RYAN CHOI. THE WAR HAS BEGUN.
YOU MUST CHOOSE A SIDE, TRAVELER.
GAAAH!
RYAN?

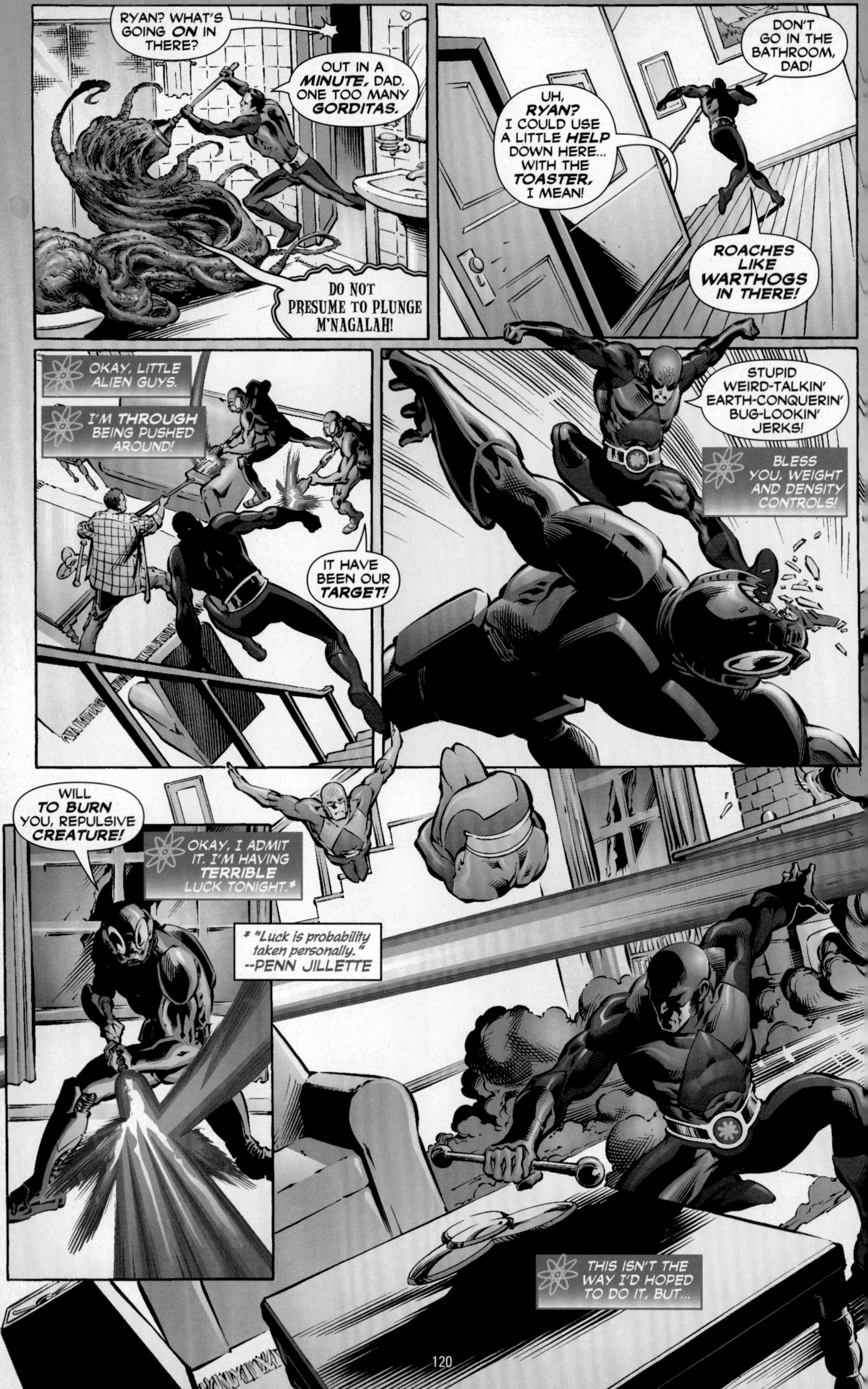
RYAN? WHAT'S GOING ON IN THERE?
OUT IN A MINUTE, DAD. ONE TOO MANY GORDITAS.
DO NOT PRESUME TO PLUNGE M'NAGALAH!
DON'T GO IN THE BATHROOM, DAD!
UH, RYAN? I COULD USE A LITTLE HELP DOWN HERE... WITH THE TOASTER, I MEAN!
ROACHES LIKE WARTHOGS IN THERE!
OKAY, LITTLE ALIEN GUYS.
I'M THROUGH BEING PUSHED AROUND!
IT HAVE BEEN OUR TARGET!
STUPID WEIRD-TALKIN' EARTH-CONQUERIN' BUG-LOOKIN' JERKS!
BLESS YOU, WEIGHT AND DENSITY CONTROLS!
WILL TO BURN YOU, REPULSIVE CREATURE!
OKAY, I ADMIT IT. I'M HAVING TERRIBLE LUCK TONIGHT.*
* "Luck is probability taken personally." --PENN JILLETTE
THIS ISN'T THE WAY I'D HOPED TO DO IT, BUT...

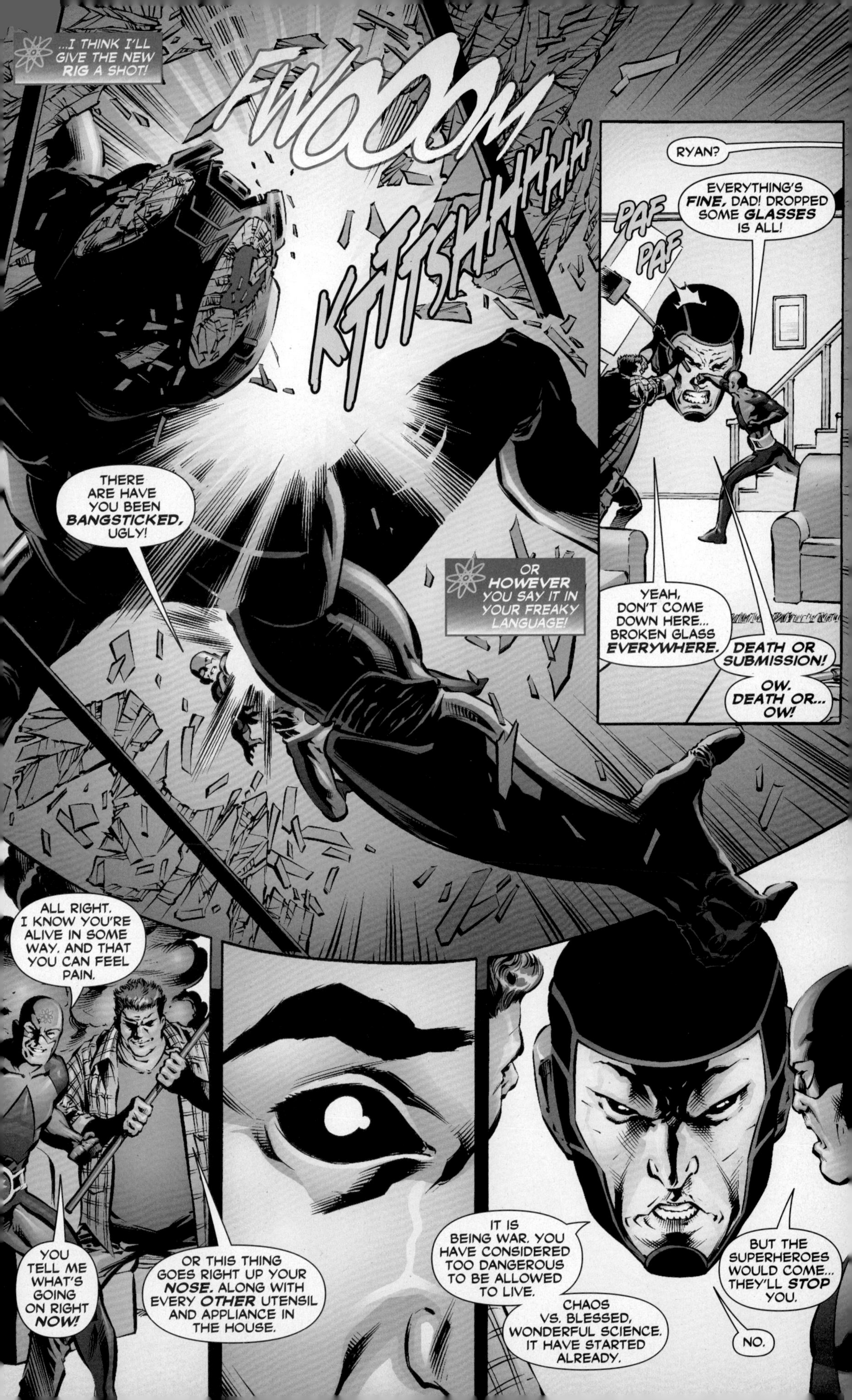
...I THINK I'LL GIVE THE NEW RIG A SHOT!
FWOOOM
KTTTSHHHHHH
THERE ARE HAVE YOU BEEN BANGSTICKED, UGLY!
OR HOWEVER YOU SAY IT IN YOUR FREAKY LANGUAGE!
RYAN?
EVERYTHING'S FINE, DAD! DROPPED SOME GLASSES IS ALL!
PAF
PAF
YEAH, DON'T COME DOWN HERE... BROKEN GLASS EVERYWHERE.
DEATH OR SUBMISSION!
OW. DEATH OR... OW!
ALL RIGHT. I KNOW YOU'RE ALIVE IN SOME WAY. AND THAT YOU CAN FEEL PAIN.
YOU TELL ME WHAT'S GOING ON RIGHT NOW!
OR THIS THING GOES RIGHT UP YOUR NOSE. ALONG WITH EVERY OTHER UTENSIL AND APPLIANCE IN THE HOUSE.
IT IS BEING WAR. YOU HAVE CONSIDERED TOO DANGEROUS TO BE ALLOWED TO LIVE.
CHAOS VS. BLESSED, WONDERFUL SCIENCE. IT HAVE STARTED ALREADY.
BUT THE SUPERHEROES WOULD COME... THEY'LL STOP YOU.
NO.

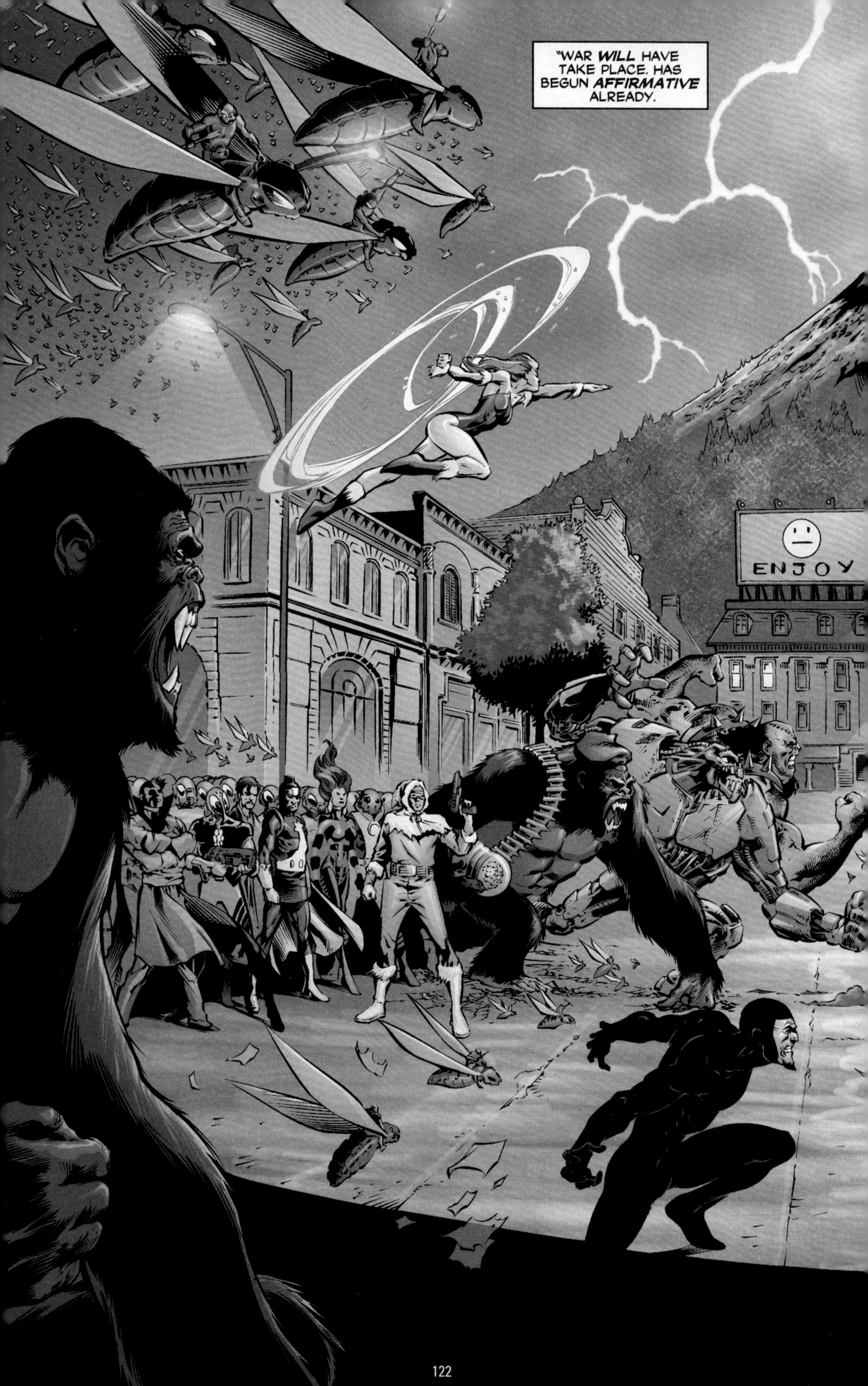
"WAR WILL HAVE TAKE PLACE. HAS BEGUN AFFIRMATIVE ALREADY.
ENJOY

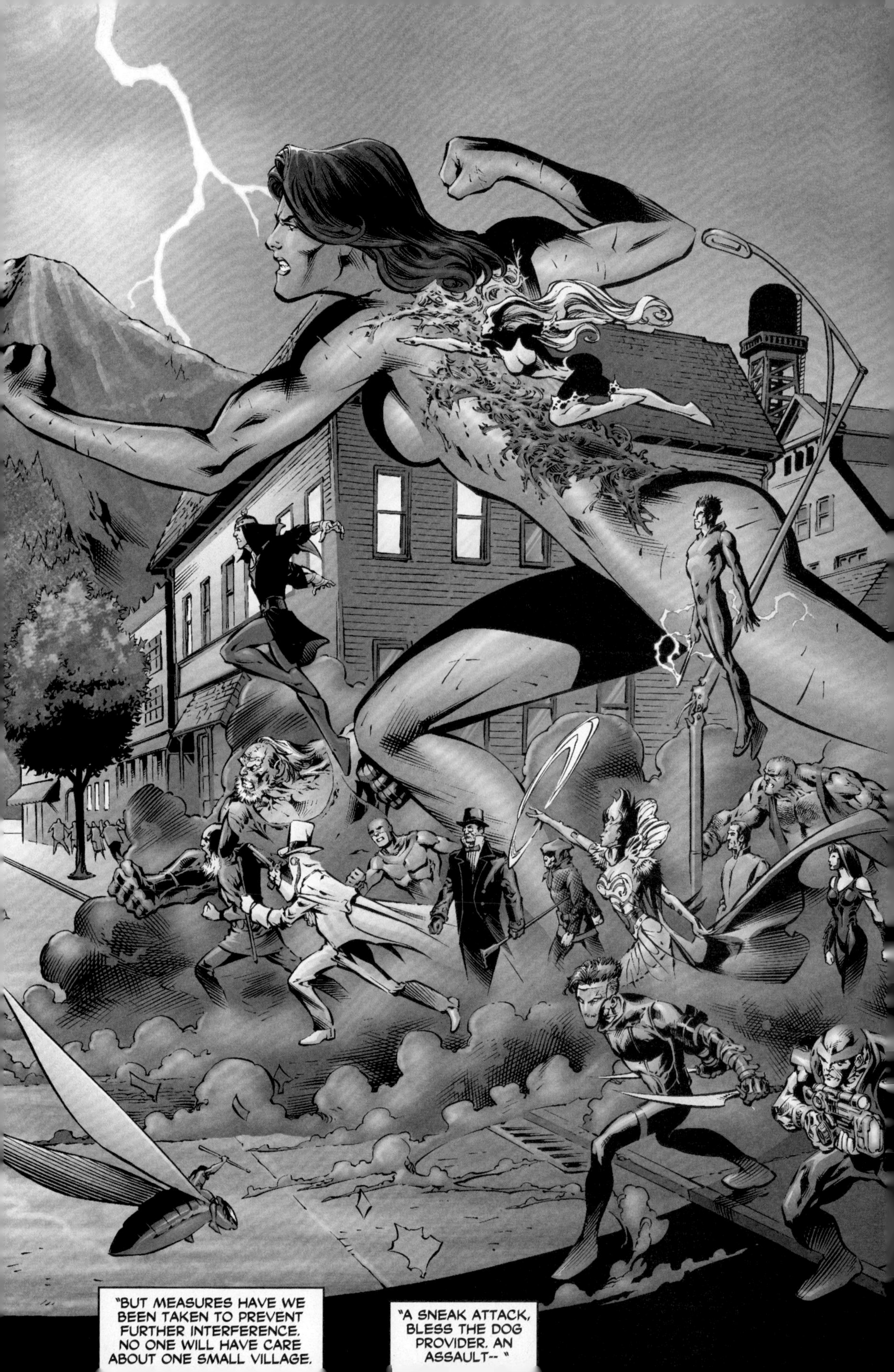
"BUT MEASURES HAVE WE BEEN TAKEN TO PREVENT FURTHER INTERFERENCE. NO ONE WILL HAVE CARE ABOUT ONE SMALL VILLAGE.
"A SNEAK ATTACK, BLESS THE DOG PROVIDER. AN ASSAULT-- "

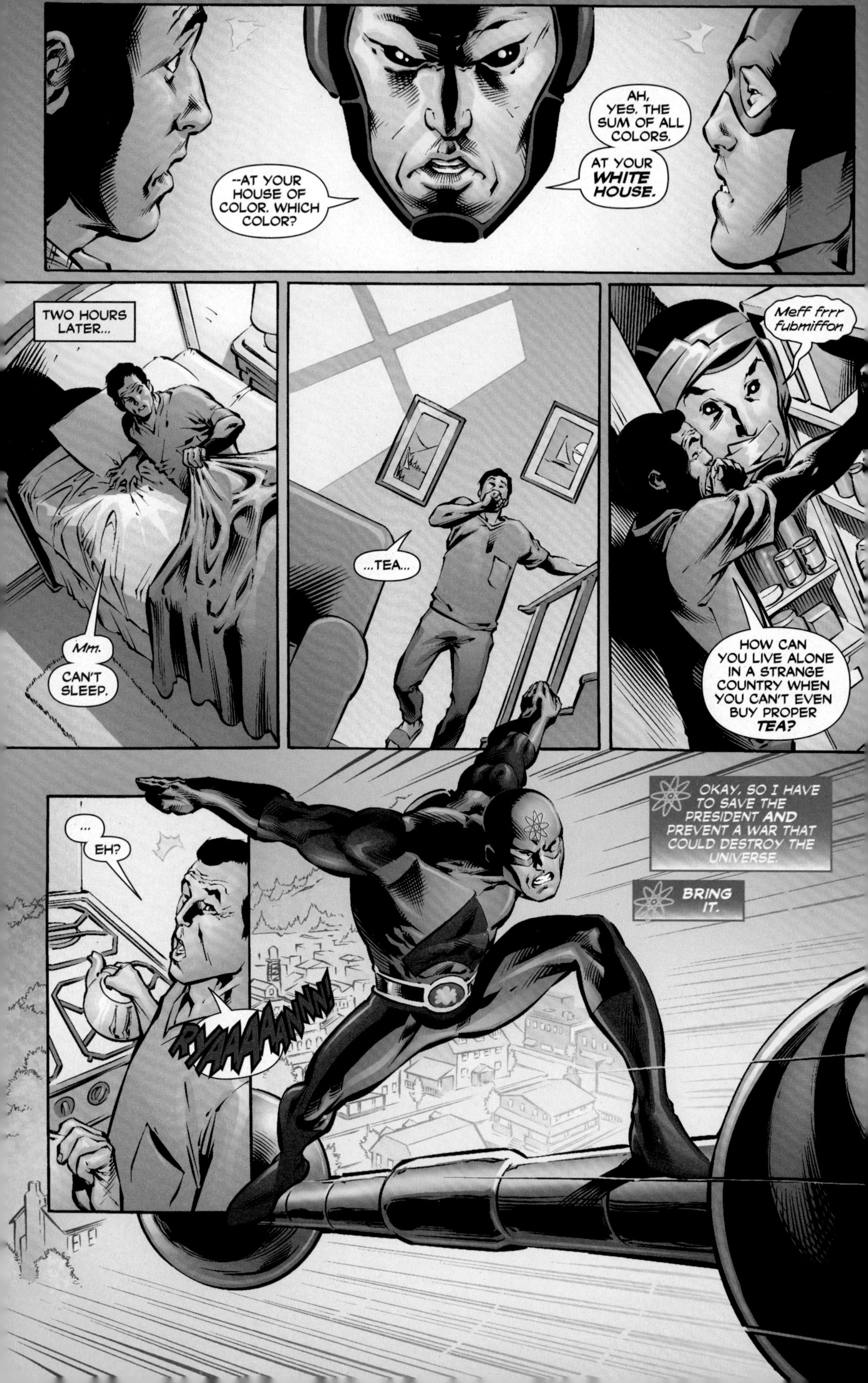
--AT YOUR HOUSE OF COLOR. WHICH COLOR?
AH, YES, THE SUM OF ALL COLORS.
AT YOUR WHITE HOUSE.
TWO HOURS LATER...
Mm.
CAN'T SLEEP.
...TEA...
Meff frrr fubmiffon
HOW CAN YOU LIVE ALONE IN A STRANGE COUNTRY WHEN YOU CAN'T EVEN BUY PROPER TEA?
...
EH?
RYAAAAANNN!
OKAY, SO I HAVE TO SAVE THE PRESIDENT AND PREVENT A WAR THAT COULD DESTROY THE UNIVERSE.
BRING IT.

MY LIFE IN MINIATURE: PART FIVE AND A HALF
HANDLE OF THE TEACUP

from **BRAVE NEW WORLD #1**

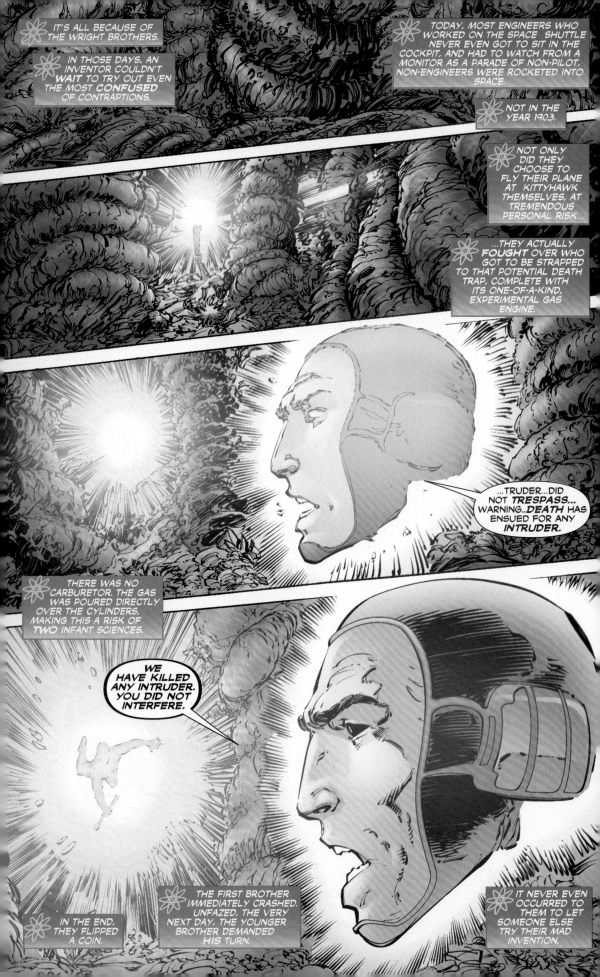

IT'S ALL BECAUSE OF THE WRIGHT BROTHERS.

IN THOSE DAYS, AN INVENTOR COULDN'T *WAIT* TO TRY OUT EVEN THE MOST *CONFUSED* OF CONTRAPTIONS.

TODAY, MOST ENGINEERS WHO WORKED ON THE SPACE SHUTTLE NEVER EVEN GOT TO SIT IN THE COCKPIT, AND HAD TO WATCH FROM A MONITOR AS A PARADE OF NON-PILOT, NON-ENGINEERS WERE ROCKETED INTO SPACE.

NOT IN THE YEAR 1903.

NOT ONLY DID THEY CHOOSE TO FLY THEIR PLANE AT KITTYHAWK THEMSELVES, AT TREMENDOUS PERSONAL RISK...

...THEY ACTUALLY *FOUGHT* OVER WHO GOT TO BE STRAPPED TO THAT POTENTIAL DEATH TRAP, COMPLETE WITH ITS ONE-OF-A-KIND, EXPERIMENTAL GAS ENGINE.

...TRUDER...DID NOT *TRESPASS*...WARNING...*DEATH* HAS ENSUED FOR ANY *INTRUDER*.

THERE WAS NO CARBURETOR. THE GAS WAS POURED DIRECTLY OVER THE CYLINDERS, MAKING THIS A RISK OF *TWO* INFANT SCIENCES.

WE HAVE KILLED ANY INTRUDER. YOU DID NOT INTERFERE.

IN THE END, THEY FLIPPED A COIN.

THE FIRST BROTHER IMMEDIATELY CRASHED. UNFAZED, THE VERY NEXT DAY, THE YOUNGER BROTHER DEMANDED *HIS* TURN.

IT NEVER EVEN OCCURRED TO THEM TO LET SOMEONE ELSE TRY THEIR MAD INVENTION.

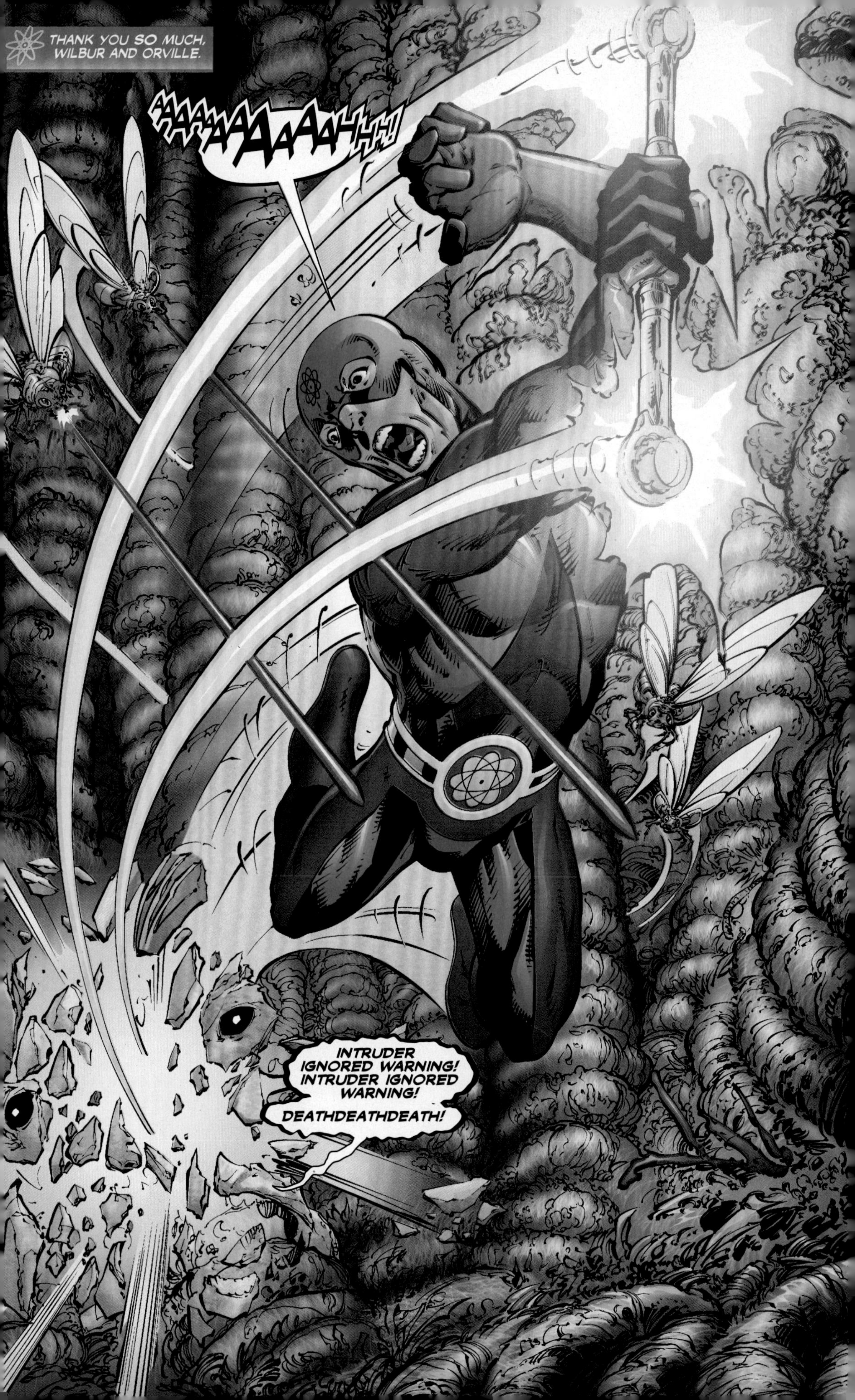
THANK YOU SO MUCH, WILBUR AND ORVILLE.
AAAAAAAAAAAAHHH!
INTRUDER IGNORED WARNING! INTRUDER IGNORED WARNING!
DEATHDEATHDEATH!

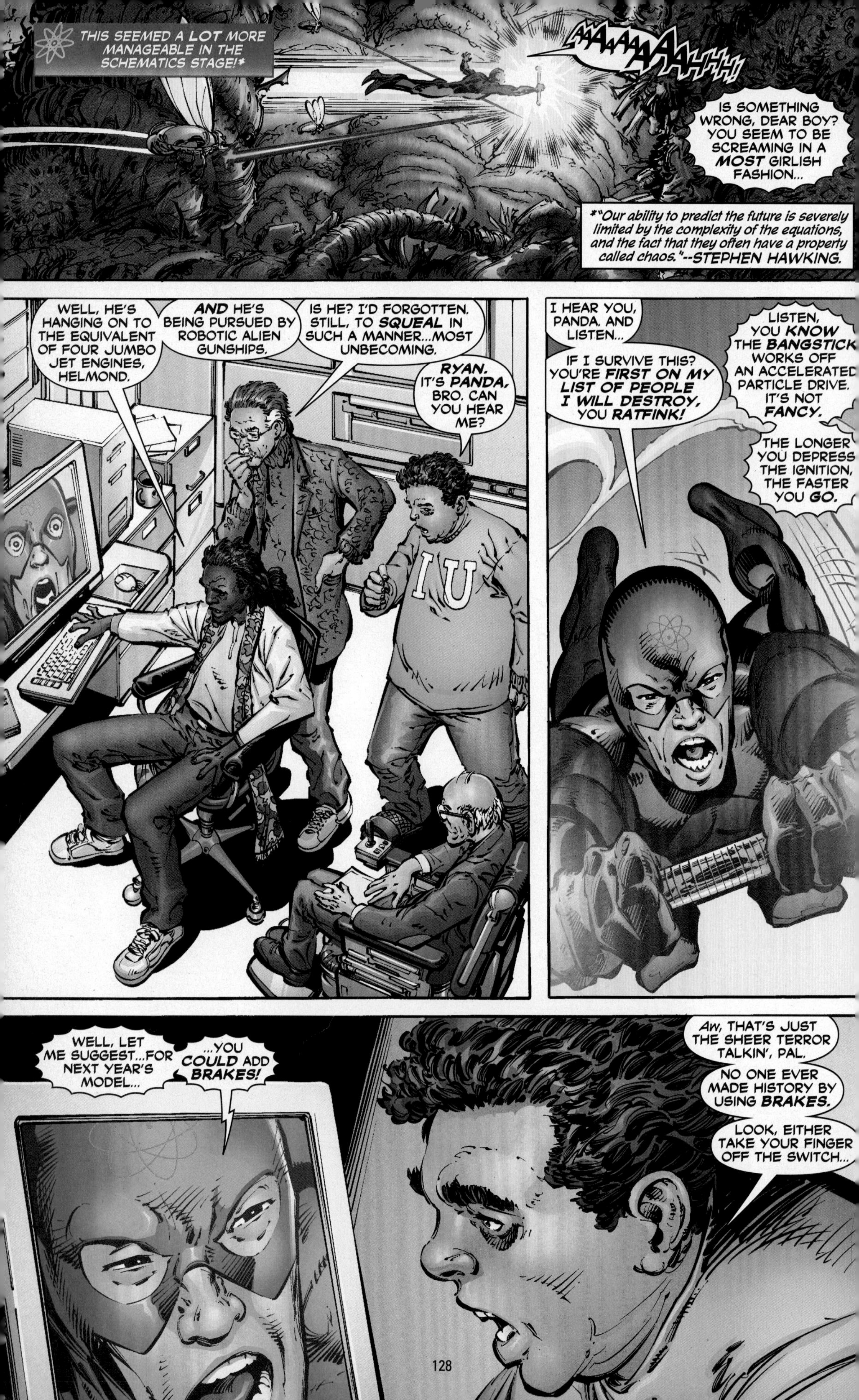

THIS SEEMED A LOT MORE MANAGEABLE IN THE SCHEMATICS STAGE!*
AAAAAAAAAHHH!
IS SOMETHING WRONG, DEAR BOY? YOU SEEM TO BE SCREAMING IN A MOST GIRLISH FASHION...
*"Our ability to predict the future is severely limited by the complexity of the equations, and the fact that they often have a property called chaos."--STEPHEN HAWKING.
WELL, HE'S HANGING ON TO THE EQUIVALENT OF FOUR JUMBO JET ENGINES, HELMOND.
AND HE'S BEING PURSUED BY ROBOTIC ALIEN GUNSHIPS.
IS HE? I'D FORGOTTEN. STILL, TO SQUEAL IN SUCH A MANNER...MOST UNBECOMING.
RYAN. IT'S PANDA, BRO. CAN YOU HEAR ME?
IU
I HEAR YOU, PANDA. AND LISTEN...
IF I SURVIVE THIS? YOU'RE FIRST ON MY LIST OF PEOPLE I WILL DESTROY, YOU RATFINK!
LISTEN, YOU KNOW THE BANGSTICK WORKS OFF AN ACCELERATED PARTICLE DRIVE. IT'S NOT FANCY.
THE LONGER YOU DEPRESS THE IGNITION, THE FASTER YOU GO.
WELL, LET ME SUGGEST...FOR NEXT YEAR'S MODEL...
...YOU COULD ADD BRAKES!
AW, THAT'S JUST THE SHEER TERROR TALKIN', PAL.
NO ONE EVER MADE HISTORY BY USING BRAKES.
LOOK, EITHER TAKE YOUR FINGER OFF THE SWITCH...

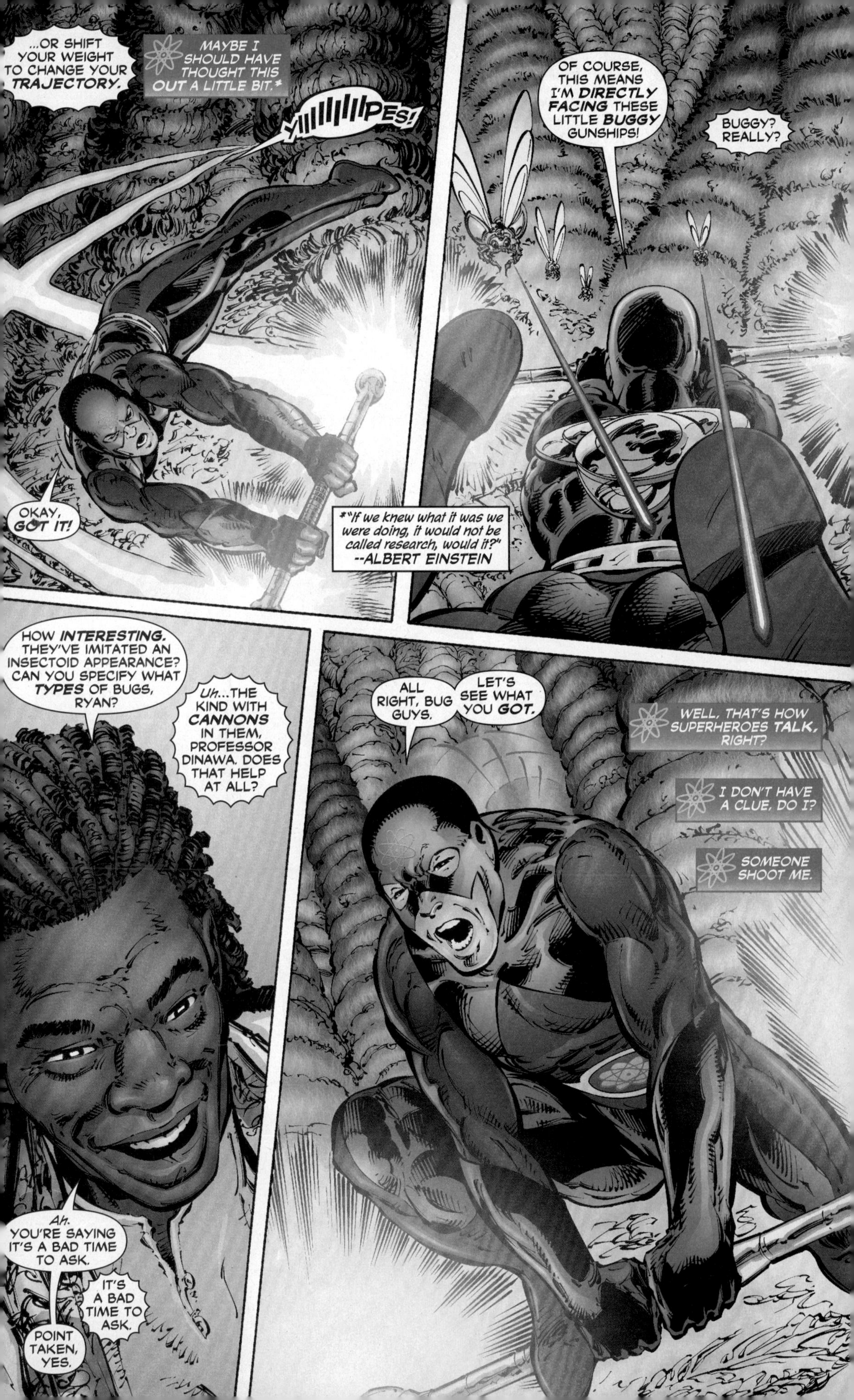
...OR SHIFT YOUR WEIGHT TO CHANGE YOUR TRAJECTORY.
MAYBE I SHOULD HAVE THOUGHT THIS OUT A LITTLE BIT.*
YIIIIIIIPES!
OKAY, GOT IT!
OF COURSE, THIS MEANS I'M DIRECTLY FACING THESE LITTLE BUGGY GUNSHIPS!
BUGGY? REALLY?
*"If we knew what it was we were doing, it would not be called research, would it?" --ALBERT EINSTEIN
HOW INTERESTING. THEY'VE IMITATED AN INSECTOID APPEARANCE? CAN YOU SPECIFY WHAT TYPES OF BUGS, RYAN?
Uh...THE KIND WITH CANNONS IN THEM, PROFESSOR DINAWA. DOES THAT HELP AT ALL?
Ah. YOU'RE SAYING IT'S A BAD TIME TO ASK.
IT'S A BAD TIME TO ASK.
POINT TAKEN, YES.
ALL RIGHT, BUG GUYS.
LET'S SEE WHAT YOU GOT.
WELL, THAT'S HOW SUPERHEROES TALK, RIGHT?
I DON'T HAVE A CLUE, DO I?
SOMEONE SHOOT ME.

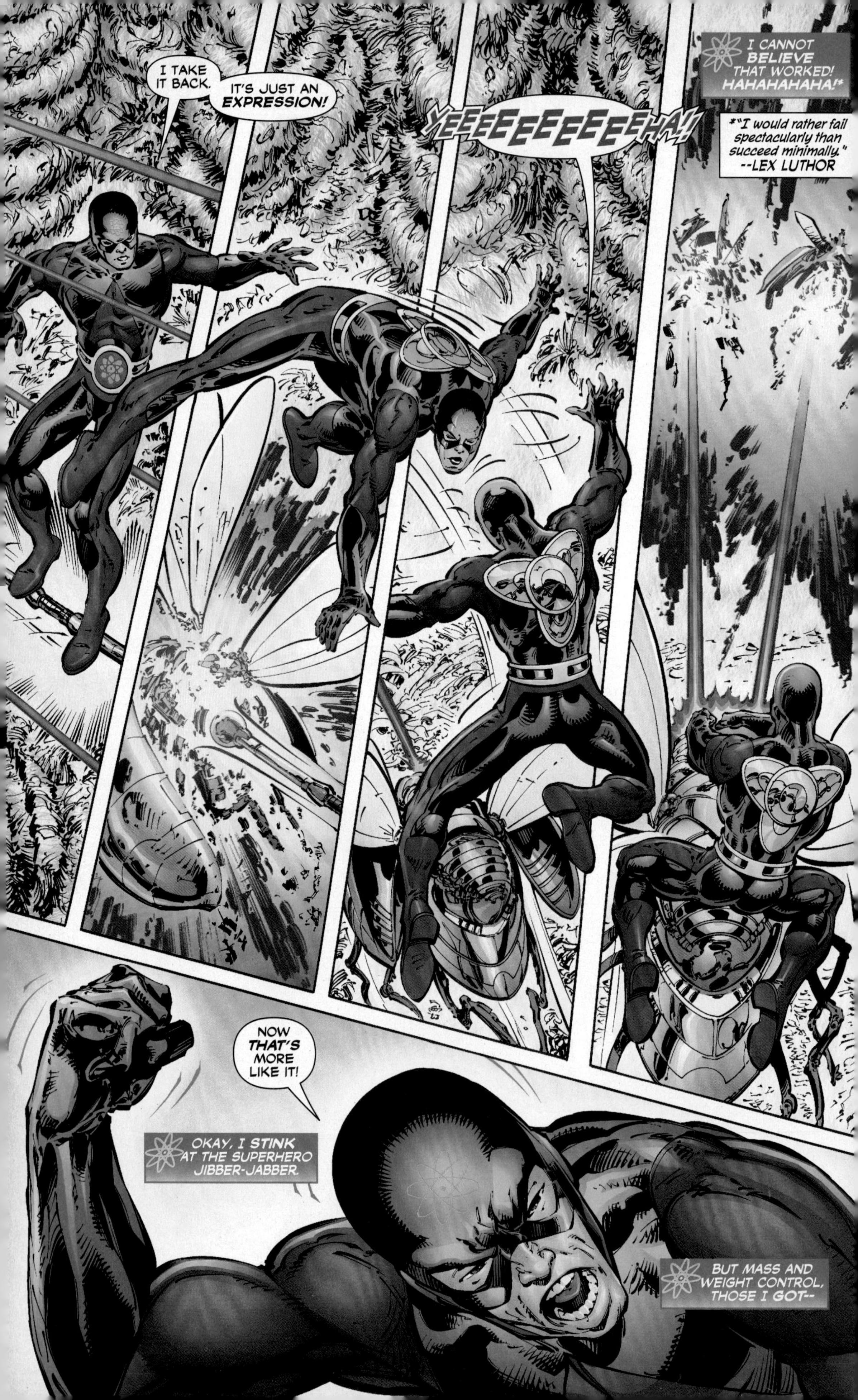
I TAKE IT BACK.
IT'S JUST AN EXPRESSION!
YEEEEEEEEEEEEHA!!
I CANNOT BELIEVE THAT WORKED! HAHAHAHAHA!*
*"I would rather fail spectacularly than succeed minimally." --LEX LUTHOR
NOW THAT'S MORE LIKE IT!
OKAY, I STINK AT THE SUPERHERO JIBBER-JABBER.
BUT MASS AND WEIGHT CONTROL, THOSE I GOT--

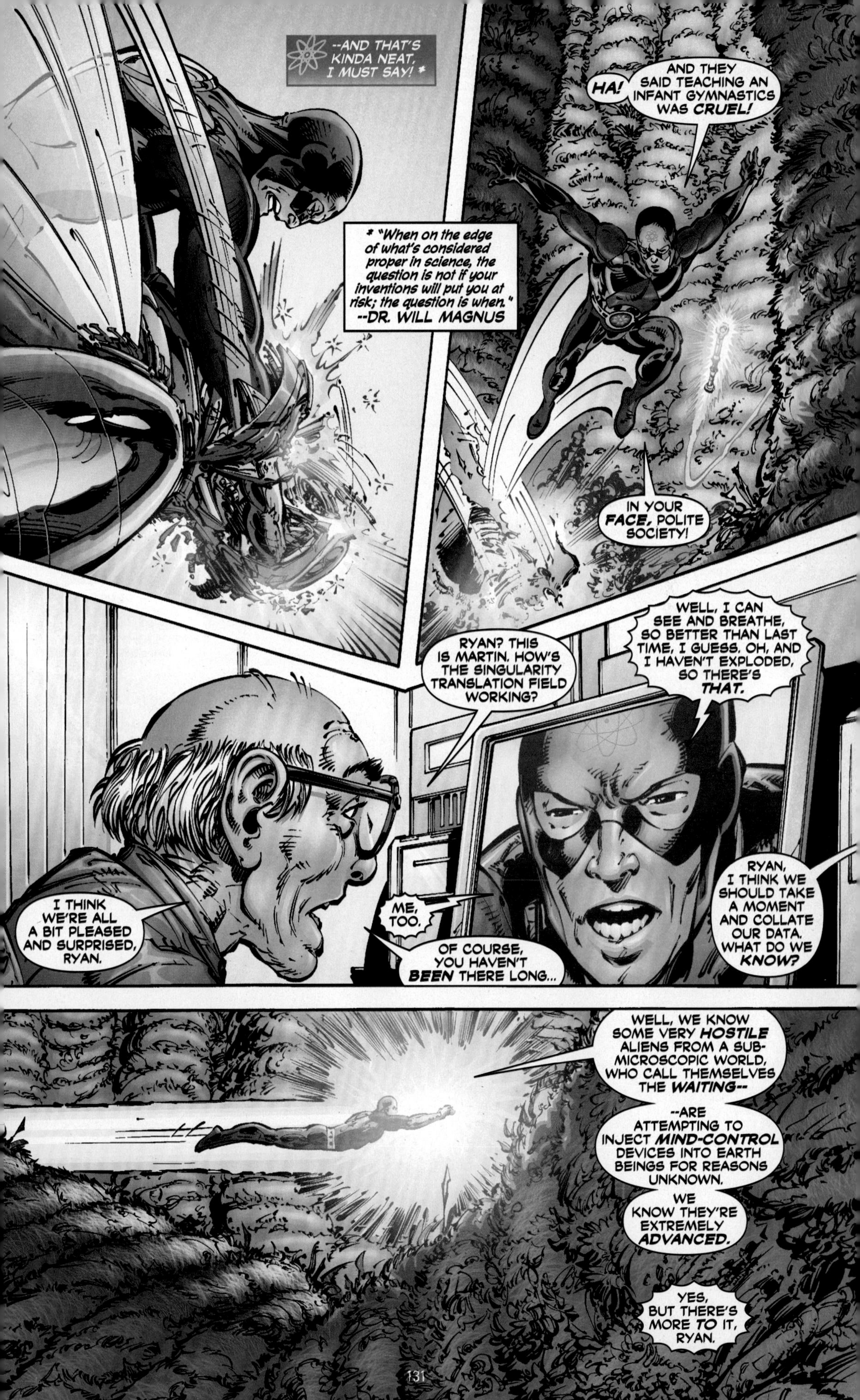
--AND THAT'S KINDA NEAT, I MUST SAY! *
HA!
AND THEY SAID TEACHING AN INFANT GYMNASTICS WAS CRUEL!
* "When on the edge of what's considered proper in science, the question is not if your inventions will put you at risk; the question is when." --DR. WILL MAGNUS
IN YOUR FACE, POLITE SOCIETY!
RYAN? THIS IS MARTIN. HOW'S THE SINGULARITY TRANSLATION FIELD WORKING?
WELL, I CAN SEE AND BREATHE, SO BETTER THAN LAST TIME, I GUESS. OH, AND I HAVEN'T EXPLODED, SO THERE'S THAT.
I THINK WE'RE ALL A BIT PLEASED AND SURPRISED, RYAN.
ME, TOO.
OF COURSE, YOU HAVEN'T BEEN THERE LONG...
RYAN, I THINK WE SHOULD TAKE A MOMENT AND COLLATE OUR DATA. WHAT DO WE KNOW?
WELL, WE KNOW SOME VERY HOSTILE ALIENS FROM A SUB-MICROSCOPIC WORLD, WHO CALL THEMSELVES THE WAITING--
--ARE ATTEMPTING TO INJECT MIND-CONTROL DEVICES INTO EARTH BEINGS FOR REASONS UNKNOWN.
WE KNOW THEY'RE EXTREMELY ADVANCED.
YES, BUT THERE'S MORE TO IT, RYAN.

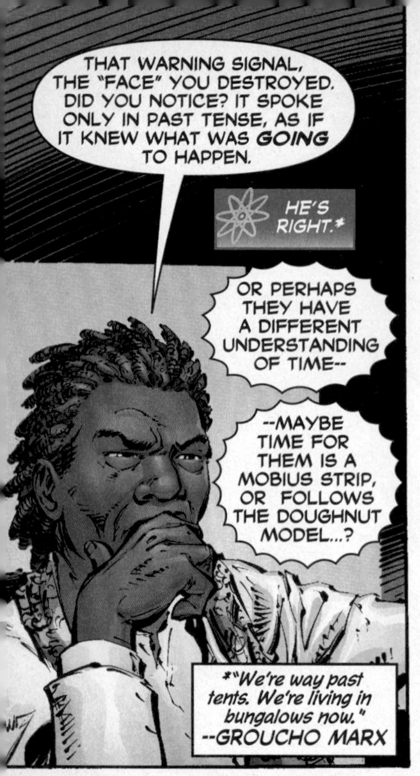
THAT WARNING SIGNAL, THE "FACE" YOU DESTROYED. DID YOU NOTICE? IT SPOKE ONLY IN PAST TENSE, AS IF IT KNEW WHAT WAS **GOING** TO HAPPEN.
HE'S RIGHT.*
OR PERHAPS THEY HAVE A DIFFERENT UNDERSTANDING OF TIME--
--MAYBE TIME FOR THEM IS A MOBIUS STRIP, OR FOLLOWS THE DOUGHNUT MODEL...?
*"We're way past tents. We're living in bungalows now." --GROUCHO MARX

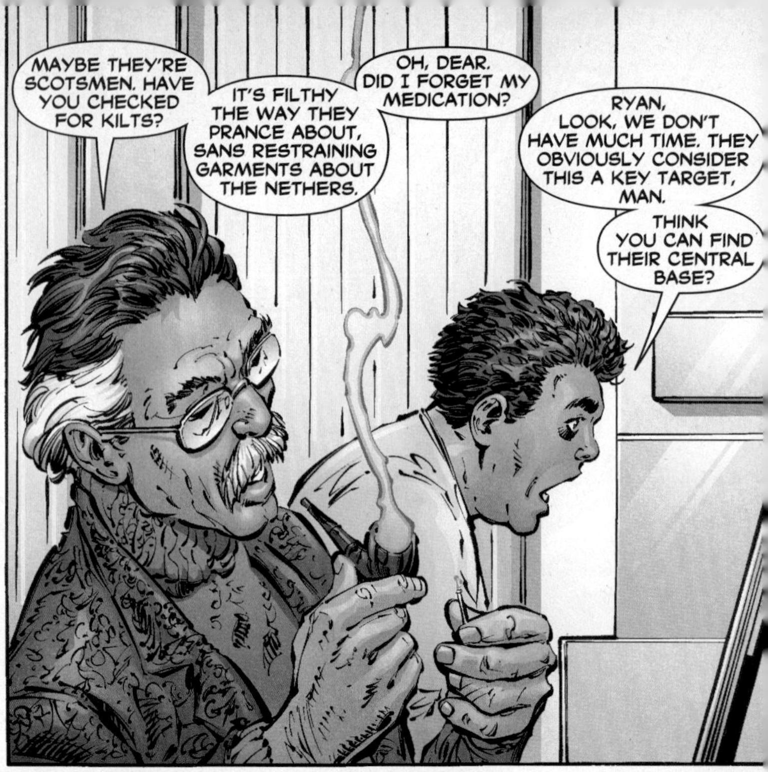
MAYBE THEY'RE SCOTSMEN. HAVE YOU CHECKED FOR KILTS?
IT'S FILTHY THE WAY THEY PRANCE ABOUT, SANS RESTRAINING GARMENTS ABOUT THE NETHERS.
OH, DEAR. DID I FORGET MY MEDICATION?
RYAN, LOOK, WE DON'T HAVE MUCH TIME. THEY OBVIOUSLY CONSIDER THIS A KEY TARGET, MAN.
THINK YOU CAN FIND THEIR CENTRAL BASE?

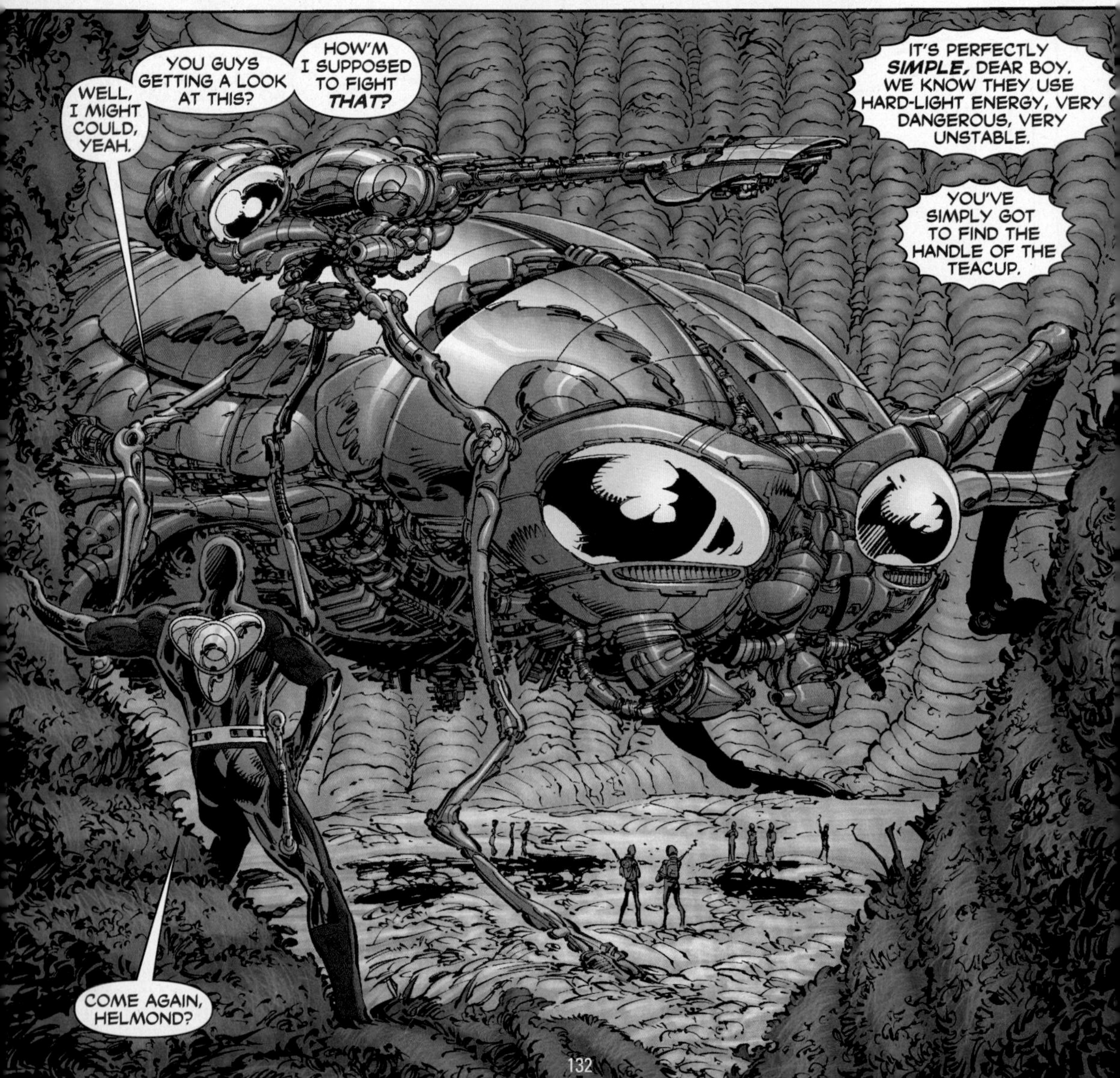
YOU GUYS GETTING A LOOK AT THIS?
HOW'M I SUPPOSED TO FIGHT **THAT?**
WELL, I MIGHT COULD, YEAH.
IT'S PERFECTLY **SIMPLE,** DEAR BOY. WE KNOW THEY USE HARD-LIGHT ENERGY, VERY DANGEROUS, VERY UNSTABLE.
YOU'VE SIMPLY GOT TO FIND THE HANDLE OF THE TEACUP.
COME AGAIN, HELMOND?

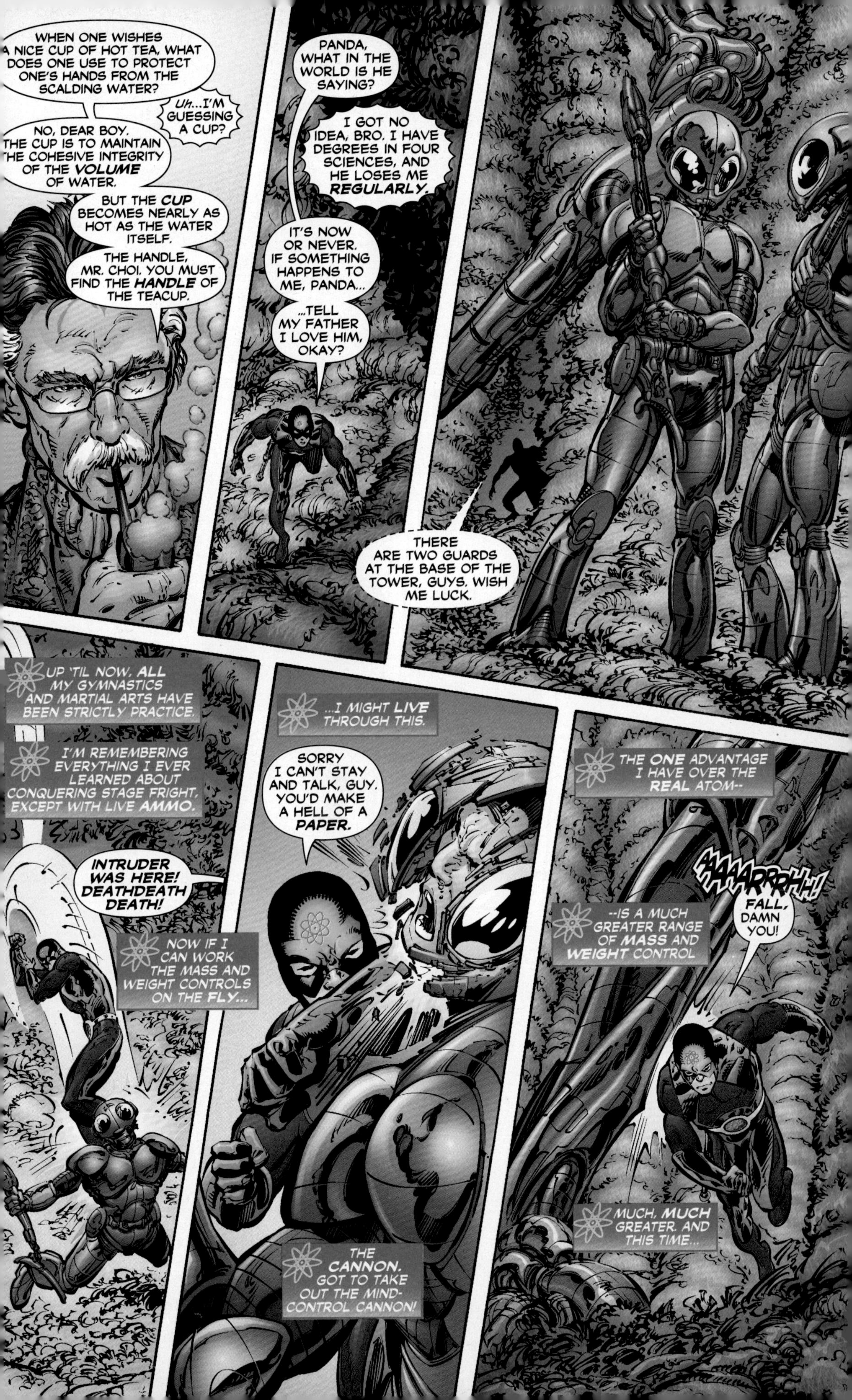
WHEN ONE WISHES A NICE CUP OF HOT TEA, WHAT DOES ONE USE TO PROTECT ONE'S HANDS FROM THE SCALDING WATER?
Uh...I'M GUESSING A CUP?
NO, DEAR BOY. THE CUP IS TO MAINTAIN THE COHESIVE INTEGRITY OF THE VOLUME OF WATER.
BUT THE CUP BECOMES NEARLY AS HOT AS THE WATER ITSELF.
THE HANDLE, MR. CHOI. YOU MUST FIND THE HANDLE OF THE TEACUP.
PANDA, WHAT IN THE WORLD IS HE SAYING?
I GOT NO IDEA, BRO. I HAVE DEGREES IN FOUR SCIENCES, AND HE LOSES ME REGULARLY.
IT'S NOW OR NEVER. IF SOMETHING HAPPENS TO ME, PANDA...
...TELL MY FATHER I LOVE HIM, OKAY?
THERE ARE TWO GUARDS AT THE BASE OF THE TOWER, GUYS. WISH ME LUCK.
UP 'TIL NOW, ALL MY GYMNASTICS AND MARTIAL ARTS HAVE BEEN STRICTLY PRACTICE.
I'M REMEMBERING EVERYTHING I EVER LEARNED ABOUT CONQUERING STAGE FRIGHT, EXCEPT WITH LIVE AMMO.
INTRUDER WAS HERE! DEATHDEATH DEATH!
NOW IF I CAN WORK THE MASS AND WEIGHT CONTROLS ON THE FLY...
...I MIGHT LIVE THROUGH THIS.
SORRY I CAN'T STAY AND TALK, GUY. YOU'D MAKE A HELL OF A PAPER.
THE CANNON. GOT TO TAKE OUT THE MIND-CONTROL CANNON!
THE ONE ADVANTAGE I HAVE OVER THE REAL ATOM--
AAAAARRRHH!
--IS A MUCH GREATER RANGE OF MASS AND WEIGHT CONTROL
FALL, DAMN YOU!
MUCH, MUCH GREATER. AND THIS TIME...

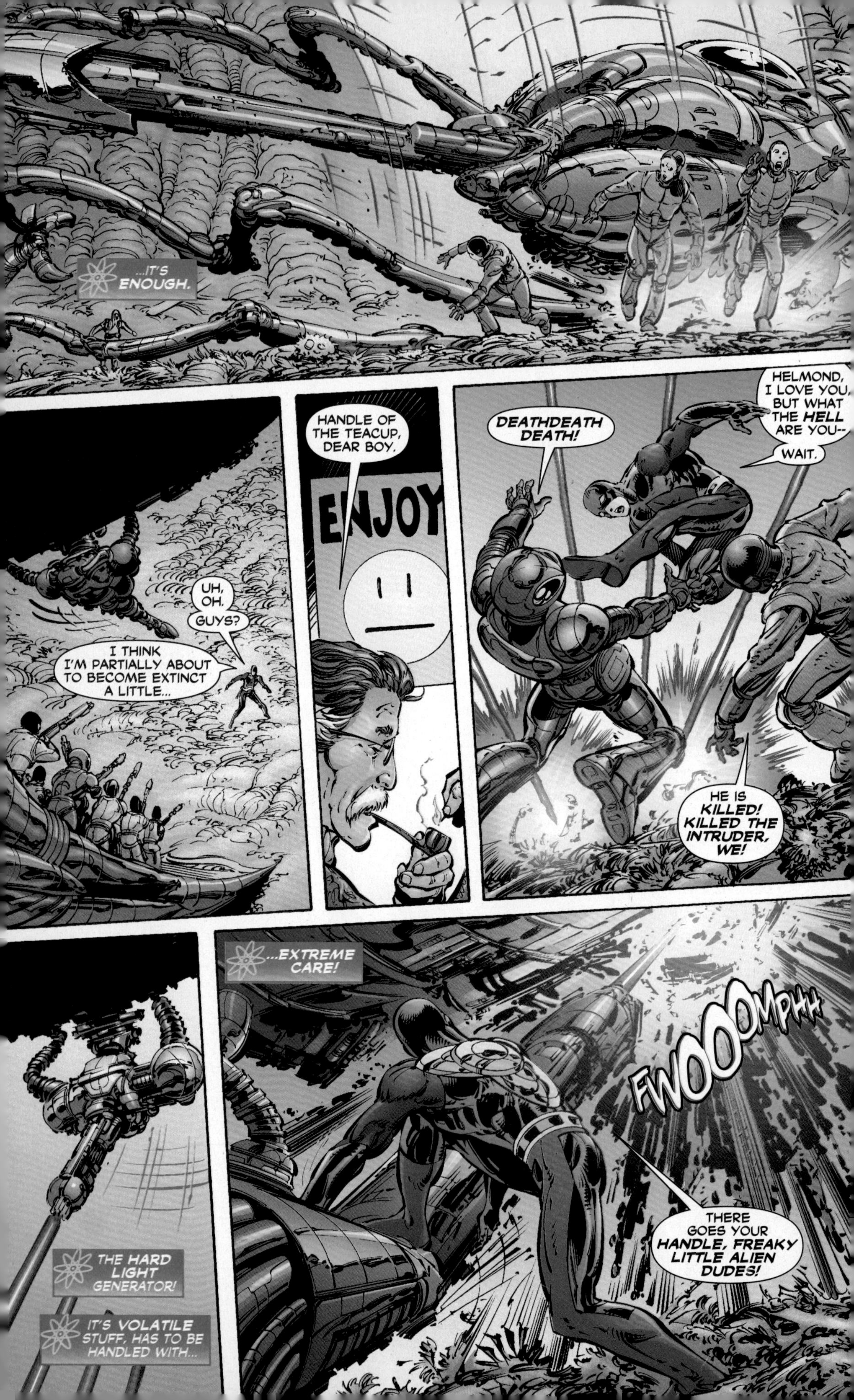
...IT'S ENOUGH.
UH, OH, GUYS?
I THINK I'M PARTIALLY ABOUT TO BECOME EXTINCT A LITTLE...
HANDLE OF THE TEACUP, DEAR BOY.
ENJOY
DEATHDEATH DEATH!
HELMOND, I LOVE YOU, BUT WHAT THE HELL ARE YOU--
WAIT.
HE IS KILLED! KILLED THE INTRUDER, WE!
THE HARD LIGHT GENERATOR!
IT'S VOLATILE STUFF, HAS TO BE HANDLED WITH...
...EXTREME CARE!
FWOOOMPHH
THERE GOES YOUR HANDLE, FREAKY LITTLE ALIEN DUDES!

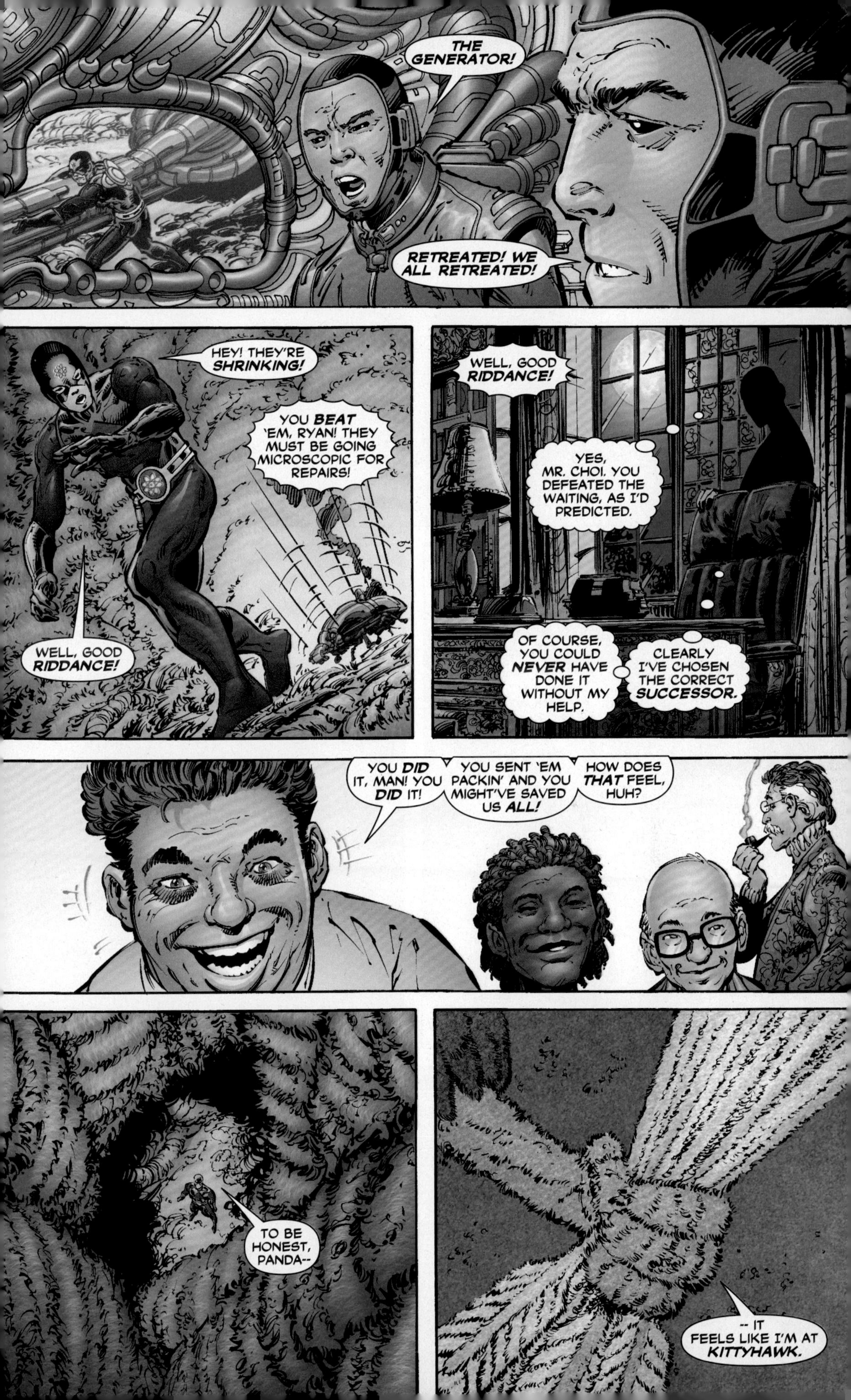
THE GENERATOR!
RETREATED! WE ALL RETREATED!
HEY! THEY'RE SHRINKING!
YOU BEAT 'EM, RYAN! THEY MUST BE GOING MICROSCOPIC FOR REPAIRS!
WELL, GOOD RIDDANCE!
WELL, GOOD RIDDANCE!
YES, MR. CHOI. YOU DEFEATED THE WAITING, AS I'D PREDICTED.
OF COURSE, YOU COULD NEVER HAVE DONE IT WITHOUT MY HELP.
CLEARLY I'VE CHOSEN THE CORRECT SUCCESSOR.
YOU DID IT, MAN! YOU DID IT!
YOU SENT 'EM PACKIN' AND YOU MIGHT'VE SAVED US ALL!
HOW DOES THAT FEEL, HUH?
TO BE HONEST, PANDA--
-- IT FEELS LIKE I'M AT KITTYHAWK.

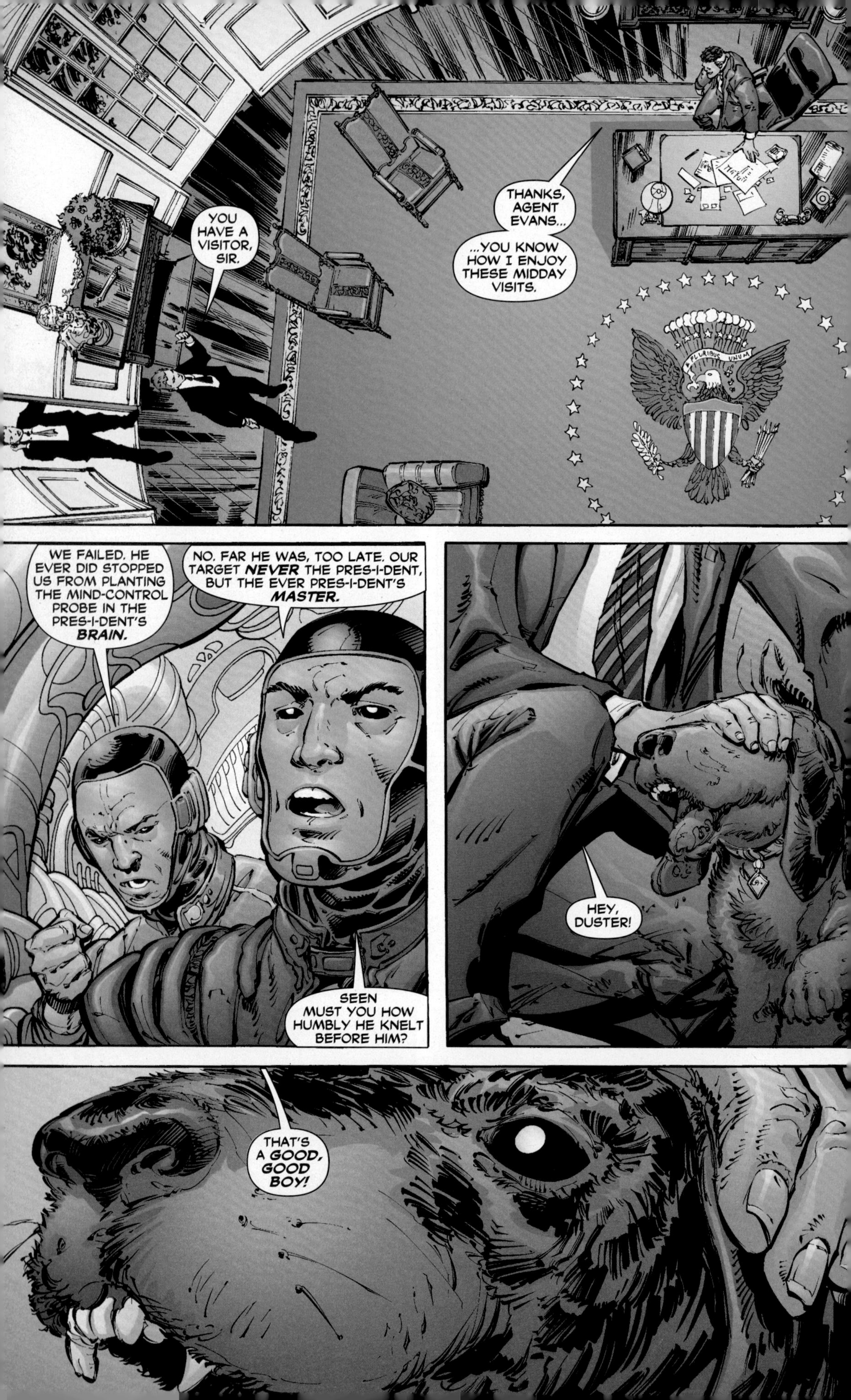
YOU HAVE A VISITOR, SIR.
THANKS, AGENT EVANS...
...YOU KNOW HOW I ENJOY THESE MIDDAY VISITS.
E PLURIBUS UNUM
WE FAILED. HE EVER DID STOPPED US FROM PLANTING THE MIND-CONTROL PROBE IN THE PRES-I-DENT'S **BRAIN.**
NO. FAR HE WAS, TOO LATE. OUR TARGET **NEVER** THE PRES-I-DENT, BUT THE EVER PRES-I-DENT'S **MASTER.**
SEEN MUST YOU HOW HUMBLY HE KNELT BEFORE HIM?
HEY, DUSTER!
THAT'S A **GOOD, GOOD BOY!**

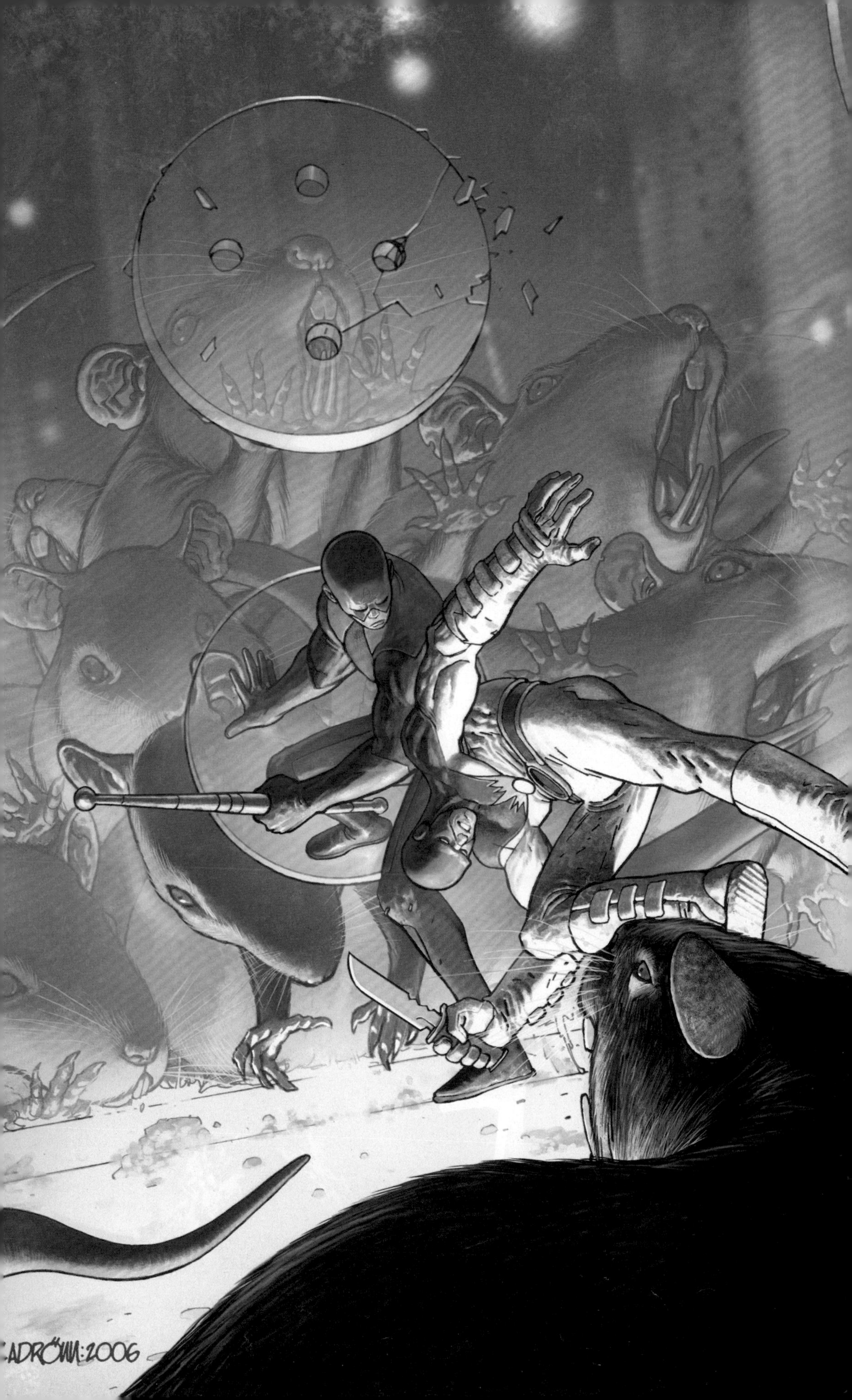
CADRÖNN:2006

MY LIFE IN MINIATURE: PART SIX
CHARGED PARTICLES

from **THE ALL NEW ATOM #6**
Cover by **Ladronn**

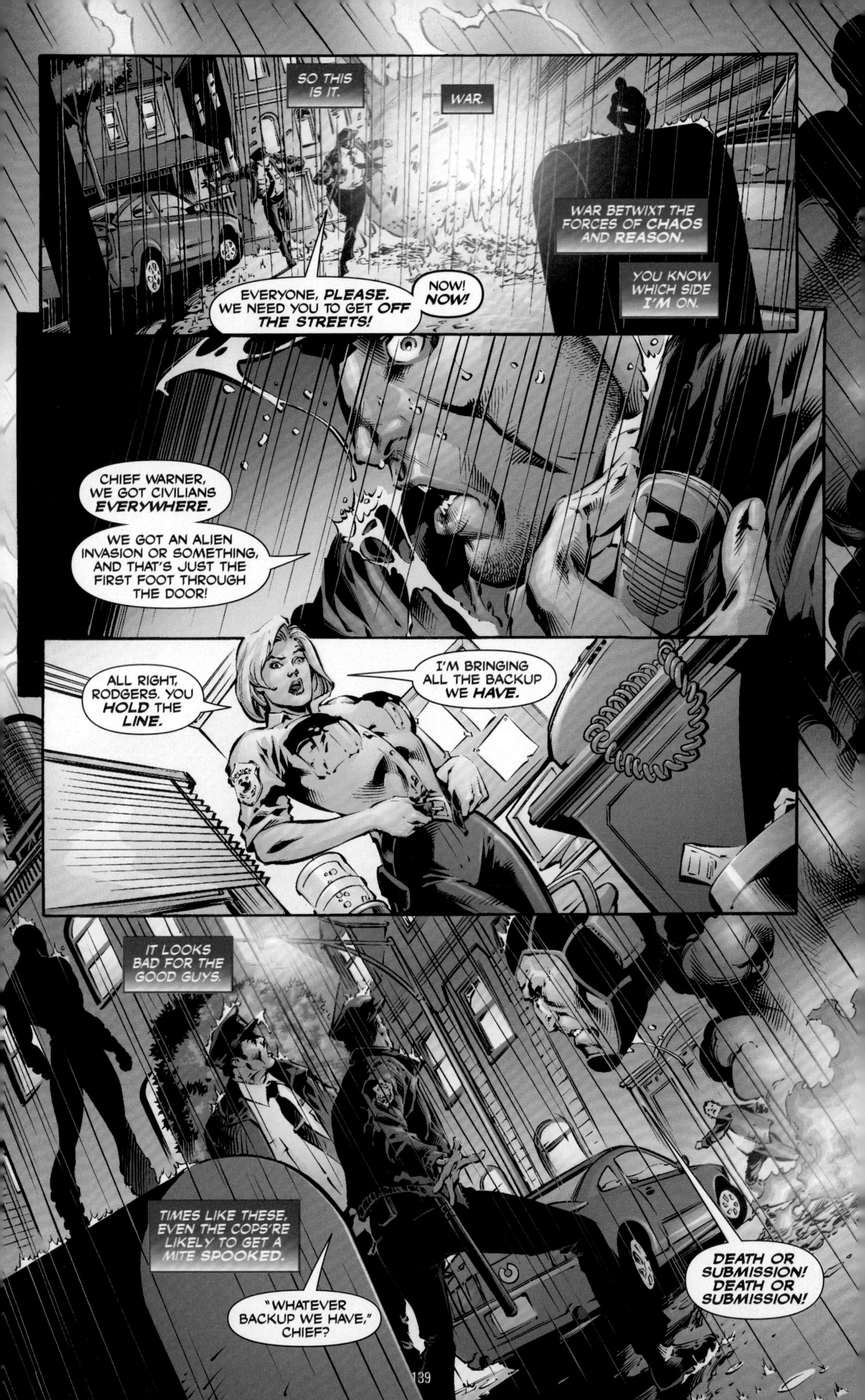
SO THIS IS IT.
WAR.
WAR BETWIXT THE FORCES OF CHAOS AND REASON.
YOU KNOW WHICH SIDE I'M ON.
EVERYONE, PLEASE. WE NEED YOU TO GET OFF THE STREETS!
NOW! NOW!
CHIEF WARNER, WE GOT CIVILIANS EVERYWHERE.
WE GOT AN ALIEN INVASION OR SOMETHING, AND THAT'S JUST THE FIRST FOOT THROUGH THE DOOR!
ALL RIGHT, RODGERS. YOU HOLD THE LINE.
I'M BRINGING ALL THE BACKUP WE HAVE.
IT LOOKS BAD FOR THE GOOD GUYS.
TIMES LIKE THESE, EVEN THE COPS'RE LIKELY TO GET A MITE SPOOKED.
"WHATEVER BACKUP WE HAVE," CHIEF?
DEATH OR SUBMISSION! DEATH OR SUBMISSION!

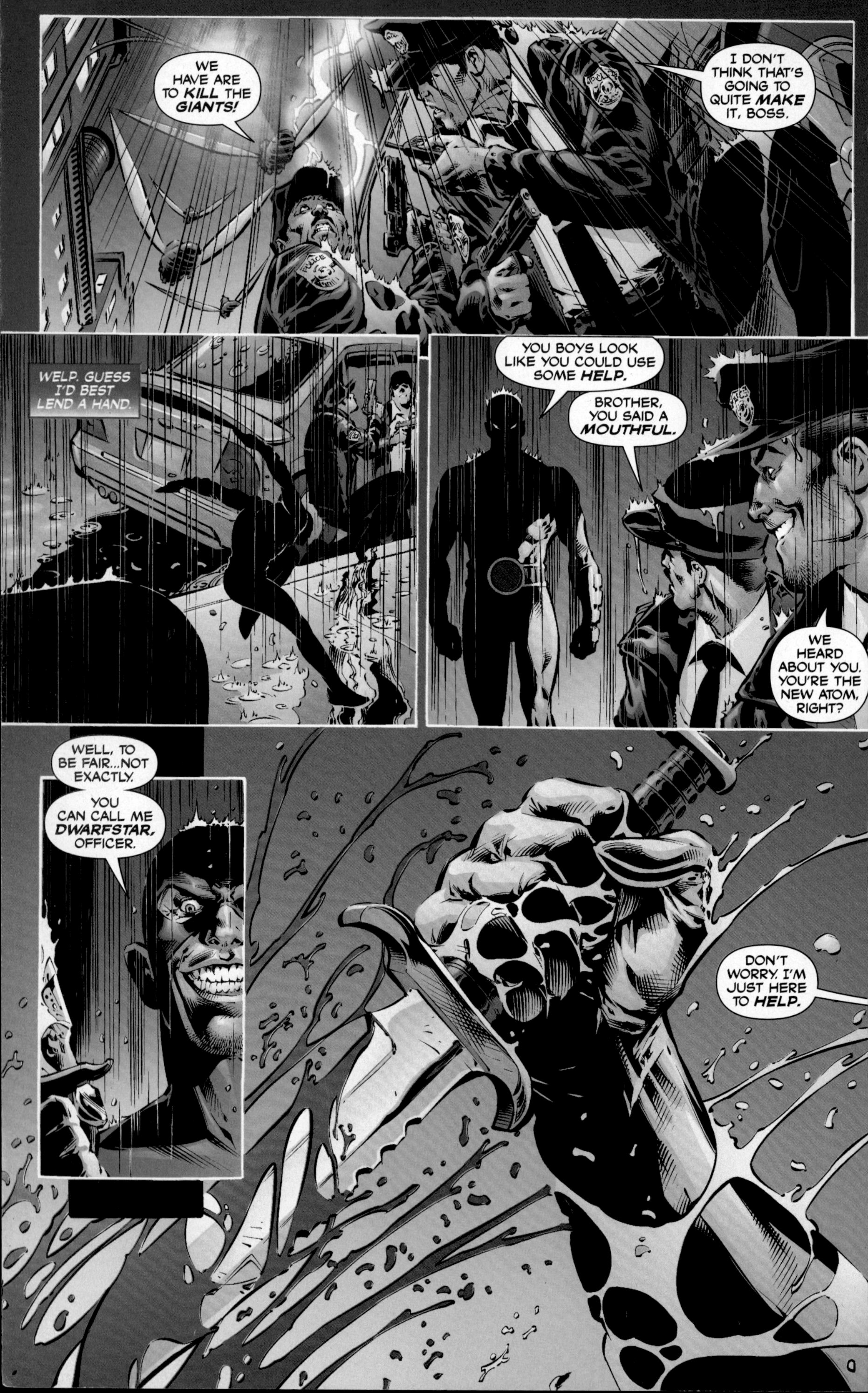
WE HAVE ARE TO KILL THE GIANTS!
I DON'T THINK THAT'S GOING TO QUITE MAKE IT, BOSS.
WELP. GUESS I'D BEST LEND A HAND.
YOU BOYS LOOK LIKE YOU COULD USE SOME HELP.
BROTHER, YOU SAID A MOUTHFUL.
WE HEARD ABOUT YOU. YOU'RE THE NEW ATOM, RIGHT?
WELL, TO BE FAIR...NOT EXACTLY.
YOU CAN CALL ME DWARFSTAR, OFFICER.
DON'T WORRY. I'M JUST HERE TO HELP.

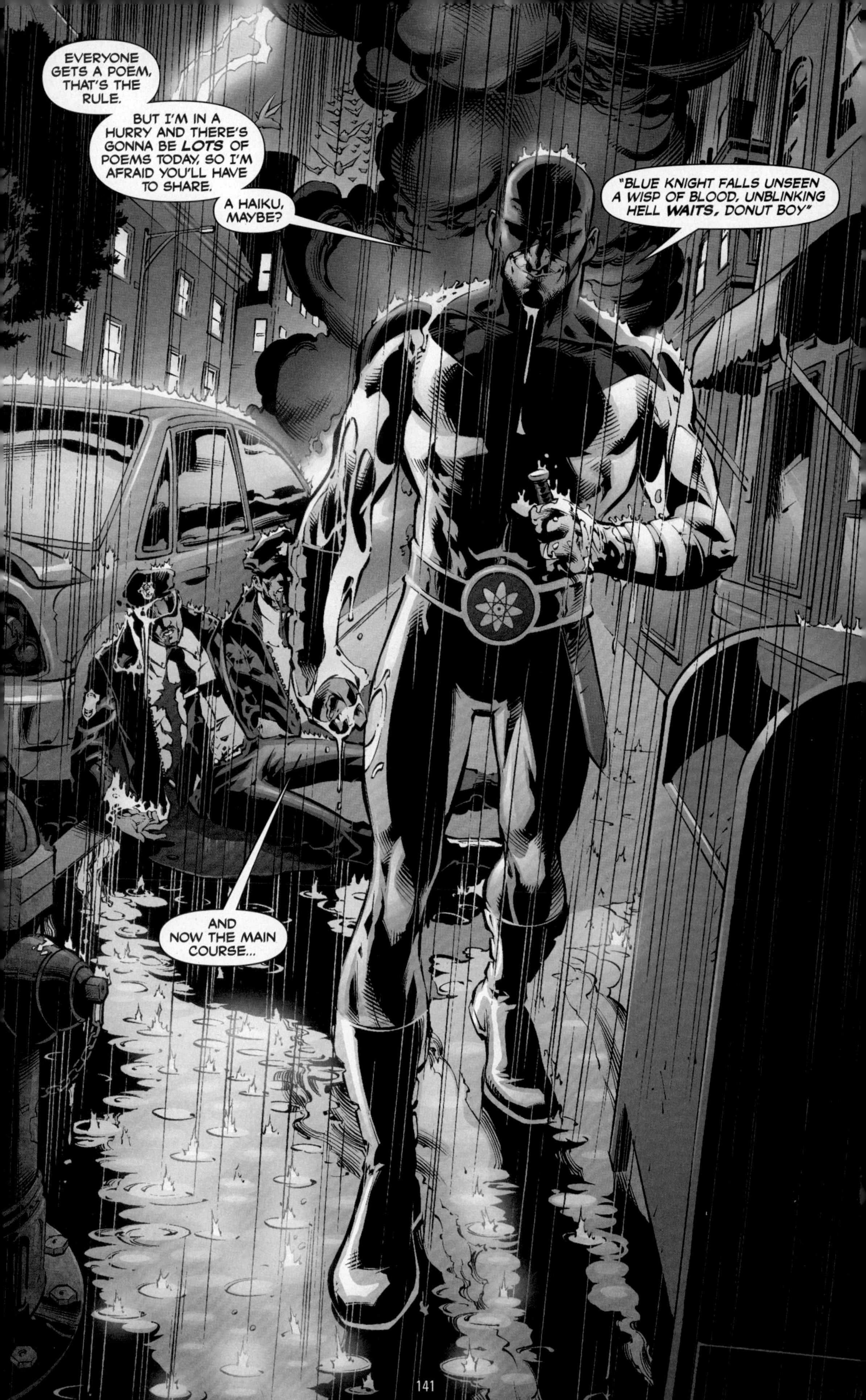
EVERYONE GETS A POEM, THAT'S THE RULE.
BUT I'M IN A HURRY AND THERE'S GONNA BE LOTS OF POEMS TODAY, SO I'M AFRAID YOU'LL HAVE TO SHARE.
A HAIKU, MAYBE?
"BLUE KNIGHT FALLS UNSEEN A WISP OF BLOOD, UNBLINKING HELL WAITS, DONUT BOY"
AND NOW THE MAIN COURSE...

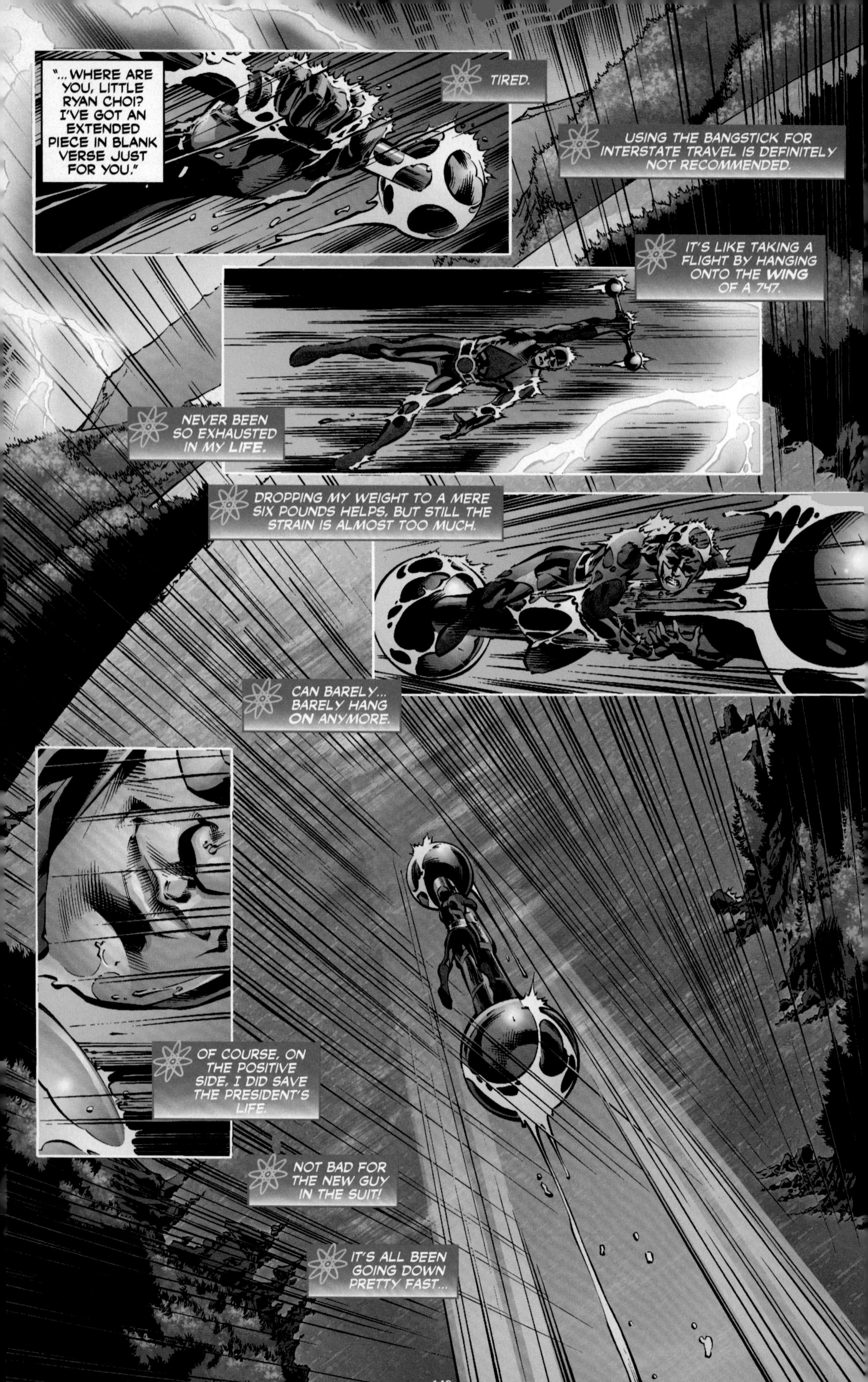
"...WHERE ARE YOU, LITTLE RYAN CHOI? I'VE GOT AN EXTENDED PIECE IN BLANK VERSE JUST FOR YOU."
TIRED.
USING THE BANGSTICK FOR INTERSTATE TRAVEL IS DEFINITELY NOT RECOMMENDED.
IT'S LIKE TAKING A FLIGHT BY HANGING ONTO THE WING OF A 747.
NEVER BEEN SO EXHAUSTED IN MY LIFE.
DROPPING MY WEIGHT TO A MERE SIX POUNDS HELPS, BUT STILL THE STRAIN IS ALMOST TOO MUCH.
CAN BARELY... BARELY HANG ON ANYMORE.
OF COURSE, ON THE POSITIVE SIDE, I DID SAVE THE PRESIDENT'S LIFE.
NOT BAD FOR THE NEW GUY IN THE SUIT!
IT'S ALL BEEN GOING DOWN PRETTY FAST...

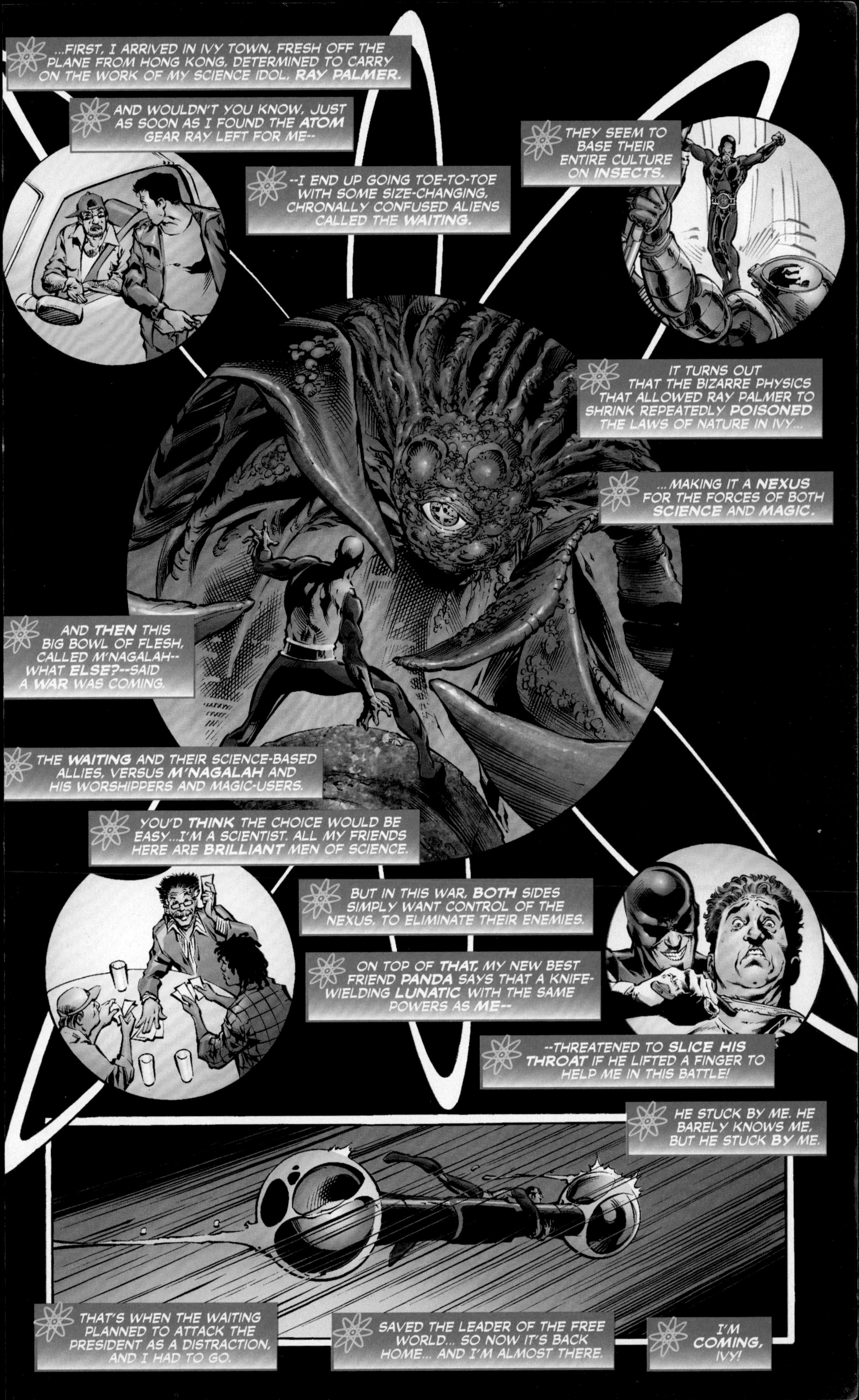
...FIRST, I ARRIVED IN IVY TOWN, FRESH OFF THE PLANE FROM HONG KONG, DETERMINED TO CARRY ON THE WORK OF MY SCIENCE IDOL, RAY PALMER.
AND WOULDN'T YOU KNOW, JUST AS SOON AS I FOUND THE ATOM GEAR RAY LEFT FOR ME--
--I END UP GOING TOE-TO-TOE WITH SOME SIZE-CHANGING, CHRONALLY CONFUSED ALIENS CALLED THE WAITING.
THEY SEEM TO BASE THEIR ENTIRE CULTURE ON INSECTS.
IT TURNS OUT THAT THE BIZARRE PHYSICS THAT ALLOWED RAY PALMER TO SHRINK REPEATEDLY POISONED THE LAWS OF NATURE IN IVY...
...MAKING IT A NEXUS FOR THE FORCES OF BOTH SCIENCE AND MAGIC.
AND THEN THIS BIG BOWL OF FLESH, CALLED M'NAGALAH-- WHAT ELSE?--SAID A WAR WAS COMING.
THE WAITING AND THEIR SCIENCE-BASED ALLIES, VERSUS M'NAGALAH AND HIS WORSHIPPERS AND MAGIC-USERS.
YOU'D THINK THE CHOICE WOULD BE EASY...I'M A SCIENTIST. ALL MY FRIENDS HERE ARE BRILLIANT MEN OF SCIENCE.
BUT IN THIS WAR, BOTH SIDES SIMPLY WANT CONTROL OF THE NEXUS, TO ELIMINATE THEIR ENEMIES.
ON TOP OF THAT, MY NEW BEST FRIEND PANDA SAYS THAT A KNIFE-WIELDING LUNATIC WITH THE SAME POWERS AS ME--
--THREATENED TO SLICE HIS THROAT IF HE LIFTED A FINGER TO HELP ME IN THIS BATTLE!
HE STUCK BY ME. HE BARELY KNOWS ME, BUT HE STUCK BY ME.
THAT'S WHEN THE WAITING PLANNED TO ATTACK THE PRESIDENT AS A DISTRACTION, AND I HAD TO GO.
SAVED THE LEADER OF THE FREE WORLD... SO NOW IT'S BACK HOME... AND I'M ALMOST THERE.
I'M COMING, IVY!

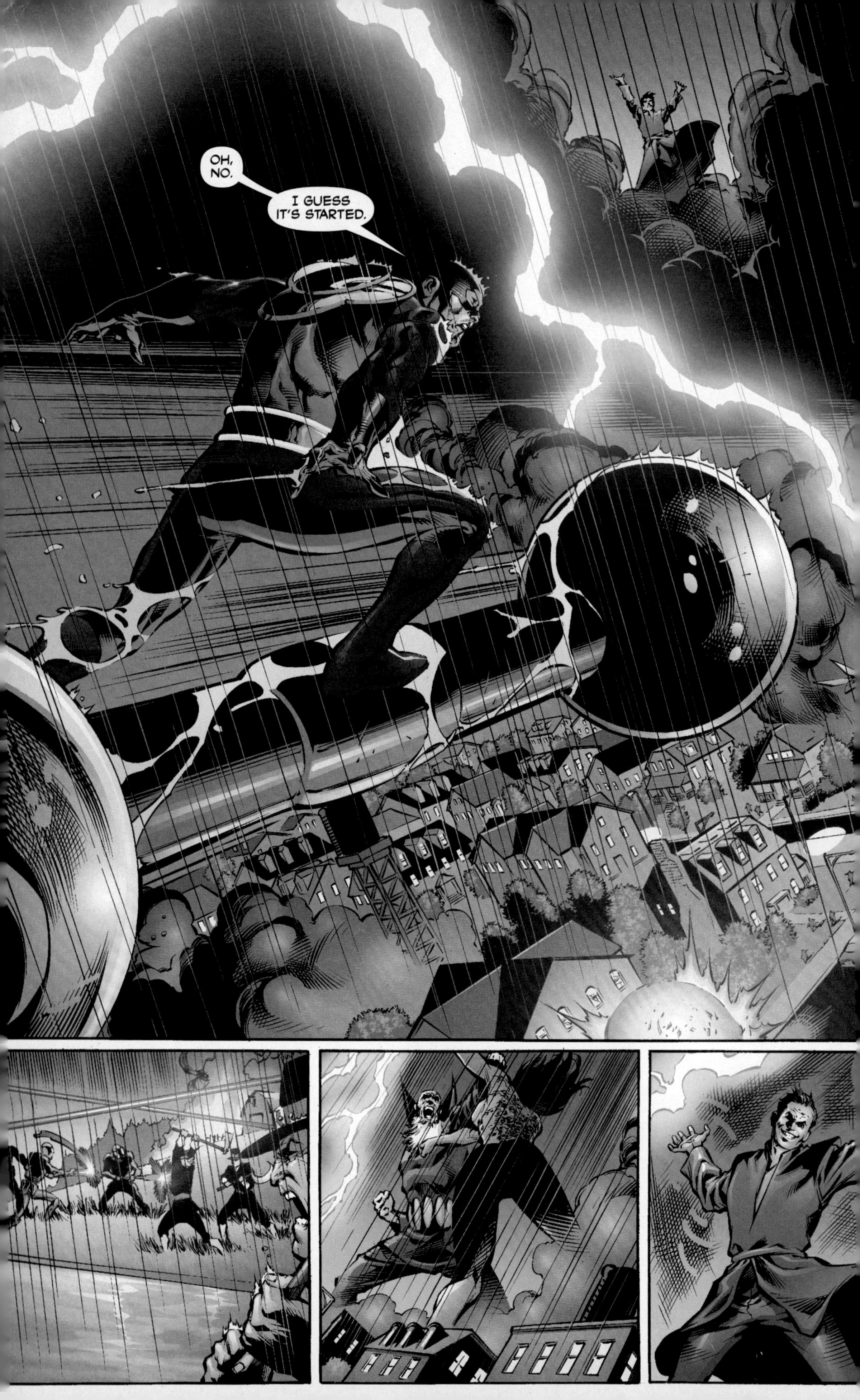
OH, NO.
I GUESS IT'S STARTED.

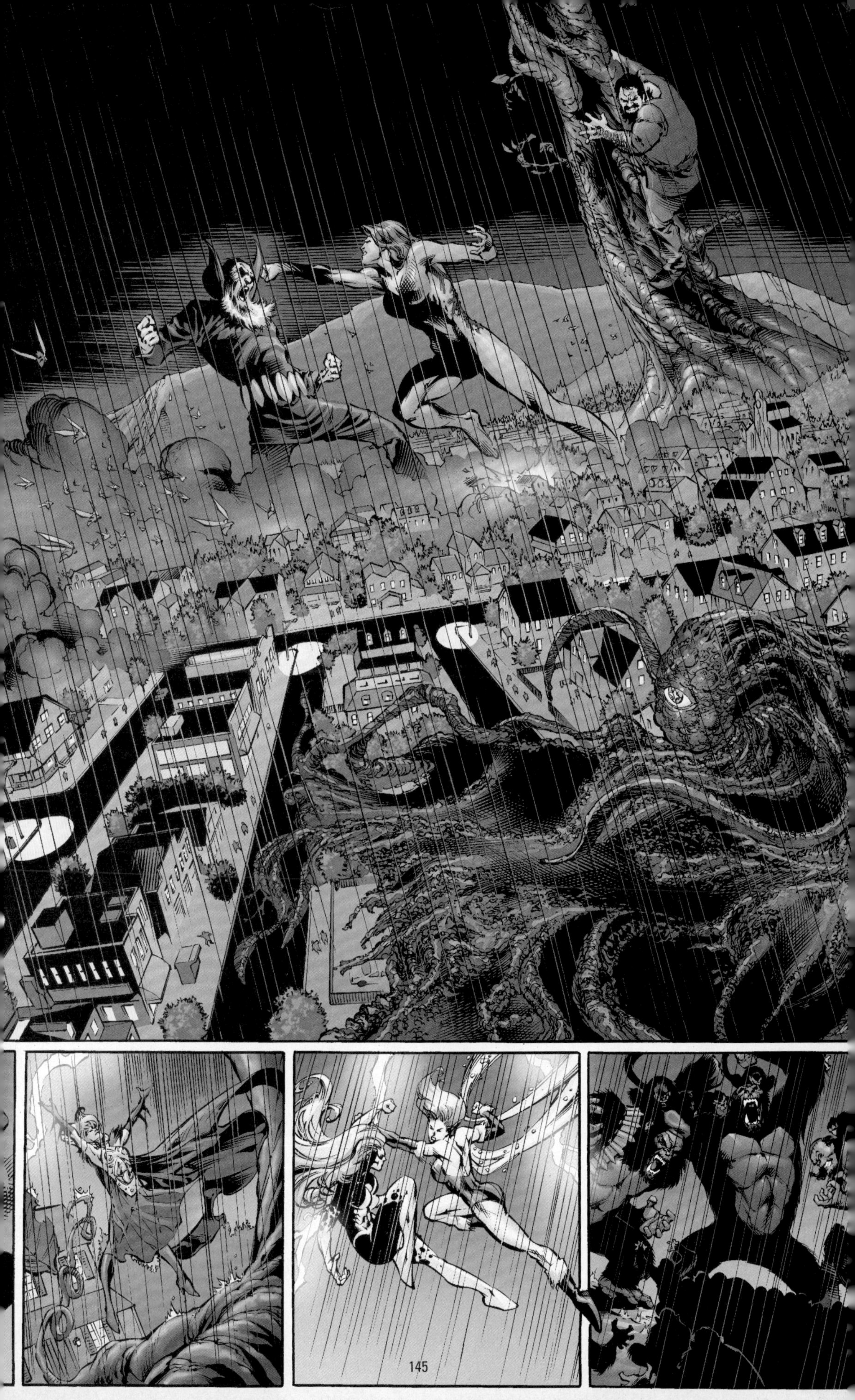

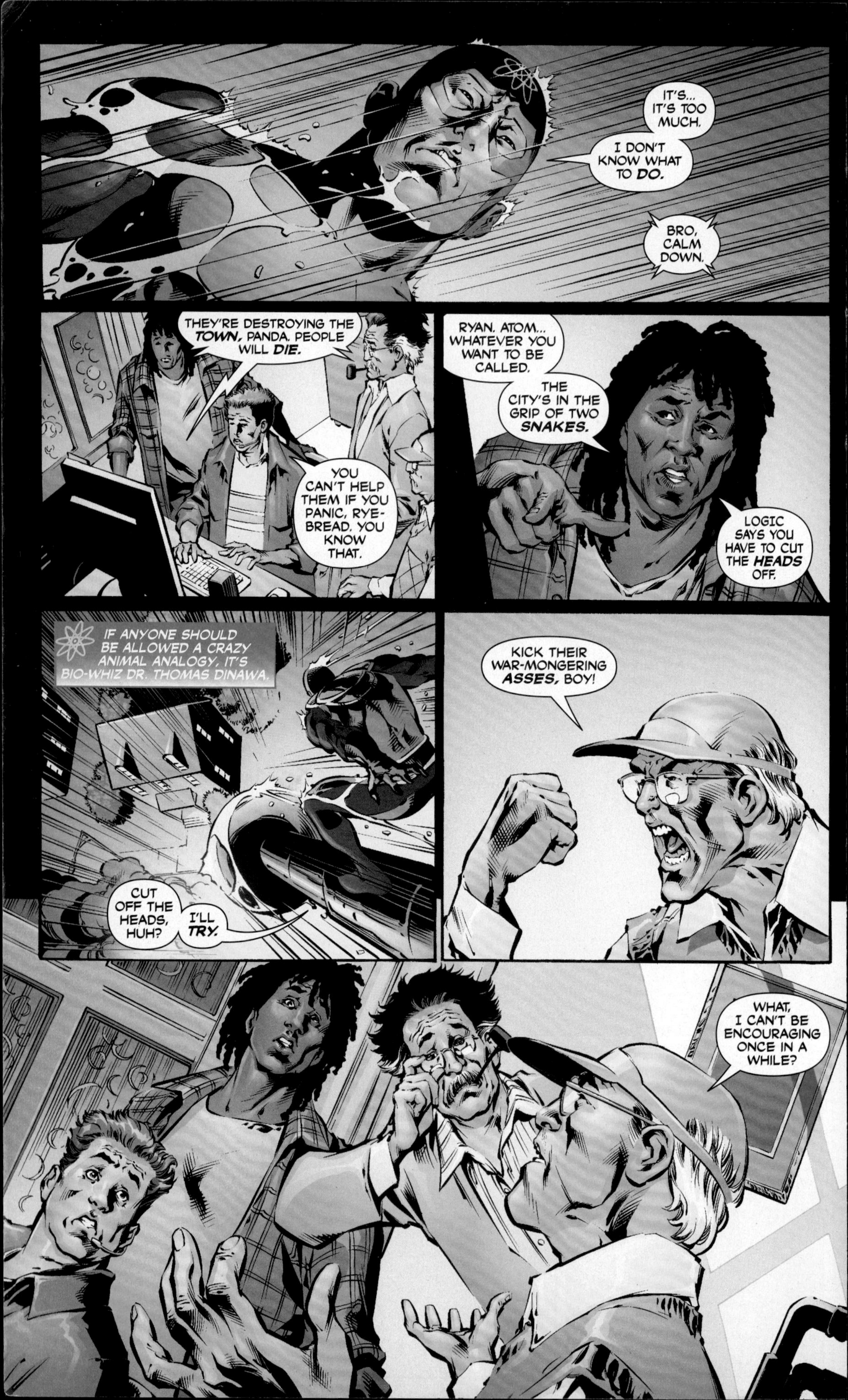
IT'S... IT'S TOO MUCH.
I DON'T KNOW WHAT TO **DO.**
BRO, CALM DOWN.
THEY'RE DESTROYING THE ***TOWN,*** PANDA. PEOPLE WILL ***DIE.***
YOU CAN'T HELP THEM IF YOU PANIC, RYE-BREAD. YOU KNOW THAT.
RYAN. ATOM... WHATEVER YOU WANT TO BE CALLED.
THE CITY'S IN THE GRIP OF TWO ***SNAKES.***
LOGIC SAYS YOU HAVE TO CUT THE ***HEADS*** OFF.
IF ANYONE SHOULD BE ALLOWED A CRAZY ANIMAL ANALOGY, IT'S BIO-WHIZ DR. THOMAS DINAWA.
CUT OFF THE HEADS, HUH?
I'LL ***TRY.***
KICK THEIR WAR-MONGERING ***ASSES,*** BOY!
WHAT, I CAN'T BE ENCOURAGING ONCE IN A WHILE?

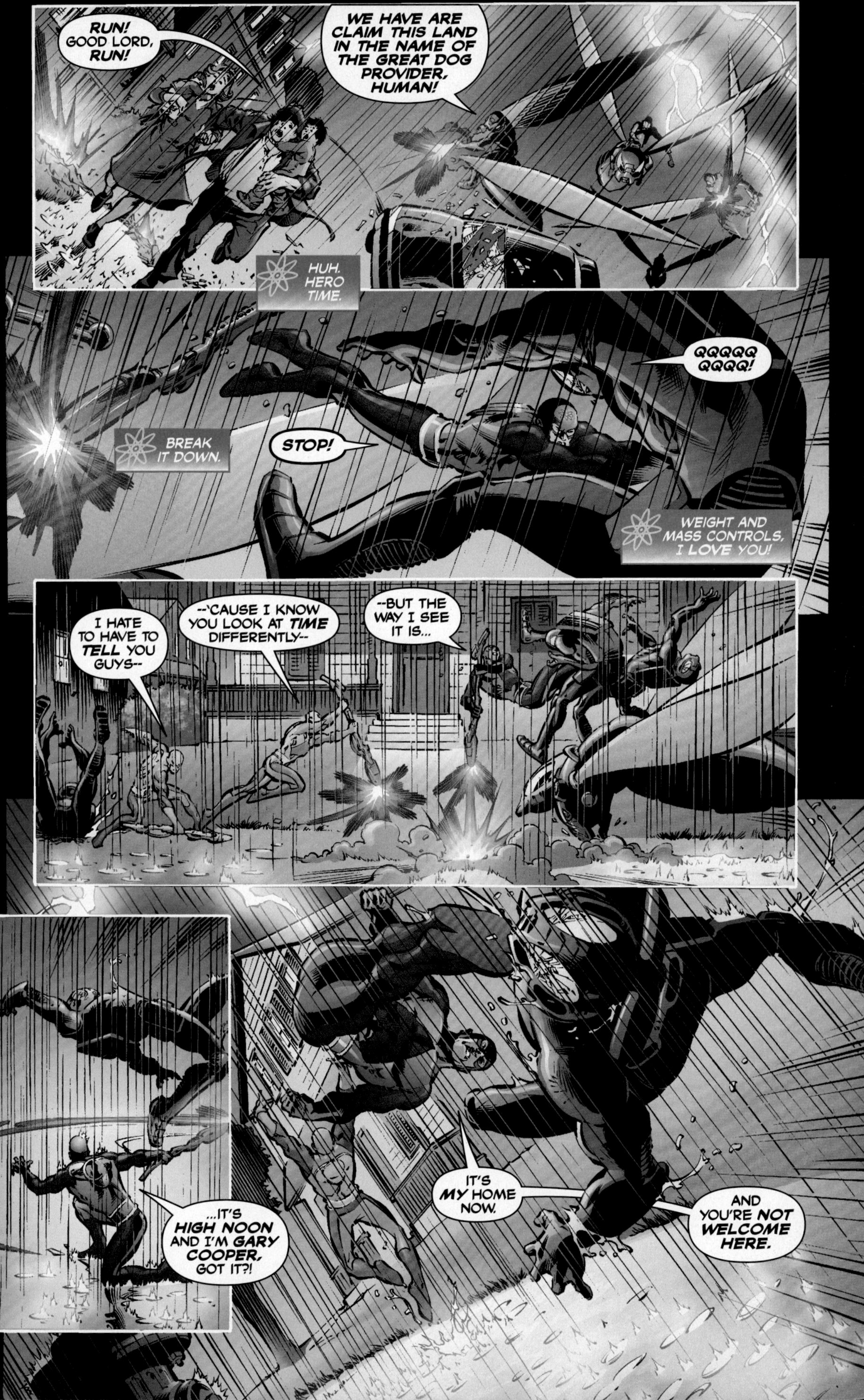
RUN! GOOD LORD, RUN!
WE HAVE ARE CLAIM THIS LAND IN THE NAME OF THE GREAT DOG PROVIDER, HUMAN!
HUH. HERO TIME.
QQQQQ QQQQ!
BREAK IT DOWN.
STOP!
WEIGHT AND MASS CONTROLS, I LOVE YOU!
I HATE TO HAVE TO TELL YOU GUYS--
--'CAUSE I KNOW YOU LOOK AT TIME DIFFERENTLY--
--BUT THE WAY I SEE IT IS...
...IT'S HIGH NOON AND I'M GARY COOPER, GOT IT?!
IT'S MY HOME NOW.
AND YOU'RE NOT WELCOME HERE.

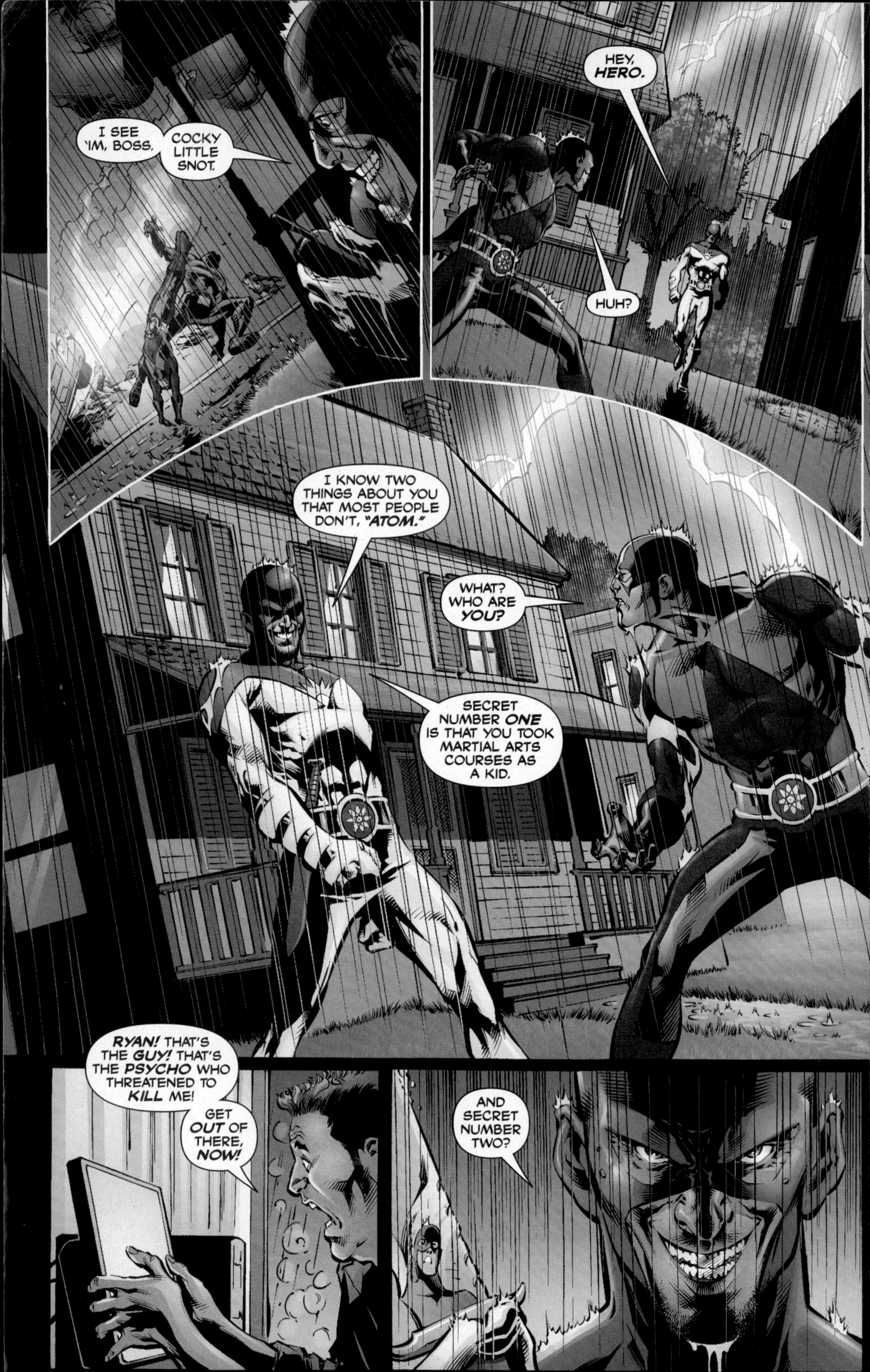
I SEE 'IM, BOSS.
COCKY LITTLE SNOT.
HEY, HERO.
HUH?
I KNOW TWO THINGS ABOUT YOU THAT MOST PEOPLE DON'T, "ATOM."
WHAT? WHO ARE YOU?
SECRET NUMBER ONE IS THAT YOU TOOK MARTIAL ARTS COURSES AS A KID.
RYAN! THAT'S THE GUY! THAT'S THE PSYCHO WHO THREATENED TO KILL ME!
GET OUT OF THERE, NOW!
AND SECRET NUMBER TWO?

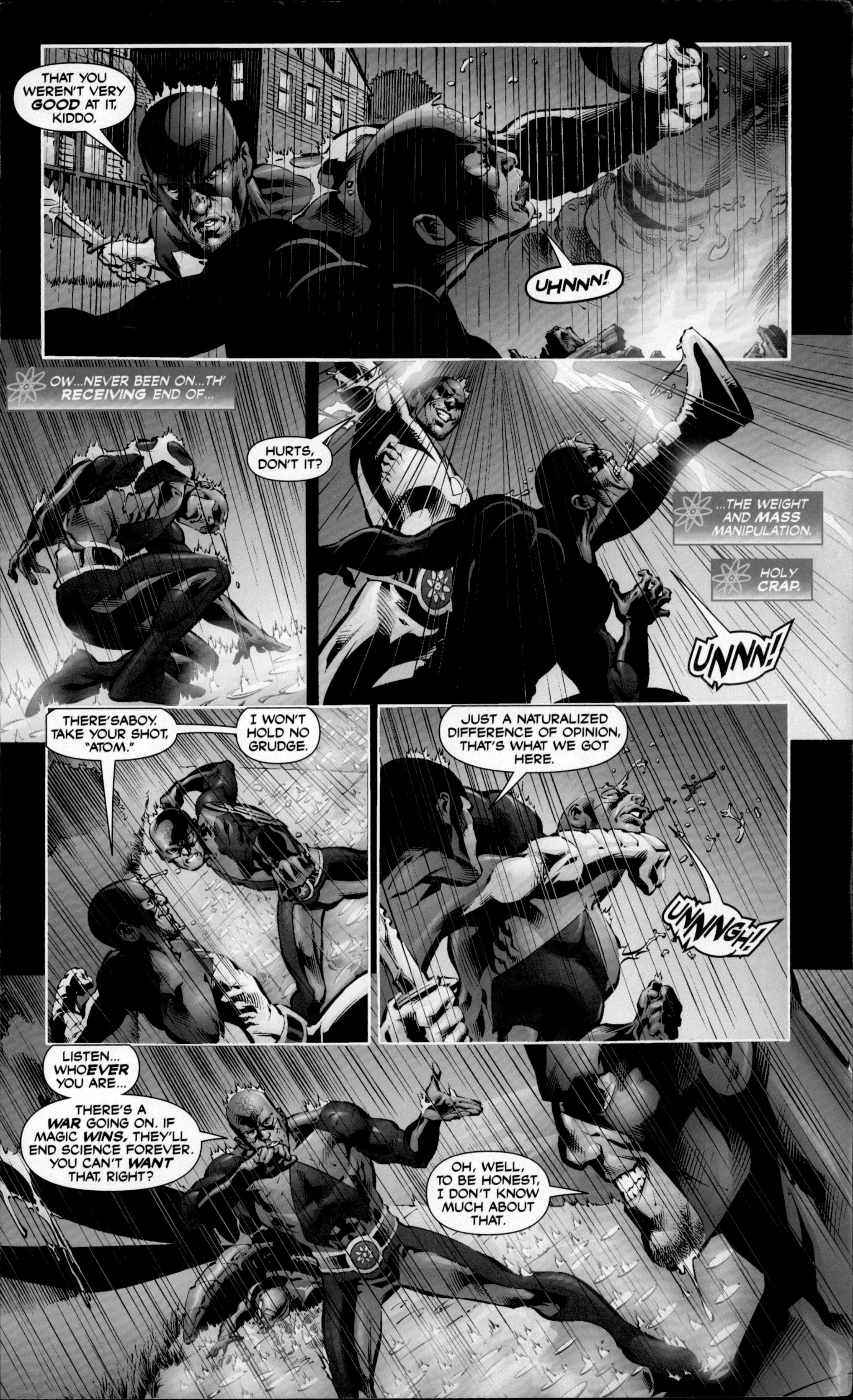
THAT YOU WEREN'T VERY GOOD AT IT, KIDDO.
UHNNN!
OW...NEVER BEEN ON...TH' RECEIVING END OF...
HURTS, DON'T IT?
...THE WEIGHT AND MASS MANIPULATION.
HOLY CRAP.
UNNN!
THERE'SABOY. TAKE YOUR SHOT, "ATOM."
I WON'T HOLD NO GRUDGE.
JUST A NATURALIZED DIFFERENCE OF OPINION, THAT'S WHAT WE GOT HERE.
UNNNGH!
LISTEN... WHOEVER YOU ARE...
THERE'S A WAR GOING ON. IF MAGIC WINS, THEY'LL END SCIENCE FOREVER. YOU CAN'T WANT THAT, RIGHT?
OH, WELL, TO BE HONEST, I DON'T KNOW MUCH ABOUT THAT.

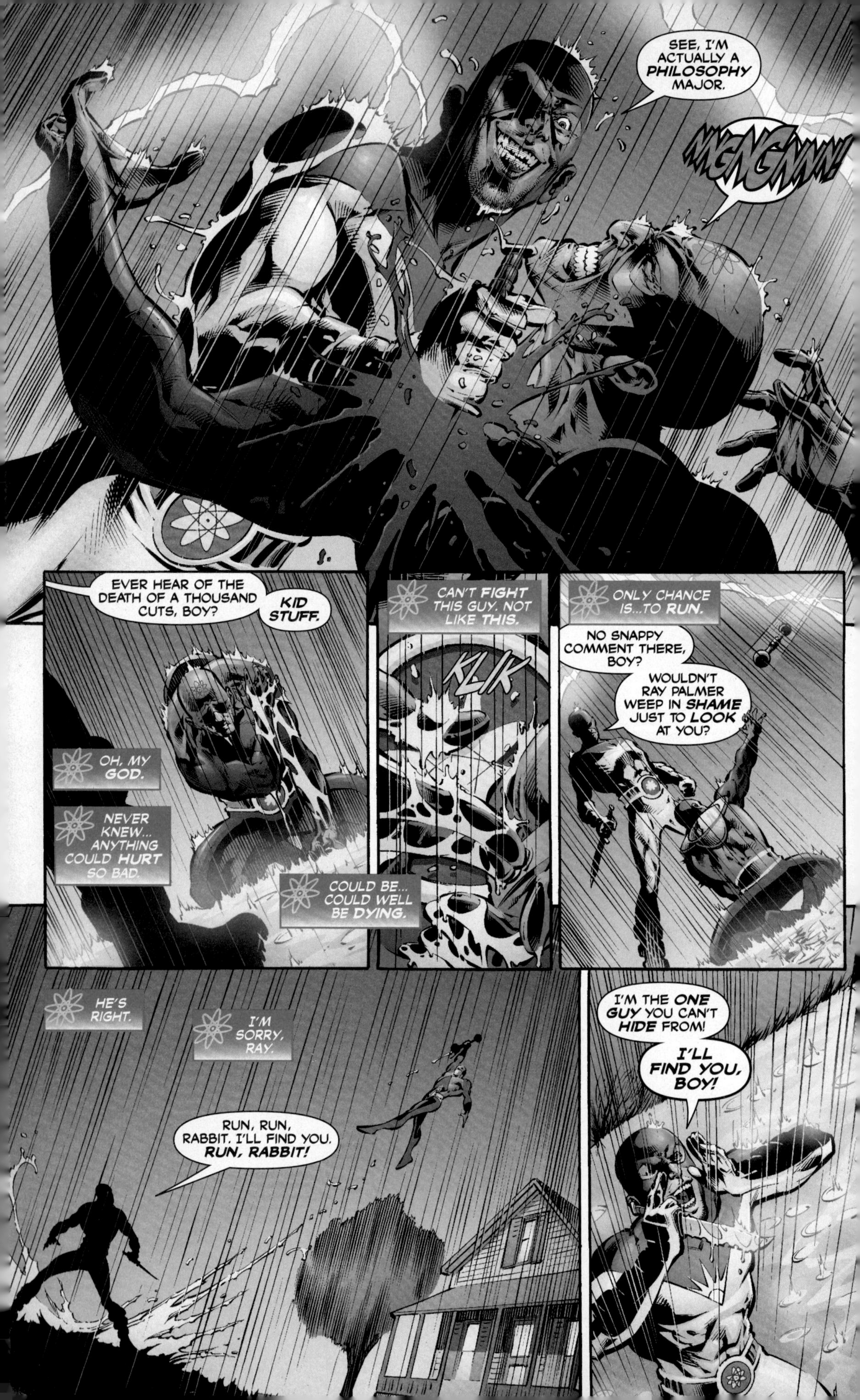
SEE, I'M ACTUALLY A PHILOSOPHY MAJOR.
NNGNGNNN!
EVER HEAR OF THE DEATH OF A THOUSAND CUTS, BOY? KID STUFF.
OH, MY GOD.
NEVER KNEW... ANYTHING COULD HURT SO BAD.
CAN'T FIGHT THIS GUY. NOT LIKE THIS.
KLIK
COULD BE... COULD WELL BE DYING.
ONLY CHANCE IS...TO RUN.
NO SNAPPY COMMENT THERE, BOY?
WOULDN'T RAY PALMER WEEP IN SHAME JUST TO LOOK AT YOU?
HE'S RIGHT.
I'M SORRY, RAY.
RUN, RUN, RABBIT. I'LL FIND YOU. RUN, RABBIT!
I'M THE ONE GUY YOU CAN'T HIDE FROM!
I'LL FIND YOU, BOY!

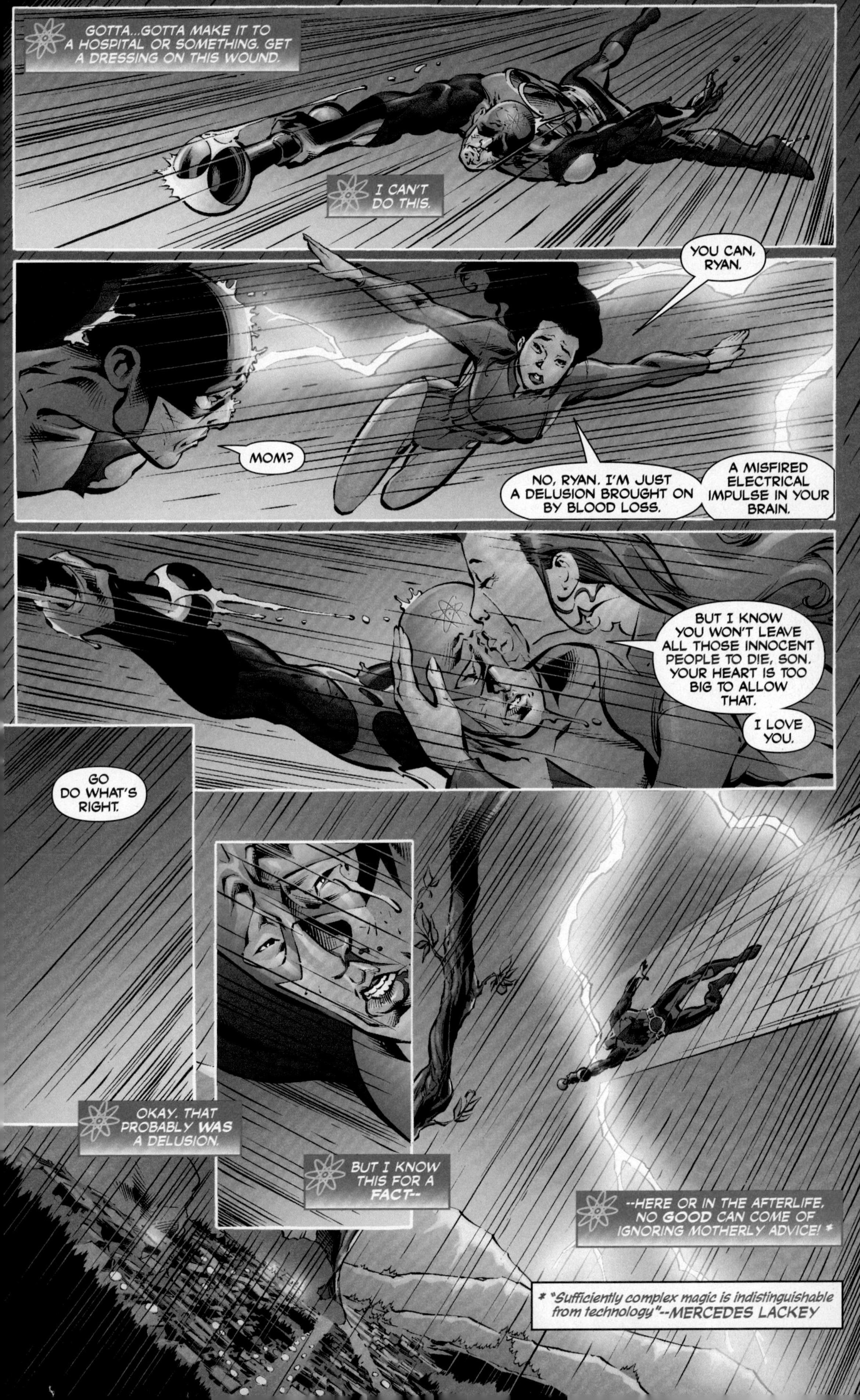
GOTTA...GOTTA MAKE IT TO A HOSPITAL OR SOMETHING. GET A DRESSING ON THIS WOUND.
I CAN'T DO THIS.
YOU CAN, RYAN.
MOM?
NO, RYAN. I'M JUST A DELUSION BROUGHT ON BY BLOOD LOSS.
A MISFIRED ELECTRICAL IMPULSE IN YOUR BRAIN.
BUT I KNOW YOU WON'T LEAVE ALL THOSE INNOCENT PEOPLE TO DIE, SON. YOUR HEART IS TOO BIG TO ALLOW THAT.
I LOVE YOU.
GO DO WHAT'S RIGHT.
OKAY. THAT PROBABLY WAS A DELUSION.
BUT I KNOW THIS FOR A FACT--
--HERE OR IN THE AFTERLIFE, NO GOOD CAN COME OF IGNORING MOTHERLY ADVICE! *
* "Sufficiently complex magic is indistinguishable from technology"--MERCEDES LACKEY

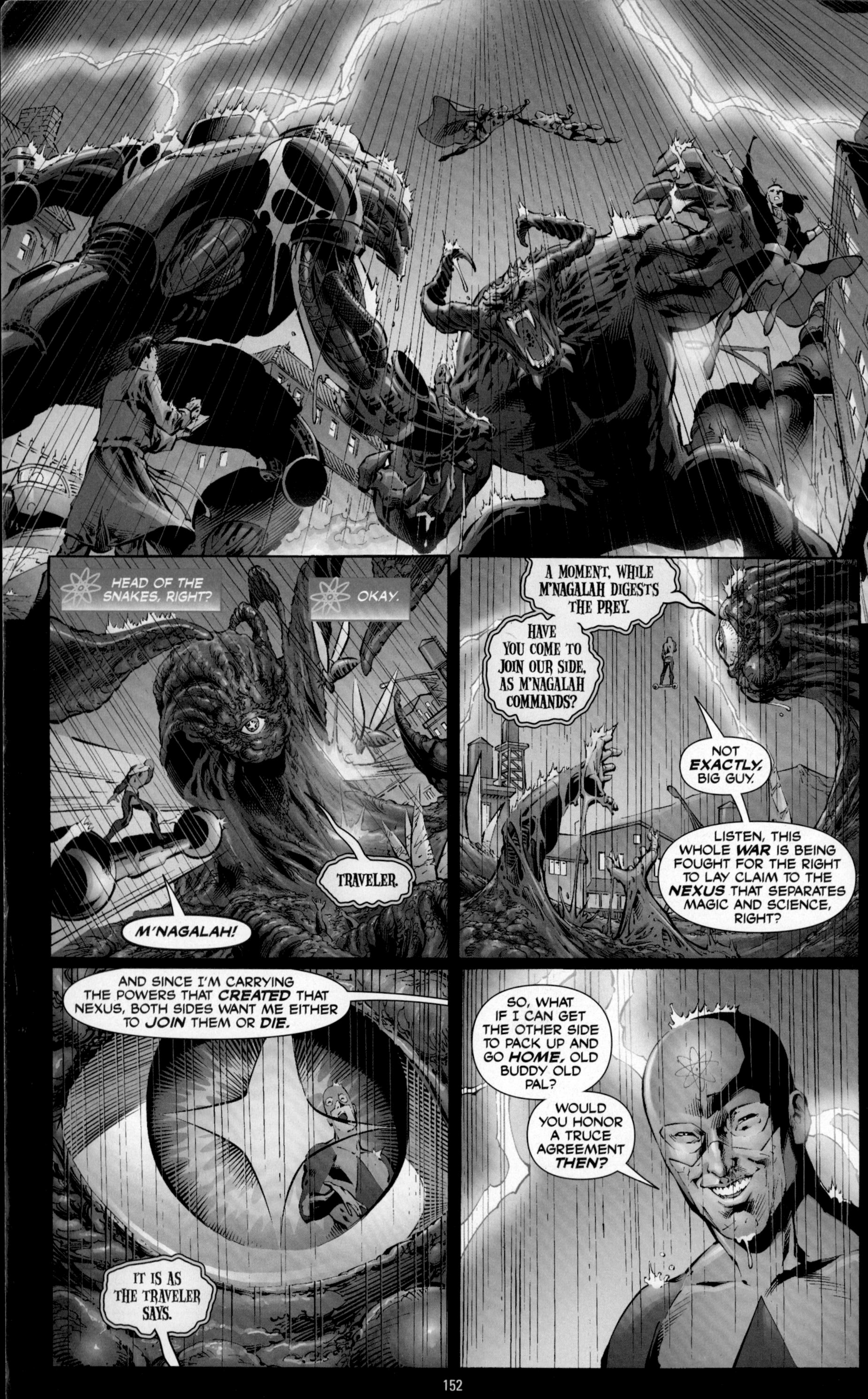
HEAD OF THE SNAKES, RIGHT?
OKAY.
M'NAGALAH!
TRAVELER.
A MOMENT, WHILE M'NAGALAH DIGESTS THE PREY.
HAVE YOU COME TO JOIN OUR SIDE, AS M'NAGALAH COMMANDS?
NOT EXACTLY, BIG GUY.
LISTEN, THIS WHOLE WAR IS BEING FOUGHT FOR THE RIGHT TO LAY CLAIM TO THE NEXUS THAT SEPARATES MAGIC AND SCIENCE, RIGHT?
AND SINCE I'M CARRYING THE POWERS THAT CREATED THAT NEXUS, BOTH SIDES WANT ME EITHER TO JOIN THEM OR DIE.
IT IS AS THE TRAVELER SAYS.
SO, WHAT IF I CAN GET THE OTHER SIDE TO PACK UP AND GO HOME, OLD BUDDY OLD PAL?
WOULD YOU HONOR A TRUCE AGREEMENT THEN?

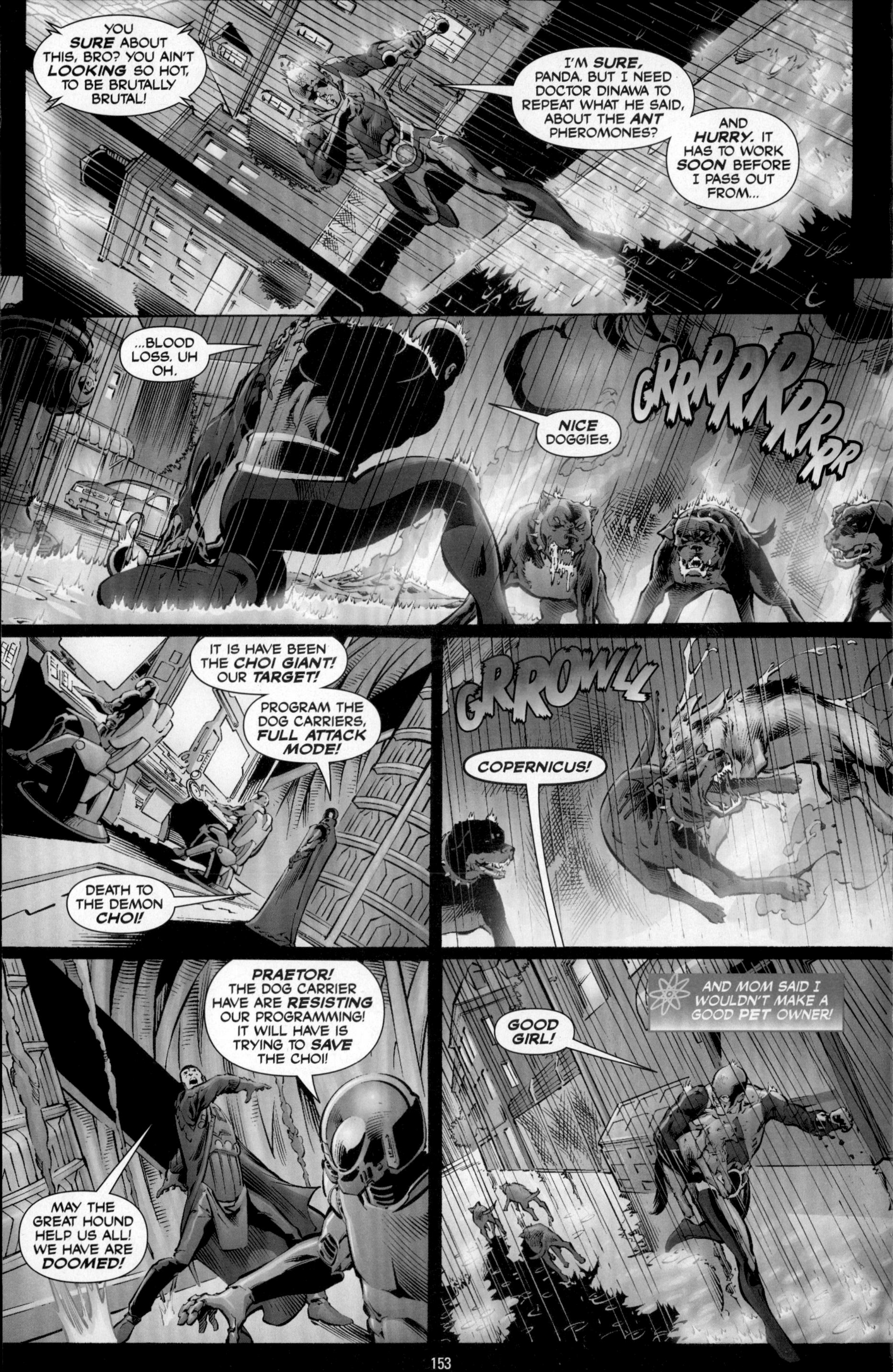
YOU SURE ABOUT THIS, BRO? YOU AIN'T LOOKING SO HOT, TO BE BRUTALLY BRUTAL!
I'M SURE, PANDA. BUT I NEED DOCTOR DINAWA TO REPEAT WHAT HE SAID, ABOUT THE ANT PHEROMONES?
AND HURRY. IT HAS TO WORK SOON BEFORE I PASS OUT FROM...
...BLOOD LOSS. UH OH.
GRRRRRRRRRR
NICE DOGGIES.
IT IS HAVE BEEN THE CHOI GIANT! OUR TARGET!
PROGRAM THE DOG CARRIERS, FULL ATTACK MODE!
DEATH TO THE DEMON CHOI!
GRROWLL
COPERNICUS!
PRAETOR! THE DOG CARRIER HAVE ARE RESISTING OUR PROGRAMMING! IT WILL HAVE IS TRYING TO SAVE THE CHOI!
MAY THE GREAT HOUND HELP US ALL! WE HAVE ARE DOOMED!
AND MOM SAID I WOULDN'T MAKE A GOOD PET OWNER!
GOOD GIRL!

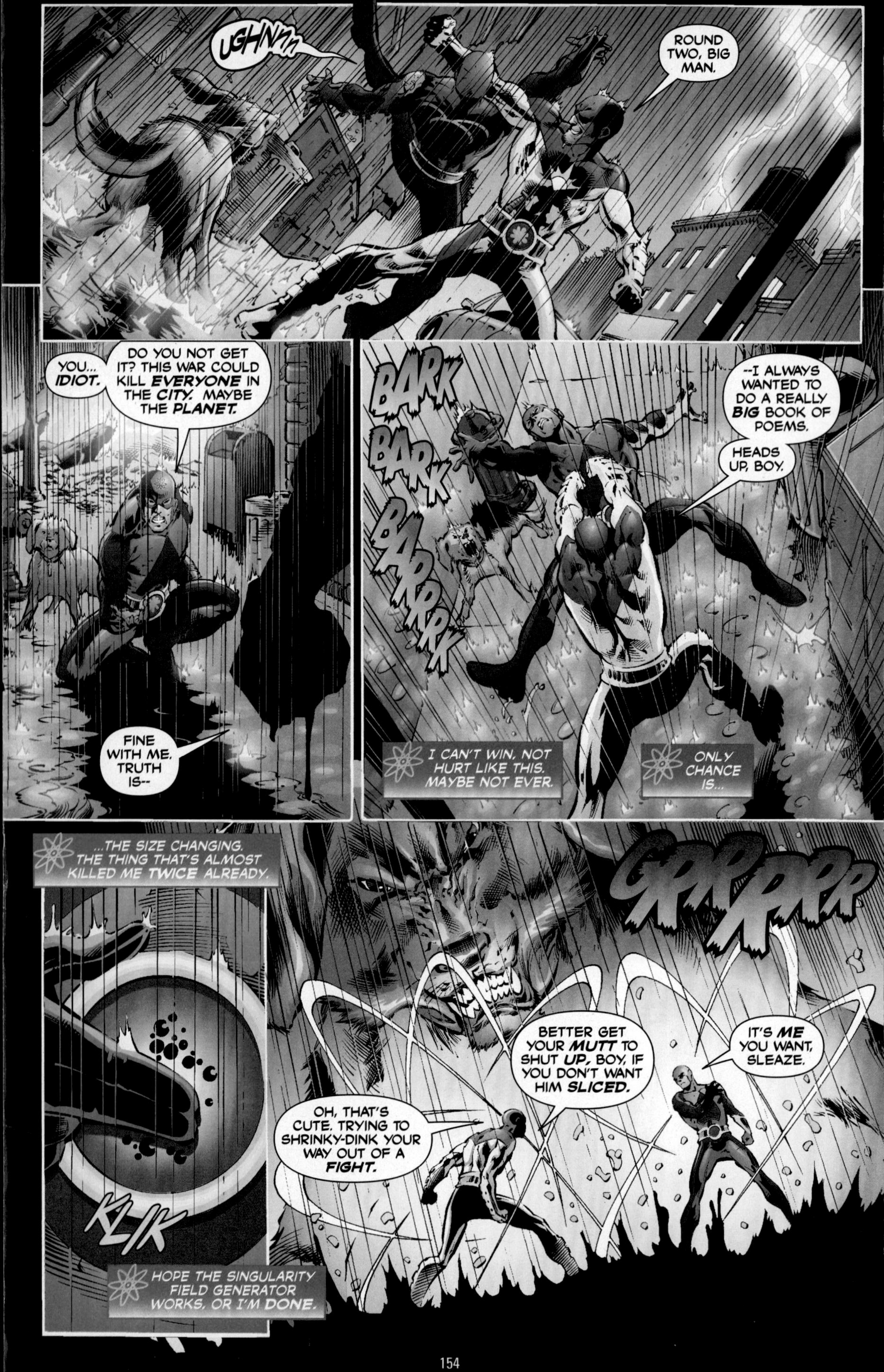

UGHN'N
ROUND TWO, BIG MAN.
YOU... IDIOT.
DO YOU NOT GET IT? THIS WAR COULD KILL EVERYONE IN THE CITY. MAYBE THE PLANET.
FINE WITH ME. TRUTH IS--
BARK
BARK
BARRRRK
--I ALWAYS WANTED TO DO A REALLY BIG BOOK OF POEMS.
HEADS UP, BOY.
I CAN'T WIN, NOT HURT LIKE THIS. MAYBE NOT EVER.
ONLY CHANCE IS...
...THE SIZE CHANGING. THE THING THAT'S ALMOST KILLED ME TWICE ALREADY.
KLIK
HOPE THE SINGULARITY FIELD GENERATOR WORKS, OR I'M DONE.
GRRRRR
OH, THAT'S CUTE. TRYING TO SHRINKY-DINK YOUR WAY OUT OF A FIGHT.
BETTER GET YOUR MUTT TO SHUT UP, BOY, IF YOU DON'T WANT HIM SLICED.
IT'S ME YOU WANT, SLEAZE.

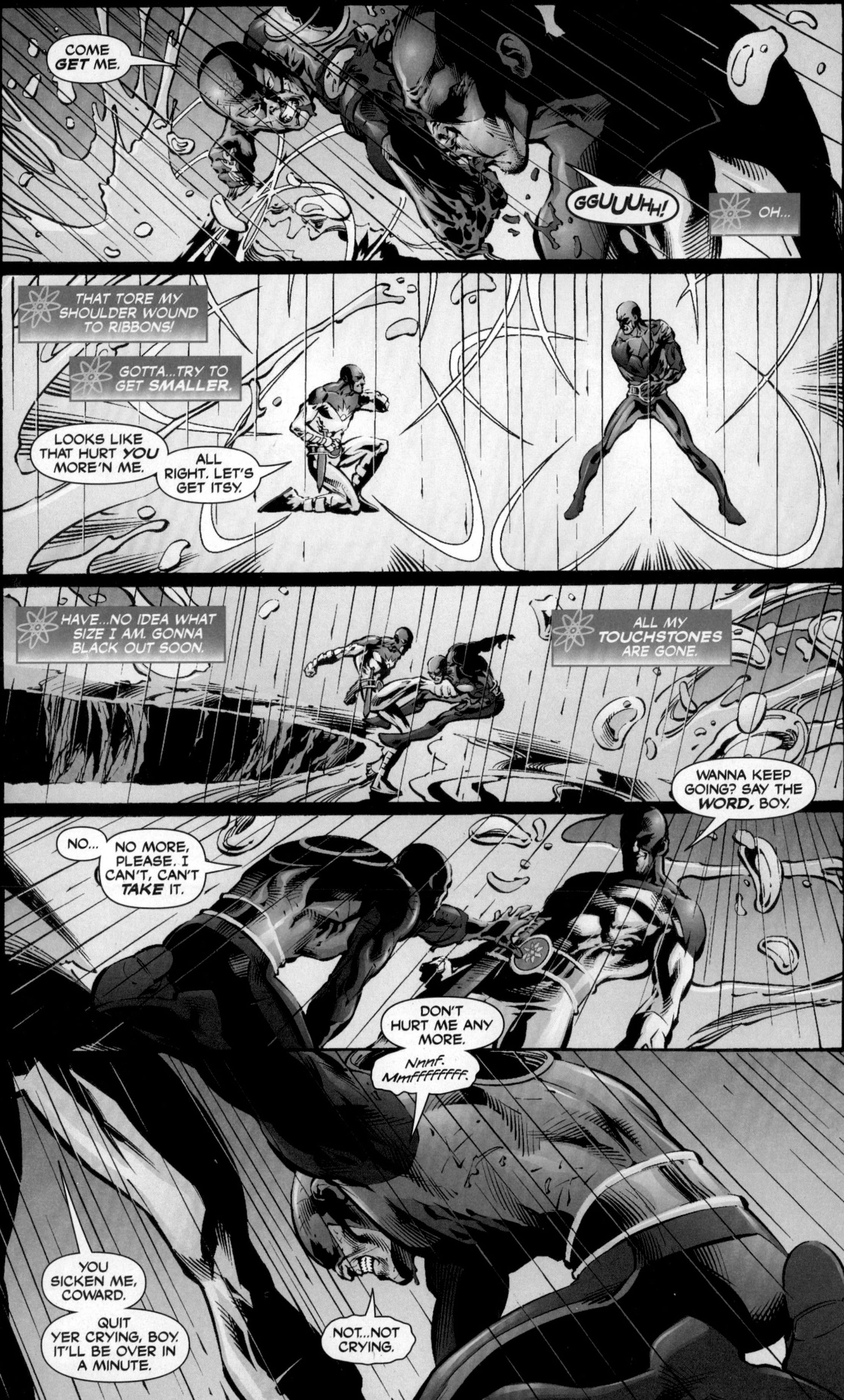
COME GET ME.
GGUUUHH!
OH...
THAT TORE MY SHOULDER WOUND TO RIBBONS!
GOTTA...TRY TO GET SMALLER.
LOOKS LIKE THAT HURT YOU MORE'N ME.
ALL RIGHT. LET'S GET ITSY.
HAVE...NO IDEA WHAT SIZE I AM. GONNA BLACK OUT SOON.
ALL MY TOUCHSTONES ARE GONE.
WANNA KEEP GOING? SAY THE WORD, BOY.
NO...
NO MORE, PLEASE. I CAN'T, CAN'T TAKE IT.
DON'T HURT ME ANY MORE.
Nnnf. Mmfffffffff.
YOU SICKEN ME, COWARD.
QUIT YER CRYING, BOY. IT'LL BE OVER IN A MINUTE.
NOT...NOT CRYING.

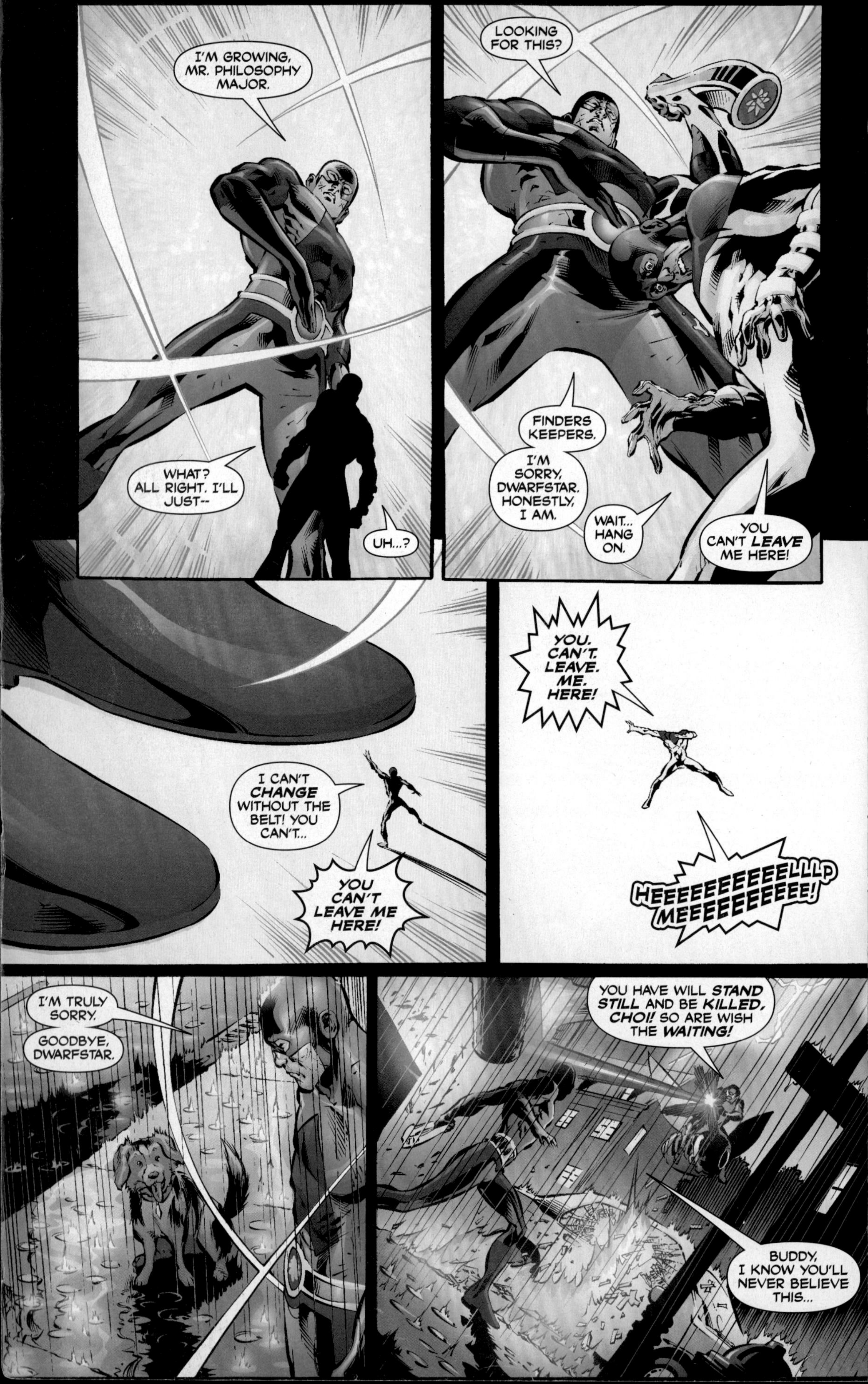
I'M GROWING, MR. PHILOSOPHY MAJOR.
WHAT? ALL RIGHT. I'LL JUST--
UH...?
LOOKING FOR THIS?
FINDERS KEEPERS.
I'M SORRY, DWARFSTAR. HONESTLY, I AM.
WAIT... HANG ON.
YOU CAN'T LEAVE ME HERE!
I CAN'T CHANGE WITHOUT THE BELT! YOU CAN'T...
YOU CAN'T LEAVE ME HERE!
YOU. CAN'T. LEAVE. ME. HERE!
HEEEEEEEEEELLLLP MEEEEEEEEEE!
I'M TRULY SORRY.
GOODBYE, DWARFSTAR.
YOU HAVE WILL STAND STILL AND BE KILLED, CHOI! SO ARE WISH THE WAITING!
BUDDY, I KNOW YOU'LL NEVER BELIEVE THIS...

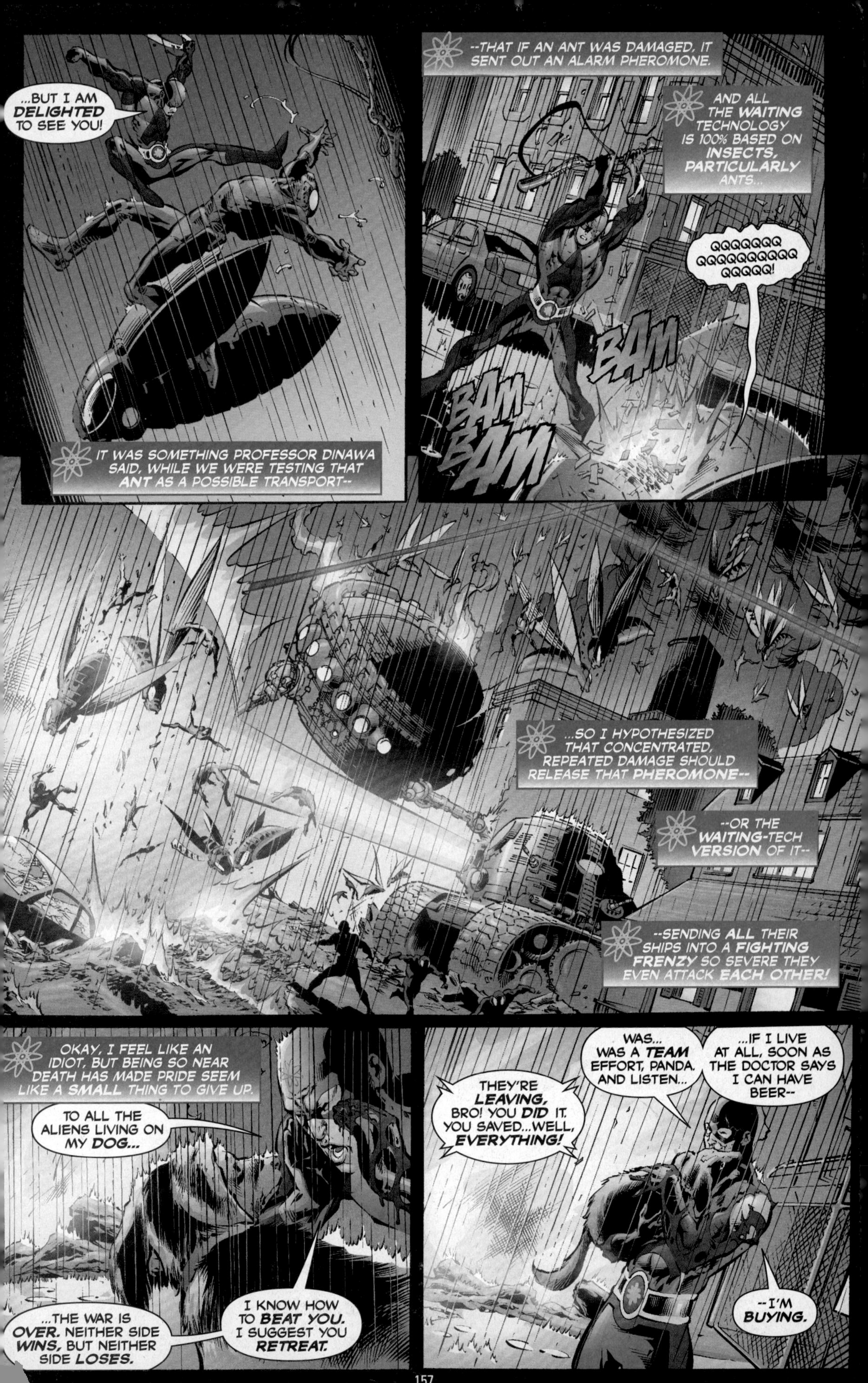
...BUT I AM DELIGHTED TO SEE YOU!
IT WAS SOMETHING PROFESSOR DINAWA SAID, WHILE WE WERE TESTING THAT ANT AS A POSSIBLE TRANSPORT--
--THAT IF AN ANT WAS DAMAGED, IT SENT OUT AN ALARM PHEROMONE.
AND ALL THE WAITING TECHNOLOGY IS 100% BASED ON INSECTS, PARTICULARLY ANTS...
QQQQQQQ QQQQQQQQQQ QQQQQ!
BAM
BAM
BAM
...SO I HYPOTHESIZED THAT CONCENTRATED, REPEATED DAMAGE SHOULD RELEASE THAT PHEROMONE--
--OR THE WAITING-TECH VERSION OF IT--
--SENDING ALL THEIR SHIPS INTO A FIGHTING FRENZY SO SEVERE THEY EVEN ATTACK EACH OTHER!
OKAY, I FEEL LIKE AN IDIOT, BUT BEING SO NEAR DEATH HAS MADE PRIDE SEEM LIKE A SMALL THING TO GIVE UP.
TO ALL THE ALIENS LIVING ON MY DOG...
...THE WAR IS OVER. NEITHER SIDE WINS, BUT NEITHER SIDE LOSES.
I KNOW HOW TO BEAT YOU. I SUGGEST YOU RETREAT.
THEY'RE LEAVING, BRO! YOU DID IT. YOU SAVED...WELL, EVERYTHING!
WAS... WAS A TEAM EFFORT, PANDA. AND LISTEN...
...IF I LIVE AT ALL, SOON AS THE DOCTOR SAYS I CAN HAVE BEER--
--I'M BUYING.

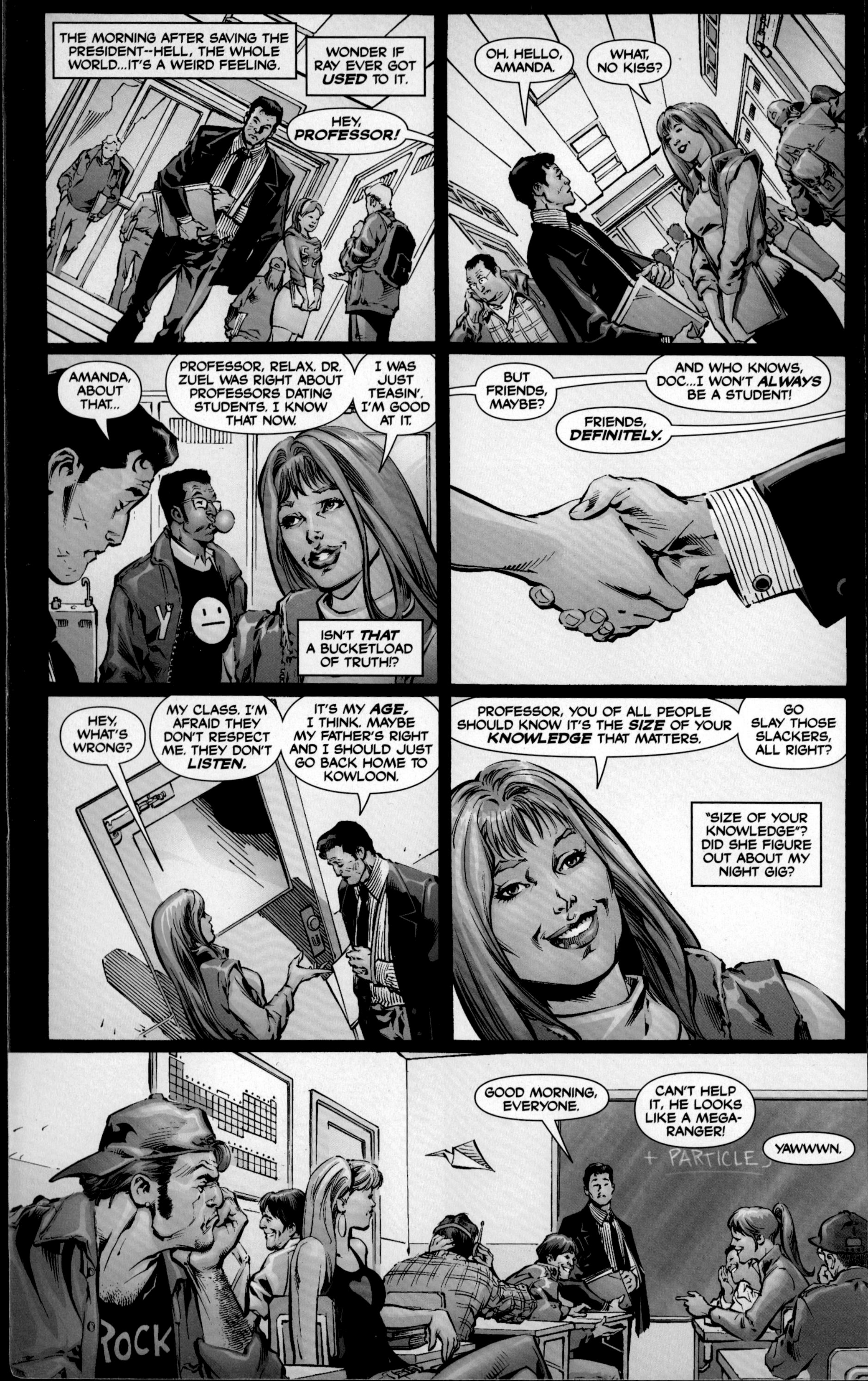
THE MORNING AFTER SAVING THE PRESIDENT--HELL, THE WHOLE WORLD...IT'S A WEIRD FEELING.
WONDER IF RAY EVER GOT USED TO IT.
HEY, PROFESSOR!
OH, HELLO, AMANDA.
WHAT, NO KISS?
AMANDA, ABOUT THAT...
PROFESSOR, RELAX. DR. ZUEL WAS RIGHT ABOUT PROFESSORS DATING STUDENTS. I KNOW THAT NOW.
I WAS JUST TEASIN'. I'M GOOD AT IT.
ISN'T THAT A BUCKETLOAD OF TRUTH!?
BUT FRIENDS, MAYBE?
AND WHO KNOWS, DOC...I WON'T ALWAYS BE A STUDENT!
FRIENDS, DEFINITELY.
HEY, WHAT'S WRONG?
MY CLASS. I'M AFRAID THEY DON'T RESPECT ME. THEY DON'T LISTEN.
IT'S MY AGE, I THINK. MAYBE MY FATHER'S RIGHT AND I SHOULD JUST GO BACK HOME TO KOWLOON.
PROFESSOR, YOU OF ALL PEOPLE SHOULD KNOW IT'S THE SIZE OF YOUR KNOWLEDGE THAT MATTERS.
GO SLAY THOSE SLACKERS, ALL RIGHT?
"SIZE OF YOUR KNOWLEDGE"? DID SHE FIGURE OUT ABOUT MY NIGHT GIG?
GOOD MORNING, EVERYONE.
CAN'T HELP IT, HE LOOKS LIKE A MEGA-RANGER!
YAWWWN.
+ PARTICLE
ROCK

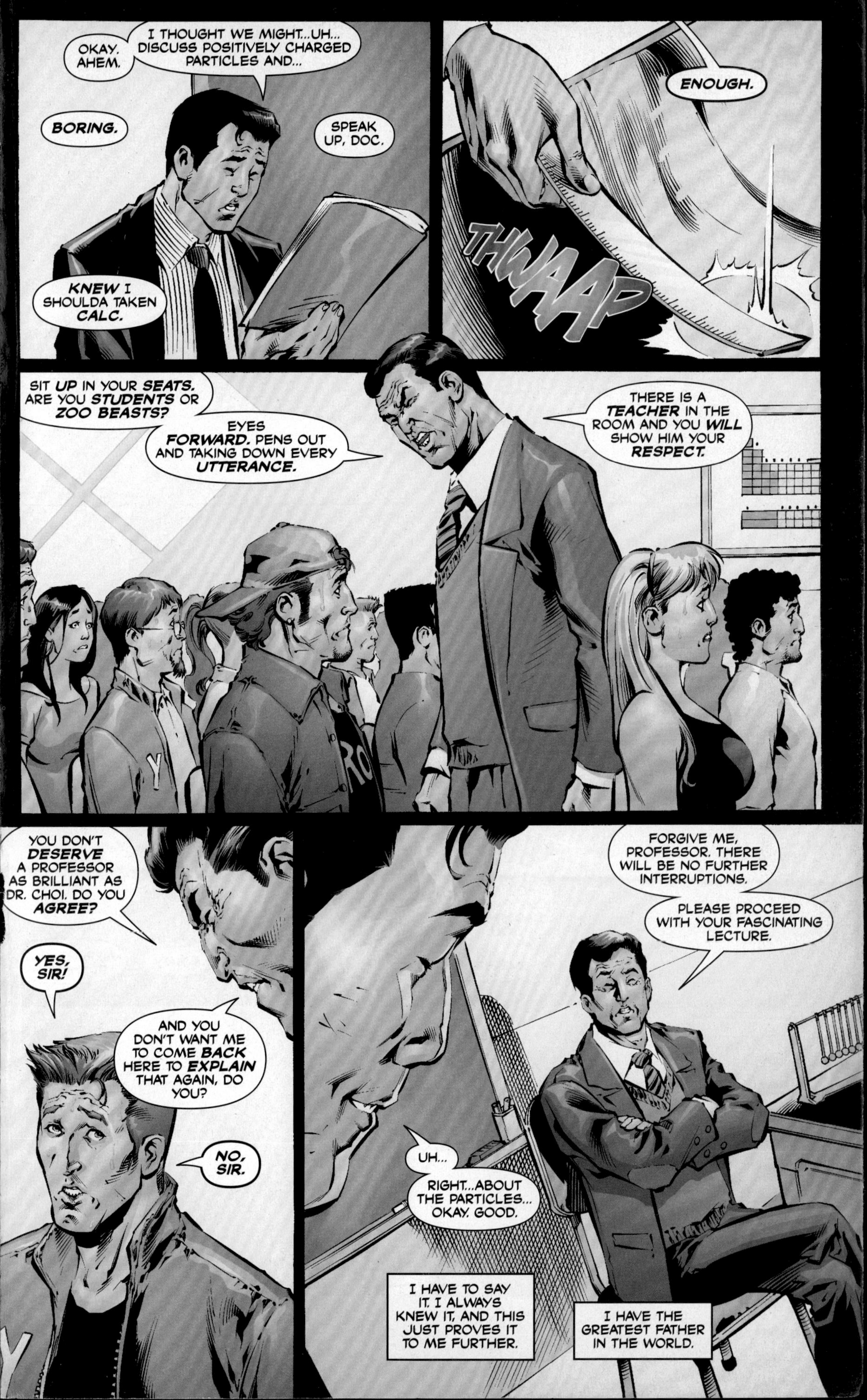
OKAY. AHEM.
I THOUGHT WE MIGHT...UH... DISCUSS POSITIVELY CHARGED PARTICLES AND...
BORING.
SPEAK UP, DOC.
KNEW I SHOULDA TAKEN CALC.
ENOUGH.
THWAAP
SIT UP IN YOUR SEATS. ARE YOU STUDENTS OR ZOO BEASTS?
EYES FORWARD. PENS OUT AND TAKING DOWN EVERY UTTERANCE.
THERE IS A TEACHER IN THE ROOM AND YOU WILL SHOW HIM YOUR RESPECT.
YOU DON'T DESERVE A PROFESSOR AS BRILLIANT AS DR. CHOI. DO YOU AGREE?
YES, SIR!
AND YOU DON'T WANT ME TO COME BACK HERE TO EXPLAIN THAT AGAIN, DO YOU?
NO, SIR.
FORGIVE ME, PROFESSOR. THERE WILL BE NO FURTHER INTERRUPTIONS.
PLEASE PROCEED WITH YOUR FASCINATING LECTURE.
UH...
RIGHT...ABOUT THE PARTICLES... OKAY. GOOD.
I HAVE TO SAY IT. I ALWAYS KNEW IT, AND THIS JUST PROVES IT TO ME FURTHER.
I HAVE THE GREATEST FATHER IN THE WORLD.

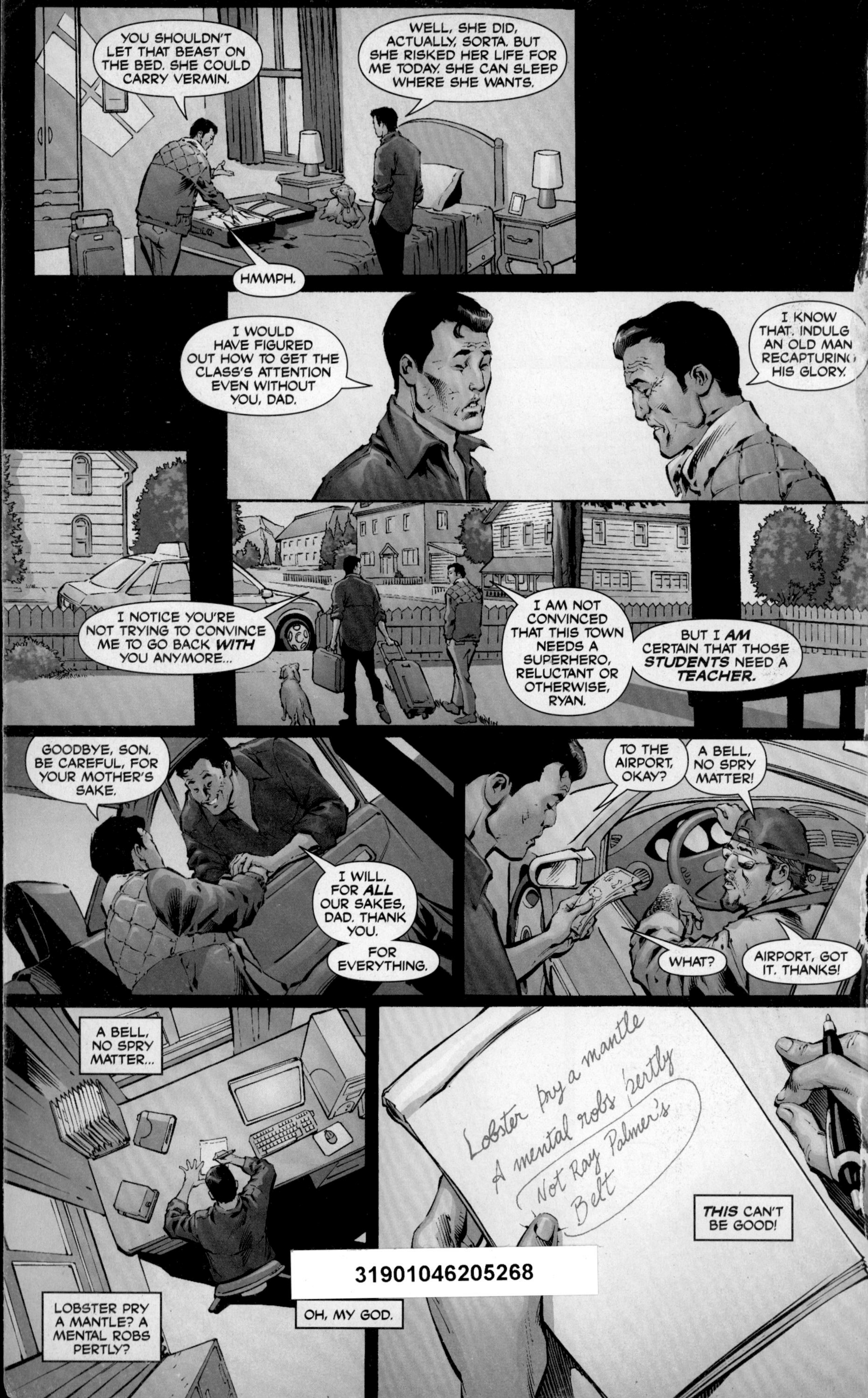

YOU SHOULDN'T LET THAT BEAST ON THE BED. SHE COULD CARRY VERMIN.
WELL, SHE DID, ACTUALLY, SORTA. BUT SHE RISKED HER LIFE FOR ME TODAY. SHE CAN SLEEP WHERE SHE WANTS.
HMMPH.
I WOULD HAVE FIGURED OUT HOW TO GET THE CLASS'S ATTENTION EVEN WITHOUT YOU, DAD.
I KNOW THAT. INDULG AN OLD MAN RECAPTURING HIS GLORY.
I NOTICE YOU'RE NOT TRYING TO CONVINCE ME TO GO BACK ***WITH*** YOU ANYMORE...
I AM NOT CONVINCED THAT THIS TOWN NEEDS A SUPERHERO, RELUCTANT OR OTHERWISE, RYAN.
BUT I ***AM*** CERTAIN THAT THOSE ***STUDENTS*** NEED A ***TEACHER.***
GOODBYE, SON. BE CAREFUL, FOR YOUR MOTHER'S SAKE.
I WILL. FOR ***ALL*** OUR SAKES, DAD. THANK YOU.
FOR EVERYTHING.
TO THE AIRPORT, OKAY?
A BELL, NO SPRY MATTER!
WHAT?
AIRPORT, GOT IT. THANKS!
A BELL, NO SPRY MATTER...
LOBSTER PRY A MANTLE? A MENTAL ROBS PERTLY?
OH, MY GOD.
Lobster pry a mantle
A mental robs pertly
Not Ray Palmer's Belt
THIS CAN'T BE GOOD!